HOW TO READ MARX'S *CAPITAL*

HOW TO READ MARX'S
CAPITAL

Commentary and Explanations on the Beginning Chapters

Michael Heinrich

TRANSLATED BY
ALEXANDER LOCASCIO

MONTHLY REVIEW PRESS
New York

Copyright © 2021 by Monthly Review Press
All Rights Reserved

Originally published as *Wie das Marxsche* Kapital *Lesen?* in two volumes by Schmetterling Verlag GmbH, Stuttgart, Germany © 2018 by Schmetterling Verlag GmbH. English translation by Alexander Locascio published by Monthly Review Press.

The translation of this work was funded by Geisteswissenschaften International Translation Funding for Work in the Humanities and Social Sciences from Germany, a joint initiative of the Fritz Thyssen Foundation, the German Federal Foreign Office, the collecting society VG WORT, and the Börsenverein des Deutschen Buchhandels (German Publishers & Booksellers Association).

Library of Congress Cataloging-in-Publication Data available from the publisher.

ISBN 978-1-58367-894-7 (paper)
ISBN 978-1-58367-895-4 (cloth)

MONTHLY REVIEW PRESS, NEW YORK
monthlyreview.org

Typeset in Minion Pro and Bliss
5 4 3 2 1

Contents*

Preface.. 13
Introduction... 19
    Why Read Capital *Today?*... 19
    Difficulties in Reading Capital..................................... 23
    How to Discuss Capital.. 25
    Various Types of Commentary.. 27
    Using the Commentary: An Initial Reading Plan...................... 30

Commentary on the Beginning of *Capital*................................. 35
Capital. A Critique of Political Economy................................. 35

Preface to the First Edition (89–93)..................................... 37
    a) The Difficulty of the Beginning, "Bourgeois Society,"
        Abstraction (89–91)... 37
    b) The Object of Investigation (90–91)................................ 38
    c) People as Personifications of Economic Categories (92).............. 40
    d) Natural Laws of Capitalist Production (90–92)....................... 41
    e) Scientific Inquiry and Social Struggles (92–93)..................... 42
    f) The Three Volumes of *Capital* (93)................................. 44

Postface to the Second Edition (94–103).................................. 45

Contents (5–10).. 45

PART ONE: COMMODITIES AND MONEY.. 47
Chapter 1: The Commodity (125–177)....................................... 47
1. The Two Factors of the Commodity: Use-Value and Value
    (Substance of Value, Magnitude of Value) (125–131)................. 47
    a) Introductory Paragraph: Wealth and the Commodity
        (Definition and Analysis) (125)................................. 47

---

*Marx's headings are in sans serif type. All other headings are the author's and are in serif type. The page references in parenthesis refer to the Penguin edition of *Capital*.

- b) Use-Value (last paragraph 125 to penultimate paragraph 126) ... 51
- c) Exchange-Value (Analysis and Construction) (last paragraph 126 to penultimate paragraph 127) 53
- d) Value and Substance of Value (final paragraph 127 to last paragraph 128)...................................... 59
  First Step of the Argument: The Common Element of the Commodities Is Not a Natural Property 59
  Second Step of the Argument: Only the Property of Being a Product of Labor Remains 62
  Third Step of the Argument: The Substance of Value Is Abstract Human Labor...................................... 63
- e) Magnitude of Value and Productivity (first paragraph 128 to first paragraph 131) 68
- f) Concluding Observation: Use-Value and Value (penultimate paragraph 131) 73
- g) Comments on the First Subsection's Arguments 74
  The Commodity Character of Services........................ 74
  Supply and Demand... 75
  Conscious Action on the Part of Those Engaged in Exchange?.. 76
  Labor and Appropriation.................................... 76
  A Proof of Value Theory?................................... 77

2. The Dual Character of the Labor Embodied in Commodities (131–137) 79
   - a) Introductory Paragraph: "Crucial" for Understanding Political Economy (final paragraph 131)..................... 80
   - b) Concrete, Useful Labor (first paragraph 132 to first paragraph 134)... 81
   - c) Abstract Human Labor, Simple and Complex Labor (second paragraph 134 to first paragraph 136)................ 84
   - d) Final Remark, Physiology (last paragraph 137) 89

3. The Value-Form, or Exchange-Value (138–163).................... 92
   Introduction: The Mystery of Money (138–139) 93
   (a) The Simple, Isolated, or Accidental Form of Value (139–154) 98
   1. The two poles of the expression of value: the relative form of value and the equivalent form 99
   2. The relative form of value 100
      (i) The content of the relative form of value................. 100
      (ii) The quantitative determinacy of the relative form of value.. 106

		3.	The Equivalent Form....................................	108

- 3. The Equivalent Form 108
  - *The First Peculiarity of the Equivalent Form* 110
  - *The Second Peculiarity of the Equivalent Form* 113
  - *The Third Peculiarity of the Equivalent Form*................ 114
  - *Excursus on Aristotle*..................................... 116
- 4. The Simple Form of Value Considered as a Whole 118
  - *The Independent Presentation of Value as Exchange-Value* 118
  - *Insufficiencies of the Simple Form of Value*................... 122
  - *Passing Over to the Expanded Form of Value (Characteristics of Conceptual Development)* 123
- (b) The Total or Expanded Form of Value (154–157) 125
  - (1) The expanded relative form of value 125
  - (2) The particular equivalent form............................ 127
  - (3) Defects of the total or expanded form of value 127
- (c) The General Form of Value (157–162)......................... 129
  - (1) The changed character of the form of value................. 129
    - *The Historical Appearance of the Forms of Value* 129
    - *The Changed Character of the Relative Form of Value*........ 130
    - *The Changed Character of the Equivalent Form* 132
  - (2) The development of the relative and equivalent forms of value: their interdependence........................... 136
  - (3) The transition from the general form of value to the money form 139
- (d) The Money Form (162–163) 139

- 4. The Fetishism of the Commodity and Its Secret (163–177)........ 143
  - a) "Whence, then, arises the enigmatic character of the product of labour, as soon as it assumes the form of a commodity?" (163–165) 144
  - b) The "Peculiar Social Character of the Labour which Produces Commodities"—Retroactive Socialization (second paragraph 165 to second paragraph 166).................. 151
  - c) Knowledge of Value and "Objective Semblance" (third paragraph 166) 157
  - d) The Society's Movement Taking on a Life of its Own, and Its Content (second paragraph 167).......................... 161
  - e) "Objective Forms of Thought" (*Objektive Gedankenformen*) (second paragraph 168 to second paragraph 169)........... 166
  - f) Forms of Production Not Based on Commodity Production (third paragraph 169 to last paragraph 173)................ 170
  - g) Religion and Mode of Production (second paragraph 172 to first paragraph 173)....................................... 174

  h) Commodity and Value in Political Economy: The Analysis of Fetishism as a Precondition for a Critique of Political Economy (second paragraph 173 to 177) 177

Chapter 2: The Process of Exchange (178–187) 187
  a) The New Level of Abstraction in Chapter 2.................. 187
  b) The Process of Exchange and Commodity Owners (Private Owners) (178 to first paragraph 179)...................... 188
  c) The Contradictory Requirements of the Exchange Process and Its Solution: Money (179 to first paragraph 181)......... 192
  d) The Historical Development of Commodity Exchange and Money (third paragraph 181 to third paragraph 184) 198
  e) Money-Form and Money Fetish (last paragraph 184 to 187) 202

Chapter 3: Money, or the Circulation of Commodities (188–244)..... 208
1. The Measure of Values 210
  a) Immanent Measure of Value and Money as Its Necessary Form of Appearance (188)................................ 212
  b) Price and Ideal Money (189–190) 217
  c) Measure of Values and Standard of Prices (191 to second paragraph 195)... 219
  d) Price and Value (last sentence of 195 to 198) 222

2. Means of Circulation 226
  (a) The Metamorphosis of Commodities 227
   The Social Metabolism and Its Form Aspect (198 to third paragraph 199) 227
   Introduction to the Investigation of the Metamorphosis of the Commodity (last paragraph 199 to fourth paragraph 200)... 233
   C – M. The First Metamorphosis: Sale (Supply and Demand on the Market for Commodities, Realization of the Price of the Commodity, Realization of the Ideal Use-Value of Money) (last paragraph 200 to first paragraph 205) 234
   M – C. Second Metamorphosis: Purchase (second paragraph 205 to first paragraph 206)............................... 242
   The Completed Metamorphosis as a Whole (second paragraph 206 to second paragraph 207) 243
   The Difference Between the Circulation of Commodities and the Exchange of Products, "Social-natural Connections," The Possibility of Crisis (third paragraph 207 to 209)........ 245

	(b)	The Circulation of Money 252
		The Circulation of Commodities and the Semblance Generated by It (210 to third paragraph 212) 252
		The Amount of the Means of Circulation, Critique of Quantity Theory (final paragraph 212 to 220)..................... 254
	(c)	Coin. The Symbol of Value 258
		Coin in the Process of Circulation (second paragraph 222 to second paragraph 224) 259
		The "Law Peculiar to the Circulation of Paper Money" (third paragraph 224 to first paragraph 225) 260
		The Symbol of Money (second paragraph 225 to 227) 262
3.	Money... 265	
	(a)	Hoarding.. 267
		The Hoard as a New Function of Money (227–228) 267
		"The Lust for Gold," "The Hoarding Drive" (229 to third paragraph 231) 270
		The Function of Hoards for the Economy as a Whole, Consequences for the "Law Peculiar to the Circulation of Paper Money" (last paragraph 231) 274
	(b)	Means of Payment.. 274
		Money's New Function, New Economic Characteristics (232 to second paragraph 234) 274
		Means of Payment and Monetary Crisis (last paragraph 234 to first paragraph 237)................................... 278
		The Total Amount of Money in Circulation (second paragraph 237 to 240)... 281
	(c)	World Money 283

PART TWO: THE TRANSFORMATION OF MONEY INTO CAPITAL .. 287
Chapter 4: The General Formula for Capital 287

a)	Historical Preconditions and Conceptual Point of Departure (first three paragraphs 247)	287
b)	Differences in Form Between C – M – C and M – C – M (last paragraph 247 to third paragraph 250)	289
c)	The Different Content of Each Form of Circuit: Capital as Valorized Value (last paragraph 250 to 253)	291
d)	The Capitalist (254 to first paragraph 255)	294
e)	Value as "Automatic Subject" and "Self-Moving Substance Which Passes Through a Process of Its Own" (second paragraph 255 to 257)...	296

Chapter 5: Contradictions in the General Formula 302
    a) Presentation of the Problem (258 to first paragraph 259) 302
    b) The Circulation of Commodities "In Its Pure Form":
         The Exchange of Equivalents (second paragraph 259 to
         first paragraph 262). 303
    c) The Exchange of Non-Equivalents (third paragraph 262
         to second paragraph 266) 304
    d) "Antediluvian Forms" of Capital (third paragraph 266 to 267) . . 306
    e) Valorization in Production? (first two paragraphs 268) 308
    f) The Result: Paradoxical Requirements of the Presentation
         (second paragraph 268 to 269). 309

Chapter 6: The Sale and Purchase of Labor-Power 313
    a) On the Way to Solving the Puzzle: The Specific Commodity
         Labor-Power (Free Will and Objective Compulsion)
         (270 to third paragraph 272). 313
    b) The "Historical Imprint" of Economic Categories (second
         paragraph 273 to first paragraph 274) 315
    c) The Value of the Commodity Labor-Power (Class Struggle)
         (second paragraph 274 to first paragraph 279). 318
    d) Illustration and (Moral) Critique (footnote 14) 324
    e) The Use-Value of the Commodity Labor-Power (second
         paragraph 279 to first paragraph 280) 326
    f) The Sphere of Circulation and the Sphere of Production,
         Freedom, and Coercion (280). 327

PART THREE: THE PRODUCTION OF ABSOLUTE
    SURPLUS-VALUE. 332
Chapter 7: The Labor Process and the Valorization Process 332
1. The Labor Process. 332
    a) General Characteristics of the Human Labor Process,
         the "Nature" of Human Beings (second paragraph 283
         to first paragraph 284) 333
    b) The Object of Labor, Instruments of Labor, Objectified
         (Concrete) Labor (second paragraph 284 to second
         paragraph 287). 335
    c) Product, Means of Production, Productive Labor, and
         (Concrete) Living Labor (third paragraph 287 to
         fourth paragraph 290) 337
    d) Levels of Abstraction of the Presentation
         (last paragraph 290 to first paragraph 291). 339

  e) The Labor Process as the Process by Which the Capitalist Consumes Labor-Power (the "Rebel" Workers) (second paragraph 291 to 292) 340

2. The Valorization Process 342
  a) The Process of Creating Value (third paragraph 293 to second paragraph 298) 342
  b) The "Secret of Profit-Making" Revealed (third paragraph 298 to second paragraph 302) 344
  c) Conceptual Demarcations and Simple vs. Complex Labor (fourth paragraph 302 to 306) 347
  d) Looking Ahead 349

Appendix 1: Marx's Critical Economic Writings 355
Appendix 2: The Universality of Labor as a Social Characteristic of "Labor that Posits Exchange Value" (from the *Contribution to the Critique of Political Economy* [1859], MECW 29: 273–275) 366
Appendix 3: A Paradoxical Form of Value (from *Das Kapital*, First Edition, [1867], MEGA II/5: 42–43, English: Dragstedt [1976, 32–34]) 370
Appendix 4: Value-Objectivity as Objectivity Held in Common (from *Ergänzungen und Veränderungen zum ersten Band des Kapitals* [1871–72], MEGA II/6: 29–32) 375
Appendix 5: The "Transition to Capital" (from "Original Text of *A Contribution to the Critique of Political Economy*" (*Urtext*) [1858], MECW 29: 478–499) 382
Appendix 6: Levels of Abstraction and the Course of Argument in the First Seven Chapters of *Capital* 391
  1. What Is Being Abstracted From 391
  2. Value, Money, and Fetish at Different Levels of the Presentation 392
  3. "Theoretical Developments" and Historical Process 395

Glossary 399
Bibliography 403

Preface

In many Western European countries, the student movement of the late 1960s and 1970s brought a renewed interest in Marx. Along with it came interpretations of Marx that questioned the well-trodden paths pursued by many socialist and communist parties. The time was also marked by the emergence not only of important contributions dealing with *Capital* but also key manuscripts such as the *Grundrisse* and *Theories of Surplus Value*. Hence, one can rightly speak of a "new reading of Marx" that overcame the one-sided economic orientation of previously dominant readings. At the same time, dealing with Marx became almost a mass phenomenon. Among students and young academics—primarily within the social sciences and teaching environment—hardly anything could be done without Marx, at least if one wanted to be considered enlightened and progressive. These changes influenced many students, apprentices in the skilled trades, young workers, and a number of trade union activists. In West Germany and West Berlin, *Capital* courses sprang up at many universities, either as official courses or as self-organized reading groups, and it was not only students who participated. Talk of the "contradiction between use-value and value" or the "overaccumulation of capital" became a must in many discussions. However, knowledge of Marx often remained superficial, and the majority of participants in *Capital* courses got stuck somewhere in the first volume. Engaging with Marx was in part a mere fashion, even though it was more than that.

Invoking Marx may have been part of the German Democratic Republic's official self-conception, but the omnipresent "Marxism-Leninism" taught in its schools and institutions of higher education generally consisted of more or less catchy sayings and textbook-like abbreviations of the "classics." It served mainly as an ideology justifying "really existing socialism." Truly rigorous discussions focused on the text of Marx's *Capital*—not just the manuals of "Political Economy of

Capitalism and Socialism"—only occurred in small circles of experts. In the 1970s, when the new Marx-Engels Gesamtausgabe (MEGA) began to publish all Marx and Engels's surviving texts and manuscripts, the discussion in the GDR became increasingly interesting and more substantial in content, but it did not extend throughout the society.

In the West, belief in the possibility of rapid political and social change played a part in making the broad engagement with Marx fashionable. In the 1960s, the student movement developed in just a few years, stirring up life in the sleepy Federal Republic of Germany. Similar things happened in other countries. Meanwhile, in the so-called Third World there came to exist armed movements aiming at social revolution—movements that, like the Vietcong, took on the United States, the leading capitalist power. It seemed plausible that, if Marxism could just spread in the working class of the Global North, then a revolutionary perspective would also be possible there. In the early 1970s the predominantly student founders of the various German "K-groups" (communist circles and small parties) believed this, as did many others.

Toward the end of the 1970s, however, the optimistic hopes that marked the decade's beginning began to crumble. The Vietcong, the North Vietnamese army, and the Khmer Rouge managed to expel the U.S. military and the U.S.-maintained governments from South Vietnam and Cambodia. However, it soon became clear that there was hardly an emancipatory perspective in the development-oriented dictatorships of "really existing socialism" that came to power. In the case of the Khmer Rouge in Cambodia, its taking power led to mass murder of the domestic population. The hope for a revolutionary transformation of the working class in the Global North was likewise disappointed. It appeared that the revolutionary spark was just as unlikely to spread to the masses there as in other countries where class struggle was initially much more developed, regardless of whether they pursued the traditionalist path of building a "Marxist-Leninist" cadre party or the deliberately non-centralist unifying organizational approaches of groups such as the Socialist Bureau in Germany. Demonstrations and paint bombs no longer provoked or even unsettled politicians and the media, as they had in the late 1960s. Many leftists regarded the frustration of their own political expectations as merely a "crisis of Marxism"—a diagnosis they often adopted uncritically from France and Italy, where it had originated under different social conditions. These former activists opted to not question their earlier inflated expectations that had now run aground— that is, their own process of appropriating and applying Marx's theory. Instead, they simply perceived these expectations as the authentic result of Marx's theory, concluding now from their own disappointment that this theory had failed.

From the late 1970s and into the 1980s, many of those who had thrived on grand theoretical designs a few years earlier (often using them as rhetoric to dominate people) now proclaimed the end of great theories in general and of Marx's theory in particular. If the trend only a few years back was Marxism, now it became fashionable to reject it with a gesture of sober disillusionment. It was common to encounter the figure of the knowledgeable, detached old leftist, who allegedly knew his Marx very well, but now understood that what Marx had said with regard to the working class, capitalism, and politics was no longer relevant. Especially after the collapse of really existing socialism in the period 1989–1990, it seemed as if Marx's theory was forever washed up. Even those approaches that had long criticized authoritarian Soviet-style state socialism with the help of Marx's theory lost their credibility in the general rejection of social alternatives.

Nevertheless, the end of the old confrontation between blocs did not lead to either a more peaceful state system or a more stable (or even more social) capitalism. Wars and crises occurred with greater frequency than in previous decades, and the standards of social security that wage earners had achieved in Western Europe and North America during the "economic miracle" came under constant attack in an onslaught that continues even today. However, starting in the second half of the 1990s, we have witnessed growing signs of resistance at various levels. Many protests have remained limited in scope; they often merely resist immediate changes for the worse or demand "better" policies from the state, which is supposed to protect its citizens from capital's impositions. However, there is a change in the social climate, albeit limited and slow, and it appears that the neoliberal hegemony that has existed since the early 1980s, with its idolization of markets and competition, is beginning to crack.[1]

Since the end of the 1990s, there has been a renewed interest in Marx's theory in Germany and in other countries. Even if the discussion has by no means reached the intensity it had in the West in the 1970s, it seems that a new generation of politically active people from different backgrounds—regardless of whether they come from the East

---

1. I wrote most of this preface in early 2008, just before the financial crisis started. This crisis shattered neoliberalism as an ideology but not as a practice, as was demonstrated by the aftermath of the crisis and the subsequent treatment of the increased state debt.

or the West—is in the process of appropriating Marx's critique of political economy. This appropriation is accompanied by a far lower level of political expectation than in the 1970s, and it does not appear to be so pompous as before. Instead, an open-minded, interested attitude prevails, without expecting Marx's theory to provide the final answers to all important questions. Not bad as conditions for serious engagement!

However, nowadays the social framework that would allow for a more intense, problem-free study of Marx's theory does not exist. People who want to address *Capital* today cannot count on finding appropriate courses at a university or in its environment, and things are usually not much better elsewhere, such as in the educational programs of trade unions. There is hardly any engagement with Marx in established academic institutions anymore—though this also encourages people to engage with his work outside of institutional constraints. The present volume is intended to assist those who are interested. It is meant for individuals or groups without any special prior knowledge, who wish to read *Capital* intensively and accurately on their own.

The first two chapters of *Capital* are the most difficult parts of the entire book and present major problems for readers. Nevertheless, these initial chapters are of central importance for Marx's later arguments, so understanding them is especially important. That's why this volume comments in detail on these chapters. On the one hand, it should make reading easier; on the other, it should clarify the contents of these chapters and what is frequently overlooked during a first reading. Hence, they could help even those who have already read the beginning of *Capital* to learn something new.

The first chapters of *Capital* deal with the interrelationship between value, labor, and money. Marx had already dealt many times with this problem, which is central to his critique of political economy. He addresses it at the beginning of the *Grundrisse* (1857–58) and in the *Contribution to the Critique of Political Economy* (1859). A treatment of the issue is later found in the first edition of *Capital* (1867), only to be revised considerably in the second edition (1872–73). These different versions are not mere repetitions; their differences sometimes express advances in knowledge or changes in emphasis but sometimes also problematic simplifications. Therefore, it seemed to make sense to comment not only on the most recent versions, which appear in most editions of *Capital*, but also to deal with other versions. I resort to Marx's alternative treatments of the issue not only in the continuous commentary, but also in appendices 2 to 4. In this way, I hope to provide a more rigorous engagement with Marx's value theory for both those who are just beginning to read *Capital* and for more "advanced" readers.

When this book first appeared in German in 2008, it dealt only with the first two chapters of *Capital*. However, it became clear to me that a commentary on the first two chapters was far from enough to resolve all the difficulties of beginning *Capital*. In that regard, chapter 3 is considerably easier to read than chapter 1, but it is frequently received in a very superficial way. Moreover, after the challenges of the first two chapters, one wishes to get quickly to chapter 4, which finally deals with capital! Although chapter 3, with its 56 printed pages, is a bit longer than the lengthy chapter 1, readers often consider little more than its account of money's basic functions and too often overlook the chapter's important contribution to the analysis of form. Indeed, chapter 3 might be the most underestimated chapter of the entire first volume. Moving forward in the book, chapters 4 to 6 (which constitute a single chapter in the German edition) are easily understandable. However, the investigation into form-analysis in chapter 4 is frequently left by the wayside, while chapter 6 is sometimes rather crudely simplified. Finally, chapter 7 not only provides observations supplementing those in the previous three chapters, it demonstrates how Marx makes the transition to analyzing capitalist production. For these reasons, a commentary on chapters 3 to 7, dealing with all of these kinds of difficulties, seemed to be called for.

In the Preface to *Capital*'s first edition, Marx writes that chapter 1 (which in later editions became Part 1, "Commodities and Money" and was subdivided into three chapters) summarizes the content of the earlier *Contribution to the Critique of Political Economy* (1859). However, he adds that "many points only hinted at in the earlier book are here worked out more fully, while, conversely, points worked out fully there are only touched upon in this volume" (89). The first part of this statement applies primarily to the initial two chapters of *Capital*: Marx improved the presentation in *Capital* compared to the *Critique* in these chapters, more fully developing points that he merely hinted at before. In chapter 3, the reverse is true. It contains some important additions to the earlier account, but treats many issues in a much more cursory fashion. For this reason, my commentary appeals repeatedly to the *Contribution to the Critique* and its more thorough arguments when dealing with chapter 3.

In *Capital*, Marx's account of how money transforms into capital in chapter 4 immediately follows his presentation of money and the circulation of commodities. However, in the so-called *Urtext* from 1858, published in English as the "Outline of the Critique of Political Economy," there is another section immediately before, which Marx did not incorporate into *Capital*. This section, called the "Transition to Capital," contributes to understanding the connection between chapter 4 and the first three chapters. For that reason, Appendix 5 reproduces and comments on parts of this section of the *Urtext*. By contrast, Appendix 6 deals with the text of *Capital*, specifically the levels of abstraction and the sequence of presentation in its first seven chapters. This appendix is not an introduction to the first seven chapters, but rather an overview of their structure for those who have already read them.

The preceding remarks are meant to clarify the difference from the method I pursued in *An Introduction to the Three Volumes of Karl Marx's Capital* (Heinrich 2012). That book aims to provide an initial overview of all three volumes of *Capital*. I have said many times that the *Introduction* cannot substitute for one's own reading of Marx's text; it only offers limited assistance to those who want to undertake an independent reading of *Capital*. Value theory does play an important role in the *Introduction* (the chapter on value is the most extensive one), but I could only address the theoretical elements most important to understanding *Capital*'s overall argument. This new book, by contrast, undertakes a *detailed* engagement with the *actual text* of *Capital*.

In the course of working on this book, I was aided by others who read and criticized the drafts. For their extremely interesting discussions, helpful observations, and critical readings of my manuscripts, I would like to give special thanks to Valeria Bruschi, Andrei Draghici, Ingo Elbe, Alex Gallas, Andreas Hirt, Kolja Lindner, Urs Lindner, Hermann Lührs, Antonella Muzzupappa, Arno Netzbandt, Sabine Nuss, Paul Sandner, Oliver Schlaudt, Anne Steckner, Ingo Stützle, and Wolfgang Veiglhuber. For the precise translation I want to thank Alex Locascio, and for his excellent work as editor, Chris Gilbert.

Introduction

Why Read Capital *Today?*

These days, it's not at all clear why one would undertake an intensive reading of *Capital*. The first volume was published in 1867, more than 150 years ago. It's reasonable to doubt whether the analyses contained in the book are still relevant today. Hasn't a lot changed since then? It is not only right-wing critics of Marx who claim that *Capital* has lost much of its relevance, but also a number of leftist critics of capitalism. Ultimately, one has to read *Capital* oneself to respond to the question. However, I wish to offer a few arguments beforehand for why it still makes sense to read *Capital* today.

Marx wrote *Capital* during the 1860s and 1870s in London. In the mid-nineteenth century, the capitalist mode of production was most advanced in England—with France, Germany, and the United States following at a great distance. At the time, London represented *the* capitalist center *par excellence*. It was the center of world finance and the beating heart of the capitalist world. Both Parliament and the press debated economic questions far more comprehensively and intensively than in other countries. In the first half of the nineteenth century, "political economy" (the contemporary term for the science of economics) developed most fully in England, and the British Museum in London held the world's largest collection of economic literature. In that sense, it was an enormous stroke of luck that Marx, pressured by the Prussian government, had been forced to leave Paris and move to London; in fact, there was no better place in the world for him to study capitalism.

Marx had already begun research into economics before arriving in London. Looking backward, he would claim that he resolved in London to "start again from the very beginning" (MECW 29: 265). In 1851, Marx believed that he would be "finished with the whole economic shit in five weeks' time" (letter to Engels from April 2, 1851, corrected translation of MECW 38: 325). However, Marx proved completely wrong: the "economic shit" would occupy him until the end of his life in 1883. The studies that Marx began in London initially led to his compiling a plethora of excerpts of economic literature. From 1857 forward, he wrote a number of extensive manuscripts, from which *Capital* ultimately emerged (an overview of these various manuscripts can be found in Appendix 1).

Marx took many of the examples in *Capital* from the English capitalism of his time. But *Capital*'s object is by no means English capitalism, nor is it the capitalism of the nineteenth century. Marx's intent is not to examine a particular capitalism or a specific phase of capitalist development, but rather—as he emphasizes in the Preface to the first edition—the fundamental laws of capitalism. Marx aims to depict what he calls at the end of the third volume the "ideal average" of the capitalist mode of production (*Capital* III: 970). He is concerned with what makes capitalism *capitalism*. Whether we speak of capitalism in England during the nineteenth century or in Germany at the beginning of the twenty-first century, there must be something in common that allows us to use this term. Marx aims to identify and describe precisely this common element that we encounter in *every* capitalism.

This means that Marx argues at a very high level of abstraction. Consequently, his presentation is still of interest today and is by no means limited to the nineteenth-century context. That does not guarantee that Marx's account is accurate; that has to be tested by reading it. However, one cannot claim that what Marx discusses is outmoded. In a certain sense, *Capital* is even more suited for the twentieth and twenty-first centuries than it was for the nineteenth century (which also speaks for its analytical robustness). This is because Marx's analysis assumes that a number of developments had already matured, which were actually just starting to appear in the nineteenth century. Today they are much more pronounced.[2]

In contrast, the claims that Marx's theory has been refuted by capitalist development have repeatedly vanished into thin air. During the "economic miracle" of the 1960s, it may have been widely accepted that capitalism was constantly increasing society's prosperity and finally functioning free of crises, but today such a statement sounds simply ridiculous. Since the 1970s, capitalism has proven crisis-prone in both the "first" and "third" worlds, confirming Marx's more than hundred-

---

2. This point will not be further elaborated here. A brief effort to explain the "economic miracle" of the 1960s on the basis of Marx's theory can be found in my *Introduction* (Heinrich 2012: 118ff.).

year-old analysis of capitalism's mode of functioning. Moreover, it's also obvious that the development of capitalism is repeatedly accompanied by the production of misery—of various kinds and in the most diverse contexts—as Marx concluded at the end of the first volume.

Hence, to the extent that one pays attention to *Capital*'s content, one cannot claim that the work lacks relevance to the present (a topicality that *Capital*'s critics rarely have). However, caution is warranted to not overestimate *Capital*'s analytic reach. We should not forget that every capitalism is historically embedded; it does not exist in the world as an "ideal average" but rather in a particular historical, social, and cultural context. Therefore Marx's arguments, carried out on an abstract level, cannot by themselves offer an exhaustive analysis of each historical capitalism that we encounter, even if supplemented with contemporary data. In order to understand how contemporary capitalism has developed and where it is going, we require much more analysis than is found in *Capital*.

Even recognizing that Marx's analysis is not obsolete, one can still ask if it's necessary to actually read *Capital* in the original. Perhaps a summary of its conclusions would suffice? Yet every such summary, with its emphases and exclusions, bears the stamp of its author's perspective, and one can only assess the original work on the basis of an independent reading. Furthermore, an introduction can at best *state its conclusions*, but offers little in the way of *justification* for these conclusions.

However, one can still ask why reading *Capital* is important if not engaged in scholarly work on the book's themes. *Capital* is a "scientific" work, meaning that its claims have to be justified in a way that can be comprehended and criticized by others, but it is not an economic study in a narrow professional sense. Rather, *Capital* is concerned on a fundamental level with the specific manner of capitalist "socialization" or "social constitution" (*Vergesellschaftung*), that is, the always conflict-ridden and crisis-prone formation of the social fabric. This social fabric appears to be largely "objective" (*versachlicht*), a relationship between things, in which prices, interest, stock prices, and so on have an independent existence. Relations of domination and exploitation disappear behind apparently "objective compulsions" (*Sachzwänge*). Both everyday consciousness and political economy take this objectivity for granted, without questioning the social conditions that allow it to emerge at all. Marx refers to the objectification of social relations as *fetishism*. In analyzing the economic foundations of this mode of socialization and uncovering the fetishism inherent to it, he provides both a critique of spontaneous forms of everyday consciousness (forms that tend to subordinate our perceptions of economic relations to varying degrees) and of the science that operates within these fetishistic forms: political economy. For that reason, Marx is not engaged in political economy but rather, as *Capital*'s subtitle emphasizes, a "critique of political economy."

By exposing the fundamental structures of capitalist socialization, Marx points out their contradictory and destructive character. The accumulation of wealth in one part of society is accompanied by the accumulation of misery (in its various forms) in another. The development of social labor's productive force goes hand in hand with the destruction of human beings and nature. Moreover, all this occurs not due to the "greed" of the capitalist or because of a "savage" insufficiently regulated capitalism. Instead, it results from the capitalist "logic of valorization," which necessarily reduces human beings and nature to mere means of valorization and making profits.

Capitalism exists in various social and political contexts, and the capital relation has historically been politically regulated in widely diverse ways. But the dynamic of crisis—inextricably bound up with the capitalist mode of production—constantly demolishes all modes of regulation, every "class compromise" that is achieved. It is not so much exaggerated forms of capitalism but rather capitalism's normal functioning that makes a self-determined "good" life impossible. For that reason, Marx is not concerned with promoting a different *distribution* of wealth within the existing capitalist mode of socialization, but rather with *overcoming* it altogether. *Capital* provides crucial elements of the basic knowledge that is needed to fundamentally change social structures. Therefore, it is interesting not only for people doing scholarly work, but also for everybody interested in changing those structures.

What is presented in *Capital*'s three volumes constitutes a coherent whole. Thus, we cannot simply pick out a few interesting parts and deal with them alone. Regardless of the knowledge obtained this way, it would be distorted in some way or other. Nor should we only read the first volume. For example, the third volume presents key categories that are necessary to understanding capitalism, such as profit and interest (and this sequence is not arbitrary, since the treatment of these categories in the third volume is prepared by the preceding material). For instance, if we pay attention only to the first volume of *Capital*, then there's the danger of equating "surplus value" with profit, which is definitely wrong. At the end of the day, the first volume is only fully comprehensible in the context of the two volumes that follow it. This even applies to the commodity form, which Marx analyzes at the beginning of the first volume. The commodity is by no means fully characterized in chapter 1, which bears the title "The Commodity," but rather only at the end of the third volume. The presentation in *Capital*'s three volumes forms an indissoluble unity, which can only really be understood and applied when one has dealt with all three volumes. Such an undertaking is certainly strenuous and time-consuming. Yet along with the political usefulness of such a project, engaging with the three volumes is also a fascinating intellectual adventure.

Difficulties in Reading Capital

Reading Marx's *Capital* is not easy. The beginning of the first volume is itself one of the most difficult parts of the entire work. This is not due to complicated language or incomprehensible jargon; what is complicated are the interconnections presented. A superficial reading can contribute to the belief that one has understood everything because the language is usually rather simple. However, reading carefully makes one aware that the arguments sometimes elude understanding. Nor is it easy to encounter satisfactory answers to the questions that emerge when comparing Marx's arguments with one's own perceptions.

Faced with such difficulties, one frequently encounters two very different kinds of advice, both of which I regard as useless. The first is the suggestion that Marx's presentation is "dialectical." In order to really understand what Marx meant, we are told, one needs to address the dialectic of German philosopher Georg Friedrich Wilhelm Hegel (1770–1831). On numerous occasions, Marx indeed engaged critically with Hegel's philosophy, and it influenced him. However, this influence does not consist simply in Marx having "adopted" or "applied" a few elements of Hegel's philosophy, which we should thus try to extract from Hegel's work. In the Postface to the second edition of *Capital*'s first volume, Marx writes that he "coquetted" with the "mode of expression peculiar to him [Hegel]" in *Capital* (Marx 1976: 103). Marx did not *accept* Hegel's conclusions, but rather a certain awareness of the requirements of scientific presentation and the problems that accompany it. By "coquetting" with Hegel's mode of expression, Marx evoked that philosopher and paid homage to him. Nevertheless, Marx nowhere gives even the slightest hint that, in order to understand his own work, it's necessary to first read Hegel. Turning to Hegel's works could lead to even greater problems of understanding than *Capital*, and Hegel's relation to Marx could become less clear. I do not recommend *preparing for* a first reading of *Capital* by reading Hegel. Only *after* reading *Capital* does it make any sense to turn to Hegel and discuss the question of what Marx learned from him.

The second kind of advice is that one needs to prepare for reading *Capital* by examining Marx's other writings. However, understanding Marx's "early writings" is also difficult—for example, the "Paris Manuscripts" of 1844, where he developed his theory of "alienation." Moreover, one soon runs into Hegel again and the philosopher Ludwig Feuerbach (1804–1872), whose influence there is significant. Furthermore, it's an open question whether Marx's theory of alienation plays a role in *Capital* at all, or whether he proceeds from completely different assumptions. Also, Marx's simpler "economic" texts, such as "Wage Labor and Capital" or "Value, Price, and Profit," are not the best preparation for *Capital*. The first piece of writing is based on talks composed long before *Capital*, and therefore does not represent the same level of knowledge. The second text derives from a talk Marx prepared when he had already begun working on *Capital*, but he did so reluctantly, since the context required making a number of problematic simplifications. Instead of using these in some ways deficient expositions, it's better to begin directly with *Capital* without making any detours.

Reading *Capital* also leads to difficulties because of our own preconceptions. We employ terms like *value*, *money*, and *capital* in everyday life, associating them with certain meanings that are not always identical to those Marx assigns to the terms. Frequently, we project ideas—regarded as self-evident—onto Marx's text. This is especially true if one has studied economics for a few semesters and assumes that certain supposedly "elementary" relationships always apply. Approaching Marx with such schemes in mind makes it hard to follow his argument, because we are always looking for the familiar.

Secondary sources *about* Marx are also often problematic. There is a truncated, somewhat skewed conception of Marx's arguments in traditional "worldview Marxism." After Marx's death, this kind of Marxism began to take shape in late nineteenth-century German Social Democracy, and it continued after the First World War as Marxism-Leninism. (For more on "worldview Marxism," see chapter 1.3 of my *Introduction* and Elbe 2006 on the various versions of Marxism.) Too often, the role of this stunted Marxism was simply to provide formulas for everyday propaganda and justify the policies of socialist or communist parties. Such a Marxism, in a still more truncated form, also became the stuff of textbooks and the media, while playing an important role in shaping what people think they know about Marx based on a diffuse general knowledge. Everyday notions about Marx and Marxism, however, have precious little to do with *Capital*'s real arguments. For that reason, we should treat one's own prior knowledge with a healthy dose of mistrust.

How to Discuss Capital

When reading a text like *Capital*, we try to understand individual terms and statements and then apply what we have learned to everyday life in capitalism, drawing political conclusions, and so on. For those with no prior knowledge, the usual approach might be to concentrate on the text, attempting to solve problems by reading things more carefully. We might also put problems aside momentarily, hoping they will be clarified on arriving at later parts of the text. In principle, such a text-oriented method is the best way to address *Capital*.

However, people approach things differently, if they are further along in reading Marx's work and are familiar with other philosophical and economic texts or secondary literature about *Capital*. Then they tend to resort to certain terminological grids, such as those involving "essence and appearance," "dialectic," "alienation," "ideology," and "the critique of ideology." Using these concepts, people sometimes rush to explain what Marx "actually" meant," or what he "basically" intended to say. A good portion of the secondary literature about *Capital* proceeds in a similar manner.

In all these approaches, however, the reader pushes the text of *Capital* into the background; it becomes no more than a source for catchphrases and quotations. Frequently, the reader no longer bothers to ascertain whether and to what extent such terminology even shows up in the text. For example, *Capital* already mentions "to appear" (*erscheinen*) and "appearance" (*Erscheinung*) or "form of appearance" (*Erscheinungsform*) in chapter 1, but "essence" (*Wesen*) shows up only a few times much later in the first volume. Marx makes some remarks about the "dialectic" in *Capital*'s Preface and Postface, but the term rarely appears in the text. Similarly, "alienation" (*Entfremdung*) does not occur at all in the first volume, although a few passages contain the adjective "alienated" (*entfremdet*), and while the term does appear a few times in the third volume, it is used only in a general sense. Nowhere does the "essence of man" (*Wesen des Menschen*), which was so important in the Paris Manuscripts of 1844) appear in *Capital*, and the word "ideology" only pops up two or three times in a general, unspecific sense. Of course, even if a term does not appear—or rarely appears—in Marx's work, it still might be helpful in explaining the text. However, an interpreter who introduces such a term must show that it connects with a specific passage and says something meaningful. Unfortunately, some discussions and books about *Capital* fail to connect their interpretive schemes to the text.

Marx always strove to argue as precisely as possible. Discussions about Marx's texts should also strive to be as precise as they can be. One should regard with suspicion all claims that *Capital* is "actually" about something not stated explicitly in a specific passage, but which allegedly emerges in view of the overall context. Even those just beginning to deal with *Capital* should not be intimidated by the actual or supposed knowledge of others, but rather *always demand an exact justification for the theses being put forward*. If some make statements about Marx's *Capital*, then we should always ask *which passages of the text* support their claims. Based on these passages, we can debate their claims. In contrast, an ill-defined "overall context" or something that's "actually clear" cannot be discussed.

Some leftists, when asked for textual evidence for their interpretation of Marx, complain that the point is not to merely interpret the text or get at what Marx meant. They disavow "academic" debates, insisting rather on *using* the texts: *The point is politics and the critique of capitalism*. In fact, all of this is simply a way to evade justifying their claims. Do not be impressed by such evasive maneuvers. Using the arguments and analyses of *Capital* in political debates presupposes knowing what the arguments and analyses really *are*. This knowledge cannot be acquired by handpicking individual quotations or speculating, but only by examining Marx's text in a precise way.

Discussions of *Capital* require focusing on the text. While reading, we should pay close attention to the concepts and arguments. When Marx explains a concept, how does he justify what he is presenting? Which expressions does Marx use and which does he avoid? What presuppositions does he make? When does the text offer information explicitly (state it directly), and when does it give the material only implicitly (state it indirectly)? We should also carefully pay attention to the chapter titles and subheadings that Marx selected. Further, for every chapter and subsection, we should ask what constitutes its *unity* (why this particular information is contained here) and what relation that section has to earlier material. Is the subsequent chapter a further development of preceding material, or does it initiate a new level of argumentation? What is important is not only the *content* of Marx's specific arguments, but also the *overall structure of his reasoning*. We should keep this overall structure in mind when considering every chapter, section, and volume.

Finally, we should always be careful, if applying concepts from early on in *Capital* to the capitalist reality around us, to check whether it is really possible at that stage of the text. Marx's argument develops through a process involving numerous intermediate steps. He claims to

Introduction

present the capitalist mode of production—but only in the three volumes of *Capital as a whole*. If Marx begins his presentation analyzing the commodity, but initially abstracting it from money and prices, then the commodity he analyzes is not yet identical with those commodities we see in shop windows with price tags affixed. The *early results* of Marx's analysis therefore *cannot* be related *directly* to the phenomena of everyday life that surround us.

Various Types of Commentary

This book is meant to help individuals or groups who want to deal rigorously with *Capital*. To make an independent reading easier, it offers an extended commentary on the beginning of *Capital*. That commentary analyzes the structure and plausibility of Marx's reasoning, while also addressing questions and objections that frequently arise during a first reading. The commentary is detailed, first because of the complexity of what is dealt with in *Capital*'s beginning chapters, and second because it tries to show *how* we should read and discuss such a text and what we should pay attention to during the reading.

There are two fundamentally different ways of commenting upon a text like *Capital*. Relying upon knowledge of the three volumes of *Capital* and further works by Marx, a commentator can try to explain what Marx means in any given passage, what hidden references the text contains, and so on. The aim is to reveal things that are not obvious to first-time readers of *Capital*. For example, Marx uses the word "wealth" in the first sentence of chapter 1 without explaining it. This kind of commentator might clarify what Marx understands by "wealth," relying on his later arguments. This procedure might help some readers, but it forces them to rely on the commentator. Since they are just beginning the book and aren't familiar with the reasoning that follows, the readers aren't able to judge whether the commentator is correct in explaining what Marx means by "wealth." In this way, the commentator becomes an authority, and only after reading *Capital* can they retrospectively evaluate or debate his commentary. The danger is that, until then, one is forced to read *Capital* through the commentator's lenses, accepting his approach to the work's content.

Another type of commentary refers exclusively to the text in question. It carefully analyzes the work, examining what the arguments in a particular passage can and cannot justify, and pointing to what is implicit in the text. The interpretation is based only on the passage under consideration and the already covered sections of the work. For example, if the initial sentence of chapter 1 has the word "wealth" without further explanation, then the commentator would indicate that we do not know what Marx means by "wealth" at this point, and we certainly do not yet know if it coincides with our use of the word. So the word "wealth" in the first sentence is a placeholder that has to be filled in during the course of Marx's later reasoning. When deeper into Marx's text, the reader can return to this first sentence and the word "wealth." Such a commentary initially leaves a few problems open. It must constantly point out that until we reach a certain point in the text, some questions cannot be answered. However, this type of commentary has the advantage that readers can check its claims directly against the text; the arguments don't have to be taken on faith, and the commentator does not become an authority.

My commentary in what follows is basically of the second type. One of my motives is that I want readers to be able to check my arguments. More important, however, is that I take seriously Marx's claim to present a *scientific* work. Marx by no means presupposed knowledge of other texts in order to read *Capital*, and his claim to be "scientific" simply means that he attempts to present his arguments as precisely and transparently as possible. Attentive readers should be able to follow his arguments directly, and if necessary criticize them. Hence, my primary concern here is *following Marx's arguments* and what can actually be said faced with *each passage of the text* (also perhaps what cannot be said). It is not about all the references that might occur to someone familiar with Marx's work.

I could not, however, limit myself entirely to this kind of commentary, for two reasons. First, Marx's starting point when writing *Capital* often involved adapting common terminology, certain debates, and economic science that had reached a certain level. He could more or less presuppose such knowledge among his readers. With respect to the literary allusions, Marx could assume they would be understood by educated strata. Since that time much has changed: debates have gone in different directions, terminology has been modified, and today's readers have different everyday knowledge than their late nineteenth-century counterparts. For that reason, contemporary readers can benefit from a number of explanations. For example, the term "political economy," which is part of *Capital*'s subtitle, was in fact very common in Marx's time. These days, however, it's seldom used, and usually with a different meaning than in the nineteenth century. Hence the term needs clarification, but it cannot be done solely with Marx's text.

The second reason why the work calls for a more extensive commen-

Introduction

tary—not throughout the entire work, but at certain points—is a certain ambiguity and uncertainty in specific parts of Marx's text. Commenting on every instance of ambiguity would take us back to the first type of commentary. However, I am concerned with specific ambiguities in Marx's theory of value. What Marx presents in the initial chapters of *Capital* is the result of a laborious research process, which constantly led him to develop new presentations and revise earlier ones (see Appendix 1). Marx faced a twofold problem. On the one hand, he sought to grasp the general form of capitalist socialization on the basis of the interrelation between commodity, labor, value, and money (which involved a fundamental critique of economic science). On the other hand, he worked to present that interrelation in a way that was both precise and comprehensible. It would have been miraculous if Marx had entirely succeeded in solving both problems. Since he planned to further revise the text of *Capital* for the third German edition and the English translation (neither of which did he survive to see), he obviously did not assume that all such problems had been solved.

In the following commentary, I have refrained from using conceptual or terminological schemes that seem unambiguous but which Marx avoided or only rarely used (the manner of proceeding that I criticized above). Instead, I refer to *other texts by Marx relevant to value theory* that have a clear relationship to the passage under examination. I do not seek to explain *Capital*'s beginning sections on the basis of passages that come much later; by using a purported philosophical background; or even by relying on a diffuse "general context." Rather, I attempt to resolve the ambiguities in the *existing version* of *Capital*'s beginning by considering *other versions* of this beginning—above all, from the first edition of *Capital* and the revision manuscript "Ergänzungen und Veränderungen" for the second edition. I quote brief passages from these versions in the commentary, whereas I use the appendices to reproduce and comment on some of the longer pertinent passages.

Sometimes, I briefly address secondary literature on *Capital*. A detailed engagement with the extensive body of secondary sources would overload this commentary. Nonetheless, it seemed appropriate at certain points to refer to "classical" critics of Marx or to specific interpretations when it leads to a better understanding of the passage in question.

Therefore, the commentary works on two different levels, which are visually distinguished in the printed text:

1) The main text of the commentary deals with each specific passage selected from *Capital*. Readers can check all my arguments against

the quoted text. Beyond that, the only information required is general knowledge regarding people and concepts, which can be found in a dictionary.
2) However, if I use information that doesn't have this general character, but refers specifically to additional texts by Marx or other authors, then these sections are prefaced with the word "Addendum" and presented in a smaller font.

Reading groups should carefully separate these two levels. They should always distinguish between an argument justified by what Marx *writes in a passage*, which can therefore be immediately verified, and an argument referring to *other texts* (not familiar to everyone) that frequently require interpretation.

Using the Commentary: An Initial Reading Plan

Under no circumstances should the commentary be read *before* Marx's text. Much of it would be incomprehensible since it presupposes reading the text. Moreover, doing so might lead to seeing Marx's text only through the lens of the commentary. The aim of the commentary is not to provide a quick overview of the beginning of *Capital*. Rather, it is a workbook, meaning that one should *work with it* and with *Capital*. It is best to proceed in three steps:

1. Focus on a small section of *Capital*, read it *thoroughly*, and *take notes* on all questions and uncertainties that arise. Such notes are not just an aid to memory; they force one to formulate problems clearly. Moreover, attempting to articulate a problem in a way that others can understand often clarifies it.
2. Next, and only after an independent effort to understand a given passage, read the commentary on it. An open copy of *Capital* should be placed alongside the commentary in order to closely track what it refers to.
3. Finally, reread the corresponding passage in *Capital*, while correcting your notes from the first step, since some of the problems recorded there might have been resolved and new ones might have arisen.

A comment on the *footnotes* in *Capital*: the first volume of *Capital* contains about a thousand footnotes. These days, that's not at all unusual in a large-scale scientific work. In Marx's time, however, such a comprehensive apparatus of notes, with the many sources cited, was extraordinary. In this way, Marx underscored the meticulousness of his work, the scientific character of which he emphasized in the Preface. Many footnotes merely contain quotations from older authors, which Marx does not discuss further. In such notes, Marx is pointing out that an idea of his has already been expressed before, or he is providing an example of a view he criticizes in the text. However, Marx intends such footnotes primarily for the scholarly public, and one should not dwell on footnotes consisting primarily of quotations during a first reading of *Capital*. Above all, it would be an error to begin reading the authors mentioned, since your reading of *Capital* would never be completed! By contrast, there are a number of footnotes where Marx further elaborates his own ideas; these should be discussed just as carefully as the main text. I comment on such footnotes here in the same way as on the main text.

Appendices 2, 3, and 4 should be read only *after* dealing with the first three subsections of the first chapter of *Capital*. Appendix 1 may be read beforehand. Appendices 5 and 6 should be read only after the first seven chapters of *Capital*. The appendices deal with texts by Marx providing supplementary arguments to claims made in *Capital*. In commenting on these additional texts, I presuppose familiarity with the preceding commentary and the corresponding passages of *Capital*.

If a group reads *Capital*, everyone should use the same edition. In German, the standard edition of the first volume is: Karl Marx, Friedrich Engels, *Werke*, Band 23 (MEW 23), Dietz Verlag Berlin, which follows the text of the fourth edition of 1890. For the English-language version of this commentary, all page references are from the edition published by Penguin Classics: Karl Marx, *Capital Volume 1* (1976), translated by Ben Fowkes. In the commentary, I make reference to other works by Marx contained in Karl Marx, Friedrich Engels, *Gesamtausgabe* (MEGA), Berlin 1975ff. (roman numerals refer to divisions, arabic numerals to the volume number), and, to the extent that an English translation exists, I refer to the *Marx Engels Collected Works* (MECW) published by Lawrence and Wishart.

In the quotations from Marx (sans serif font), I have preserved all of Marx's emphases. In the commentary headings, I have retained all of Marx's titles (sans serif font) but have sometimes introduced further itemizations (serif font).

It is specifically the beginning of *Capital* that gives rise to many questions. For that reason, I recommend that when beginning to read the work (or when carrying out discussions in working groups), focus on *very small sections* of the text. With groups, it's better to meet frequently (once a week is best) with enough time to discuss a small section, rather than meeting less often and discussing longer sections. The following division appears reasonable to me, with the caveat that during a meeting, the reader could undertake less, but never *more*, than the specified passage:

1. Preface to the First Edition (89–93), the beginning of chapter 1.1 (125–27)
2. The rest of chapter 1.1 (final paragraph 127 to 131)
3. All of chapter 1.2 (131–37)
4. The beginning of chapter 1.3 (138–44)
5. The middle of chapter 1.3 (144–54)
6. The rest of chapter 1.3 (154–63)
7. The beginning of chapter 1.4 (163–69)
8. The rest of chapter 1.4 (final paragraph 169 to 177)
9. All of chapter 2 (178–87)
10. chapter 3.1 (188–98)
11. The beginning of chapter 3.2 (198–209)
12. The rest of chapter 3.2 (210–27)
13. chapter 3.3 (227–44)
14. chapter 4 (247–57)
15. chapters 5 and 6 (258–80)
16. chapter 7 (283–306)
17. Review of the first seven chapters

After reading the first seven chapters, you may take bigger steps. At the end of the first volume, it would be good to do a complete review of all arguments presented up to that point. A recommended supplementary reading is the "Results of the Immediate Process of Production" (*Capital Volume I*, 948–1084). This is a chapter that Marx originally intended as the conclusion of the first volume, but did not incorporate into the final work. Many arguments in the chapter were integrated into the text of *Capital*, but there are a few ideas in it that either do not appear at all there or appear less clearly.

After the first volume, you should definitely read *Capital*'s second and third volumes. The argument of the three volumes constitutes a coherent whole. As mentioned above, important categories are missing from the first volume; for example, it does not address *profit, the rate of profit, interest,* or *credit*. Moreover, what you learn in the first book about *value, money, surplus value*, and other concepts becomes fully understandable only when familiar with the content of all three volumes.

Introduction

There are two different English translations of *Capital*'s first volume. Both contain a considerable number of misleading or even wrong translations. Additionally, the same German term is sometimes translated differently. In a few cases, it was necessary to correct the existing translation, with the corrected translation being added in brackets to the quote. Sometimes the German term that Marx used is inserted inside the quote for greater clarity.

Commentary on the Beginning of *Capital*

Capital: A Critique of Political Economy

The work's main title, *Capital*, makes clear that Marx is not concerned with "the economy" in a general, transhistorical sense, but rather with a *historically specific* mode of production: the capitalist mode of production.

People often pay attention to the work's main title, but not the subtitle, *A Critique of Political Economy*. To begin with, the term "political economy" requires some explanation. It is not Marx's invention, and is by no means intended to emphasize the "political" character of economic issues, as is sometimes supposed. In ancient and medieval scholarship, the word "economy" stood for "housekeeping" (the Greek word *oikos* means "house"). The economy of the entire polity only became an independent topic of investigation in the early modern period. To distinguish the latter from household economy, people began to speak in the seventeenth century of "political economy." In England and France during the nineteenth century, this was the usual term applied to what today is roughly called "economics." It was only toward the end of the nineteenth century that the term "economics" became the usual one in the English language. Through the early nineteenth century, Germans still spoke of *Nationalökonomie.*

A book's subtitle often tries to explain or clarify the meaning of the title. In choosing the subtitle *A Critique of Political Economy*, Marx implies two things: first, that he is not just aiming to *depict* capitalist relations, but also *critiquing* them; second, that he is not critiquing just individual theories or conclusions, but rather the whole of political economy—the *entire science* expressing these relations.

ADDENDUM: The twin tasks of depicting capitalist relations and critiquing economic science are not separable. For Marx, they mutually condition each other. In a letter to Lassalle (February 22, 1858), Marx describes his project as follows:

> The work I am presently concerned with is a *Critique of Economic Categories* or, IF YOU LIKE, a critical exposé of the system of the bourgeois economy. It is at once an exposé and, by the same token, a critique of the system. (MECW 40: 270)

Marx's letter to Kugelmann from December 28, 1862, also makes clear his aim of criticizing an entire science. There, Marx places *Capital* among the "*scientific* attempts to revolutionise a science" (MECW 41: 436, emphasis in the original). Marx also stresses the *scientific* character of his critique in this letter. In effect, he does not contrast *critique* and *science*.

The works of Scottish economist Adam Smith (1723–1790) and English economist David Ricardo (1772–1823) dominated political economy until the second half of the nineteenth century. Marx considered them the most important representatives of "classical" political economy and refers to them frequently in *Capital*. However, the 1870s brought the "marginalist revolution" in economics. Instead of basing a commodity's value on the labor expended in its production, as Smith and Ricardo did, marginalism focuses on utility—or more exactly "marginal" utility, which is the increase in utility that an additional good yields. By the end of the nineteenth century, the "classical" political economy of Smith and Ricardo was considered obsolete. The "neoclassical" school dominant today in universities and economic research institutes is the direct heir of the marginal utility school. Since Marx also saw a connection between value and expended labor, neoclassical economists consider him to be part of "classical" political economy and therefore obsolete. They do not pay attention to Marx's aim of *critiquing* the *entirety* of economic science. Also they completely ignore the question of whether Marx's critique remains limited to classical political economy, or if it is indeed so fundamental that it also applies to modern economic theories.

We cannot decide in advance how and whether Marx redeems his claim to criticize an entire science: that claim must be demonstrated by a reading of *Capital*.

I will comment on the title of Book I, "The Process of Production of Capital," when discussing the table of contents.

Preface to the First Edition (89–93)

In prefaces, one does not usually find scholarly arguments but rather an author's declaration of intent about what he wishes to present and how he intends to proceed. On their own, such statements do not prove anything at all. They merely offer an initial orientation that the reader can verify in the text that follows, which is why I will return to the Preface at appropriate moments. Here, I limit myself to addressing only the most salient points; the *systematic* commentary begins with the text of chapter 1.

A) The Difficulty of the Beginning, "Bourgeois Society," Abstraction (89–91)

Marx begins by pointing out that *Capital* is the continuation of *A Contribution to the Critique of Political Economy*, published in 1859 (MECW 29: 257–417). He adds that the content of that work is summarized in chapter 1 of *Capital*. (Marx is referring to "Commodity and Money," chapter 1 of the first edition of *Capital*; from the second edition forward, it was made into the first *section* bearing the same name, but is now subdivided into three chapters.)

Marx calls attention to the specific difficulties of the beginning, which is dedicated to presenting the commodity. He observes that a complete body is easier to study than an individual cell, while claiming that for

> bourgeois society, the commodity-form of the product of labour, or the value-form of the commodity, is the economic cell-form. (90)

ADDENDUM: Here, Marx does not specify what he means by the term "bourgeois society" (*bürgerliche Gesellschaft*, sometimes translated also as "civil society"). However, he goes into somewhat more detail in the Preface to the *Contribution to the Critique of Political Economy*. Marx speaks there of the "material conditions of life, the totality of which Hegel, following the example of English and French thinkers of the eighteenth century, refers to with the term "civil society" (*bürgerliche Gesellschaft*—Trans.) (MECW 29: 262). These "English and French thinkers of the eighteenth century" examined the social relations of emerging capitalism, where individuals pursued their particular economic interests in the market. In his *Philosophy of Right*, Hegel sums up these new relationships as "bourgeois society" or "civil society" (*bürgerliche Gesellschaft*), which he locates between the intimate realm of the family and the public-political realm of the state (Hegel 1991: § 182). When Marx speaks of "bourgeois society," he has these modern capitalist relations in mind. The same holds when he speaks later on in *Capital* of the "bourgeois mode of production" (174n34)

Only after addressing Marx's analysis of the commodity will we be able to discuss what he means by claiming that the commodity form is bourgeois society's "economic cell-form."

Marx calls attention to a further point:

> In the analysis of economic forms neither microscopes nor chemical reagents are of assistance. The power of abstraction must replace both. (90)

This remark shows that Marx intends to do more than simply *describe* the immediately visible phenomena of capitalism. However, to understand the central role of abstraction in *Capital*, we will need to get deeper into Marx's arguments. At the beginning of chapter 1, we will return to the question of abstraction.

B) THE OBJECT OF INVESTIGATION (90–91)

> What I have to examine in this work is the capitalist mode of production, and the relations of production and forms of intercourse [*Verkehrsverhältnisse*] that correspond to it. Until now, their locus classicus has been England. This is the reason why England is used as the main illustration of the theoretical developments I make. (90)

It's not surprising, in light of *Capital*'s title, that Marx defines the object of his investigation as the "capitalist mode of production." What is remarkable are the distinctions he makes. Marx contrasts his "theoretical developments" and their "illustration" in the English context. His focus is not the analysis of English capitalism, but rather these "theoretical developments." In the next paragraph, he says this about his theoretical focus:

> Intrinsically, it is not a question of the higher or lower degree of development of the social antagonisms that spring from the natural laws of capitalist production. It is a question of these laws themselves, of these tendencies winning their way through and working themselves out with iron necessity. (90)

Marx is thus concerned neither with one historical phase of capitalist development nor with the historical sequence of capitalist development's individual stages, but rather with the "laws" of the capitalist mode of production. There are many historical passages in *Capital*. However, based on what Marx says here, we can assume that the historical presentation is subordinated to the "theoretical development." For a further discussion of this subordination, see the last point in Appendix 6.

The aforementioned "laws" apply not only to a specific phase of capitalism, but wherever capitalism is the predominant mode of production. For that reason, Marx says somewhat later on:

> It is the ultimate aim of this work to reveal the economic law of motion of *modern society*. (92, emphasis M.H.)

My emphasis makes clear the general character of Marx's account; how it refers not to a specific society, but rather to modern-capitalist society *as such*, in contrast to feudal or ancient society.

Only by reading *Capital* can we decide whether Marx actually succeeds in providing such a universal account, or whether he sometimes confounds specific and transitory traits of the capitalist mode of production with universal laws of capitalism. What is clear, however, is Marx's *intention*.

ADDENDUM: There are two formerly common ways of reading *Capital* that conceived of the work's object in a way that contradicts Marx's intention, even if the advocates of these interpretations failed to see the contradiction. The first reading originates with Karl Kautsky (1854–1938), who was considered the leading theoretical mind of social democracy after the death of Friedrich Engels (1820–1895). Kautsky held that Marx primarily aimed to describe the *historical development* of capitalism. The second reading is mostly popular in the context of Marxism-Leninism. It contends that Marx analyzed the *competitive capitalism* of the nineteenth century. Later on, Lenin (1870–1924) continued Marx's analysis by examining the *monopoly capitalism* of the twentieth century. In the first conception, Marx is made a historian of capitalism; in the second, he becomes a theorist of a specific capitalist phase. Both ways of reading *Capital* contradict the claims Marx articulated in the Preface.

c) People as Personifications of Economic Categories (92)

Marx emphasizes that although he does not depict the capitalist and landowner with "rosy colours," he is not criticizing the behavior of individuals, because

> individuals are dealt with here only in so far as they are the personifications of economic categories, the bearers [*Träger*] of particular class-relations and interests. My standpoint, from which the development of the economic formation of society is viewed as a process of natural history, can less than any other make the individual responsible for relations whose creature he remains, socially speaking, however much he may subjectively raise himself above them. (92)

Marx is not concerned with capitalists as individual people, but only with capitalists to the extent that they "personify" something—that is, to the degree that social relations determine the logic of their actions. What this logic is and the extent to which individuals are compelled to follow it will not be discussed here. It will be dealt with later in Marx's account.

However, there is another important point. In the passage quoted, Marx refers to "categories," "class-relations," and then just "relations." Yet we must distinguish between the "category" (the scientific expression of a social relation) and the social relation itself. Whereas the latter are relations between people in a society, the former are scientific constructs, used to grasp these relations. A society consists of multiple social relations that exist *simultaneously* and mutually influence each other. Nevertheless, in a scientific account, the individual categories expressing these social relations must be developed *one after the other*. When approaching a category for the first time, we therefore cannot consider all the relationships in which the particular social relation expressed by the category stands. Later in this commentary we will return to the relationship between categories and social relations.

In the passage quoted above, Marx's language is not very precise.

People are not personifications of a category but of a social relation (to the extent that they follow this relation's logic of action). If we examine this social relation scientifically, deciphering the operating logic concealed within it, then we create a concept or category for the relation (Marx uses *concept* and *category* more or less synonymously). So it would be more precise to say that a *capitalist personifies the social relation expressed by the category of capital.* In effect, by distinguishing between *category* and *social relation* we can understand Marx's claim that "individuals" are "personifications of economic categories" as an abbreviated manner of speaking.

While reading *Capital*, we should always pay close attention to whether the text is dealing with *economic categories*—that is to say, the analysis of social relations and the *logics* of action they include (but still without taking active individuals into consideration)—or whether it is examining the *actions of individuals* as "personifications" of these categories.

D) NATURAL LAWS OF CAPITALIST PRODUCTION (90-92)

In the second quote in section B above, Marx speaks of the "natural laws of capitalist production." Likewise, the quote presented above refers to the "economic formation of society" as a "process of natural history." Such language raises the issues of how justified we are in speaking of "laws" that operate in society and economy, and whether Marx's conceptions amount to historical determinism. In fact, we can only seriously discuss such issues based on Marx's analysis, not the Preface.

Generally, we should recognize that the social and intellectual context in which Marx made these statements was completely different from today's. When Marx wrote these lines in 1867, he was opposing the predominant form of historiography, which saw history as mainly an affair of great men or great ideas, while relegating material and economic conditions to a completely subordinate role. In contrast to this subjective and idealist focus, Marx emphasized the objective, structural aspects of history. He therefore spoke provocatively of the development of an economic social formation as a "process of natural history" and of the "natural laws of the capitalist mode of production."

Historical approaches centered on individual subjects have by no means disappeared today. However, since Marx's time, even non-Marxist historical writing has, albeit to varying degrees, gotten used to reflecting on the objective and material aspects of development. Conversely, traditional worldview Marxism frequently overemphasized the objective features of history to the point of historical determinism (not the least by relying on the short account of Marx's conception of history found in the Preface to the *Contribution to the Critique of Political Economy*, which I will briefly address in the commentary on Marx's treatment of the "commodity fetish"). For that reason, one becomes suspicious today when people refer to the "natural laws" of social development without qualification. Today the discursive context is quite different from that of Marx's time, and we must therefore assume that he used this terminology in a far more open, less biased sense than people do today.

E) Scientific Inquiry and Social Struggles (92–93)

At the end of the Preface, Marx observes that in the field of political economy "free scientific inquiry" faces not only its usual enemies but also, because of its content, the "furies of private interest" (92). Marx obviously sees his own project as "scientific inquiry," which is not the same as working on behalf of particular interests.

ADDENDUM: Marx is very committed to his reasoning having a *scientific* character, as we saw above in his comments to Kugelmann on the work's title. Marx despised the idea of twisting scientific arguments to promote particular interests. In *Theories of Surplus Value*, he wrote about the economist Malthus, whom he accused of doing exactly that:

> But when a man seeks to **accommodate** science to a viewpoint which is derived not from science itself (however erroneous it may be) but from **outside**, from **alien, external interests**, then I call him "**base**." (MECW 31: 349)

Contrary to what is frequently said, Marx does not, in his own view, adopt a specific "standpoint"—that of the proletariat or a future socialist society—in order to analyze the capitalist mode of production from that perspective. However, the scientific objectivity that Marx lays claim to doesn't make science unpolitical: for example, his discoveries about the nature of capitalism and the consequences of the capitalist mode of production for the majority of people can indeed be used as a weapon in political struggle. In a letter from April 17, 1867, Marx thus refers to *Capital* as "the most terrible MISSILE that has yet been hurled at the heads of the bourgeoisie (landowners included)" (MECW 42: 358).

For Marx, change does not begin only after the elimination of capitalism. Instead, he emphasizes that capitalism itself changes:

> The present society is no solid crystal, but an organism capable of change, and constantly engaged in a process of change. (93)

The results that are "missiles" in the struggle are not dogmas, but rather the outcomes of *scientific inquiry*. For that reason, the analyses they rest upon cannot simply be accepted but must be discussed and verified. Hence, Marx writes at the end of the Preface:

> I welcome every opinion based on scientific criticism. (93)

As we can see, Marx expects anything but credulous readers!

At the same time, he emphasizes that he has never yielded to the "prejudices of so-called public opinion." Marx ends the Preface presenting a (modified) quote from Dante's *Divine Comedy* as his motto:

> "Segui ii tuo corso, e lascia dir le genti." (93) [Go on your own way, and let the people talk.]

ADDENDUM: Here, Marx picks up where he left off at the end of the Preface to the *Contribution to the Critique of Political Economy* (1859). There, he sketches his trajectory of study, adding that the sketch is intended to demonstrate how

> my views—no matter how they may be judged and how little they conform to the interested prejudices of the ruling classes—are the outcome of conscientious research carried on over many years. At the entrance to science, as at the entrance to hell, the demand must be made:
> "Qui si convien lasciare ogni sospetto / Ogni viltà convien che qui sia mortal"
> [Here all misgiving must thy mind reject. Here cowardice must die and be no more]. (MECW 29: 265)

The final quote also comes from Dante's *Divine Comedy*, in which the Roman poet Virgil guides the author Dante through the various circles of hell. The claim that scientific inquiry must cast off "misgivings" and "cowardice" refers to how the outcomes of analysis should be treated. We must stand by the outcomes of serious inquiry, regardless of how they offend the prejudices of "public opinion" or "the ruling classes."

The left also has prejudices and is often unwilling to let scientific analysis destroy its cherished opinions about a situation. Against this, Marx stresses later on in *Capital* that he is *not* interested in a critique "which knows how to judge and condemn the present, but not how to comprehend it" (638n48). Real criticism becomes impossible unless it is willing to "comprehend" without being afraid of the results.

F) The Three Volumes of *Capital* (93)

The first volume of *Capital*'s complete title is: "The Process of Production of Capital." It is striking that Marx refers to both "volumes" and "books" at the end of the Preface (93). In effect, *Capital* was to comprise four "books," which Marx wanted to publish in three "volumes."

After Marx's death, Engels published Book II as the second volume in 1885 and Book III as the third volume in 1894. The result is that today no one any longer distinguishes between "book" and "volume." Marx's manuscript *Theories of Surplus Value* was later published in the Marx-Engels Werke volumes 26.1–26.3 under the title "The 4th Volume of *Capital*." However, this text is not identical with the planned Book IV; nor is it even a direct preliminary work. Despite its many digressions, the manuscript focuses exclusively on the history of a *single* category, surplus value. This manuscript is part of the research process that led to *Capital*. The Book IV planned by Marx does not exist.

The titles of the three extant books clearly indicate that they deal with interrelated material. We can therefore consider them to be a complete work.

Postface to the Second Edition (94–103)

The Postface to the Second Edition that follows the Preface in the Penguin Classics Edition and MECW 35 should be treated as what it is: a *post*face. Marx placed it at the end of the text, and it obviously presupposes familiarity with *Capital*. The Postface contains remarks about the evolution of political economy and about Marx's manner of presentation. However, we cannot discuss these issues before entering into Marx's account. Therefore, I will only refer to the Postface later on in the commentary, when doing so can shed light on certain passages.

Contents (5–10)

As with any scientific work, it is a good idea to get a rough overview of its structure from the table of contents before beginning to read. We will not understand everything but will learn that some topics expected early appear only later on (and vice versa).

The first book of *Capital* bears the title *The Process of Production of Capital*, which has a double meaning in the original German, *Der Produktionsprozess des Kapitals*. The phrase could be either a "genitivus subjectivus" or a "genitivus objectivus." On the one hand, it could refer to a production process dominated by capital, that is, capital as the subject of the production process, *genitivus subjectivus*. On the other hand, it could refer to the process by which capital is produced, that is, capital as the object of the production process, *genitivus objectivus*. We will soon discover that both meanings are at play in the table of contents.

In the English translation, the book is divided into *eight parts*, which all contain multiple chapters (the German original has a somewhat different division into parts and chapters). Part One is called "Commodities and Money," whereas Part Two is called "The Transformation of Money into Capital." Evidently, Marx does not immediately begin by examining capital. Next come three parts dealing with the production of surplus value, where we find an analysis of the production process dominated by capital. Only *after that* comes Part Six, "Wages." This sequence should be kept in mind when reading Part Two. There, Marx addresses among other things "The Sale and Purchase of Labour-Power," but the examination of wages is still to come.

Part Seven is called "The Process of Accumulation of Capital." The second chapter in this part (the twenty-fourth chapter of the book as a whole) is titled "The Transformation of Surplus Value into Capital." Hence, this part is both about how capital is produced and how *new* capital is produced.

Part Eight is called "The So-Called Primitive Accumulation." As the part's chapter titles indicate, it deals with the historical emergence of the capitalist mode of production. As we can see, the structure of *Capital* emphasizes the difference between theoretical development and historical process mentioned in the Preface (see point B above). Tellingly, Marx *does not begin* with the historical emergence of capitalist production, but rather places it at the *end* of his analysis. That is, the historical sketch *follows* the theoretical development and presupposes it.

Since our reading begins with Part One, let's take a closer look at its structure. Part One is divided into three chapters:

Chapter 1: *The Commodity*
Chapter 2: *The Process of Exchange*
Chapter 3: *Money, or the Circulation of Commodities*

This breakdown may seem surprising: doesn't the commodity always have something to do with exchange, and doesn't exchange have to do with money (at least in the capitalist mode of production, which is what we are supposed to be examining)? Judging the usefulness of Marx's organization of the material will require reading further. However, during the course of reading, we should not only raise questions about each chapter's *content*, but also about its *unity* (the thread that runs through its material) and how it *differs* from the next chapter. It makes sense to also ask such questions at the end of each of the volume's eight parts. In doing so, consider the role of each chapter in the overall structure of the argument: Is it a matter of making the previous chapter more specific, completing it, or embarking on a new level of argumentation?

Part One: Commodities and Money

Chapter 1: The Commodity (125–77)

1. The Two Factors of the Commodity: Use-Value and Value (Substance of Value, Magnitude of Value) (125–131)

The distinction between use-value and value does not come from Marx. It is found in Adam Smith and long before that in Aristotle (384–322 BCE). However, Marx was the first to not only take up this distinction but to examine it in-depth.

a) Introductory Paragraph: Wealth and the Commodity (Definition and Analysis) (125)

The wealth of societies in which the capitalist mode of production prevails appears as an "immense collection of commodities"; the individual commodity appears as its elementary form. Our investigation therefore begins with the analysis of the commodity. (125)

Many readers will not want to dwell over this paragraph, because everything seems clear. Such readers often believe that Marx says that wealth in capitalist society is a collection of commodities, and he therefore wishes to begin by analyzing the commodity.

However, things aren't so simple. First, the passage begins with an assertion (wealth as a collection of commodities) that is questionable: in our everyday experience, the people considered "rich" are mainly those possessing a great deal of money, and money is usually not considered part of the "collection of commodities." Hence, it is an open question whether Marx and his conception of wealth are the same as the everyday one.

One should pay close attention to Marx's word choice. In my brief rendering of what many readers believe is the content of his first paragraph, I wrote that wealth "is" a collection of commodities, but Marx actually writes that it "appears as" a collection of commodities. What is the difference between "is" and "appears as"?

The verb "is" expresses a classification: "a lion is an animal" means that there might be animals that are not lions, but lions are always animals, and not, for example, plants.

"To appear as" (*erscheinen als*) is usually used in the sense of "to take the appearance of" or "to manifest itself as." It suggests the possibility of appearing *in another way*. If wealth *is* not a collection of commodities, but rather *appears* as a collection of commodities, that points to the possibility of wealth appearing as something else.

However, it does not mean that the appearance is deceptive. To speak about a possible deception, one does not use "appear" (*erscheinen*) but rather "seem" (*scheinen*). When one says, "This coin seems to be made of gold," it leaves open the possibility that the coin only looks like gold, but isn't really.

In writing that wealth "appears as" a collection of commodities, Marx is pointing to the possibility that wealth could appear as something else. Let's take another look at the first sentence: Marx emphasizes that his claim refers to "societies in which the capitalist mode of production prevails." In such a society, but not in every society, wealth "appears" as a collection of commodities.

It's obvious that Marx is distinguishing between societies where the capitalist mode of production plays only a subordinate role (or doesn't exist at all), and societies where other modes of production may exist, but the capitalist one "prevails." (He refers to such a society both as "bourgeois society," as in the Preface, and as "capitalist society"; see pages 103, 134, 667, 875.) Only in regard to capitalist society does Marx claim that wealth appears as a "collection of commodities." In other modes of production, there may be commodities (goods that are exchanged), but wealth, Marx implicitly claims, does not appear there as a "collection of commodities." Marx thus implies that the wealth of societies where other modes of production prevail will assume *different forms*, but wealth "appears" in capitalist societies in the *commodity* form.

ADDENDUM: In the first sentence of *Capital*, there is an implicit critique of Adam Smith's main economic work, *An Inquiry into the Nature and Causes of the Wealth of Nations*, published in 1776. Smith conceives the "wealth of nations" as a product of labor, regardless of the social formation. He thus begins his investigation with the division of labor. By conceiving wealth independently of society, Smith can more easily characterize capitalist relations as "natural." By contrast, Marx maintains that wealth takes on a specific form in "societies in which the capitalist mode of production prevails." His presentation does not begin with something like labor or the division of labor that is (really or seemingly) independent of the form of society. Instead, he proceeds from a specific form of wealth: wealth as a collection of commodities. That does not preclude wealth appearing in other forms in capitalist society. However, the form of wealth that is typical here, and *only here*, is the commodity form.

A final issue to consider: Marx speaks of "societies" (plural) in which the "capitalist mode of production" (singular) prevails. Evidently, Marx maintains that there is only one capitalist mode of production that, according to the Preface, is the object of his inquiry; still, he holds that there are different kinds of societies in which that mode of production prevails. It follows that his analysis of the capitalist mode of production does not address all social relations.

The word "therefore" in the second sentence in the opening paragraph suggests that Marx's decision to begin his analysis with the commodity follows from what precedes: his observation that wealth in capitalist societies appears as a collection of commodities and the commodity is its elementary form. However, this second sentence at best expresses a motivation, not a strict justification, for beginning with the commodity. For even if the first sentence is valid, it doesn't explain why we should begin with the commodity and not, for example, with money.

Basically, the first paragraph states that Marx begins his analysis with the commodity, and that he believes he has good reasons to do so. Only later in his account will we be able to see how good these reasons actually are. A frequently quoted observation from the Postface to the second edition addresses this problem, which pertains to every scientific account, not just Marx's:

> Of course the method of presentation must differ in form from that of inquiry. The latter has to appropriate the material in detail, to analyse its different forms of development and to track down their inner connection. Only after this work has been done can the real movement be appropriately presented. If this is done successfully, if the life of the subject-matter is now reflected back in the ideas, then it may appear as if we have before us an *a priori* construction. (102)

Any scientific account of a material reality presupposes the author's having acquired knowledge of it through a previous *research process*, allowing him to discover the material's "internal connections." However, the readers still have to acquire this knowledge. This means that when the author begins *presenting* his knowledge—employing concepts that are supposed to express the inner connections of his material—he has far more knowledge than the reader. The author cannot *immediately* share all the information he has acquired with the reader. Based on his prior knowledge, the author has to make certain decisions (such as where to begin and how to structure his presentation) that might initially appear arbitrary to the reader. For this reason, he might seem to be offering a construction that is "a priori" (prior to experience). Only to the extent that the readers have grasped the object can they later on verify whether the presentation was adequate.

The last sentence of the first paragraph—"our investigation therefore begins with the analysis of the commodity"—shows that Marx does not aim to *define* the commodity, but rather to *analyze* it. Marx is not simply defining what he understands by the term *commodity*. Rather, he takes the commodity as an object given in experience and analyzes it. That is to say, Marx dissects it, tracking down its particular features. He then develops concepts or "categories" (see point C of the commentary on the Preface) that express those features.

Furthermore, the first paragraph reveals something else: the commodity with which Marx begins his analysis is the commodity in *capitalism*. Exchange, commodities, and money exist in diverse modes of production—for example, in antiquity's mode of production based on slavery and in medieval feudalism. However, Marx is *not* dealing with the commodity as something universal, existing in various modes of production, but rather as the elementary form of wealth where "the capitalist mode of production prevails." Nevertheless, he has not yet explicitly spoken of capital. According to the table of contents, it is only in chapter 4 that capital itself becomes an object of inquiry. This shows that Marx initially analyzes the commodity produced *in a capitalist economy* but *in abstraction from capital*. This means that we are not yet dealing with the process of commodity production under capitalism or the sale of commodities as part of capital's circulation process (buying and selling as determined by capital). Hence, the power of abstraction that Marx speaks of early in the Preface (90) emerges right at the beginning of his account.

B) Use-Value (last paragraph 125 to penultimate paragraph 126)

> The commodity is, first of all, an external object, a thing which through its qualities satisfies human needs of whatever kind. (125)

Not everything that satisfies a human need is a commodity. But for something to be a commodity, it must satisfy some kind of need. This satisfaction of needs is now clarified in two respects. First:

> The nature of these needs, whether they arise, for example, from the stomach, or the imagination, makes no difference. (125)

That means that the *type of need* has no bearing on utility. If I assume that a certain rock protects me from evil spirits, then the rock is useful to me. Marx does not distinguish between "true" and "false" needs.

The second clarification refers to the *way of satisfying* needs:

> Nor does it matter here how the thing satisfies man's need, whether directly as a means of subsistence, i.e. an object of consumption, or indirectly as a means of production. (125)

In the paragraph that follows, Marx claims that useful things differ in terms of *quality* and *quantity*, and that it's the "work of history" to discover the uses of things. That means that their utility is not simply a given. In order to conceive something as useful, we must on the one hand have the corresponding need (both consumption and production generate needs) and, on the other hand, we have to be aware of the thing's properties. Needs of consumption and production, as well as our knowledge of things, develop historically.

The next paragraph introduces the concept of "use-value":

> The usefulness of a thing makes it a use-value. (126)

What has been stated about the usefulness of a thing, that it is both independent of the type of need and the way of satisfying it, also applies to use-value. Additionally, Marx identifies four further determinations of use-value:

First, usefulness, as Marx says, "does not dangle in mid-air" but is rather "conditioned by the physical properties of the commodity." He thus concludes:

It is therefore the physical body of the commodity itself, for instance iron, corn, a diamond, which is the use-value or useful thing. (126)

Second, use-value does not depend upon whether the appropriation of the thing's useful properties requires a lot or a little human labor.

Third, use-values are quantitatively defined; a use-value is not simply "wheat" (which is a certain *genus* of use-value), but it could be 10 kg of wheat, for example.

Fourth, Marx maintains:

Use-values are only realized [*verwirklicht*] in use or in consumption. (126)

We may add: the *use* of a thing always involves its faster or slower *consumption*.

Finally, the concept of "exchange-value" shows up in this paragraph:

They constitute the material content of wealth, whatever its social form may be. In the form of society to be considered here they are also the material bearers [*Träger*] of ... exchange-value. (126)

These two sentences contain a lot of implicit information. First, Marx no longer speaks about "wealth" indiscriminately here, as in the chapter's first sentence, but rather distinguishes the "material content" of wealth from its "social form." The *material content* of wealth in all societies consists of use-values, useful things. By contrast, the *social form* of wealth in capitalist societies—and now we can understand the opening of *Capital*—is the *commodity form*.

The use-value dimension of wealth is independent of its social form, insofar as that social form is not visible in the object itself. That is, one cannot see or taste whether wheat is a capitalistically produced commodity sold on the market or the tribute a serf pays to his lord.

Despite this, the social form of production does influence the *type and extent* of use-values produced. It is the "work of history" to discover ways of using things, and the "material content" of what is produced is by no means unaffected by society. Nonetheless, *material content* and *social form* must be carefully distinguished in our analysis.

A thing *is* a use-value based on its material properties, but it is not exchange-value in the same way. It *is not* simply exchange-value but rather, as Marx emphasizes, the "bearer" of exchange-value—and only within specific social relations. A diamond always has its hardness, but it only possesses exchange-value in a society where exchange occurs. Since use-values constitute the material content of *every form* of wealth, we don't learn anything about the *specific form* under examination here, the *commodity form*, if we look only at the commodity's use-value. Hence, we must now examine exchange-value.

Incidentally, the second sentence quoted above makes clear that when Marx examines exchange-value, he is concerned neither with the commodity in general nor with the commodity in a pre-capitalist society. Rather, he is dealing with the commodity "in the form of society to be considered here," that is to say, capitalist society.

c) Exchange-Value (Analysis and Construction)
(last paragraph 126 to penultimate paragraph 127)

Marx now analyzes exchange-value based on the exchange relation of one commodity to various other commodities. At this point, we might well be puzzled. The introductory paragraph indicated that Marx wishes to analyze the commodity *in capitalism*. But in capitalism, two commodities are not usually directly exchanged for each other. Rather, a commodity is sold for money and with this money another commodity may be purchased. The direct exchange of one product for another, without the mediation of money, is the exception, not the rule. And even in pre-capitalist societies, to the degree that exchange is a frequent occurrence, money is involved. So what is Marx considering? Clearly, it cannot be a phenomenon *typical* of capitalism.

At this point, Marx cannot simply argue that the commodity has use-value on the one hand, and is exchanged for money on the other, since money has not yet been introduced as a *category*. We may have an everyday understanding of money, but we do not yet have a scientific concept.

This means that Marx is analyzing a capitalistically produced commodity, which is normally exchanged for money, but he is doing so initially not only in *abstraction from capital* but also in *abstraction from money*. For that reason, Marx does not yet mention prices. The relation between the money price that we are familiar with in everyday life and exchange-value still has to be explained. Once again, we see the power of abstraction, mentioned in the Preface, operating here. The object of inquiry, the "commodity," is not simply *drawn* from experience. Instead, it is *constructed,* by means of abstraction, from what is empirically given.³

Why is such a construction necessary? Economic relations mutually depend on each other. Under capitalist conditions, we encounter commodities that are exchanged for money, money that buys commodities, capital that buys means of production as commodities and produces commodities, and so on. If our account is to begin with one of these relations, that relation must be extracted from its embeddedness in all the other relations. In doing so, one necessarily abstracts from a great many determinations that the relation normally involves. Later in our account, we must incorporate further determinations, and the relations initially abstracted from must be brought into play. The examination of exchange-value and the commodity does not end in the first pages of *Capital.*

Using abstraction to construct a new object (here, a commodity that is not determined by price) is a necessary step to begin the presentation. However, with every abstraction, we must ask whether precisely *this* abstraction is justified. What justifies making an exchange relation like *a quarter of wheat for x boot-polish*—an exchange that normally doesn't occur in capitalist society—the starting point for the analysis of exchange-value? In exchange mediated by money, the quarter of wheat is first sold for a certain amount of money; then, with this money, x boot-polish could be purchased. What Marx considers is not just any abstraction, but rather the overall *result* of exchange mediated by money. Whether this point of departure is adequate will be demonstrated later in his argument.

Exchange-value appears [*erscheint*] first of all as the quantita-

---

3. Lenin misunderstands this when he writes: "In his *Capital,* Marx first analyses the simplest, most ordinary and fundamental, most common and everyday *relation* of bourgeois (commodity) society, a relation encountered billions of times, viz. the exchange of commodities" (Lenin, *Collected Works,* Vol. 38, 358). But commodity exchange that is not mediated by money fails to be an everyday occurrence in bourgeois society. Wolfgang Fritz Haug takes Lenin's brief remark and turns it into the basis of an interpretation of *Capital*'s beginning section (Haug 2005: 48ff.). Haug conceives of the commodity with which Marx begins his analysis as a price-bearing commodity as might appear from the "perspective of a shopping trip" (49). He then immediately makes observations about money (50f.). This has nothing to do with Marx's argument at the beginning of *Capital.* Haug unintentionally reveals this by supporting his view with Marx quotations that aren't found at the beginning of the account in *Capital,* but rather in a later stage. What Marx really analyzes in the first pages of *Capital* is not (as Haug thinks), that "which we all know," but a construction based on an *abstraction* from what is universally familiar.

Commodities and Money

tive relation, the proportion, in which use-values of one kind exchange for use-values of another kind. This relation changes constantly with time and place. Hence exchange-value appears to [more correctly: seems to, *scheint*] be something accidental and purely relative, and consequently an intrinsic value, i.e. an exchange-value that is inseparably connected with the commodity, inherent in it, seems a contradiction in terms. (126)

Here, we must pay exact attention to the wording. Whereas in the first sentence Marx uses the verb *erscheinen* (appears), in the third sentence he uses *scheinen* (seems). "Exchange-value *appears first of all...*" means that this is only a first appreciation of exchange-value; the topic of exchange-value is thus not yet settled. What do we see at first glance? The exchange-value of a commodity is precisely what one receives for it in exchange. If a quarter of wheat exchanges for x boot-polish, then x boot-polish is the exchange-value of a quarter of wheat.

Just before, on page 126, Marx wrote that "in the form of society to be considered here," use-values are the "material bearers" of exchange-value. Now we can specify how: they are the bearers not of their own exchange-value, but of another commodity's exchange-value. In our example, the use-value "x boot-polish" is the material bearer of the exchange-value of a quarter of wheat.

Therefore, a commodity has *many different* exchange-values—as many as the various other commodities it is exchanged for. Furthermore, quantitative exchange relations vary with place and time. That's why exchange-value "seems" to be "something accidental and purely relative," and why the idea that an exchange-value could be "intrinsic" to a commodity seems to be a "contradiction in terms." If exchange-value were really something external and accidental, then it would be a contradiction to apply the adjective "intrinsic" to it.

When Marx says that exchange-value "seems" (*scheint*) to be accidental and arbitrary, he is not talking about something we simply *see* at first glance. Instead he is referring to an apparent or obvious conclusion—which could, however, also be wrong. By using the verb *scheinen*, Marx distances himself from the conclusion.

In the next paragraph, Marx tries to make clear that this apparent conclusion is in fact wrong. He considers the many different (and, one would have to add, simultaneous) exchange-values of a quarter of wheat: x boot-polish, y silk, z gold, and so on. Marx concludes that the quarter of wheat's different exchange-values must be "mutually replaceable or of identical magnitude" (127).

What does this sentence mean? The two phrases are connected by an "or," and the "or" is clearly not meant in an exclusive sense, that is, either one or the other, but rather in the inclusive sense, that is, the two statements are virtually equivalent. Is this true? It makes sense to say that the exchange-values are "mutually replaceable": y silk can replace x boot-polish as the exchange-value of a quarter of wheat, since y silk is also the exchange-value of a quarter of wheat.

However, what does their being "of identical magnitude" mean? X boot-polish and y silk are both exchange-values of a quarter of wheat. But now they are also supposed to be exchange-values "of identical magnitude." That is to say, y silk is supposed to be the exchange-value of x boot-polish, and x boot-polish is supposed to be the exchange-value of y silk. Even though the text does not explain why, it maintains that if a quarter of wheat exchanges for x boot-polish and for y silk, then x boot-polish must also exchange for y silk (and not, for example, 2y silk).

Why should this hold? When there are merely random and rare acts of exchange, it could indeed be the case that a quarter of wheat exchanges for x boot-polish or y silk, but that x boot-polish exchanges for more than y silk. However, if exchange is the *prevailing* form of economic intercourse (which is the case in capitalism), then such a situation would immediately lead to profits being made through a clever sequence of exchanges: y silk exchanges for a quarter of wheat; a quarter of wheat exchanges for x boot-polish; and x boot-polish exchanges for *more than y silk*. Through nothing more than this clever chain of exchanges, y silk would have transformed itself into *more than y silk*. The momentary existence of this kind of exchange relation cannot be excluded from the get-go. Nevertheless, if this kind of exchange relation were to exist permanently, it could only be explained by special social structures—power relations, structural information deficits, or the like. In the absence of such social structures, then, it's hard to see why people engaged in exchange would not *always* choose the favorable chain of exchanges and avoid the unfavorable ones (which would lead, however, to the favorable chain of exchange no longer existing, since nobody would be willing to opt for the unfavorable one). In reality, such structures might sometimes exist. However, we're at the beginning of the analysis and are considering the capitalist mode of production's most *general* character: the products of this mode of production have the form of commodities and exchange mediates social reproduction, but special circumstances that might foster the unequal exchanges described above are not part of the picture. That's why the statement that a commodity's various exchange-values are "of identical magnitude" makes sense.

Modern economists don't themselves question the claim that, barring special circumstances, individual acts of exchange must fulfill the condition described: if A can be exchanged for B or C, then B must also be exchangeable with C. (Formal mathematical techniques are usually applied here to demonstrate that the exchange fulfills the conditions of a so-called equivalence relation.) As we shall soon see, Marx goes a step further, in that he seeks something that in a certain respect is "behind" the relation of equivalence. For now, he draws two conclusions from the statement that the exchange-values of the same commodity are "of identical magnitude":

The valid exchange-values of a particular commodity express something equal.

and:

Exchange-value cannot be anything other than the mode of expression, the "form of appearance," of a content distinguishable from it. (127)

The bearers of a commodity's various *exchange-values* are, in the first place, certain *use-values*, which as use-values are *qualitatively different*. As "valid" exchange-values of the same commodity, they are also exchange-values *for each other* and to that extent also express something "equal," namely something *with regard to which* they are *of equal magnitude*. In some sense, a quarter of wheat, x boot-polish, and y silk are all expressions of something "equal," which is Marx's first conclusion.

Since the individual exchange-values, with their diverse material content, are qualitatively different use-values (x boot-polish is something completely different from y silk) but all express the same thing, Marx concludes that "exchange-value," that is, the quantity of a use-value that exchanges for a particular commodity, "cannot be anything other than the mode of expression" or "form of appearance" of "a content distinguishable from it"—Marx's second conclusion.

Exchange-value is thus no longer merely the *quantitative relation* in which use-values of one kind are exchanged for use-values of another kind (which is how exchange-value "first of all" appeared (126)). Now exchange-value is characterized as the *"form of appearance"* of a *"content"* that is as yet unknown to us.

Marx's mention of a "form of appearance" points to a *difference*: we now have a "content" that is not immediately visible but rather expressed in *something else*. This something else thus becomes that content's form of appearance. Form of appearance and content are not identical, but they don't just exist alongside each other coincidentally. In what follows in *Capital*, we have to pay attention not only to how this content is characterized, but also to *why* it requires a form of appearance that differs from it (the third subsection of chapter 1 provides the answer).

Our speaking of "content" and "form of appearance" might remind readers who are versed in philosophy of the distinction between "essence" and "appearance" that plays such an important role in Hegel's philosophy. But neither here nor in the whole first chapter does Marx speak of "essence"; it looks like, at least in this context, he consciously wishes to avoid such philosophical baggage. However, many interpreters introduce just that into the text. Not infrequently, Marx uses the terms "essence" (*Wesen*) and "essential/essentially" (*wesentlich*) in a common and colloquial sense—to refer to what is important or fundamental to a thing—but he sometimes uses them in a more specific sense. The relevant meaning should be elucidated based on context, and not by imposing a ready-made scheme on Marx's text. In the first volume of *Capital* in particular, Marx (unlike many of his interpreters!) is very sparing in his use of the word "essence" (*Wesen*): the term shows up for the first time on page 359 of MEW Volume 23 [page 458 of the Penguin Classics translation, where *Wesen* is translated as "nature"—Trans.].

In the next paragraph, Marx tries to demonstrate the same thing, that is, there is a "content" that is not immediately visible, using a single exchange equation (1 quarter of corn = x cwt of iron). Here two use-values are equated through exchange. If this equation is not merely coincidental but has a real significance (as is indeed the case in a society based upon exchange), then both things equated as exchange-values must have a qualitatively "common element." They must have a *quality* in common that makes them *comparable* in the first place, and they must both possess the same *quantity* of this "common element" for one to be able to speak of *equality*. This means that 1 quarter of corn and x cwt of iron must somehow be equal to a "third thing," which is neither corn nor iron. This "third thing" is the "content" that the previous paragraph refers to.

ADDENDUM: In the first edition of *Capital*, Marx refers to the common third thing as "value" in the example 1 quarter of corn exchanges for x cwt of iron, because they both have the same *value*. Hence, we can conclude that value is the *content* that is merely *expressed* by exchange-value and that exchange-value is the "form of appearance" of value. However, for now value is no more than a name. We don't know

Commodities and Money   59

anything yet about value or the "common element," the "third thing." It still has to be explained.

D) VALUE AND SUBSTANCE OF VALUE
(FINAL PARAGRAPH 127 TO LAST PARAGRAPH 128)

Marx now carries out a more detailed characterization of this "common element," or "value," and does so in three steps. First, he excludes all the natural properties of commodities from being candidates for this common element (127f.). Then he states that only one property remains, that of being products of labor (128). Finally, he presents labor, or more exactly "human labour in the abstract," as the "substance" of value (128). Objections have been raised against all three steps in the argument. We will carefully examine Marx's arguments, which occupy less than three pages.

First Step of the Argument: The Common Element of the Commodities Is Not a Natural Property

> This common element cannot be a geometrical, physical, chemical or other natural property of commodities. (127)

Why can't the common element in question be some natural property of the commodities? Marx's answer is that such natural properties only come into consideration to the extent that we are dealing with use-values. But:

> the exchange relation of commodities is characterized precisely by its abstraction from their use-values. (127)

How do we know that, in the exchange relation, an abstraction is made from the use-values of commodities? Marx's answer is that every use-value (boot-polish, silk, etc.) can be exchanged with another use-value (for example, a quarter of wheat), "provided only that it is present in the appropriate quantity" (127). Since every use-value is replaceable in the exchange relation—so Marx argues—no property of a specific use-value could matter. He then summarizes:

> As use-values, commodities differ above all in quality, while as exchange-values they can only differ in quantity, and therefore do not contain an atom of use-value. (128)

After dealing with the objections to this argument, we will return to Marx's account in *Capital*. But first we will briefly look at one issue. Marx attempts to ascertain what commodities have in common: their "value." In doing so, he does not consider the *production process of a single commodity*, but rather *the exchange relation of two commodities*. Therefore, only *based on* the exchange relation can Marx say that there is an abstraction from the use-value of the commodity, and then go on to draw further conclusions. This is important because of the long debate about whether the value of commodities is already established in production, or if it requires the unity of production and circulation (see chapter 3.4 of my *Introduction to the Three Volumes of* Capital, 52ff.). Here one must not only pay attention to what Marx says about value, but also *on what basis* he makes the statements.

There are two main arguments used to criticize Marx's rejection of use-value as a candidate for the common element we are seeking.

First Objection

One argument is that it makes no sense to abstract from use-value, since commodity owners only exchange commodities having use-values they don't need, in return for use-values they desire but don't possess. To that extent, it is nothing other than use-value that drives exchange.

What is said here about commodity owners and their thought processes is quite correct, but Marx is dealing with a different problem. Up to now in the text of *Capital*, Marx has not written of commodity *owners* and their *notions* and *motives* for exchange, but merely of *commodities*, which confront each other in an exchange *relation*. At this stage, Marx is obviously abstracting from commodity owners and their intentions.

One could wonder whether this way of proceeding is correct. If we look at an isolated exchange of water and diamonds between two travelers who encounter each other by chance in a desert, the exchange relation will be determined by whether one of the two is dying of thirst. Here, abstracting from the commodity owners would not be justified. However, as Marx makes clear as early as the first chapter's initial paragraph, he wishes to examine the commodity as the form of wealth in societies where "the capitalist mode of production prevails." Here, exchange does not occur coincidentally, but rather as the predominant form of economic intercourse. Among other things, this means that individual commodity owners usually face preexisting quantitative exchange relations that are completely independent of how they, as individuals, evaluate the usefulness of commodities. Under capitalist conditions, exchange relations have an objective character, which makes it possible for Marx to proceed by first abstracting from commodity owners and their relation to use-values.

ADDENDUM: Only in chapter 2, "The Process of Exchange," do commodity *owners* enter the picture. There Marx treats the relation of commodity owners to the use-values of their own and others' commodities (see point C in the commentary on that chapter).

Second Objection

Marx seeks the common element of exchanged commodities. It is clear that the element cannot be a *particular* property of a use-value, since exchange relations among commodities do not depend on *particular* use-values (every use-value is replaceable). However, it must *in general* be use-values that are exchanged. *Common* to the exchanged goods is, therefore, their *existence as use-values*, as useful things. The objection against Marx's reasoning is then that he mistakes the *abstraction from the particular modalities of a circumstance* that occurs in exchange with an *abstraction from the circumstance itself*: that the particularities of the use-values are not relevant does not mean that their existence as use-values is not relevant at all.[4]

Marx is aware that, as far as things being exchanged are concerned, their existence as use-values is a precondition for their being exchanged. His analysis in fact began by stating that *every* commodity is a use-value. The question, however, is whether *this* general precondition is *sufficient* to determine value. Most of the time, general preconditions don't say anything about a specific case. An example can make this clear. Every human society consists of people who live in it. In order to live, people must breathe. Breathing is therefore the precondition of every society. However, one won't discover anything about a particular society or its functioning by dealing with human breathing.

Neoclassical economics, which emerged in the last third of the nineteenth century, followed the very path laid out in this objection, by con-

---

4. Böhm-Bawerk (1949: 74ff.), who was the first to attempt a comprehensive critique of Marx's reasoning shortly after the publication of the third volume of *Capital*, made this very criticism of Marx. The "classic" refutation comes from Rudolf Hilferding (1904). However, parts of his defense of Marx were problematic. *After* reading *Capital*, a reader would do well to engage with this controversy for two reasons. On the one hand, it provides a way to check your own understanding of Marx's text. On the other hand, it is an entry point into contemporary controversies, since a good part of today's criticisms of Marx still rests on Böhm-Bawerk's arguments.

sidering exchange based on the utility or marginal utility of goods, that is, the increased utility brought by an additional unit of a good. Böhm-Bawerk, mentioned in footnote 4, was a representative of this school. However, since utility and marginal utility are purely subjective appraisals, neoclassical economists make individual commodity owners and their motivations into a self-evident point of departure for their reflections and no longer probe any deeper.

Here, we can draw an important conclusion. Because Marx's analysis initially abstracts from commodity owners, he is obviously operating initially on the level of social structure, which is always upstream from individuals and their actions, and must therefore be analyzed without reference to people's actions. Only the existence of such a level justifies Marx's statement in the Preface about people as "personifications of economic categories" (92). The fact that use-value is not a candidate for the common element we are seeking is *not* simply a result of Marx's close examination of a single exchange equation. Rather, his exclusion of use-value reflects a specific *strategy* for analyzing the exchange equation: whether we prioritize the *motives* of those acting (as in classical political economy and neoclassical economics), or whether we initially examine the *forms* that condition such activity and shape people's motives.[5] At this point in the text, we can only confirm that Marx is following the latter strategy—later on we will be able to judge whether he is *justified* in doing so.

Second Step of the Argument: Only the Property of Being a Product of Labor Remains

> If then we disregard the use-value of commodities, only one property remains, that of being products of labour. (128)

This sentence is problematic. People also exchange goods that aren't products of labor such as virgin land. Very casually, Marx restricts the world of commodities to products of labor, but this is hardly self-evident.

---

5. In Heinrich (1999) I attempt to make clear that Marx's critique of political economy constitutes a rupture with classical political economy's "theoretical field." Marx's critique of economics breaks with the fundamental assumptions about the economy and society that many quite different economic schools regard as self-evident. One of the implicit assumptions of political economy's theoretical field is that society and the economy are composed of individuals (or individual units), which then become the most fundamental units of analysis.

ADDENDUM: Marx wishes to *initially* analyze the value of commodities that are products of labor and then use it as a basis to examine the commodity form of goods that aren't products of labor. For example, the third volume of *Capital* deals with the price of virgin land in the section on ground rent. Strictly speaking, we cannot judge whether this way of structuring the book's argument is successful until we actually get to Marx's treatment of the commodity form of non-produced goods. However, one could criticize Marx for not explicitly pointing this out at the beginning of *Capital*. By contrast, in the *Contribution to the Critique of Political Economy*, Marx points out that he still must explain the exchange-value of commodities that do not contain labor (MECW 29: 302).

Third Step of the Argument: The Substance of Value Is Abstract Human Labor

Even if the common element of commodities consists in their being products of labor, they are nevertheless products of very *different concrete* acts of labor (a table is the product of carpentry, bread is the product of baking, etc.). In exchange, abstraction is made from their use-value. This abstracting from use-value also has consequences for the labor that produces the commodities:

> With the disappearance of the useful character of the products of labour, the useful character of the kinds of labour embodied in them also disappears; this in turn entails the disappearance of the different concrete forms of labour. They can no longer be distinguished, but are all together reduced to the same kind of labour, human labour in the abstract. (128)

First mentioned here, this "human labour in the abstract" is distinct from any concrete-useful labor. It has nothing to do with a *specific type* of labor expenditure, which is different from other types of labor expenditure. Marx speaks of abstract human labor, because a specific *reduction* occurs when things are *equalized in exchange*: the diverse useful types of labor are "reduced to the same kind of labor."

Nowhere does Marx claim that this reduction (which leads to abstract human labor) is *consciously* undertaken by commodity owners. As noted above, Marx is not yet concerned with commodity owners, but only with the exchange relations among commodities. His focus is therefore upon a reduction (and abstraction) that actually occurs in the exchange relation, *without the knowledge* of those participating in exchange, and which only *scientific analysis* can make visible.[6]

> Let us now look at the residue of the products of labour. There is nothing left of them in each case but the same phantom-like objectivity [*gespenstige Gegenständlichkeit*]; they are merely congealed quantities [*Gallerte*] of homogeneous human labour, i.e. of human labour-power expended without regard to the form of its expenditure. (128)

Marx describes what remains of the products of labor after abstracting from their use-value, the "residue," as a "phantom-like objectivity" [*gespenstige Gegenständlichkeit*, better translated as "spectral objectivity" —Trans.] At first glance, one might overlook such an expression or see it as merely a stylistic idiosyncrasy. Taking Marx's text seriously, however, means that we should ask about the significance of such an expression. Even after abstracting from their properties as use-value, labor products still represent something "objective" (*Gegenständliches*). However, this objectivity can no longer be grasped by the senses. If we associate it with weight, color, form, or any other quality, we always come back to use-value—but we've just abstracted from use-value! Thus, the objectivity is present but is as intangible as a ghost; hence it is a "spectral objectivity." The remainder of the sentence, in which this residue is described as "merely congealed quantities of homogeneous human labor," points in a similar direction. Something coagulate or jelly-like (*Gallerte*) is objective, but one cannot grasp it.

But what is this "spectral objectivity," this "coagulate"? Marx is seeking the "common element" in commodities that are exchanged. In exchange there occurs an abstraction from all characteristics related to use-value; only a "spectral objectivity" remains. Marx concludes that this is the common element, usually referred to as "value." The "spectral objectivity" is nothing other than the *value-objectivity* of commodities, as distinct from their objectivity as use-values:

> All these things now tell us is that human labour-power has

---

6. This kind of abstraction, which is not based on a mental process but rather on a certain relation (here, the exchange relation of commodities), may be referred to as a "real abstraction" in contrast to a mental abstraction. Sohn-Rethel (1973) was the first to make this distinction, which is very useful for interpreting Marx's value theory.

been expended to produce them, human labour is accumulated in them. As crystals of this social substance, which is common to them all [*Als Kristalle dieser ihnen gemeinschaftlichen gesellschaftlichen Substanz*], they are values—commodity values [*Warenwerte*]. (128)

Marx's first reference to "labor-power" occurs in the penultimate paragraph on page 128 (not only in the passage just quoted, but also in the preceding sentence). Labor-power is literally the "power" to work, but it does not only refer to physical power; labor-power means the *ability* or capacity to work. The "expenditure" of labor-power that Marx refers to here is the application of that ability: labor itself. This labor creates the product; for that reason, one could say that labor is "accumulated" in products. Labor may be something dynamic and procedural, but it comes to a standstill in the finished product: fluid labor has congealed in it. That's why Marx speaks of "crystals" in the next sentence: commodities, as crystallizations of this substance (labor), are "values."

What Marx explains here in an abbreviated way is frequently summarized by saying that labor is the substance of value. This statement is seen as an abridged version of Marx's theory of value. However, one must pay close attention to how Marx uses the terms "labor" and "substance."

Which labor is the substance of value? Marx by no means speaks of labor, always and everywhere, as the substance of value; rather, he speaks of *equal human labor* or *abstract human labor* as value's substance. But abstract human labor is not simply a matter of, for example, a carpenter making a table or a tailor fashioning a coat. We first obtain this abstract human labor *as a result of a process of abstraction:* that is, when abstraction takes place in the *exchange relation* from the use-values of the products exchanged, and thus from the useful character of the different labor activities. This implies that abstract labor only exists in a *specific* social context, not in every society. Abstract human labor expresses a purely *social* determination of labor, only found in societies based on exchange.

In what sense does Marx speak of "substance"? The concept of substance is a loaded one in the history of philosophy. Aristotle uses the term to describe what is essential or permanent in a thing, in contrast to its purely coincidental, changeable characteristics. Substance is, as it were, the "inside" of something, the bearer of its properties. Marx, however, speaks of a "social substance, which is common to them all" (*gemeinschaftliche gesellschaftliche Substanz*). It is firstly a "social" substance; secondly it is "common" to the goods exchanged. What is meant here by "social" and "common" needs to be examined more closely.

The substance in question is *abstract human labor*, thus something purely *socially* determined. In that sense, one could say this substance is itself a *social* substance: it does not express any natural qualities, but rather a specific *social relationship*.

ADDENDUM: Marx had already spoken of "value" at this point in *Capital*'s first edition. Before dealing with the substance of value, he stated concisely:

> Commodities as objects of use or goods are corporeally different things. Their reality as *values* forms, on the other hand, their *unity*. This unity does not arise out of nature but out of society. (Dragstedt 1976: 9)

Since value's existence is something social, the substance of value must also be something social.

Marx also emphasizes that commodities have this social substance "in common" (*gemeinschaftlich*). This statement is linguistically ambivalent. Does "in common" mean that each of the exchanged products contains this substance by itself and are each thus objects of value in their own right? In that case, if we place them beside each other, we can say they have something in common—in the sense that, if two people individually own cars, then they have car ownership in common. Or does "in common" here mean that the two products only collectively share the substance through their relationship with each other, just as two people can own a car together without each owning a car individually?

ADDENDUM: In *Capital*'s first edition, Marx wrote: "The common social substance which merely manifests itself differently in different use-values, is—labour" (Dragstedt 1976: 9). It sounds very similar to the sentence of the second edition, page 128, quoted above. However, what Dragstedt and Fowkes both translated as "common" are two different German words. In the first edition, Marx used "*gemeinsam*" (common) whereas in the second he changed it to "*gemeinschaftlich*" (in community). The latter is derived from "*Gemeinschaft*" (community). In fact, the sentence on page 128 would be better translated as "As crystals of this social substance, which they all hold in community..." That Marx changed from "*gemeinsam*" to "*gemeinschaftlich*" is a strong hint that he had in mind the second meaning mentioned above.

Let's summarize Marx's argument. It starts with the exchange relation between two commodities, then turns to the process of abstraction from their use-values that occurs in exchange and—as part of this abstraction—the reduction of the various types of useful labor to equal human labor or abstract human labor. Abstract human labor, as the substance of commodities' value, does not emerge on the basis of the *individual* commodity but is based on the exchange relation between commodities. If we consider only a single product and thus only *one* kind of labor expenditure, we cannot speak of "equal" human labor, for *equality* refers to something common to the *various* types of useful labor. This suggests that the "commonality" of the substance of value should be understood in the second sense mentioned above. Abstract human labor is not an *individual* product's substance of value. Only when products stand in a certain relationship to each other, namely in the exchange relation, are they commodities and objects of value. In that relation, abstract human labor is their common substance. Whenever we speak about an "individual" commodity in what follows, what is meant is a commodity in the exchange-relation with another commodity and not a commodity outside or before the exchange-relation.

ADDENDUM: Marxists hotly debate whether individual producers "create" value *in production*, independent of exchange,[7] or whether value only exists as a result of the reduction that occurs in the exchange of labor products, that is, as a result of production *and* exchange. Our arguments so far support the second interpretation. In a manuscript written in 1871–72 as preparation for the second edition of *Capital*, Marx explicitly addresses this point. He says this about products being exchanged:

> *Neither is in and of itself value-objectivity* [*Wertgegenständlichkeit*]; they are this only insofar as that this *objectivity is held in common* by them. Outside of their relationship with each other—the relationship in which they count as equal—neither coat nor linen possess value-objectivity or objectivity as congelations of human labor per se. (MEGA II/6: 30)

When Marx speaks here of "common" value-objectivity, his use of the term coincides exactly with the second sense of common mentioned above (on this manuscript, see Appendix 4).

This concludes Marx's three-step argument that aims to ascertain the "common element" of commodities. In the next paragraph (last one on page 128), Marx briefly recapitulates his presentation up to now, high-

---

7. This interpretation was dominant not just in traditional Marxism. It is also found among authors who appear to be critics of that tradition, such as Robert Kurz or Norbert Trenkle (see my debate with Trenkle in the journal *Streifzüge*, 1998–99).

lighting three terms containing the word "value": *use-value*; *exchange-value* as something independent from it; and *value* as the "common element" in commodities that presents itself "in the exchange relation, or in the exchange-value of the commodity" (this the "content" or "third thing" mentioned on page 127). Marx asserts that "the progress of the investigation will lead us back to exchange-value as the necessary mode of expression, or form of appearance, of value." For now, however, value must be considered "independently of its form of appearance" (128).

It's important to note the difference between exchange-value and value: the *exchange-value* of a commodity—for example, a quarter of wheat—is the quantity of *use-values* that is obtained by exchanging it (for example, x cwt iron). By contrast, the *value* of a commodity is that "spectral objectivity" possessed by the commodity (in exchange) as an *embodiment of abstract human labor*. Exchange-value is the "form of appearance" or "mode of expression" of this value—in being equated with x cwt iron, the value of a quarter of wheat becomes visible.

That exchange-value is the *form of appearance* of value does not mean that it's less important than value, which, by the way, is also true of the other forms of appearance mentioned in *Capital*. Exchange-value is in fact so important that Marx devotes the entire third section of chapter 1 to it.

e) Magnitude of Value and Productivity
(first paragraph 128 to first paragraph 131)

Marx's account so far has presupposed that value has a quantitative determination: 1 quarter of corn = x cwt iron "signifies that a common element of identical magnitude" exists in the two things (127). However, this quantitative character has not yet been *explained*. So far Marx's account has dealt only with value's form of appearance (exchange-value) and substance (abstract human labor). The *magnitude of value* must therefore be examined.

> A use-value, or useful article, therefore, has value only because abstract human labour is objectified [*vergegenständlicht*] or materialized in it. How, then, is the magnitude of this value to be measured? By means of the quantity of the "value-forming substance [*wertbildende Substanz*]," the labour, contained in the article. This quantity is measured by its duration, and the labour-time is itself measured on the particular scale of hours, days etc. (129f.)

It seems straightforward to trace the magnitude of value back to a quantity of labor substance. That is because, if labor is the substance of value, then the magnitude of value must depend upon the quantity of labor, and the quantity of labor is measured by a duration of time.

However, things aren't so simple: the substance of value is not simply "labor," but rather "abstract human labor" (as Marx's first sentence in this paragraph emphasizes again). Yet we don't know how *abstract human labor* should be measured. A clock is only good at measuring the time a *specific individual* uses to perform a *specific act of useful labor*: carpenter X requires two hours of labor today to manufacture a normal kitchen table. So we can certainly measure a quantity of *individually expended, concrete useful labor*. However, what does this measurement imply about the quantity of value-creating, *abstract human* labor involved? Can we conclude that, if the table is exchanged, then the carpenter's two hours of concrete labor count as two hours of value-creating, abstract human labor? Marx makes clear in the next paragraph that this cannot be automatically assumed.

He emphasizes that it is *not* the labor time *actually* required *by an individual producer* that creates value. This is his explanation:

> However, the labour that forms the substance of value is equal human labour, the expenditure of identical human labour-power. The total labour-power of society, which is manifested in the values of the world of commodities, counts here as one homogeneous mass of human labour-power, although composed of innumerable individual units of labour-power. (129)

So far value-forming labor—"equal human labor"—has been characterized as that which remains of concrete useful labor when one abstracts from its concrete-useful character in exchange. That is, Marx has only spoken about two distinct acts of useful labor that, by exchanging their products, are reduced to equal human labor. Now, by contrast, he refers to the "total labour-power of society," albeit qualifying it as something "manifested in the values of the world of commodities." Why does Marx now refer to the whole of commodity-producing labor?

In section C above, we stressed that exchange is not an isolated phenomenon in the capitalist mode of production, but rather the prevailing form of economic intercourse. We also saw that individual acts of exchange are connected with one another because a commodity's various exchange-values are equal in magnitude. In an isolated act of exchange, *this* wheat, produced by Producer A with his individual labor-power, stands opposite *this* silk, produced by Producer U with her individual labor-power. However, the wheat and silk here are, as commodities, part of the *entire* world of commodities, and are connected with the entire world of commodities via the entirety of exchange relations. As a commodity, it doesn't matter whether the wheat was produced by Farmer A or B; nor does it matter whether the silk as a commodity was made by silk-spinner U or V. Furthermore, it is irrelevant whether the wheat as a commodity exchanges for silk or for boot-polish. In a capitalist economy, each act of exchange is part of a totality of interconnected exchange acts. Moreover, within this entirety of interconnected exchanges, *all* useful acts of labor whose products are exchanged are reduced to equal human labor, and the individual differences between labor-powers are erased; for example, that one producer is able to produce faster, more powerfully, or more skillfully than another. Marx can therefore say that the "total labour-power of society, which is manifested in the values of the world of commodities, counts here as one homogeneous mass of human labour-power," namely as labor-power that expends "equal human labor." It is not in every society that the plurality of individual labor-powers count as *one* labor-power. Only in commodity-producing societies is that the case, and even there, only to the extent that labor-power is expended to produce commodities.

Individual labor-power expended to produce commodities only counts "to the extent that it has the character of a socially average unit of labour-power and acts as such" (129). What "creates value" is therefore not individually required labor-time, but rather the labor-time that an average labor-power needs to produce a commodity. Marx refers to this labor-time as "socially necessary labor-time":

> Socially necessary labour-time is the labour-time required to produce any use-value under the conditions of production normal for a given society and with the average degree of skill and intensity of labour prevalent in that society. (129)

Socially necessary labor-time depends, therefore, on two factors:

- "the conditions of production normal for a given society," that is, the state of technology, science, and infrastructure considered normal;
- "the average degree of skill and intensity of labor," that is, the normal qualification of labor-power and normal intensity of labor.

In the paragraph that follows, Marx summarizes his conclusions:

> What exclusively determines the magnitude of the value of any article is therefore the amount of labour socially necessary, or the labour-time socially necessary for its production. The individual commodity counts here only as an average sample of its kind. (129)

To the extent that the magnitude of a commodities value depends upon the quantity of socially necessary labor required to produce it (a point we will return to), Marx concludes:

> The value of a commodity is related to the value of any other commodity as the labour-time necessary for the production of the one is related to the labour-time necessary for the production of the other. (130)

The last two quotations are often taken to mean that the magnitude of value is already determined in production and therefore prior to exchange. But what determines value is not the individual labor-time actually expended in production. It is rather, as Marx writes elsewhere, the "socially necessary labor-time." Socially necessary labor-time is an "average magnitude" that depends upon "normal" production conditions. But it is only through market exchange that the normal state of technology and worker qualification can be determined. What is "normal" depends upon the kinds of producers that actually appear on the market. Spinning yarn by hand is only a "normal" condition of production if most yarn offered on the market is spun by hand. However, if most yarn on the market is machine spun, then hand spinning is no longer a normal production condition. Socially necessary labor-time depends upon the normal or average production conditions, but only in exchange does the average come to *exist* that determines socially necessary labor-time. Therefore, only through the exchange of products can individually expended labor-time actually be reduced to value-creating, socially necessary labor-time.

ADDENDUM: It is the process of competition among individual capitals that imposes "socially necessary labor-time." However, this process will not be dealt with here, since the category of capital has not yet been developed. Volume 1, chapter 3, 201ff., deals with the competition among commodity owners, and chapter 12 contains a first anticipation of the competition between individual capitals as a process of enforcing socially necessary labor-time. However, it is only in the third volume of *Capital* that Marx treats competition systematically.

The question remains, however, whether the reduction to socially necessary labor-time serves to fully explain the quantitative determination of value. At this point, two questions always come up. First, what about *different types* of concrete labor? Is all labor contributing to socially necessary time reduced to "equal human labor" to the same extent? Does, for example, an hour of *unskilled* labor devoted to collecting fallen fruit count as the same amount of value-forming abstract human labor as an hour of a goldsmith's highly skilled work? Marx addresses the relation between "simple" and "complex" labor later in chapter 1. Second, doesn't the relation between supply and demand play some role in determining the magnitude of value? I will return to this question below in the comments on the first subsection.

Another question should be addressed here. So far, we have only discussed the labor-time expended directly in production. Nevertheless, every production process also uses raw materials, intermediate products, and tools. How do they influence the finished product's magnitude of value? Marx first answers this question explicitly in the second subsection of chapter 7; however, we can already formulate an answer here. What is socially necessary to produce a specific product is not only the labor expended in the final stage of production (for example, the labor of a spinner who spins cotton into yarn on a spindle), but also the (socially necessary) labor required for the intermediate products (cotton) and the means of production (spindle). In this way, the spun cotton's value is completely incorporated into the yarn's value. The same goes for the spindle's value, to the degree that it wears out: if one spindle is used to create 1,000 pounds of yarn, then 1/1000th of the value of the spindle is incorporated into a pound of yarn.

In the next paragraph (130–31), Marx observes that the socially necessary labor-time which determines the magnitude of a commodity's value varies because of changes over time in both the social conditions of production and the workers' skill levels (their qualification). *Labor's productivity* or *productive power* (*Produktivkraft*) changes, that is, the amount of product that a worker can produce within a certain unit of time.

When the production of a certain commodity undergoes changes in productivity, it changes the quantity of labor that is socially necessary for its production and therefore the magnitude of the commodity's value. In effect, if productivity increases (that is, more products can be produced in the same amount of time), then the magnitude of value of an individual commodity decreases (a smaller amount of labor-time is required for its production). By contrast, if labor's productivity declines, then the commodity's magnitude of value will increase.

Commodities and Money 73

In this paragraph, Marx also mentions that diamonds are very rare, which means that finding them requires a great deal of labor-time. He expresses doubt that diamonds have ever been sold for their full value. Implicitly, Marx is rejecting the perspective that attributes commodities' value to their "rarity"; in fact, the rarity of diamonds means that much labor has to be expended to obtain them.

Works of art represent a special kind of rarity (a popular question in reading groups at this point): they are unique. Since unique things are not "average specimens," it makes no sense to talk here about "socially necessary labor-time" and "magnitude of value." Such unique objects are sold for whatever a buyer is willing to pay, and so value theory of any kind is out of place.

f) Concluding Observation: Use-Value and Value (penultimate paragraph 131)

The last paragraph contains a summary of Marx's account of use-value and value. He begins by stating:

> A thing can be a use-value without being a value. This is the case whenever its utility to man is not mediated through labour. Air, virgin soil, natural meadows, unplanted forests, etc. fall into this category. (131)

With the exception of air, all the use-values listed here are also sold. They therefore have exchange-value, but not value. This is possible because people acquire such goods as private property and sell them. But it remains to be clarified how their exchange-value is determined. As already noted in D above, Marx does so in the third volume of *Capital*. The argument of chapter 1 continues:

> A thing can be useful, and a product of human labour, without being a commodity. He who satisfies his own need with the product of his own labour admittedly creates use-values, but not commodities. In order to produce the latter, he must not only produce use-values, but use-values for others, social use-values. (131)

Not every useful product of human labor is a commodity. In a footnote, Engels points out that a use-value is not simply a commodity because it has been produced for others; it must also have been obtained through *exchange*. If I consume my own product, then this product would be a *use-value*, but not a *commodity*. The same holds if I produce something that is consumed by somebody else, but they don't obtain it through exchange—whether I gave it as a present or was obliged to cede it to them (for example, a medieval peasant's tribute in kind). The commodity form is always bound to *exchange*. A product only has *value* if it is *exchanged*. Whether a specific expenditure of labor produces value or not, doesn't depend on the labor's *content*, for example, the "meaningfulness" or "importance" the product of the labor has. It is merely a question of whether the product is *exchanged* or not. Hence, the claim that a certain kind of labor activity (for example, unpaid caring for a sick relative) does not create value, because the product is not sold, does not in any way mean that this labor is unimportant.

For a product to be exchanged or sold, it must be a use-value for the purchaser. Therefore, Marx concludes the paragraph saying:

> Finally, nothing can be a value without being an object of utility. (131)

g) Comments on the First Subsection's Arguments

The following comments address questions that frequently come up about the argument of this entire subsection.

First Comment: The Commodity Character of Services

When examining use-value at the beginning of the subsection, Marx states that the commodity is "first of all, an external object, a thing which through its qualities satisfies human needs of whatever kind" (125). Also, in the concluding final paragraph, the word "thing" comes up many times. It might appear that Marx considers only tangible things—objects like wheat, iron, boot-polish, but not services like cutting hair, giving piano lessons, or artists' performances—as commodities. However, he does not explicitly exclude services from the realm of commodities.

The question of the commodity character of services and how their value is determined is quite relevant. It is common to hear the opinion that the transition from "industrial society" to "service society" has completely changed capitalism, making Marx's analysis of value formation obsolete. In the second volume of *Capital* (2:134f.) Marx deals more extensively with the commodity character of services. However, even with the arguments developed thus far, we can begin to address the issue.

Commodities and Money 75

The difference between products of labor that are objects and services is a purely material one. A stand-alone product has a certain durability and does not need to be consumed right away, although with considerable differences, since a wardrobe could be in inventory for a year before I use it, whereas a bread roll should be consumed the same day it is baked. A service differs from this only in that *the times of production and consumption coincide*: a taxi driver produces a change of location that I consume in the moment; the barber produces an improvement of my appearance, the consumption of which begins with the act of production.

But the *commodity form* has nothing to do with the *material* properties of a thing. Instead, the *commodity form* is a *social* property, whose existence depends upon the nature of the social bond; a use-value becomes a commodity when it is transmitted to somebody else via exchange. The cake I bake for my guests is not a commodity, any more than the magic trick I perform for them. By contrast, if I sell the cake on the market and perform as a magician there (charging admission), then both are commodities. What is decisive for the *commodity form* is whether or not the transmission of a thing or service takes place through exchange. A service can therefore be just as much of a commodity as a material product.

Selling a service must be distinguished from *wage labor*. If I employ a worker by paying a wage, then I buy his or her *labor-power* (the ability to work), and use it as I see fit. I can then sell the product that results from this expenditure of labor-power. As the *customer* of a taxi driver, I merely buy a service (a change in location). However, as the *boss* of a taxi driver, I buy his or her labor-power (the ability to work, in this case to drive a car), pay a wage, and sell a change of location to customers. Chapter 6 in *Capital* deals with the buying and selling of labor-power.

SECOND COMMENT: SUPPLY AND DEMAND

Readers of *Capital* frequently ask about the relevance of supply and demand. For example, what if a certain product is produced with the average level of skill and conditions of production, but the total amount produced goes beyond the (paying) demand, that is, supply exceeds demand? Does that have an influence upon the magnitude of value?

Marx does not deal explicitly with this problem here. In the final paragraph of this subsection, he emphasizes that it's a *precondition* of products that assume the commodity form that they be "use-values for others, social use-values" (131). If a thing is useless, then "so is the labour contained in it; the labour does not count as labour, and therefore creates no value" (131). Based on this, we can discuss the problem of supply and demand. If a specific product is produced within the socially necessary labor-time, but the amount produced exceeds the *paying* social demand, then part of what has been produced is *useless* (under the conditions of commodity production) and thus does not represent "social use-value." The labor used to produce the excess amount is therefore also useless and not value-creating. As far as exchange is concerned, this could mean that a part of what is produced is not exchanged, but the rest is exchanged according to its content of socially necessary labor (in terms of the state of technology, organization, and skill). It could also mean that all of what is produced can be sold, but that every individual commodity (which, as emphasized above, only counts as an average example of its type) represents a correspondingly smaller magnitude of value. In this respect, the extent to which the total labor expended in a branch creates value does depend upon demand. Marx develops this thought explicitly in chapter 3 (201–2; see also my *Introduction*, 51f.).

Third Comment: Conscious Action on the Part of Those Engaged in Exchange?

In the course of our account so far, it's become clear that Marx is not examining commodity owners and their motivations or actions, but rather "the commodity" (as the title of chapter 1 clearly indicates). However, the result we've arrived at, that commodities as values represent nothing other than abstract human labor, raises a couple of questions. Do those engaged in exchange *know* this? Do they exchange their commodities in certain proportions because they know the amount of labor necessary for their production? In the first subsection of chapter 1, which we've been dealing with up to now, Marx does not say anything about this problem. In the chapter's fourth subsection, however, he explicitly mentions commodity owners' lack of awareness concerning their own actions (166f.). We will return to this problem below.

Fourth Comment: Labor and Appropriation

If we claim that only labor creates value, it raises the question of whether only the worker has the right to appropriate the product created. If we answer this question affirmatively, it might easily lead to condemning capital gain as "illegitimate" (because the profit is not derived from the capitalist's own labor). Did Marx make such a connection between labor and rightful appropriation? There is no indication of this in the first subsection, which is what we've covered so far.

Before Marx, the labor theory of value, as formulated by Adam Smith and David Ricardo, led some people to draw such conclusions. In the 1830s, the "Left Ricardians" argued that if the worker's labor creates all value, then this value should belong to the worker. Ferdinand Lassalle (1825–1864) likewise demanded the "undiminished proceeds of labor," a demand that became popular in the German Labor Movement of the 1860s. Later in the labor movement, Marx's labor theory of value was often seen as an attempt to prove that capital's profits were unjustified or even a "theft" of the worker. Conventional economic science's rejection of the labor theory of value in the nineteenth century has much to do with the consequences that were being drawn from the theory. By proving that not only labor but also capital creates value, conventional economics aimed to legitimate the capitalist's appropriation of profit.

ADDENDUM: Nevertheless, Marx is not trying to criticize profit as "illegitimate." In chapter 6, he proves that the valorization of capital does not violate the laws of commodity exchange, but actually complies with those laws. And in chapter 24 of the first volume, under the subsection titled "The Inversion Which Converts the Property Laws of Commodity Production in Laws of Capitalist Appropriation," Marx makes an important—albeit brief and frequently misunderstood—critique of the ideas circulating about the connection between labor and appropriation (see Heinrich 1999: 375ff.). He also explicitly criticized Lassalle's demand for the "undiminished proceeds of labor" (MECW 24: 84). Additionally, Marx rejects the opinion attributed to him that the surplus value appropriated by the capitalist amounts to "robbery" of the worker (MECW 24: 535). Marx did not aim to merely critique *distribution* within capitalist commodity production. Rather he critiqued the capitalist mode of production, with the aim of *abolishing* it.

FIFTH COMMENT: A PROOF OF VALUE THEORY?

Marx provides only a brief argument that it is *labor* that is expressed in value (128). As a consequence, there has been a great deal of debate about whether Marx provided an adequate "proof" of the "labor theory of value" (a term he himself never used). So let's ask whether Marx aspired to formulate such a proof.

As indicated in my commentary on the Preface (under D), changes in the scientific context must be taken into account. When Marx formulated his theory of value, Smith and Ricardo's "labor theory of value" was still the prevailing theory. In effect, the thesis that value expresses the labor-time needed for a commodity's production was not an extraordinary one in Marx's day. That's why Marx saw no need to provide an extensive "proof" that labor is the exclusive substance of value. Instead, he emphasized the *differences* between his theory of value and that of classical political economy.

Today, the scientific context is radically different: neoclassical economics is now the predominant economic theory, and it does not even inquire into the value behind price or about value's substance; its only interest is in price relationships, which are explained through utility or marginal utility ratios. Neoclassical economics views any kind of "labor theory of value" as scientifically obsolete, and therefore sorely in need of justification.

The search for a "proof" of the "labor theory of value" at the beginning of *Capital* often turns on a misunderstanding of Marx's argumentation. The supposition is that Marx takes an arbitrary, individual pair of objects of exchange (like 1 quarter wheat for x cwt iron), and then, on the basis of their exchange, he establishes that what is equated in this process is abstract human labor. It should be clear by now that Marx isn't arguing in this way.

ADDENDUM: If Marx were arguing based on the exchange of an individual pair of objects, then he would have to assume that empirically ascertained exchange relations, at least on average (that is, disregarding short-term fluctuations), correspond to the magnitude of value of the commodities exchanged. As he advances in his presentation, Marx emphasizes that this is precisely *not* the case. In a footnote in chapter 5, he notes that "average prices do not directly coincide with the values of commodities" (269n24; see also 329n9). But if commodities are by no means exchanged at their values, then one also cannot attempt a proof based on observing empirical acts of exchange. Marx has been examining the commodity *in capitalism* from the beginning, but he is initially *abstracting from capital*. Determining "average prices," however, presupposes a developed analysis of capital, and doing so first becomes possible in connection with the treatment of profit and average profit. Marx deals with the formation of average prices in the third volume of *Capital* under the heading "Transformation of Commodity Values into Prices of Production." Until then, he argues on the *assumption* (which he frequently emphasizes is just that) that exchange relations are determined by the magnitude of value of the commodities, that *commodities exchange at their value*. Marx doesn't deny that exchanging at value isn't the norm in a capitalist economy. However, he holds that capitalist relations can only be depicted by using value theory as *the starting point*. Whether this is true can only, in fact, be evaluated at the end of the third volume, after we have followed Marx's overall argument.

If Marx does not intend to provide a "proof" of the labor theory of value in this first subsection, what are his arguments trying to do?

He is simply beginning to analyze the commodity and indicating those areas where his theory of value constitutes a critique of classical political economy's labor theory of value. Marx can only hint at these areas of divergence at the beginning of the presentation; later, however, he will take them up again. Of particular importance are the following:

- The distinction between *material content* and *social form*, which pertains not only to commodities, and was largely ignored by classical political economy.
- It is not just *labor* that creates value, but rather *abstract human labor*. The second subsection of chapter 1 deals in greater detail with the distinction between concrete, useful labor versus abstract human labor, a distinction not known by political economy.
- The substance of value is something held *in community* (*gemeinschaftlich*), which commodities only have through exchange. The consequences of this will become clear in the course of the third subsection's analysis of the value-form.
- Marx describes value-objectivity (*Wertgegenständlichkeit*) as "phantom-like" (*gespenstig*, better translated as "spectral"), which is somewhat surprising—what do ghosts have to do with the economy? In the fourth subsection, which deals with the fetish character of the commodity, this will become clearer, as will political economy's bias within this "spectral" framework.

Many introductions and summaries of Marx's *Capital* assume that this first subsection contains everything essential about value theory. The essential thing is taken to be that "labor creates value." But that merely reduces Marx's theory of value to its starting point, the contemporary discourse of classical political economy. Making that assumption leads to completely overlooking the points that constitute a *critique* of classical political economy, which may be mere hints in the first subsection but are elaborated in later subsections. This critique is not just a question of economic science's technical details, but rather of its fundamental approach to understanding and analyzing capitalist society.

2. The Dual Character of the Labor Embodied [correct: Represented] in Commodities (131–37)

The title should be read carefully: the topic is not the dual character of "labor" per se, but rather the dual character of the labor "embodied in [*dargestellt*, better translated as "represented in"] commodities." Marx is discussing a specific historical form of labor.

a) Introductory Paragraph: "Crucial" Distinction for Understanding Political Economy (final paragraph 131)

Marx picks up on the first subsection's exposition here: the commodity initially appeared "as an object with a dual character, possessing both use-value and exchange-value." Marx would have been more precise had he spoken instead of use-value and *value* here (as he does in the first subsection's title). In the next sentence, Marx's language becomes more exact:

> In so far as it [labor] finds its expression in value, it no longer possesses the same characteristics as when it is the creator of use-values. (132)

The first subsection has already addressed this; here it is to be merely "further elucidated." Hence it is not a new level of argumentation, nor a new set of concepts, but rather a deeper examination of the previous section's themes.

Why is a deeper examination called for? Marx emphasizes that the "twofold nature of the labour contained in commodities" is "crucial to an understanding of political economy" (131). What does that mean exactly? The original German phrase "*das Verständnis der politischen Ökonomie*" is ambiguous; just like the title of the first book it can be either a *genitivus subjectivus* or a *genitivus objectivus*. That is, it could mean, on the one hand, political economy's understanding of something (the themes it investigates); or, on the other hand, the understanding that one has of political economy. Since in the first section Marx did not deal with scholarship about the commodity, but rather began by first presenting his own analysis, it's likely that he had the genitivus subjectivus in mind. That is, the "dual character" of commodity-producing labor is "crucial" to grasping what political economy endeavors to understand— namely, the commodity, money, capital, etc.

Marx also emphasizes that he was "the first to point out and examine critically" this issue. That implies, in turn, that political economy *before* Marx could not fully succeed in carrying out its analysis of the commodity and other derivative analyses, since it failed to clarify this crucial point. As we read further into Marx's exhaustive discussions of labor's

Commodities and Money 81

"dual character," we should pay attention to whether it is in fact "crucial" to our understanding, and whether Marx makes clear how political economy fails by not elucidating this crucial issue.

b) Concrete, Useful Labor
(first paragraph 132 to first paragraph 134)

The following observations take as their starting point two commodities: a coat and 10 yards of linen. Both are use-values satisfying specific needs. A use-value results from specific productive activity, and Marx refers to the labor that creates a specific use-value as "useful labor."

Qualitatively different use-values result from qualitatively different acts of useful labor. There is a *social division of labor* in the diverse totality of useful labor activities. About this social division of labor, Marx states:

> This division of labour is a necessary condition for commodity production, although the converse does not hold; commodity production is not a necessary condition for the social division of labour. (132)

The social division of labor is a *necessary* condition of commodity production, but not a *sufficient* one: there can be a social division of labor without products being exchanged for each other, as Marx emphasizes by referring to historical examples and the division of labor within a factory.

> Only the products of mutually independent acts of labour, performed in isolation, can confront each other as commodities. [Corrected translation: Only the products of autonomous and mutually independent private acts of labor can confront each other as commodities.] (132)

Here, Marx indicates the most general social precondition of commodity exchange and he introduces for the first time an emblematic term for it: labor must be expended through *private acts of labor* that are independent of each other.

The social division of labor means that the various labor activities are *materially dependent* on each other (the tailor who makes a coat relies upon others to produce the necessary cloth, needles, etc.). However, in commodity production the individual acts of labor are carried out *inde-*

pendently of each other—only on the market do the products of labor meet. Although the individual commodity producer attempts to estimate what he can sell on the market, he decides *privately*—independently of other producers—what to produce and how much. And it is only on the market that he learns whether his decisions were correct.

In the first subsection of chapter 1, Marx speaks of "individual units of labor-power" and the "individual hour of labour" (129). This "individual" labor expenditure should not be confused with "private labor." When Marx speaks of individual labor expenditure, he's referring to the difference between individual A and individual B (for example, A works faster than B). By contrast, "private labor" refers to a specific social context where the various acts of labor take place: that the individual acts of labor are "private" means that they are executed independently of one another and are not coordinated. If these individual acts of labor were coordinated, it would no longer be private labor. However, in that case, the acts of labor would still be individual acts of labor and would still exhibit individual differences.

Finally, it must be remembered that up to now, Marx is abstracting from capital, but is still examining the capitalistically produced commodity (see the commentary on the first paragraph of 125). This means that "producers" are not just individual people, but also entire *capitalist enterprises*. These enterprises produce "privately," that is, independently from other capitalist enterprises. And they exhibit "individual" differences. For example, some enterprises will produce with more modern techniques than others and be able to produce the same amount of product in a shorter period of time.

In the last paragraph starting on page 132, Marx observes that attaining a certain level of the social division of labor is a precondition of commodity production, and that the division of labor constantly deepens as commodity production extends. In the next paragraph, however, Marx notes that whether a coat is exchanged is irrelevant to its use-value. It's also irrelevant to its use-value whether tailoring is an independent trade. Here, we could object that products improve with progress in the division of labor, so that the division of labor *does* have an influence upon use-value. However, Marx's point is merely that the coat's use-value—independently of exchange and the division of labor—is always the result of a specific useful labor activity. About this useful labor, he writes:

> Labour, then, as the creator of use-values, as useful labour, is a condition of human existence which is independent of all forms

of society; it is an eternal natural necessity which mediates the metabolism between man and nature, and therefore human life itself. (133)

It seems self-evident to us today that all societies require useful labor activity that provides use-values. However, the sentence's language is anything but self-evident. In pre-capitalist societies, different kinds of useful labor frequently had diverse social and cultural connotations. Even today, some labor activities are frowned upon and others are popular. In medieval feudalism and in antiquity, however, particular activities were closely associated with the society's conceptions of honor. Also, specific groups of people had "estates" that either allowed or forbade them to engage in certain jobs. Bringing all these different activities together under the single term "useful labor" is therefore a mental abstraction that first becomes possible in a society where individual acts of labor have largely lost such cultural connotations. That means that this apparently simple and trivial sentence about useful labor as a condition of human existence, which is independent of all forms of society, can only be formulated under the conditions of modern capitalist society.

The same can also be said about the term "use-value": mentally associating quite different goods, products, and services as use-values first becomes possible in a society in which these things and services possess a common *form* that is indifferent to their concrete content. This indifferent-to-content form is the value-objectivity of commodities, which is the predominant social form of things and services in capitalist societies. Only when most things and services are present as commodities can one mentally compare these various objects and services and ask what they have in common beyond the commodity form, establishing that they are all "use-values."

ADDENDUM: In the "Introduction" of 1857, Marx discusses, using the example of labor, how the possibility of forming certain abstractions depends on social conditions (see *Grundrisse*, 103f.).

In the final paragraph on *Capital*'s page 133, Marx finally addresses the question of what creates value and wealth: labor alone or both labor and nature. To respond, however, it's necessary to clarify whether the question refers to use-value or value in exchange.

As use-values, things are "combinations of two elements, the material provided by nature, and labour" (133). Marx's answer is not original, as his reference to William Petty indicates. He states:

Labour is therefore not the only source of material wealth, i.e. of the use-values it produces. (134)

Nature plays a role in creating *use-value*, but not in creating value. The latter, in contrast to use-value, is a purely social quality. It only exists in a society based on exchange. That's why nature cannot have a share in creating value.

c) Abstract Human Labor, Simple and Complex Labor (Second Paragraph 134 to First Paragraph 136)

Marx begins by summarizing what has already been developed in the first subsection of chapter 1 (128): "As values, the coat and the linen have the same substance, they are the objective expressions of homogeneous labour" (134). Tailoring and weaving, however, are qualitatively different labor activities. They are only homogeneous if one disregards their differences. In that way, both labor activities become simply the expenditure of human labor-power. Now comes a new thought:

> Tailoring and weaving, although they are qualitatively different productive activities, are both a productive expenditure of human brains, muscles, nerves, hands etc., and in this sense both human labour. (134)

This sentence is obviously meant to describe the "homogeneous labor" that is expressed in value. However, the remark is problematic in two respects. First, if we reduce labor to the expenditure of brains, muscles, and nerves, then it is far from homogeneous. Individual acts of labor differ from each other precisely because they require different amounts and proportions of brains, muscles, and nerves. Second, Marx has emphasized several times—in the title and at the beginning of this subsection—that he is discussing the dual character of "the labor represented in the commodity." But *every* kind of labor, whether it is represented in commodities or not, can be reduced to the expenditure of brains, muscles, etc. We will return to this problematic statement when discussing the final paragraph of this subsection.

The same paragraph introduces another issue. Marx distinguishes here between "simple average labor" and "complex labor." Simple average labor is the expenditure of simple labor-power,

> the labour-power possessed in his bodily organism by every ordi-

nary man, on the average, without being developed in any special way. (135)

At first, it sounds like Marx is characterizing labor-power solely on the basis of the human being's biological capacity. However, in the next sentence, Marx clarifies that he is not referring to labor-power as something biologically given, but rather socially produced. In particular, he adds that simple average labor is present in all societies but "varies in character in different countries and at different cultural epochs."

Simple labor-power involves all the abilities that are normally expected of a given society's members. For example, in the centers of capitalism today, one may assume that the vast majority of workers can read and write. Just two hundred years ago, these were high-level qualifications that only a minority possessed. Marx describes all labor activities requiring no more than skills possessed by the great majority as "simple average labor." He refers to labor activities requiring further qualifications as "complex labor."

Through the process of exchange, the products of *simple average labor* are equated as values to the products of complex labor; in that way, both simple average labor and complex labor are reduced to value-creating, equal human labor. However, they are reduced to value-creating abstract human labor in different measures:

> More complex labour counts only as *intensified*, or rather *multiplied* simple labour, so that a smaller quantity of complex labour is considered equal to a larger quantity of simple labour. (135)

An hour of a specific complex labor activity (for example, goldsmithing) might be reduced to three times as much abstract human labor as an hour of simple labor. In that case, what is produced by an hour of such work will have the same value in exchange as that produced by three hours of simple labor. It is not uncommon to abbreviate this by saying that an hour of goldsmithing creates three times as much value as an hour of simple labor. Strictly speaking this is wrong, however, since goldsmithing is concrete useful labor and does not create value any more than the simple labor of collecting fallen fruit; both merely produce use-value. Only abstract human labor creates value. It is just that goldsmithing and collecting fallen fruit are reduced to abstract human labor in different proportions.

In footnote 15, Marx emphasizes that the equating of different labor activities does not have to do with the different wages paid in the various sectors of the economy, but only with the value of the commodity in which the labor is objectified. He adds:

> At this stage of our presentation, the category of wages does not exist at all. (135n15)

The wording of this sentence merits careful reading. Marx does not write, for example, that we are considering social relations where wage labor does not exist, thus prior to the capitalist mode of production. Rather, he emphasizes that the "category" of wages does not yet exist at this *stage of his presentation*. Our commentary on the Preface (in point C) stressed the importance of distinguishing between social relations and the categories through which these relations are grasped. That distinction becomes important here, too. As Marx makes clear as early as page 125, in the first subsection's initial paragraph, he is dealing with the capitalist mode of production from the very start. The social relations and circumstances of wage labor, capital, the commodity, money, and so on, simultaneously form part of this reality from the beginning. However, the *categories* expressing these relations must be presented one after another. Marx began his presentation with the category of "the commodity." But other categories, such as *wages*, do not yet exist at this *stage of the presentation*. That is, these categories cannot yet enter into the arguments, nor can we say anything about them yet.

If complex types of labor are equated to specific portions of simple labor through exchange, then determining these proportions is of interest. However, Marx limits himself to saying that the proportions are not consciously set:

> The various proportions in which different kinds of labour are reduced to simple labour as their unit of measurement are established by a social process that goes on behind the backs of the producers; these proportions therefore appear to the producers to have been handed down by tradition. (135)

Marx points out that in the ensuing presentation he will assume that the labor expended is always simple labor, so that converting from complex to simple labor is not necessary.

Some critics have criticized Marx for being unable to determine these proportions more exactly. Among them is Böhm-Bawerk, mentioned earlier. However, it's doubtful whether these proportions *could be determined at all*, given the very general level of Marx's arguments (see the commentary on the Preface, point B).

ADDENDUM: In chapter 7, Marx returns briefly to the relation between simple and complex labor and points to the influence of "accidental" factors:

> The distinction between higher and simple labour, "skilled labour" and "unskilled labour," rests in part on pure illusion or, to say the least, on distinctions that have long since ceased to be real, and survive only by virtue of a traditional convention; and in part on the helpless condition of some sections of the working class, a condition that prevents them from exacting equally with the rest the value of their labour-power. Accidental circumstances here play so great a part that these two forms of labour sometimes change places. (305n19)

This characterization of what counts as complex labor includes social prejudices and power relations. The historically strong or weak positions of certain groups also play an important role. Beyond the factors that Marx mentions, there are also asymmetrical gender relations, which lead to activities usually carried out by women being counted as "simple" labor, in contrast to similar activities that might be primarily carried out by men. Moreover, the concrete ways that simple and complex labor are hierarchized differ from country to country, and within a country they change over time. The exact proportions in which complex labor is reduced to simple labor become manifest in exchange.[8]

In the three paragraphs that follow (final paragraph 135 to third paragraph 136), Marx summarizes his characterizations of concrete useful labor and abstract human labor. He states that the various labor activities, due to their *different qualities*, yield different *use-values*. However, these different labor activities only become the *substance of value* insofar as abstraction is made from these different qualities causing the different acts of labor to count as labor of *equal quality*. The *magnitude* of value, in turn, depends upon the *quantity* of this labor of equal quality contained in the commodity.

The next two paragraphs (136 fourth paragraph to 137 second paragraph) deal with the interrelation between concrete useful labor and abstract human labor, on the one hand, and the productivity of labor, on the other. Initially, Marx repeats one of the first subsection's conclusions (see 130f.): if labor productivity increases in the production of a certain article, then this article can be created with less socially necessary labor-

---

8. See chapter 3.3 of my *Introduction* for a discussion of the three reductions occurring in exchange: individually expended labor-time to socially necessary labor; complex labor to simple labor; and the labor actually expended in a branch to the labor that is in fact required to satisfy paying demand in the society (Heinrich 2012: 48–52).

time; provided all other circumstances remain the same, the magnitude of the article's value will decrease (136).

In the next paragraph, Marx brings up another issue. A larger quantity of use-values constitutes a greater amount of *material* wealth than a smaller quantity. If labor productivity increases, then more material wealth can be produced in the same time period. Productivity "always" means "the productivity of concrete useful labor" (137). If we abstract from the useful character of labor, then productivity ceases to count. Abstract human labor "performed for the same length of time, always yields the same amount of value, independently of any variations in productivity" (137). The dual character of the labor represented in commodities explains the seeming paradox that an increased mass of use-value can represent less value: this can happen when, due to increased productivity, a larger mass of use-values is created with less (socially necessary) labor-time than the original mass of use-values.

From the final paragraph of page 135 to the first paragraph of 137, Marx compares concrete useful labor and abstract human labor from various perspectives. He does not elaborate on an issue mentioned in the second paragraph on page 133. There, Marx emphasized that *useful labor* "is a condition of human existence which is independent of all forms of society." Based on this, one might wonder how things stand with *abstract human labor*, but Marx doesn't address that question here.

ADDENDUM: In the much briefer juxtaposition of useful and abstract labor in the *Contribution to a Critique of Political Economy* (1859), Marx is clearer on this point than in *Capital*. Take into account that in this earlier text, Marx does not yet distinguish between the terms exchange-value and value. However, after characterizing useful labor as a condition of human existence, he continues:

> On the other hand, the labour which posits exchange-value is a specific social form of labour. For example, tailoring if one considers its physical aspect as a distinct productive activity produces a coat, but not the exchange-value of the coat. The exchange-value is produced by it not as tailoring as such but as abstract universal labour, and this belongs to a social framework not devised by the tailor. (MECW 29: 278)

After reading the initial chapter's first subsection, it shouldn't surprise us that value-creating labor, which Marx refers to here in his earlier language as "the labor that posits exchange-value," is "a specific social form of labor." In that subsection, Marx already made clear that the substance of value, "abstract human labor," is a "social" substance and by no means

Commodities and Money 89

a natural one. It pertains to a specific social context, that of commodity production.

It is important to note this difference here. At the beginning of the subsection now being examined, Marx referred to commodity-producing labor's dual character as "crucial" to an understanding of political economy. Further, when pointing out that he was the first to make the distinction, Marx is indirectly accusing political economy of not having this crucial insight. But if useful labor is an independent condition for the existence of all human life, and abstract human labor is a *specific social form*, then lack of clarity concerning this difference leads to *the specifically social* being confused with *that which is independent of social form*: what is specifically social comes to be seen as something natural and inevitable.

d) Final Remark, Physiology
(last paragraph 137)

> On the one hand, all labour is an expenditure of human labour-power, in the physiological sense, and it is in this quality of being equal, or abstract, human labour that it forms the value of commodities. On the other hand, all labour is an expenditure of human labour-power in a particular form and with a definite aim, and it is in this quality of being concrete useful labour that it produces use-values. (137)

Marx appears to be merely summarizing his conclusions here. However, if one takes a closer look at the wording, some problems emerge. For one, Marx speaks of "all" labor (without further qualification) being both abstract human labor that creates value and concrete useful labor that produces use-values. But in fact only the labor that produces *commodities* creates value. Marx has made clear, both in the title of this subsection and in the initial paragraph, that he is concerned with the labor *represented in commodities*. For that reason, it makes sense to understand the expression "all labour" as an abbreviation for "all labor *represented in commodities*."

However, the property of labor that Marx now claims as its value-creating character, the expenditure of labor in the physiological sense, is by no means bound to commodity production. Every type of labor, whether that of a slave or Robinson Crusoe on a deserted island, is always both the expenditure of labor-power in the physiological sense (the expenditure of "brains, muscles, nerves, hands" as Marx puts it on page 134) and useful activity. It's problematic that Marx uses such a transhistorical characteristic of labor to characterize abstract human labor.

The first subsection of chapter 1 introduced abstract human labor. There it was shown to result from the reduction—characteristic of the exchange relation—of the various concrete useful acts of labor to equal labor. This reduction is not an action of individual commodity owners, but rather a social process consummated in exchange. The abstract human labor resulting from this *social process of reduction* does not express a physiological property of labor, but rather a purely *social* one. Of course, it's true that every labor expenditure is based upon physiological processes: the exertion of "brains, muscles, nerves, hands." But such an abstraction says nothing about the abstraction happening in the social process under examination here. By the same token, one could say that all people are "equal" to the extent that they breathe. But physiological equality doesn't say anything about social relations, nor about the legal relations under which humans count as "equal." Abstractions derived from physiological commonalities, and those expressing a social way of "being equal," are two completely different things.

ADDENDUM: In subsequent chapters, Marx does not return to this "physiological" characterization of abstract human labor; it is not a fundamental part of his argument (the only other allusion to it is in the fourth subsection of this chapter). Moreover, the first edition of 1867 contains no reference to physiology. There Marx writes in summary:

> It follows from the preceding not that there are two differing kinds of labour lurking in the commodity, but rather that the *same* labour is specified in differing and even contradictory manners—in accordance with whether it is related to the use-value of the commodity as labour's *product* or related to the *commodity-value* as its merely *objective* expression. Just as the commodity must be above all else an object of use in order to be a value, just so does labour have to be before all else useful labour—purposeful, productive activity—in order to count as *expenditure* of *human labour-power* and hence as simple *human labour*. (Dragstedt 1976:16)

How should we understand the reference to physiology in the second edition? At best, it is a clumsy presentation. Less favorably, it might express some ambivalences in Marx's argument.[9]

---

9. In the 1920s, Russian author I. I. Rubin pointed out the difference—in a book that is still worth reading—between "social" and "physiological" characterizations

In footnote 16, at the end of this subsection, Marx deals briefly with Adam Smith's justification of the labor theory of value. According to Smith, equal quantities of labor always have the same value for the worker. Marx criticizes Smith for confusing "his determination of value by the quantity of labour expended in the production of commodities with the determination of the values of commodities by the value of labour." Marx has already discussed the (socially necessary) labor-time required for the production of a commodity, but has not yet dealt with the "value of labor." From his contrasting the two, we can see that Marx strictly distinguishes between "value-creating labor" and "the value of labor." However, he does not yet explain the difference.

ADDENDUM: In chapter 19, when dealing with wages, Marx addresses for the first time the expression "the value of labor"—and above all criticizes this expression. Wage laborers do not sell a specific product, but rather (or so it seems) their "labor." Thus, we might ask how the "value of labor" is determined. In chapter 6, however, Marx demonstrates that the wage laborer does not sell his or her "labor," but rather his or her "labor-power," meaning the ability to perform labor. Hence, chapter 19 deals with the illusion prevailing in everyday life that "labor" itself is sold, and that wages pay the "value of labor."

Marx then mentions an anonymous predecessor of Smith who, instead of confusing the quantity of value-creating labor with "the value of labor" as Smith does, writes that in exchange, a man "cannot make a better estimate of what is a proper equivalent, than by computing what cost him just as much labour and time" (138n16).

This predecessor may not be making the same mistake as Smith, but he does argue—in this respect, just like Smith—that the exchange relation emanates from the subjective estimation of those involved in exchange: because these people know that the same quantity of labor is contained in both products they are willing to exchange them in specific quantities. This kind of argument is still problematic: at most, those engaged in exchange know the amounts of concrete labor required in production. Such labor, however, is not identical with value-creating, abstract human labor. In this sense, it's problematic that Marx does not criticize Smith and his predecessor's shared assumption that those engaged in exchange

---

of abstract labor. He saw this as primarily a problem of Marx's presentation (Rubin 1973: 134ff.). However, I have shown that Marx's critique of political economy exhibits not just problems of presentation but also fundamental ambiguities (see Heinrich 1999).

know what they're doing. By contrast, in the fourth subsection, which deals with the commodity's fetish character, Marx will emphasize that those exchanging commodities "do not know" what they are doing.

ADDENDUM: In his 1859 *Contribution to the Critique of Political Economy*, Marx deals with the passage from Adam Smith quoted in footnote 16. In this earlier work, he likewise criticizes Smith's confusion of value-creating labor and the value of labor, but adds as a criticism of Smith that he

> mistakes the objective equalisation of unequal quantities of labour forcibly brought about by the social process for the subjective equality of the labours of individuals. (MECW 29: 299)

In this way, Marx makes it clear that Smith mistakes an objective social process, which occurs "behind the backs" of the actors, with an expression of their subjective will.

3. The Value-Form, or Exchange-Value (138–63)

At the beginning of the first subsection, Marx mentions exchange-value: initially, he characterizes it as the quantitative exchange relation between two use-values (126) and later as value's form of appearance (127, 128). But until now Marx has not yet used the term "value-form" (except in the Preface). The title of this new subsection implies that Marx is using "exchange-value" and "value-form" synonymously, but the term value-form more explicitly points to it being a form, a manifestation of value.

This subsection is considerably longer than the previous two, and Marx breaks it down into further sections and subsections. The first edition's Prefaces pointed out that the beginning is difficult, especially its examination of the value-form:

> To the superficial observer, the analysis of these forms seems to turn upon minutiae. It does in fact deal with minutiae, but so similarly does microscopic anatomy. With the exception of the section on the form of value, therefore, this volume cannot stand accused on the score of difficulty. (90)

In 1867, Friedrich Engels and Ludwig Kugelmann read the galley proofs of the first edition. Both recommended that Marx simplify his presentation of the value-form. While the first volume was being typeset and proofread, Marx wrote an appendix, "The Value-Form" (translated to English in *Capital and Class*: 4, Spring 1978, 130–50).

Commodities and Money

About this appendix, Marx would say that he tried to present things "as simply and even as schoolmasterly as possible" (MEGA II/5, 12). For the second edition, published in 1872/73, Marx reworked this dual presentation. (In the process, he wrote a manuscript called "Ergänzungen und Veränderungen" which is commented on in Appendix 4 of this book.) The second edition's analysis of the value-form is much closer to Marx's "simple" appendix than it is to the analysis that appeared in the first edition's chapter 1. Even so, it is not identical to that appendix. Hence, the analysis of the value-form exists in three different versions. Our commentary focuses on the revised version of the second edition contained in Volume 23 of the Marx-Engels-Werke, which is the basis for both the English translation of *Capital* Volume I used here and the one in Marx-Engels Collected Works, Volume 35. However, on some occasions it's helpful to refer to the two other versions. Appendix 3 of this book contains the final part of the first version, which was completely replaced in the later versions.

INTRODUCTION: THE MYSTERY OF MONEY (138–39)

The first page and a half serves as an introduction to the entire subsection. Its first paragraph:

> Commodities come into the world in the form of use-values. … However, they are only commodities because they have a dual nature, because they are at the same time objects of utility and bearers of value. Therefore they only appear as commodities, or have the form of commodities, in so far as they possess a double form, i.e. natural form and value-form. (138)

Here, Marx summarizes one of the findings from the first subsection: commodities have a dual character, use-value and value. There's nothing new here. Nevertheless, Marx's emphasis is now different: "However, they are *only* commodities because they have a dual nature" (italics mine). The idea is that only if use-values actually have a value-form, their own manifestation of value, are they commodities.

This is expressed in the manner of using the verb "appear" here (*erscheinen*; see also the commentary on the initial paragraph of chapter 1). "To appear" is equated with "to have": "Therefore they only *appear* as commodities, or *have* the form of commodities" (italics mine). Thus "appear" in this context means: they only *perform as* or *are* commodities, to the extent that they have a dual character.

In the second paragraph, Marx summarizes the "objectivity of commodities as values": "not an atom of matter" enters into it. As early as the first chapter's first section, Marx characterized the value of commodities as a "residue" obtained when one abstracts from all of a commodity's use-value characteristics, and he called it a "spectral objectivity" (128). Now he emphasizes value's phantom-like character more fully than in the first subsection:

> We may twist and turn a *single* commodity as we wish; it remains impossible to grasp it as a thing possessing value. (138, emphasis M.H.)[10]

But why can't we grasp value-objectivity in a single commodity? This is due to the social character of the substance of value, which was emphasized in the first subsection. The substance of value, abstract labor, is not inherent to a single commodity, but rather held in common by two commodities that are exchanged. Marx summarizes this thought:

> However, let us remember that commodities possess an objective character as values only in so far as they are all expressions of an identical social substance, human labour, that their objective character as values is therefore purely social. (138)

As a specific product, an *individual* commodity is simply the outcome of a particular useful and individual labor activity—a given table is the result of a particular labor activity, of carpentry, as well as the expression of the individual labor of, perhaps, the especially slow carpenter X. The table can only become an expression of *equal human* labor through exchange, when confronting other commodities. Then the various particular and individual acts of labor are reduced to equal human labor. From this "purely social" character of value-objectivity, Marx says that it follows "self-evidently" that

---

10. "Dame Quickly" suddenly appears in the text two sentences prior to this quote. Marx is referring to a character from Shakespeare's *Henry IV*. In the play, Falstaff says to the innkeeper named Quickly that she is neither fish nor fowl, "a man knows not where to have her," whereupon she replies, somewhat suggestively, "any man knows where to have me" (*Henry IV* Part 1, 3.3). About Marx's enthusiasm for Shakespeare, his son-in-law Paul Lafargue wrote: "His respect for Shakespeare was boundless: he made a detailed study of his works and knew even the least important of his characters. His whole family had a real cult for the great English dramatist; his three daughters knew many of his works by heart." (Fromm 1961: 173)

it can only appear in the social relation between commodity and commodity. (139)

Taken in isolation, this sentence could seem to mean that a commodity's value-objectivity is already present prior to and outside of exchange; it merely "appears" within exchange, in the sense of *becoming visible*. However, this is obviously not what Marx means. In highlighting just before that value-objectivity is "purely social," Marx underscored that it cannot be a *single* thing's property. Marx expressed the same thing explicitly in the manuscript from 1871–72 (with which we will deal in Appendix 4; see also the commentary on page 128). In the first paragraph of this subsection, Marx used "appear" and "have" interchangeably. That can only mean: commodities *have* value-objectivity *only* in the social relation of one commodity to another—which is why it first comes to light here. Prior to and outside of this relation, they are mere use-values: they are on the way to becoming commodities, but far from being commodities. When Marx speaks of the value of a *single* commodity (or its magnitude of value), he always *presupposes a value-relation to another commodity*, of which the individual commodity is a part.

The end of the second paragraph reads:

In fact we started from exchange-value, or the exchange relation of commodities, in order to track down the value that lay hidden within it. We must now return to this form of appearance of value. (139)

The first subsection introduced exchange-value as a quantitative relation in which one commodity exchanges for another (126–27). After examining exchange-value, Marx concluded that it must be the form of appearance of a distinct content, of value, and he found abstract human labor to be value's substance. It is this series of connections that Marx alludes to when he writes here that we started from exchange-value in order to track down value. The reference to the "return" to exchange-value makes it clear that the third subsection picks up on the arguments of the first subsection and not the second (which merely looked deeper into a theme from the first subsection). It's also evident that Marx does not open a completely new level of investigation in this third subsection. After having characterized the *substance* and *magnitude* of value in the first subsection, Marx is concerned here with the *form* of value, which he had only mentioned earlier, but not analyzed.

The third paragraph clarifies Marx's subject matter in this subsection:

> Everyone knows, if nothing else, that commodities have a common value-form which contrasts in the most striking manner with the motley natural forms of their use-values. I refer to the money-form. Now, however, we have to perform a task never even attempted by bourgeois economics. That is, we have to show the origin of this money-form, we have to trace the development of the expression of value contained in the value-relation of commodities from its simplest, almost imperceptible outline to the dazzling money-form. When this has been done, the mystery of money will immediately disappear. (139)

Since this paragraph contains a great deal of information, it calls for extensive commentary. First, we should note that the topic of money is raised here for the first time. However, one must read the text carefully: Marx is not talking about *money*, but rather the money-*form*. Without elaborating further, he thus distinguishes between the *money-form* as a specific form of value—that is, a specific manner of expressing value—and *money* as the material manifestation of this expression of value.

ADDENDUM: The first chapter's third subsection deals with the *money-form*, and *money* itself first becomes a topic in chapter 2. Only afterward, in chapter 3, are the *functions of money* addressed. This, however, is where most economic theories begin their analyses of money. In that sense, the structure of Marx's argumentation itself expresses a fundamental critique of mainstream economic theories: they take as a self-evident point of departure something that must first be explained.

In the first sentence, Marx asserts that "everyone knows" the money-form. What is to be investigated now is the "origin of this money-form." Its origin is unknown not only to the man in the street, but even to "bourgeois economics." Here Marx uses the term "bourgeois economics" for the first time. He is obviously referring to hegemonic economic science. (A more exact determination of "bourgeois economics" appears further on in the fourth subsection of this chapter, which deals with the commodity's "fetish character," and will be discussed in the commentary in point E below.) Marx does not accuse bourgeois economics of having wrongly understood this "origin," or of presenting it incompletely. Instead, he says that it has "never even attempted" such a presentation. Bourgeois economics was obviously completely unaware that something had to be presented here at all. So Marx claims to be entering an entirely new theoretical territory.

Commodities and Money 97

But what does "the origin of the money-form" mean? The word for "origin" in the original German text is "Genesis," which means emergence or development. However, in what sense are we talking about development here? A seemingly obvious interpretation is "historical development," as if Marx were wanting to briefly retrace the historical development that has led to modern money. In traditional Marxism, this interpretation is very common (see for example Mandel 1968: 49ff.).

A few things already encountered in the text, however, contradict the interpretation of "origin" as historical development. First, Marx never says anywhere that he aims to provide a *historical* narrative recounting money's emergence. Second, the history of money begins in pre-capitalist times, but Marx has said many times that his object of investigation is the commodity *in capitalism*, and we are still analyzing the commodity. Third, Marx writes that showing "the origin of this money-form" was something "bourgeois economics" did not even attempt. If Marx's "origin of the money-form" were a brief history of money, then this statement about bourgeois economics would be simply wrong. Histories of money had existed for a long time, and Marx knew the literature very well. In fact, when Marx wrote critically on the history of economic theory—for example in *Theories of Surplus Value*—he never accused bourgeois economists of overlooking or inadequately treating the historical emergence of money. If Marx indeed wanted to show something not present *at all* in bourgeois economics, then it must be something other than the historical emergence of money.

A phrase near the end of this paragraph, the "mystery of money," hints at what this other thing might be. Marx writes that showing the "origin of the money-form" will cause the "mystery of money" to disappear. Still, he does not explain what the mystery of money consists of. In everyday life, money doesn't appear to be mysterious: money is what we use to buy all commodities. However, it's not really clear *why* we can buy everything with money. That money possesses value is not itself sufficient. Other commodities also possess value; nonetheless, we can't go shopping with any old commodity. It's unlikely that it has to do with a property of the *material* used for money (for example, a property of gold), since these materials have changed many times in history. Marx's wording suggests that only the money-*form* will explain why we can buy all commodities with money.

Three new terms appear in this subsection's page-and-a-half introduction (138–39): value-form *(Wertform)*, expression of value *(Wertausdruck)*, and value-relation *(Wertverhältnis)*. The title makes clear that Marx uses exchange-value and value-form interchangeably. He does not further define the terms "expression of value" and "value-relation," which show up in the last two paragraphs of this introduction. There, "expression of value" is clearly used as a synonym for exchange-value and value-form, whereas "value-relation" deals with the relationship between two commodities in terms of their value. However, we must distinguish between the mere *exchange relation* and *value-relation*. The first section considered the "exchange relation" of two commodities, concluding that there is a "common element" of equal magnitude in both: value (127). If we speak of the "value-relation" of two commodities, then value is already presupposed as a result of the examination of the exchange relation: now the exchange relation is considered based on the relation of the commodity values within it. For this reason, Marx writes that "the relation between the values of *two* commodities" provides "the simplest expression of the value of a *single* commodity" (emphasis M.H.). However, Marx is subsequently not very strict in using the term "value-relation"; he sometimes uses it interchangeably with "expression of value."

a) The Simple, Isolated, or Accidental Form of Value (139–54)

x commodity A = y commodity B or:
x commodity A is worth y commodity B.
(20 yards of linen = 1 coat, or: 20 yards of linen are worth 1 coat)

Why does Marx refer to this form of value as "simple, isolated, or accidental"? It is *simple*, because it is based on just two commodities. It is *isolated*, because it has no relationship with other value-relations. It is *accidental*, because the commodities related to each other are chosen at random; instead of linen and a coat, they could be wheat and iron or silk and boot polish, etc.

Marx's formula following the subheading characterizes this form of value using two expressions connected by an "or": on one side is an equality relationship and on the other is the polar relationship "is worth" (more on the polar relationship shortly). There has been much debate about this line's meaning. Critics, for their part, accuse Marx of inadmissibly equating polarity and equality. However, the formula following the subheading merely expresses, in a schematic way, the thought formulated at the end of the preceding introductory section: the value-relation of two commodities (x commodity A = y commodity B) provides the simplest expression of a commodity's value (x commodity A is worth y commodity B).

1. The Two Poles of the Expression of Value: The Relative Form of Value and the Equivalent Form

> The whole mystery of the form of value lies hidden in this simple form. Our real difficulty, therefore, is to analyze it. (139)

Just like the first chapter's opening sentence, "The wealth of societies..." (125), Marx reveals here a *result* of his research process: the decisive information for understanding the forms of value is already there in the simple form of value. Readers will only be able to judge whether this is actually the case after reaching the end of Marx's analysis of the forms of value.

However, this sentence provides a hint that helps us unravel the "mystery of money." If "the whole mystery of the form of value" (including that of the money-form) is already there in this simple form of value, then the solution to the mystery of money should reveal itself here, and not only in dealing with the money-form itself.

Marx considers the *exchange relation* between two commodities in the first subsection after introducing exchange-value. In the *exchange relation*, in which two commodities of equal value are exchanged, both commodities play the same role in revealing their shared "common element." Their equality of value is a symmetrical relationship.

In the *value-form* (or the *expression of value*), the two commodities play different roles. The relationship is not symmetrical: the first commodity (20 yards of linen) plays an *active* role, expressing its value in the second commodity (1 coat); the second commodity plays a *passive* role, as merely the material for the expression of value. With this distinction, the "minutiae" referred to in the first edition's Preface start to emerge! In what follows, we'll have to pay close attention to discover the point of dealing with such minutiae.

Marx describes the value of the first commodity as "relative value." The first commodity is in the *relative form of value*, whereas the second commodity is in the *equivalent form*. The terms "relative value" and "equivalent" were already in use before Marx. What is new here is that Marx has introduced the concept of *form* and undertakes a detailed analysis of the value-forms.

About the relative form of value and the equivalent form, Marx has the following to say:

- They are mutually dependent; that is, one form can't do without the other.

- They are mutually exclusive; that is, the same commodity cannot occupy both forms simultaneously.

These characteristics lead Marx to speak of two "poles" because they mutually condition and exclude each other; the "relative form of value" and "equivalent form" resemble the magnetic north and south poles.

Marx further observes that the expression of value "20 yards of linen are worth 1 coat" also includes the converse, "1 coat is worth 20 yards of linen." Why is that the case? This expression of value is based on the exchange-relation *20 yards of linen exchange for 1 coat*. This exchange-relation, which merely refers to the exchange of two commodities of equal value, is symmetrical: it can be turned around to say that *1 coat is exchanged for 20 yards of linen*. From this reversed exchange-relation, it follows that "1 coat is worth 20 yards of linen."

2. The Relative Form of Value
(i) The Content of the Relative Form of Value

Pay close attention to subheading (i) here. Marx wishes to examine the *content* of a specific *form*.

ADDENDUM: The entire section on the value-form is concerned with the content of the respective value-forms. In chapter 1 of the first edition, Marx identifies what is fundamentally new about his form analysis. He writes that "the economists have overlooked the form-content of the relative value-expression (subjected as they are to the influence of material interests)." (Dragstedt 1976: 22)

In the first paragraph's beginning sentence, Marx states what he is pursuing: he wishes "to find out how the simple expression of the value of a commodity lies hidden in the value-relation between two commodities" (140). But don't we already know that? If the value-relation is "20 yards of linen = 1 coat" then it contains the expression of value "20 yards of linen are worth 1 coat." What more do we have to find out?

In the first two paragraphs, Marx distinguishes between the *quantitative* and the *qualitative* aspects of the value-relation: in every value-relation, two commodities stand in a certain quantitative proportion. But it is precisely this quantitative relation that Marx wishes to initially abstract from (point ii that follows addresses the quantitative relation). If a value-relation exists at all between two things, regardless of the quantitative proportion, it implies the two things possess a *common quality* with regard to which they can be compared. Marx writes in the first paragraph that they must be "commensurable magnitudes" (141). As *use-values*, the linen and the coat are qualitatively distinct, but as *values* they are qualitatively equal.

In footnote 17, Marx accuses the economists who have dealt explicitly with the form of value of two things. First, they confused the form of value and value itself. Let's take note of the difference: commodities are *values* as objectifications of abstract human labor. By contrast, the *form of value* (exchange-value) is the expression of the commodity's value in a specific amount of another commodity. Second, Marx accuses the economists of overlooking the value-form's *qualitative* aspect by only dealing with the *quantitative* side. The current section proposes to deal with this qualitative aspect that economists overlooked.

ADDENDUM: Samuel Bailey (1791–1870) is mentioned by name in footnote 17. There is an important background to this apparently passing reference. In *A Contribution to the Critique of Political Economy* (1859), Marx analyzed the value-form briefly, integrating it into the exchange process, which in *Capital* became the object of chapter 2. If Marx considerably expanded the part on the value-form in *Capital*, separating it from the analysis of the exchange process, it was primarily because in the meantime he had dealt comprehensively (in *Theories of Surplus Value*, 1861–63) with Bailey's critique of Ricardo's labor theory of value. That engagement with Bailey made Marx aware of the inadequacy of his own presentation.

Marx's first two paragraphs point out that *quantitative comparability* presupposes that both things can be reduced to *the same unit*, but the third paragraph begins by emphasizing that both commodities, linen and coat, play *different* roles in the expression of value. The value of the linen is what is being expressed. How is that possible? Marx's answer: the coat "counts" as a form of existence of value, as a thing of value. Here again we must pay careful attention to the wording. In itself, the coat *is not simply* a thing of value; rather, it's a concrete and material coat, a use-value. Only in a specific relation does the coat *count* as a thing of value.

Marx's reasoning in this paragraph points to a fundamental difference between, on the one hand, the equation of the two commodities in the exchange-relation, and, on the other, the expression of the value of a commodity through another commodity. He explicitly explains this difference in the next paragraph:

> If we say that, as values, commodities are simply congealed quantities of human labour, our analysis reduces them, it is true, to the level of abstract value [corrected translation: an

abstraction, value], but does not give them a form of value distinct from their natural forms. It is otherwise in the value relation of one commodity to another. The first commodity's value character emerges here through its own relation to the second commodity. (141f.)

This paragraph calls for a thorough commentary. Here, Marx juxtaposes two different levels, separating them by "it is otherwise." His language is somewhat misleading: the first sentence talks about "our analysis," but the second and third sentences focus on the "value relation." Thus Marx seems to be confronting the analysis (the dissection, formation of categories, etc.) with specific relations. But conceiving the value relation is likewise the outcome of a certain analysis. This means that what Marx is actually confronted here are *two different levels of analysis* of the commodity.

The first sentence deals with the *analysis of the exchange-relation* of commodities, addressed in the first subsection of chapter 1. There, Marx started with the exchange-relation 1 quarter of corn = x cwt of iron, concluding that both things contain a "common element" of the same magnitude (127). He determines that this common element was value. In the first sentence in the paragraph above, Marx quotes his own text, with a subtle modification. On page 128, he argues that, on abstracting from the useful character of products of labor, nothing remains other than a spectral objectivity. They become "merely congealed quantities of homogeneous human labor," and as crystallizations of this "social substance, which is common to them all," they are *values*.

Now Marx emphasizes that this analysis has only reduced commodities to the "level of an abstraction, value" (*Wertabstraktion*, literally "value-abstraction"), a term he has not used up to now. What does he mean by this? Value is based on an abstraction: abstracting from the properties of the commodity as a use-value and, along with it, abstracting from the concrete, useful properties of the labor that produced the commodity. As values, commodities are "congealed" homogeneous human labor, but that cannot be grasped in a single commodity. If one says that "commodities are values," that reduces them to an *abstraction*, as when one says that dogs, cats, and tigers are animals.

Now, Marx confronts this "value-abstraction," which is the outcome of the analysis of the exchange relation, with the "value-form," which has not yet been reached in the analysis.

The second level addressed in the paragraph quoted above is the *analysis of the value-relation*. Why does Marx say "it is otherwise" with regard to the "value relation of one commodity to another"? First of all, it's important that the analysis of the value-relation builds on the analysis of the exchange relation: it presupposes the value-abstraction obtained from the analysis of the exchange relation. What is now "otherwise" is that the "value character" arises from a relationship to *another* commodity. This means that the analysis of the value relation no longer shows value as a mere abstraction, as a "spectral objectivity" (128). Instead, the value of one commodity (linen) is here *expressed* by another commodity (coat). Thus the linen obtains a *value-form distinct from its natural form* that is not at all spectral, but perceptible to our senses. The next paragraph makes clear how the specific character of value-creating labor is expressed in the relationship to another commodity.

The coat and the linen result from different types of concrete labor. If one equates "the coat as a thing of value" to the linen, then these different types of labor are also equated to each other. Marx says this about the equation of the two commodities:

> The expression of equivalence between different sorts of commodities . . . brings to view the specific character of value-creating labour, by *actually* reducing the different kinds of labour embedded in the different kinds of commodity to their common quality of being human labour in general. (142, emphasis M.H.)

In summary, we can say this about the two levels: The result of Marx's analysis of the *exchange-relation* was that the commodities as values are reduced to congealed homogeneous human labor. In the *value-relation*, this result is already a *component* of the relation being analyzed. Through their equation as things of value, these distinct, concrete types of labor are *actually* reduced to equal, abstract human labor.

In the second subsection of chapter 1, Marx claimed to be "the first to point out and examine critically" (132) the dual character of commodity-producing labor. However, he was by no means the first person to talk about it, as footnote 18, which deals in part with Benjamin Franklin (1706–1790), makes clear. Franklin was mostly known for his work as a natural scientist (he invented the lightning rod) and as a politician (he was an author of the U.S. Declaration of Independence), but he also worked in the area of economy. Franklin conceived trade as the exchange of *one type of labor* for *another type of labor*, concluding that value must be calculated in terms of *labor*. According to Marx, with that reflection Franklin abstracts from the particularities of the individual acts of labor, without the importance of his discovery becoming clear to him. Marx asserts: "He states this without knowing it" (142). The content of Franklin's text thus goes far beyond the author's knowledge or intentions. In Marx's reception of economic literature, his deciphering of such surplus meanings often plays an important role.

But what is the difference between Franklin and Marx? The obvious one is that Marx knows what he's saying (the dual character of labor as crucial to understanding a commodity-producing economy) and also puts emphasis on it, whereas Franklin remains unaware. However, the difference goes even deeper. Marx developed the dual character of commodity-producing labor from an *analysis of the exchange-relation*. Franklin merely takes up a de facto expression of labor's dual character in the *value relation* of the commodities, without really being aware of what is expressed there. Why is he unaware of it? Franklin has not grasped the "value abstraction," which results from the analysis of the exchange relation.

The next paragraph begins by observing that, to express the linen's value, it's not enough "to express the specific character of the labour which goes to make up the value of the linen." This is because:

> Human labour-power in its fluid state, or human labour, creates value, but is not itself value. It becomes value in its coagulated state, in objective form. (142)

It follows that

> the value of the linen as a congealed mass of human labour can be expressed only as an "objectivity" [*Gegenständlichkeit*], a thing which is materially different from the linen itself and yet common to the linen and all other commodities. (142)

Marx adds that "the problem is already solved" and reveals the solution in the next paragraph. The linen's value finds its "objective" shape in the coat. In the value-relation of the linen to the coat, the coat counts as

> a thing in which value is manifested, or which represents value in its [the thing's] tangible natural form. (143)

We should pause here in our reading. Marx has emphasized many times that we cannot grasp value in a single commodity. In the immediately preceding paragraph, Marx writes that the linen's value must be expressed in a materially distinct "objectivity." None of that seems to hold for the coat. The coat is supposed to simply represent value "in its [the coat's] tangible natural form." Marx addresses this issue when he writes:

> A coat as such no more expresses value than does the first piece of linen we come across. (143)

Nevertheless, Marx has just claimed exactly that the coat expresses value! How can we reconcile these divergent statements? Marx immediately unveils the solution to the puzzle:

> This proves only that, within its value-relation to the linen, the coat signifies more than it does outside it, just as some men count for more when inside a gold-braided uniform than they do otherwise. (143)

Taken in *isolation*, the linen and coat are both merely use-values. Neither expresses value. That the coat expresses value through *its natural form* is not one of its intrinsic properties; it possesses this property *only within* the linen-coat exchange relationship. For that reason, Marx's frequent use of the phrase "to count as" (*gelten*) is very precise: the coat "is" not a form of value's existence; rather it "counts as" a form of value's existence (see 141 third paragraph, 142 final paragraph, and 143 second paragraph). This is a *relationship of validation (Geltungsverhältnis)*.

Marx explains why a relationship of validation of this kind is present within the value-relation in the next paragraph. The coat is the "bearer of value," without this being visible in the coat itself. But in the expression "20 yards of linen are worth 1 coat," the coat *only* counts as value. It follows that:

> Nevertheless, the coat cannot represent value towards the linen unless value, for the latter, simultaneously assumes the form of a coat. (143)

The kind of validation at work here is neither something agreed upon by those engaged in exchange, nor imposed by the state. Rather, it is a relation that is structurally generated by an economy based upon exchange. In the next paragraph, Marx recaps once more:

> Hence, in the value-relation, in which the coat is the equivalent of the linen, the form of the coat counts as the form of value. (143)

Now a new perspective on the relation emerges:

> The value of the commodity linen is therefore expressed by the physical body of the commodity coat, the value of one *by the use-value of the other*. (143, emphasis M.H.)

With that, the task posed above (in the third paragraph, 142) of expressing the linen's value as an "objectivity" materially distinct from itself is solved: in the physical body of the coat, the linen obtains a value-form distinct from its own natural form.

The next paragraph states:

> We see, then, that everything our analysis of the value of commodities previously told us is repeated by the linen itself, as soon as it enters into association with another commodity, the coat. Only it reveals its thoughts in a language with which it alone is familiar, the language of commodities. (143)

Marx uses lyrical language here to restate the comparison between the two levels of analysis sketched in the last paragraph on page 141, "If we say that . . ." The first subsection of chapter 1 dealt with the "analysis of commodity value" which led to "the level of an abstraction, value" (141, corrected translation). Now, the third subsection is concerned with the value-form as an "objective" expression of value. At this new level, the same characterizations appear, albeit with a specific guise, that of the "language of commodities," that is, the relation of commodities to each other.

The final paragraph furnishes the most concentrated and abstract summary of the "content" of the relative form of value:

> Commodity A, then, in entering into a relation with commodity B as an object of value [*Wertkörper*], as a materialization of human labour, makes the use-value B into the material through which its own value is expressed. (144)

(II) THE QUANTITATIVE DETERMINACY OF THE RELATIVE FORM OF VALUE

In point (ii), Marx now turns to addressing a subject that he had deliberately abstracted from in point (i). In the first paragraph of this new subsection, Marx begins by stating that the form of value "must not only express value in general, but also quantitatively determined value, i.e. the magnitude of value" (144). He then states that an equal amount

Commodities and Money

of the "substance of value" is contained in both commodities in the value expression, and this implies that "the quantities in which the two commodities are present have cost the same amount of labour or the same quantity of labour-time" (145).

Marx speaks only of *labor* here. However, since he was just talking about the substance of value, he clearly means *value-creating labor*, that is, *abstract human labor*. What creates value is not individually expended labor-time, but rather "socially necessary labor-time" (see the first section of chapter 1, under point E), and only to the extent that it satisfies "social need" (see the comments on the first subsection regarding supply and demand).

Now Marx seeks to investigate the influence of the changes in both commodities' values on the expression of value. In investigating this, the causes of such changes are irrelevant—that is, whether they result from changes in the productivity of labor (Marx mentions this case on page 145) or changes in social need.

In footnote 20, Marx calls attention to his using the word "value" in the ensuing analysis not only to describe the "quality" of value (for example, when he says that a commodity has both use-value and value), but also for the "quantity" in which this quality is present, that is, for the particular *magnitude of value*.

Marx now identifies four cases where the magnitude of value of one or the other of the commodities changes, considering their effects upon the expression of value. Recall that on numerous occasions above we have stressed that value-objectivity is not a property of the individual product, that an isolated commodity does not really exist. But aren't we now talking about the value of an individual commodity? We are still engaged in examining the value-form contained in the value-relation between two commodities. *Within* the value-relation, we can indeed speak of a commodity and its value, but not *independently* of such a value-relation.

Marx now considers the form of value at two distinct moments in time. He postulates the occurrence of various combinations of changes in the social conditions of production. Then he considers each one's influence on the relative expression of value. However, the change in the commodity's value and the change in the expression of its value do not occur in temporal succession, but rather simultaneously. That the socially necessary labor-time (for example, in the production of linen) has changed, and how much, is first shown in exchange. It is only then that we can speak of changes in the value of the linen.

Here are the four cases:

1. The value of the linen changes; the value of the coat remains constant. In this case, the "relative value," that is, the value of linen expressed in coats, changes in accordance with the change in the linen's value.
2. The value of the linen remains constant; the value of the coat changes. In this case, the relative value of the linen changes in an inverse relation to the coat's value.

   Comparing cases 1 and 2, it becomes evident that we can't see whether the change in relative value results from a change in the magnitude of the linen's value or from an inverse change in the magnitude of the coat's value.
3. The magnitudes of the value of the linen and the coat both change; they do so in the same direction "and the same proportion," that is, by the same percentage. In this case, the relative value of the linen remains the same.
4. The magnitudes of the value of the linen and the coat both change; they do so either not in the same direction or not in the same proportion. Each possible com*bination corresponds to a repeated application of cases 1 to 3.*

With that, Marx has dealt with all of the possible changes in the values of the linen and coat and their influence upon the relative value of the linen. Marx now sums up the results:

> Thus real changes in the magnitude of value are neither unequivocally nor exhaustively reflected in their relative expression, or, in other words, in the magnitude of the relative value. (146)

In footnote 21, Marx describes this non-correspondence as the "lack of congruence between the magnitude of value and its relative expression" (146). In the section on the money-form, we will return again to this lack of congruence.

3. The Equivalent Form[11]

In the first sentence here, as earlier in point 1, Marx stresses the active role of the commodity that occupies the relative form of value, emphasizing that it "impresses a form of value" upon the second commodity. He goes on:

---

11. The Penguin edition subordinates "iii) The Equivalent Form" to "2. The relative value form." However, in the German original this is not a subsection of 2, but at the same hierarchical level as 2.

Commodities and Money 109

> The commodity linen brings to view its own existence as a value through the fact that the coat can be equated with the linen although it has not assumed a form of value distinct from its own physical form. The coat is directly exchangeable with the linen; in this way the linen in fact expresses its own existence as a value [*Wertsein*]. The equivalent form of a commodity, accordingly, is the form in which it is directly exchangeable with other commodities. (147)

The first sentence of the quotation merely summarizes the results of the investigation of the relative form of value. The next two sentences, however, assert something new: the linen expresses that the coat "is directly exchangeable" with it and that the equivalent form "is the form in which it is directly exchangeable with other commodities."

What does "form in which it is directly exchangeable" mean? As it is, the coat can exchange "directly" for linen. But what would it mean to be not directly exchangeable? This can be clarified by looking at three commodities. Assume that not only 20 yards of linen, but also 10 kg of iron, are exchanged for a coat; in that case, we can conclude that 20 yards of linen and 10 kg of iron have the same magnitude of value. But that is far from saying that 20 yards of linen are also exchangeable for 10 kg of iron. The case is different with the coat. Since for both the linen and the iron, the coat serves as the *material expression of value*—that is, for both value takes the shape of the coat and both exchange for the coat—the coat is *directly exchangeable* for both. But the 10 kg of iron in our example can only exchange for 20 yards of linen, if it is first exchanged for a coat, and then the coat for the 20 yards of linen. The iron is thus not "directly" exchangeable, but rather only exchangeable in a *mediated* way (with the coat serving as the medium). Why? Because the iron, in its *natural form*, does not already count as a *form of value*.

Marx observes in the next two paragraphs how, with the equivalent commodity (in our case, the coat), the *proportion* in which it is exchanged is by no means given. Instead, the quantitative relation of exchange depends upon the magnitude of value of both commodities. Marx thoroughly described this dependence in section 2. *The relative form of value*, subsection (ii).

Marx points out another property of the equivalent form. The magnitude of value of the linen, that is, the commodity that occupies the relative form of value, is expressed in a specific quantity of coat, the commodity that occupies the equivalent form of value. In contrast, the magnitude of value of the coat (the commodity occupying the equivalent form) is not expressed; the equivalent commodity always appears as no more than a *specific quantity of a thing.*

After these introductory remarks, Marx highlights three "peculiarities of the equivalent form."

The First Peculiarity of the Equivalent Form

Use-value becomes the form of appearance of its opposite, value. (148)

This proposition was already demonstrated when we examined the content of the relative form of value. There, Marx noted that the linen can only express its value in the coat if value takes on the form of a coat for it (143). But it is merely coincidental that the coat occupies the equivalent form. Any other commodity could occupy the coat's position, which would mean that that commodity's useful character would count directly as a manifestation of value. For that reason, Marx can make the more general claim here that use-value becomes the manifestation of value.

In the quote, Marx describes value as the "opposite" of use-value. He is referring to the fact that use-value and value are not only different, but to a certain degree are defined in opposing ways. The use-value of a commodity is based upon its usefulness, which depends on concrete material properties of the body of the commodity. By contrast, we obtain the value of a commodity by abstracting from its use-value: value is a social characteristic (analogous oppositions are the basis of Marx's using the term "opposite" in relation to the two other peculiarities).

Just as on page 127, where Marx described exchange-value as a "form of appearance" of a content distinct from it, Marx uses the term "form of appearance" without saying that there is some "essence" appearing. In this passage, it's clear that this would be nonsensical: we would have to conceive of value as the "essence" of use-value.[12]

---

12. This doesn't mean that similar nonsense about Marx can be written without harming one's academic reputation in Germany. Thus Jürgen Habermas, considered one of the most important contemporary German social philosophers, writes: "Marx analyzes the double form of the commodity as a use-value and an exchange-value, as well as the transformation of its natural form into the value form; for this purpose he draws upon Hegel's concept of abstraction and treats the relation between use-value and exchange-value like that between essence and appearance. Today this presents us with difficulties; we cannot employ unreconstructed basic concepts from Hegel's logic just like that. The extended discussion on the relation of

Marx makes two additional observations. First, that this "substitution"—Marx uses the term "quid pro quo"—of one thing for another (the switching of use-value and value, page 148) occurs only *within* the value-relation (as he already noted on page 143). Second, because no commodity can relate to itself as value, it *must* relate to another commodity as its equivalent, thus making the latter's physical existence into a form of value. From this we can conclude: the "substitution" of value for use-value that occurs in the commodity occupying the equivalent form is *necessary* in order to express the value of the commodity that occupies the relative form of value.

Marx uses the example of measuring weight to explain how this "substitution" takes place. You can't see the weight of a sugar loaf. It is expressed by putting it on a balance in relation to a few pieces of iron. The pieces of iron do not represent anything other than weight, just as the coat in the expression of value only counts as value. Marx emphasizes, however, that at this point "the analogy ceases," because the iron represents "a natural property common to both bodies."

> But in the expression of value of the linen the coat represents a *supra-natural* property: their value, which is something purely social. (149, emphasis M.H.)

If value isn't natural, it must be something "supra-natural." Here, Marx reintroduces the spectral metaphor from the first subsection of chapter 1, where he referred to the commodity's "spectral objectivity" (128).

In the next paragraph, Marx begins by emphasizing that the *relative form of value* reveals that value is something social; the value of the commodity that occupies the relative form is expressed in something distinct from its own body. The reverse is the case with the *equivalent form*:

> The equivalent form consists precisely in this, that the material commodity itself, the coat for instance, expresses value just as it is in its everyday life, and is *therefore endowed with the form of value by nature itself*. (149, emphasis M.H.)

Marx's *Capital* to Hegel's *Logic* has illuminated these difficulties rather than resolved them. I shall therefore not go any deeper into the analysis of the commodity form" (Habermas 1984: 357). First of all, Habermas overlooks that Marx completely avoids Hegel's concept of "essence" in his analysis of the commodity in *Capital*. Leaving that aside, there is no passage in Marx's work that speaks of exchange-value as a form of appearance of use-value, as Habermas insinuates.

Whereas the relative form of value expresses something social, the equivalent form *seems* to express something natural. However, value is not natural but social. For that reason, neither the coat nor any other commodity body can possess the form of value "by nature." It must be an "illusion" (*Schein*), but where does it come from? Marx's answer:

> Admittedly, this holds good only within the value-relation, in which the commodity linen is related to the commodity coat as its equivalent. However, the properties of a thing do not arise from its relations to other things, they are, on the contrary, merely activated by such relations. The coat, therefore, seems to be endowed with its equivalent form, its property of direct exchangeability, by nature, just as much as its property of being heavy or its ability to keep us warm. Hence the mysteriousness of the equivalent form, which only impinges on the crude bourgeois vision of the political economist when it confronts him in its fully developed shape, that of money. (149)

Here, Marx distinguishes between properties that exist only *within a relationship* and properties inherent to *the thing itself*. In connection with the first type of property, Marx frequently uses "to count" (*gelten*); in connection with the second type, he opts for "to be" (*sein*). Thus the coat "counts" as a thing of value (but only within the value-relation), whereas it "is" made of wool (the property *being made of wool* does not depend upon a relation).

It's often the case that that which *counts* within a relationship is merely the expression of something that *is* outside of the relationship. Thus with the previous example of the measuring weight: the pieces of iron count as a direct expression of weight in relation to the sugar loaf. This validation (*Geltung*) is possible because the pieces of iron also have weight independently of their relationship to the sugar loaf. If this example were taken as a model, then the coat would *apparently* have the equivalent form in the value-relation to the linen, because it also has the equivalent form outside of this relation, that is, "by nature." But this isn't the case; the illusion, or semblance (*Schein*), is misleading (Footnote 22 on page 149 is instructive in this sense).

Let's briefly go over the relationships discussed so far:

- The linen's value *appears* as, or takes the form of (*erscheint*) a coat. The coat is the *form of appearance* of the linen's value. This is *not an*

- *illusion*; value really does appear this way (on the difference between the German verbs *erscheinen* and *scheinen*, see page 48 above).
- The physical body of the commodity coat *counts* (*gilt*) as the embodiment of value, but only within the value-relation to the linen.
- The coat *is* (*ist*) made of wool (this is the case independently of any relation).
- The coat *seems* (*scheint*) as a *thing*—as a physical body—to directly *be* value (*unmittelbar Wert zu sein*); it seems (*scheint*) to directly possess the equivalent form. This semblance or illusion (*Schein*) is *wrong*, since a property that is only valid within a relation is being confused here with one that also exists outside of the relation.

In the section's very first sentence Marx emphasized that the linen impresses the equivalent form on the coat. However, the linen's *active* behavior (mentioned in point 1, where it appeared to be only a question of "minutiae") is not visible. What the linen "impresses" on the coat, the coat *seems* (*scheint*) to have by natural endowment; a *social relationship* thus seems (*scheint*) to be a *property of a thing*.

It is precisely this, Marx continues, that constitutes the "mysteriousness of the equivalent form" that "impinges on the crude bourgeois vision of the political economist" when he faces it in money. Marx points out that the illusion can still be easily dispelled in the case of the simple form of value, but that is no longer possible with money. Here, then, we have made the first step toward solving the "mystery of money."

The Second Peculiarity of the Equivalent Form

The second peculiarity of the equivalent form is dealt with in only three paragraphs, in a presentation beginning with the second paragraph on page 150. There, Marx draws a conclusion from the first peculiarity: if the body of the equivalent commodity, which is the product of a specific act of concrete labor, counts directly as a manifestation of value—that is, as the embodiment of abstract human labor—then the concrete labor that created this useful thing "counts" as "abstract human labour's form of realization."

In the next paragraph, Marx writes: "But in the value expression of the commodity the question is *stood on its head*" (150, emphasis M.H.). That is to say, the abstract does not stand for the common property of various concrete things; instead, concrete labor counts here as "the tangible form of realization of abstract human labour" (150).

ADDENDUM: In the appendix to the first edition of *Capital*, at the corresponding passage, Marx provides an instructive example of this inversion:

> This *inversion* [*Verkehrung*] by which the sensibly concrete counts only as the form of appearance of the abstractly general and not, on the contrary, the abstractly general as property of the concrete, characterises the expression of value. At the same time, it makes understanding it difficult. If I say: Roman Law and German Law are both laws, that is obvious. But if I say: Law [*Das Recht*], this abstraction [*Abstraktum*] *realises itself* in Roman Law and in German Law, in these concrete laws, the interconnection becomes mystical. (*Capital and Class* 4, Spring 1978: 140)

In the next paragraph, Marx summarizes the foregoing:

> The equivalent form therefore possesses a second peculiarity: in it, concrete labour becomes the form of manifestation of its opposite, abstract human labour. (150)

The Third Peculiarity of the Equivalent Form

The third peculiarity is dealt with in just one paragraph (final paragraph of page 150). It follows directly from the second, stating that the concrete labor that produces the body of the equivalent commodity counts directly as an expression of abstract human labor. For this reason, "like all other commodity-producing labour, it is the labour of private individuals, it is nevertheless labour in its directly social form" (150). About the third peculiarity, Marx writes:

> Private labour takes the form of its opposite, namely labour in its directly social form. (151)

So far Marx has discussed private labor only once: in the second subsection of chapter 1, Marx pointed out that only products of private labor can become commodities (132, corrected translation on page 81 of this book). Now, he not only mentions private labor, but also its "opposite": "labor in its directly social form." What does Marx mean by "directly social form [*unmittelbar gesellschaftliche Form*]"?

ADDENDUM: Once again, Marx's text in the appendix to the first edition of *Capital* goes into greater detail. However, we have to keep in mind that whereas Fowkes translated "unmittelbar gesellschaftliche Form" as "directly social form,"

Dragstedt translated the same term in the appendix to the first edition as "immediately social form."

> *Products of labour* would not become *commodities*, were they not products of separate *private labours* carried on independently of one another. The *social interconnection* of these private labours exists materially, insofar as they *are members of a naturally evolved social division of labour* and hence, through their products, satisfy wants of *different kinds*, in the *totality* [*Gesamtheit*] of which the similarly *naturally evolved system of social wants* [*naturwüchsiges System der gesellschaftlichen Bedürfnisse*] consists. This *material* social interconnection of *private labours* carried on independently of one another is however only *mediated* and hence is realised only through the exchange of their products. The product of private labour hence *only* has *social form* insofar as it has *value-form* and hence the form of *exchangeability* with other products of labour. It has *immediately social form* [*unmittelbar gesellschaftliche Form*] insofar as its own bodily or natural form is *at the same time* the form of its exchangeability with other commodities or *counts as value-form for other commodities*. However, as we have seen, this only takes place for a product of labour when, through the *value relation of other commodities to it*. It is in *equivalent-form* or, with respect to other commodities, *plays the role of equivalent*. The *equivalent* has *immediately social form* [*unmittelbar gesellschaftliche Form*] insofar as it has the form of *immediate exchangeability with other commodities*, and it has this form of immediate exchangeability insofar as it *counts* for other commodities as the *body of value*, hence *as equal* [*als Gleiches*]. Therefore the definite useful labour i.e. as labour contained in it also counts as *labour in immediately social form*, which possesses the form of equality with the labour contained in *other* commodities. (*Capital and Class* 4. Spring 1978, 140)

Marx first emphasizes that in commodity production, individual labor activities take place independently of each other—namely as *private acts of labor*—but still have a *material* interconnectedness. All these private acts of labor require certain intermediate products that are supplied to them by other labor activities. However, these private labor activities only become socially interconnected through the *exchange* of their products. For that reason, Marx writes that their material interconnectedness is *mediated* by exchange. That has consequences: the product of private labor does not have *social form* immediately as a product of concrete labor— as a certain use-value—but only when it obtains a *value-form* through exchange and thus becomes interchangeable. Therefore private labor activity creating some sort of product is normally *not* "labor in *immediately* (or directly) social form." It first becomes labor in social form owing to *mediation*, and that mediation is exchange, which gives the product of private labor a value-form. This mediation can occur or fail to occur (if the product is not exchanged, meaning that it does not obtain a value-form). Only private labor that produces the body of the equivalent commodity is "labor in *immediately* social form," since the equivalent commodity is immediately (or directly) exchangeable.

When Marx speaks here of "labor in immediately (or: directly) social form" as the "opposite" of "private labor," we should remember that we are talking about a society based upon exchange. In *that kind of* society, labor with an immediately social form is that labor whose product is *immediately exchangeable*. This is albeit a very specific form of the immediately social. In a society *not based upon exchange*, labor with an immediately social form would have very different characteristics (we will touch on this issue in the commentary on page 169ff.).

Excursus on Aristotle

In the first edition's Preface, Marx claimed that people sought to unravel the value-form "in vain for more than 2,000 years" (90). What this sweeping time frame refers to becomes explicit here: Aristotle was the first to analyze the value-form. The purpose of Marx's excursus on Aristotle, however, is not to interpret his thought. Rather, as Marx states, it aims to make, not all three peculiarities, but "the two peculiarities of the equivalent form we have just developed . . . still clearer" (151).

Marx emphasizes two of Aristotle's insights. First, "the money-form of the commodity is only a more developed aspect of the simple form of value" (151). Second, the value-relation of two commodities requires that there be an "essential identity" between the two sensually different things, which makes them "commensurable." However, Aristotle concludes that it's impossible for such things to be equal and breaks off his analysis. Marx comments:

> Aristotle therefore himself tells us what prevented any further analysis: the lack of a concept of value. (151)

Aristotle encountered the *money-form* empirically and reduced it to the simple *form of value*. However, he did not have a *concept of value* that could explain the equality presupposed by the expression of value. Aristotle did not succeed at doing what Marx did in the first subsection of chapter 1: decoding exchange-value as a form of appearance of a content that commodities hold in common, and determining this common content as equal human labor or abstract human labor.

Why didn't he succeed? In the final paragraph of this excursus, Marx mentions that the primary impediment to knowledge in Ancient Greek society was the social conditions. The society depended on slave labor, leading to an inequality of labor-power:

> The secret of the expression of value, namely the equality and equivalence of all kinds of labour because and in so far as they are human labour in general, could not be deciphered until the concept of human equality had already acquired the permanence of a fixed popular opinion. This however becomes possible only in a society where the commodity-form is the universal form of the product of labour, hence the dominant social relation is the relation between men as possessors of commodities. (152)

This paragraph doesn't just point out the socially based impediments to Aristotle's thought; implicitly, it provides much more. Marx speaks here of "the concept of human equality" as a "fixed popular opinion." What does that mean? It's widely recognized today that "all people are equal," which is frequently invoked against racism and discrimination. In fact, people are very unequal: both in terms of their abilities and their social situation, as well as with regard to their social rights, which depend these days, for example, on the passport one has within a country's borders. The idea that there is an abstract equality among people—the basis for the validity of universal "human rights," among other things—is not at all a necessary conclusion in the face of this de facto inequality. In ancient and feudal societies, such notions of equality were rare and would have seemed rather abstruse. This doesn't mean that people did not resist oppression and discrimination, but they usually did so without a universal claim to human equality.

Here, Marx stresses that a notion's *plausibility*, which is what he means by "fixed popular opinion," depends on everyday social reality. In a society where people face each other primarily as commodity owners, every person plays the role of a *property owner*. The content and extent of this property varies, but the owners of property are all equal *insofar as* they freely dispose of their property. This fundamental equality of commodity owners appears to be their essential characteristic; their inequality with regard to extent of their property seems an individual peculiarity. Under these conditions, the notion that there is a fundamental equality among people—expressed as an equality of commodity owners—becomes plausible. It's different in ancient and feudal societies, where there was commodity production without it being predominant. There, no level of fundamental equality existed: slaves and free people, peasants and lords faced each other as fundamentally unequal. The notion of human equality had no foundation in such social conditions.

Marx justifies this excursus on Aristotle because it is supposed to make "still clearer" the last two peculiarities of the equivalent form. To what extent does he succeed, and why doesn't it make the first peculiarity clearer?

The first peculiarity, in which the natural form of the equivalent commodity becomes the form of value, is evident. We can clearly express it by saying that, if 20 yards of linen are *worth* a coat, the coat counts as the physical manifestation of the linen's value. The two other peculiarities, however, have nothing to do with the equivalent commodity itself. Instead, they relate to the labor that produced the equivalent commodity. Understanding these two peculiarities presupposes the concept of value: the insight that the commodities as values are the objectification of equal human labor. If we don't have this concept of value then what is evident in exchange—that the coat is the form of value of the linen—appears impossible. So it's clear that there's a fundamental difference between the first peculiarity and the other two.

With that, something else becomes clear. In the first subsection of chapter 1, where Marx began to examine exchange-value, I stressed that he is not considering price-bearing commodities, that is, commodities that exchange for money. Instead he is considering a commodity that exchanges for another commodity—a case that is unusual in developed capitalism (see point C in the commentary on the first subsection). It remained to be seen whether Marx could have introduced money at that stage. Now it's clear that doing so was *not* possible. The money-form's undeveloped manifestation is the simple form of value, as Aristotle already recognized. In order to analyze it, we have first to analyze what makes commodities *commensurable* at all. It is therefore necessary to determine the substance of value before the analysis of the value-form. So the excursus on Aristotle also makes it clear that Marx's sequence of presentation so far represents an objective necessity.

4. The Simple Form of Value Considered as a Whole[13]

The Independent Presentation of Value as Exchange-Value

In the first paragraph, Marx summarizes both the qualitative and

---

13. The Penguin edition subordinates this section to "2. The relative value form" but in the German original this section is at the same hierarchical level as 2 and "3. The equivalent form."

Commodities and Money

quantitative results of his considerations, and concludes with the sentence:

> The value of a commodity is independently expressed through its presentation [*Darstellung*] as "exchange-value." (152)

A clarification follows:

> When, at the beginning of this chapter, we said in the customary manner that a commodity is both a use-value and an exchange-value, this was, strictly speaking, wrong. A commodity is a use-value or object of utility, and a "value." It appears as the twofold thing it really is as soon as its value possesses its own particular form of manifestation, which is distinct from its natural form. This form of manifestation is exchange-value, and the commodity never has this form when looked at in isolation, but only when it is in a value-relation or an exchange relation with a second commodity of a different kind. Once we know this, our manner of speaking does no harm; it serves, rather, as an abbreviation. (152)

What's wrong with saying that a commodity "is" exchange-value? A commodity "is" something double: use-value and an object of value. But it is not exchange-value; it *has* exchange-value, when *another* commodity expresses its value.

In the first subsection of chapter 1, Marx emphasized that value's substance is a substance "common" to the commodities exchanged. Value-objectivity is therefore an objectivity held *in common*, as Marx stresses in the manuscript "Ergänzungen und Veränderungen" (see Appendix 4). For that reason, if Marx speaks here of the value of *a* commodity, it's only possible because we are singling out one member in a presupposed exchange relation between two commodities (as we already pointed out in the commentary in (ii) on the "quantitative determinacy of the relative form of value").

Marx's clarification here about the difference between value and exchange-value is useful. However, one will look in vain for a passage at the "beginning" of *Capital* (that is, in the first subsection) stating that the commodity is use-value and exchange-value. The only such passage is found in the second subsection's first paragraph (131f.).

ADDENDUM: The first time Marx refers to there being a wrong manner of speaking "at the beginning of this chapter" is in the revisions he made of the first edition in the manuscript "Ergänzungen und Veränderungen" (MEGA II/6: 22). There, the header for the first subsection of chapter 1 is: "The Two Factors of the Commodity: Use-Value and Exchange-Value" (MEGA II/6: 3). So it's correct to speak of a wrong manner of speaking at the beginning of chapter 1, but only in reference to this revised header. However, Marx later corrected the header before printing, but retained the reference to the wrong manner of speaking.

The next paragraph begins:

> Our analysis has shown that the form of value, that is, the expression of the value of a commodity, arises from the nature of commodity-value, as opposed to value and its magnitude arising from their mode of expression as exchange-value. (152)

What does this mean? The initial problem of the analysis of the value-form was that value cannot be grasped in an individual commodity. It requires an objective form that is distinct from the body of the commodity whose value is to be expressed. This form is exchange-value: another commodity's body, which *counts* directly as a manifestation of value. In this way, Marx showed that the "nature of commodity-value" makes the value-form necessary—that is, the *nature of value* is incomprehensible in a single commodity, as a result of the substance of value being an "in common" and "social" substance, which in turn, means that the objective expression of a commodity's value can only happen through another commodity. Put differently, value is the basis of the value-form.

In many debates about Marx's concept of value, the sentence quoted above has been taken as proof that Marx assumes that value exists *prior to* and *independent* of exchange, with exchange being where value later acquires a value-form. This was based on interpreting the phrase "arising from" as pointing to a *temporal* sequence, with the moment of *arising* being equated with the moment of exchange. But the sentence quoted doesn't refer to time at all. It's not about a temporal sequence, but rather a *structural* relationship of *simultaneously* existing moments that condition each other.

In the rest of the paragraph, Marx accuses various economic schools, including mercantilism and the free trade school, of adhering to the opposite position: the "delusion" that value arises from its mode of expression as exchange-value. "Mercantilism" refers to an economic theory and policy that recommends that in foreign commerce countries maintain trade surpluses. In terms of value, more should be sold abroad

Commodities and Money 121

than purchased, so that money—the "finished form" of the commodity's equivalent form in Marx's language—flows into the country. The free trade school, by contrast, doesn't promote trade surpluses, but trade that is as extensive as possible. For that reason, Marx refers to them as "pedlars of free trade" who are primarily interested in the quantitative aspect of the value expression. Whether these schools have succumbed to the "delusion" mentioned by Marx—and if so to what extent—would require a more extensive discussion of their views, which is not possible here.

In the next paragraph, Marx says once more that in the expression of the value of commodity A, its natural form only counts as use-value, whereas commodity B's natural form (which expresses the value of commodity A) only counts as the form of value. He comments on this as follows:

> The internal opposition between use-value and value, hidden within the commodity, is therefore represented on the surface by an external opposition, i.e. by a relation between two commodities such that the one commodity, *whose own* value is supposed to be expressed, counts directly only as a use-value, whereas the other commodity, *in which* that value is to be expressed, counts directly only as exchange-value. Hence the simple form of value of a commodity is the simple form of appearance of the opposition between use-value and value which is contained within the commodity. (153)

This is the first time that Marx refers to the relation between use-value and value as an "opposition." Nevertheless, in characterizing the first "peculiarity of the equivalent form," he did refer to value as the *opposite* of use-value. In both cases, the reference to an "opposition" emphasizes the opposing characteristics of use-value and value. To the extent that use-value and value are opposites, one can speak of the commodity containing an "internal opposition." Because the expression of value distributes this opposition between two poles, the "internal" opposition of the commodity becomes an "external" opposition of two commodities.

In the next paragraph, Marx points out that products of labor are not commodities in all forms of society, but only where the labor used to make such products is represented as their "objective" property, as value. Since this representation occurs by means of the value-form, Marx concludes:

> It therefore follows that the simple form of value of the commodity is at the same time the simple form of value of the

product of labour, and also that the development of the commodity-form coincides with the development of the value-form. (154)

Here Marx emphasizes the inseparable connection between the value-form of the commodity and the commodity form of the product of labor. Conversely, this means that without the value-form, we cannot speak of the commodity form of the product of labor. But the value-form *only* exists in the exchange-relation—so if there is no exchange-relation, there is no commodity.

The meaning of the word "development" will become clearer after we've gone over the next three paragraphs.

Insufficiencies of the Simple Form of Value

We perceive straight away the insufficiency of the simple form of value: it is an embryonic form which must undergo a series of metamorphoses before it can ripen into the price-form. (154)

In a cursory fashion, Marx refers to the simple form of value here as an "embryonic form" that ripens into the "price-form." Up to now, he hasn't mentioned the price-form. Price is usually understood as the exchange-value of a commodity expressed in money. However, we will have to wait until we get to the money-form, before understanding how the simple form of value is the "embryonic form" of the price-form.

The next paragraph addresses the "insufficiency" of the simple form of value, which Marx says is "perceived straight away." At each pole, there is a defect due to the individual character of the form. For the first time, Marx speaks of the "simple" relative form and the "single" equivalent form. So far, Marx has only spoken of the relative form of value and the equivalent form, without qualifying them. But if there are *different* forms of value—at this point, we've only discussed the simple form of value—then there must also be *different* relative forms and equivalent forms.

Marx identifies the following as insufficiencies:

- Through the *simple relative form of value*, the value of commodity A is differentiated from its own use-value. But commodity A only stands in an exchange-relation to a *single* commodity B. The simple form of value does not express commodity A's qualitative equality (as value) to all other commodities.

- The equivalent commodity B is no more than a *single equivalent commodity*; it only has the character of direct exchangeability in relation to a *single* commodity.

Why are these "insufficiencies"? The section called "Content of the Relative Form of Value" argued that expressing the value of commodity A required an *objective* expression. The simple form of value provides an objective expression, namely the physical body of commodity B. However, this form of value does *not* express *everything* that characterizes the value of commodity A: it doesn't express that commodity A, as an object of value, is qualitatively equal to *all* other commodities. In that sense, the simple form of value is an "insufficient" expression of commodity A's value.

It has already been emphasized many times that in the expression of value, commodity A plays an active role and commodity B plays a passive role. The simple relative form of value's insufficiency is therefore reflected in the simple equivalent form: commodity B is the equivalent for only a *single* commodity. Strictly speaking, we cannot yet judge whether the equivalent form is also insufficient, since we don't yet have a standard by which to judge an equivalent form's insufficiency. However, we may guess that the simple equivalent form is insufficient if we think about the money-form that we're familiar with in everyday life: everything that functions as money is an equivalent for *all* commodities.

Passing Over to the Expanded Form of Value (Characteristics of Conceptual Development)

The final paragraph claims that the simple form of value "automatically passes over" into a more complete form. What happens in this transition? By "passing over," Marx obviously means not just a rhetorical transition from one argument to the next, but rather a transition rooted in the object of investigation. What kind of *passing over* is it? Let's take a closer look at Marx's reasoning.

Marx's first argument is that the simple form of value

> only expresses the value of a commodity A in one commodity of another kind. But what this second commodity is, whether it is a coat, iron, corn, etc., is a matter of complete indifference. (154)

Why is the nature of the second commodity "a matter of complete indifference"? Marx is analyzing the "form of value," and for the analysis of *form*, it's a matter of indifference whether value was expressed in a coat, iron, or corn. In any case, the value of the linen finds an objective form distinct from its own use-value. And regardless of whether the equivalent commodity is a coat, iron, or corn, we can always recognize the three peculiarities of the equivalent form.

Marx's second argument is that, if the second commodity is a matter of indifference for the expression of value, then commodity A has not *one*, but *many* simple forms of value. Taken together, these many simple forms of value yield a new form of value. As the next heading indicates, it is the "total or expanded form of value."

To what extent can we say that the transition from the simple to the expanded form of value occurs "automatically"? A form doesn't *do* anything, either by itself or by compulsion. By "automatically," Marx evidently means that no new determinations are required for this transition. We need only *consider* the determinations already arrived at (the indifference of the concrete physical shape of the equivalent commodity) in order to obtain the new form.

This is obviously not a *historical* development of a kind where commodity A initially only traded for commodity B, which provided the simple form of value, but then (later in time) further commodities appeared alongside commodity B, so that now commodity A could also be exchanged for commodity C, commodity D, commodity E, etc. Apart from there being no reference to a historical transition in Marx's text, the claim that the nature of the equivalent commodity is "indifferent" only makes sense if many different types of commodities are simultaneously available that can all assume the role of the equivalent.

However, if it's not a historical development, what kind of development is it? We obtained the simple form of value by randomly selecting two commodities from the "immense collection of commodities" and considering their value-relation. It's a "single" form of value not because it was the only possible one, but because *we considered it in isolation*. In the single form of value, a relation that is by no means typical of developed capitalism is being considered. Instead, using the power of abstraction, a simple relation is *constructed*, which allows us to eventually understand what's typical for capitalism. This simple, constructed relation is first analyzed. That analysis provides determinations, whose consideration leads to a new object, which is in turn analyzed. The transition from the simple form of value to the expanded form is not a historical transition, *which we are merely describing*; rather, it is a transition to a new level of analysis, *which we are carrying out*. It's a *conceptual development*—a development of our conceptual constructions—that aims to dissect of what is always mixed up and interconnected in capitalist reality, so that we can understand it.

Marx declared earlier that "the development of the commodity-form coincides with the development of the value-form" (154). It's now clear that what he was talking about is not a historical but a *conceptual development*. As I said in the commentary on the first subsection of chapter 1, the exchange-value of commodity A introduced there—namely the amount of another commodity B that one obtains in exchange-value—is not a typical exchange-value in capitalism, since exchange usually involves money. As the first sentence of chapter 1 demonstrates, Marx wishes to analyze the commodity in developed capitalism. However, he initially considers the commodity in abstraction from the capitalist process of production and from money. That is, Marx examines a commodity that is *conceptually* undeveloped, leaving out a number of properties characteristic of commodities in capitalism, such as the price form. The *undeveloped commodity-form* we have dealt with so far must now be *conceptually developed further*. When Marx asserts that the development of the commodity-form coincides with that of the value-form, he is saying that the *further conceptual development* of the commodity-form occurs through the *further conceptual development* of the value-form (and not, for example, through further determination of the substance or magnitude of value).

B) THE TOTAL OR EXPANDED FORM OF VALUE (154–57)

Why does Marx refer to this form of value as "total or expanded"? It is expanded in relation to the simple form of value: the linen only coincidentally expresses its value in the coat. If we take into account that the linen can also express its value in other commodities, we are "expanding" what is already contained in the simple form of value. The new form of value obtained thereby is "total": it encompasses all possible expressions of the linen's value.

(1) The expanded relative form of value

In the first part of A, Marx observed that the value-form consists of two poles, the relative form of value and the equivalent form. Only at the end of A did Marx speak of the "simple relative form of value" and the "single equivalent form." Now, Marx straightaway uses the more precise expression in the subsection heading, referring to the "expanded relative form of value."

Marx points out how things have advanced compared with the simple relative form of value. Since the value of the linen is now expressed in all other physical commodities, "It is thus that this value first shows itself as being, in reality, a congealed quantity of undifferentiated human labour" (155). In this form of value, the linen now stands in a social relation to "the world of commodities" (155). For this reason:

> The endless series of expressions of its value implies that, from the point of view of the value of the commodity, the particular form of use-value in which it appears is a matter of indifference. (155)

Whereas Marx has now been dealing with the qualitative side of value, the next paragraph develops the new form further and deals with the quantitative side of value—its magnitude. In the simple form of value, the quantitative exchange-relation could still be accidental. This is no longer the case with the expanded form of value:

> The value of the linen remains unaltered in magnitude, whether expressed in coats, coffee, or iron. (156)

Strictly speaking, Marx had already reached this conclusion at the beginning of the first subsection of chapter 1. On page 127, he noted that if a given commodity (a quarter of wheat) exchanges for x boot-polish or y silk or z gold, then each of these various exchange-values of the same commodity must "be mutually replaceable or of identical magnitude." What Marx was considering there was basically the expanded relative form of value of a quarter of wheat. In our commentary on that earlier passage, we explained why the same commodity's exchange-values must be "of identical magnitude." Now, in the current passage, Marx concludes:

> It becomes plain that it is not the exchange of commodities which regulates the magnitude of their values, but rather the reverse, the magnitude of the value of the commodities which regulates the proportion in which they exchange. (156)

This sentence has often been understood to mean that the magnitudes of value had to be established *chronologically* prior to exchange. This kind of interpretation was then frequently linked to the notion discussed above that a commodity's value is already determined in the production process. However, the sentence quoted is not talking about a temporal sequence, but rather a *relation of regulation*. And the latter does not necessarily depend on what regulates and is regulated being in a chronological sequence.

The magnitude of a commodity's value expresses a certain social relation between producers. The basis of this relation (what is produced and what is needed) does not simply *emerge* in exchange; it is *mediated* by exchange and *only* by exchange. This is precisely what is specific about a society based upon commodity production. (We will return to this topic in the section on the fetish character of the commodity.) Commodity producers produce *privately*, independently of one another. It is not through production that they enter in a social relationship but through the exchange of their products. Only then is it revealed what counts as "socially necessary labor-time." Exchange does not determine the amount of socially necessary labor-time; it only exists in exchange, because only in exchange are the underlying average ratios formed, and, in exchange, such labor determines the quantitative exchange relations. In this sense, the commodity's magnitude of value *regulates* its exchange-relations, but both the magnitude of value and the exchange-relations always exist *simultaneously*.

(2) The particular equivalent form

Marx speaks here not of the expanded equivalent form, but rather of the "particular" equivalent form. The expanded equivalent form is the endless range of commodities that can serve as equivalents. A single commodity picked out of this range is a *particular* equivalent; it then becomes the "particular equivalent form."

Marx asserts that the "specific natural form" of each of these commodities is a *particular* equivalent form and that the specific concrete labor that produces the physical commodity counts as a *particular* form of appearance of human labor in general (156). Here, Marx shows how the first two "peculiarities" of the simple equivalent form are properties of the particular equivalent form.

(3) Defects of the total or expanded form of value

Marx first lists three defects of the expanded relative form of value:

- The relative expression of value is endless.
- It's a "mosaic of disparate and unconnected expressions of value."
- The expanded relative forms of value of different commodities vary. (They vary because in the relative value expression of commodity

A, commodity B appears, but in the relative value expression of commodity B, it's not commodity B that appears, but rather commodity A, which is missing in the relative value expression of commodity A.)

In addition, there are two defects of the equivalent form (Marx avoids using the term "expanded equivalent form"):

- There only exist particular equivalent forms, which mutually exclude each other. (This is why Marx cannot speak of the expanded equivalent form.)
- The concrete useful labor that creates the physical body of a particular equivalent commodity is only a particular expression of abstract human labor; abstract human labor does not have a unified form of appearance.

Why are these characteristics "defects"? Marx does not further discuss the issue. He obviously believes that his hints at the end of the discussion of the simple form of value suffice. There, the defects of the simple form of value are that they do not adequately express the value of commodity A. The same holds for the expanded form of value. Now, the single commodity A stands in a relationship to the entire world of commodities. That all commodities are qualitatively equal in terms of value, however, is obscured by the endless and diverse expressions of value that the expanded form of value provides. Instead of a unified expression of the value of commodity A, there are many particular expressions. In that respect, the expanded form of value insufficiently expresses the value of commodity A.

Marx now turns to another form of value arising from the expanded form of value. The expanded form of value consists of a multitude of expressions of value. In (a)(1), Marx showed how the simple form of value *x commodity A is worth y commodity B* is based on the value equation *x commodity A = y commodity B*. This can be turned around, yielding the reverse expression of value, *y commodity B is worth x commodity A*. Marx now applies this reversal to each individual equation of the expanded form of value, thereby obtaining "the general form of value."

We can see here that the transition from the expanded form of value to the general form of value is not a historical development. Rather, it is a conceptual evolution belonging to the investigation. The transition comes from considering additional characteristics that are already part of the simple form of value. Marx stresses this once again in his final sentence: "i.e. if we give expression to the converse relation *already implied in the series*..." (157, emphasis M.H.)

(c) The General Form of Value (157–162)

(1) The changed character of the form of value

> The commodities now present their values to us, (1) in a simple form, because in a single commodity; (2) in a unified form, because in the same commodity each time. Their form of value is simple and common to all, hence general. (157)

In this way, Marx identifies the two ways the new form of value represents an advance, and he explains his choice of the term "general form of value."

The Historical Appearance of the Forms of Value

Marx briefly characterizes the first two forms of value in the second and third paragraphs. Then, on page 158, he comments briefly on the historical appearance of these forms. On the one hand, the simple form of value appears where labor products are only occasionally and coincidentally exchanged. On the other hand, the expanded form of value appears when labor products are exchanged with other commodities, not exceptionally, but as a rule.

Marx makes these remarks only after analyzing the forms. Therefore his analysis of the forms is in no way based on a historical development. In fact, it's the other way around: completing the form analysis serves to indicate what's important in the historical investigation. In commenting on the introductory passage (138), I alluded to the *historical* interpretation of development in *Capital*. That interpretation alleges that the development of the value-forms represents an abstract tracing of the historical development; the "logic" of the sequence of the forms of value reflects advances in a process of historical evolution. As we have seen, Marx does not justify the transition from the simple to the expanded, and then from the expanded to the general form of value, as historical transitions, not even in a completely abstract sense. Instead, he uses the properties already present in each respective form for the conceptual construction of a new form. In the first edition, Marx completely left out the historical remarks quoted here.

ADDENDUM: It is a consistent pattern throughout *Capital* that Marx makes a remark about the pre-capitalist existence of individual forms only *after* carrying out the form-analysis. This applies to the examination of the "so-called primitive accumulation"; that is, the historical formation of the capital relation, which appears at the first volume's end, not its beginning. It also applies to the historical examination of commercial capital and interest-bearing capital, which comes *after* the presentation of the relevant category in the third volume. In this, Marx is following a methodological insight that he formulated as early as the "Introduction" of 1857, which is the complete opposite of the way the *historical* interpretation understands his mode of presentation:

> Bourgeois society is the most developed and the most complex historic organization of production. The categories which express its relations, the comprehension of its structure, thereby also allows insights into the structure and the relations of production of all the vanished social formations out of whose ruins and elements it built itself up, whose partly still unconquered remnants are carried along within it, whose mere nuances have developed explicit significance within it, etc. *Human anatomy contains a key to the anatomy of the ape*. The intimations of higher development among the subordinate animal species, however, can be understood only after the higher development is already known. (*Grundrisse*: 105, emphasis M.H.)

However, we should remember that the forms appearing in pre-capitalist modes of production that represent "intimations of higher development" are *not identical* with this "higher development," that is, the forms in capitalism. Since Marx is examining the capitalistically produced commodity exchanged for money, but initially abstracted from capital and money, neither the simple nor the expanded form of value is identical with a simple or expanded *exchange of products* without the mediation of money. The simple and expanded forms of value are conceptual constructs formed by *abstracting* from exchange mediated by money. They are not pre-capitalist manifestations of non-monetary exchange.

The Changed Character of the Relative Form of Value

In comparing the forms of value, in the first three paragraphs on page 158, Marx emphasizes that the first two forms of value merely express the value of a commodity as something distinct from its own use-value. In the fourth paragraph, he states how the general form of value represents a decisive advance:

Commodities and Money

> The value of every commodity is now not only differentiated from its own use-value, but from all use-values, and is, by that very fact, expressed as that which is common to all commodities. (158)

As a consequence:

> By this form, commodities are, for the first time, really brought into relation with each other as values, or permitted to appear to each other as exchange-values. (158)

In what sense does Marx use the word "really" here? The first two forms of value already related commodities to each other as value. So why should this relationship only "really" occur in the general form of value? The first two forms represent a relationship that does not yet express everything that characterizes value; it is only achieved by the third form, which is no longer insufficient like the first two forms. It is in this sense that Marx says that it "really" relates commodities to each other as values—just as one might say that a task is only "really" solved if the solution is complete.

On the basis of Marx's language in this passage and in similar ones, some commentators refer to Hegel's concept of reality—what is *real* is what corresponds to the *concept* of a thing—and allege that it continues in Marx's work. Further "evidence" is in the first edition's appendix, where the corresponding passage on the general form of value states: "Only through this general character does the value-form correspond to the concept of value" (*Capital and Class* 4, Spring 1978: 46). However, whether Marx actually relies on Hegel's concept of reality—or to what extent he does so—can only be meaningfully discussed when one knows somewhat more about Marx and Hegel. Still, insofar as such imprecise language can be clarified *without* referring to the history of philosophy (which appears to me possible here and in many other passages), I attempt to do so.

In the fifth paragraph on page 158, Marx addresses an additional difference between the forms of value. In the first two forms of value, the expression of value is based on a single commodity. Marx writes that it is its "private task . . . to give itself a form of value, and it accomplishes this task without the aid of the others" (159). These other commodities only appear in the passive role of the equivalent. But the situation is fundamentally different with the general form of value:

> The general form of value, on the other hand, can only arise as the joint contribution of the whole world of commodities. (159)

At this point, the obvious question is how this *joint* contribution of the whole world of commodities is possible at all. Does it not presuppose an effort of coordination, meaning that something must be doing the coordinating? Marx does not address this question. Why not? In chapter 1, he only examines the *form determinations* of the commodity, but not the process of *implementing* and *maintaining* these form determinations through people's *actions*. This latter constitutes, as mentioned above, the object of chapter 2.

Marx proceeds:

> It thus becomes evident that because the objectivity of commodities as values is the purely "social existence" of these things, it can only be expressed through the whole range of their social relations; consequently the form of their value must possess social validity. (159)

In the introduction to the subsection on the value-form, it was taken for granted—"it follows self-evidently"—that the value-objectivity of commodities, as something purely social, "can only appear in the social relation between commodity and commodity" (139). Now, instead of this rather general formulation, Marx writes that the value-objectivity of commodities can only be expressed through "the whole range" (*allseitig*) of their social relationships. Why now "the whole range"? Let's recall that being "value-creating labor" cannot be the property of an *individual* labor process, but results instead from the diverse *social processes that form the average*. The "substance of value" is thus based on a whole range of social relationships: the various acts that contribute to the average, which are carried out in exchange, set all commodity-producing labor activities in relation to each other. Therefore the value-objectivity of commodities is only adequately expressed by the "whole range" of social relationships, which is only present with the general form of value.

In the next paragraph, Marx states that the commodities in this all-around relationship are no longer just *qualitatively equal* as values, but also the magnitudes of their value are *quantitatively comparable*—through a specific quantity of linen that serves as the expression of value.

The Changed Character of the Equivalent Form

In the first sentences of the next paragraph, Marx carries over his earlier findings to the general form of value, and thus refers explicitly now to the *general* relative form of value and the *general* equivalent. On the one hand, he emphasizes the *active* role of the commodities that occupy the relative form of value: "The general relative form of value imposes the character of universal equivalent on the linen" (159). On the other hand, Marx addresses the three "peculiarities" of the equivalent form, although only the third peculiarity is addressed in any detail.

Compared with their role in the simple form of value, these three peculiarities undergo a certain change in the general form of value. In the *simple* equivalent form, we saw that use-value / concrete useful labor / private labor became the "form of appearance" of value / abstract human labor / labor in immediately social form. By contrast, with the *general* equivalent form, both the use-value of the equivalent commodity and the useful/private labor that produced the physical equivalent commodity become value's "general form of appearance" (159) / abstract human labor / labor in immediately social form. That is, we are no longer dealing with an isolated form of appearance, but rather a *general socially valid form of appearance*.

On the basis of this *general* character, Marx draws the following conclusion about the now evident "positive nature" of value-creating labor:

> In this manner the labour objectified in the values of commodities is not just presented negatively, as labour in which abstraction is made from all the concrete forms and useful properties of actual work. Its own positive nature is explicitly brought out, namely the fact that it is the reduction of all kinds of actual labour to their common character of being human labour in general, of being the expenditure of human labour-power. (159)

Why was the labor objectified in value presented "negatively" when it was without a general equivalent? In both the individual equivalent (in the simple form of value) and the special equivalent (in the expanded form of value), the concrete labor that produced the equivalent commodity was already a form of appearance of abstract labor. However, it was only the abstract human labor objectified in the value of a *single* commodity, the single commodity of the relative form of value. Accordingly, as value-creating labor, this labor was only characterized as an abstraction from *its own* concrete useful character and for that reason only "negatively" determined.

For example, if in the simple form of value iron expresses the value of wheat, then iron is the form of appearance of value, whereas the concrete labor that produces iron is the form of appearance of value-creating labor. However, in the simple form of value, only the value of a single commodity is expressed, wheat in this case. If we consider the simple form of value that expresses the value of wheat, we can only discern that the concrete labor that produces wheat does *not* create value; only the labor producing iron "counts" as creating value. Therefore, the simple form of value only serves to make a "negative" statement about the value-creating labor represented in the value of the wheat: it is *not* concrete, wheat-producing labor.

It's different with the general form of value. With the linen as the *general* equivalent, weaving becomes the form of appearance of *all* labor objectified in value. As concrete labor, none of the various labor activities creates value. But value is created, with the commodities expressing their value in the linen. Therefore weaving expresses what all these *many* concrete labor activities have *in common*: they are "human labor." Only now that the value of many different commodities is being expressed can we perceive what the many different labor activities have in common. This is the "positive nature" of value-creating labor addressed by Marx, which first emerges with the general equivalent.

One could object that this "positive nature" was evident from the very beginning. As early as page 128, when Marx was searching for exchanged commodities' common "content," he argued that there occurs an abstraction from use-value (in exchange), and there is also an abstraction from the useful character of labor activities. All the latter are reduced to "equal human labor." Therefore, what's especially new with the general form of value?

We are dealing here with the same difference, a difference between two levels of analysis, which Marx mentioned on pages 141–42. On 128–29, the *exchange-relation* of two commodities was analyzed. The results of this analysis were "an abstraction, value" (141, corrected translation) and the characterization of value-creating labor as abstract human labor. Now we are dealing with the analysis of the *value-relation* of the commodities. Here, it is the *relationship of the commodities* itself—the world of commodities that occupies the general relative form of value and relates to a single commodity as the general equivalent—that expresses this "positive nature." In the value-relation, the *result* of the analysis of the exchange relation becomes a *component* of the relation being analyzed.

With this in mind the final paragraph of this subsection should be understood:

> The general value-form, in which all the products of labour are presented as mere congealed quantities of undifferentiated

human labour, shows by its very structure that it is the social expression of the world of commodities. (160)

This "very structure" of the general form of value consists in the fact that all commodities relate to one commodity as their common expression of value. It sets all commodities into a social relationship: in that sense, the general form of value is "the social expression of the world of commodities." And *how* does the general form of value place commodities into a social relationship? Not as *use-values*, but as *values*, in that they are represented as "congealed quantities of homogeneous human labor." Marx can therefore conclude:

In this way it is made plain that within this world the general human character of labour forms its specific social character. (160)

We have to read this sentence carefully. It makes reference to "this world" which, as the preceding sentence makes clear, refers to the "world of commodities." Within the world of commodities, our aim is to determine the "specific social character" of labor; that is, what makes *privately* expended labor *social*—a component of the labor of society? Private labor only becomes social in the world of commodities if it produces a commodity, thereby representing itself not only in a use-value, but as value. And only as "homogeneous human labor" does labor represent value. In that sense, the general human character of labor *within the world of commodities* is the specific social character of labor. Outside the world of commodities—in other modes of production—things are otherwise.

ADDENDUM: Marx addresses another important aspect of the general form of value in chapter 1 of the first edition of *Capital*. What is general in commodities, common to all of them, their value and the labor represented in value, are represented in the *general equivalent* as an *individual thing*. In the first edition, Marx emphasized this property of the general equivalent form, and he also found a very instructive example for it:

In form II (20 yards of linen = 1 coat or = *u* coffee, *or* v tea *or* x iron, etc.), the form in which the linen develops *its relative value-expression,* it relates itself to each individual commodity (coat, coffee, etc.) as a *specific Equivalent,* and to all of them together as to the *environment of its specific forms of the Equivalent.* No individual species of commodity counts any longer with

> respect to the linen as simple Equivalent, as in the *particular* Equivalent, but only as *specific* Equivalent whereby the one Equivalent excludes the other. In form III (which is the reciprocal second form, and is therefore contained in it), the linen appears on the other hand as the *general form* [corrected translation: *generic form, Gattungsform*] of the Equivalent for all other commodities. It is as if alongside and external to lions, tigers, rabbits, and all other actual animals, which form when grouped together the various kinds, species, subspecies, families etc. of the animal kingdom, there existed also in addition *the animal,* the individual incarnation of the entire animal kingdom. (Dragstedt 1976: 27)

The general equivalent is an "individual incarnation" of the generic feature of commodities: they are not only use-values but values. The linen as an individual commodity stands alongside all the other individual commodities. As the general equivalent, however, the linen counts as a general and direct manifestation of value. In that way, the genus (value) stands here as an individual (in the shape of the linen), alongside all the other individuals (the other individual commodities), which in their totality constitute this genus.

2. The development of the relative and equivalent forms of value: their interdependence

In the first couple of sentences, Marx emphasizes that the development of the equivalent form is only "the expression and the result of the development of the relative form." When presenting the simple form of value on page 139, Marx began by noting that the commodity in the relative form of value plays an active role, that is, it expresses its value, whereas the commodity in the equivalent form plays a passive role, serving as the material in which value is expressed. In the next paragraph, Marx briefly identifies the various equivalent forms that result from each respective form of value.

The remaining five paragraphs of this subsection describe the evolution of the antagonism between each pole of the value-form:

- The *simple form of value* contains this antagonism, "without as yet fixing it" (160). Because the individual expression of value can be read forwards and backwards without any problem, either of the two commodities can take on the relative form of value or the equivalent form.
- In the *expanded form of value*, only *one* commodity is in the relative

form of value, *because all other commodities are not*. If one reads the expression of value backwards, it changes character and transforms into the general form of value.
- Something similar applies to the *general form of value*: *one* commodity, *because* all other commodities are not there, is in the equivalent form, which Marx describes as "the form of direct exchangeability" (161).

The commodity that serves as the general equivalent is excluded from the *general relative form of value*, otherwise, we would have 20 yards of linen = 20 yards of linen. The general equivalent can only express its value if we reverse the general form of value. Then the (former) equivalent commodity is in the *expanded relative form of value*, and expresses its value in the infinite array of other types of commodities.

After observing that the commodity serving as the general equivalent only has the form of direct exchangeability because all other commodities don't have it, Marx states in footnote 26:

> It is by no means self-evident that the form of direct and universal exchangeability is an antagonistic form, as inseparable from its opposite, the form of non-direct exchangeability, as the positivity of one pole of a magnet is from the negativity of the other pole. (161)

In the foregoing analysis of the *simple* form of value, Marx noted that the commodity in the equivalent form only counts as the direct embodiment of value *within* the value-relation. However, since the properties of things usually do not derive from their relationships to other things—as Marx notes—the commodity in the equivalent form also appears to have this form (and thus the form of direct exchangeability) "by nature" (149). This is what causes the "mysteriousness of the equivalent form" (149). The issue is that we do not see in the equivalent form that it is only the *result* of the relative form of value, that is, another commodity expressing its value through it. In the analysis of the simple form of value, this circumstance explained why the equivalent form—the form of direct exchangeability—becomes a *material* (*dinglich*) property of the commodity that occupies that role. The commodity that takes on the role of the simple equivalent *appears* to possess certain properties that allow it to become the equivalent. This *appearance* is also present in the *general* equivalent, and to an even greater degree than in the simple form of value. This is because in the simple form of value the antagonism between the relative form of value and the equivalent form was not yet "fixed" (160) and the expression of value could be read backwards without a problem. By contrast, in the case of the general form of value, this antagonism is fixed: the expression of value can no longer be reversed without changing the form.

In the rest of the footnote, Marx criticizes Proudhonian socialism. Pierre-Joseph Proudhon (1809–1865) had been an influential socialist author in France since the 1840s. He tried to scientifically justify his notions of socialism with a combination of philosophical, economic, and above all moral arguments. In 1847, Marx responded to Proudhon's major work, *The Philosophy of Poverty* (1846), with *The Poverty of Philosophy* (MECW 6). The latter, however, was still quite far from the "critique of political economy" that Marx first formulated in 1857 (see Appendix 1). The debate with Proudhon was important in forming Marx's critique of economics. In *Capital*, Marx briefly criticizes Proudhon in a few footnotes, but the critique is frankly devastating. The debate with Proudhon clearly shows how abstract theoretical deliberations can have direct political consequences.

Marx criticizes Proudhon's socialism as a false resolution of the general equivalent's semblance of independence, due to the expression of value. Right after the sentences just quoted, he writes:

> This has allowed the illusion to arise that all commodities can simultaneously be imprinted with the stamp of direct exchangeability, in the same way that it might be imagined that all Catholics can be popes. (161)

Proudhon recognizes that the equivalent commodity itself does not have any special property that makes it the equivalent. Gold or silver, for example, which historically have been general equivalents, are ordinary commodities, just like linen or coffee. However, it is wrong to conclude from this that it's possible to simply take the equivalent's privileged position away from it. Proudhon's socialism fails to recognize two things, as do all theories that presume one can retain commodity production while abolishing money. First, that the general equivalent's privileged position is only the *result* of the rest of the world of commodities relating to this one commodity as the general equivalent; and second, that this relation is necessary so that all commodities relate to each other as values.

Marx describes Proudhon's socialism as a "philistine utopia" arising from the notions of the "petty bourgeois" who "views the production of commodities as the absolute summit of human freedom and individual independence" (161n26). In Marx's time, the phrase "petty bourgeois"

Commodities and Money 139

was understood to refer to small commodity producers, artisans, independent farmers, and self-employed professionals such as doctors or lawyers. They were themselves neither wage laborers nor real capitalists, even if they had two or three employees. They therefore operated within "simple" commodity production, that is, through purchase and sale that was not mediated capitalistically, which appeared to many of them as the natural order of things. With his disparaging remarks, which he followed with others (178n2, 280, 734n10), Marx makes it clear that he does *not* value commodity production and does not view any kind of reformed commodity production as an alternative to capitalism (see in particular 734n10).

At the end of the footnote on page 161, Marx makes clear, through a literary allusion, that he not only regards Proudhon's position as wrong, but even regards all his deliberations as puffed up and unscientific. Marx does not provide a source for the lines of verse that appear there, which are a lightly modified quotation from Goethe's *Faust*. He could count on educated middle-class readers of his time being familiar with it, so they would understand his allusion. In the lines that Marx alludes to from *Faust*, Mephistopheles mocks the scientific pretensions of theology.

(3) The transition from the general form of value to the money form

Marx points out that the general equivalent form could be assumed by *any* commodity, but claims that the form first obtains "objective fixedness and general social validity" when it is permanently restricted to *one* commodity:

> The specific kind of commodity with whose natural form the equivalent form is socially interwoven now becomes the money commodity, or serves as money. It becomes its specific social function, and consequently its social monopoly, to play the part of universal equivalent within the world of commodities. (162)

If we place this *money commodity* (which historically was gold) in the position of the linen, we obtain the money form.

(D) THE MONEY FORM (162–63)

Here Marx addresses not only the money form but also the interrelation of the forms of value and will present his solution to the "mystery of money." In the first two paragraphs, he deals with the differences between the forms of value: there were actual changes of *form* in the transition from the first form to the second, and from the second form to the third; but in terms of form, the money form is not at all different from the third form, the general form of value. The advance consists only in the equivalent form having "fused" with the natural form of a certain commodity.

As emphasized above, the development of the first three forms of value does not represent a historical evolution, but rather a *conceptual* development of the *content* of the form. Since the money form does not have any *difference in form* compared to the general form of value, it cannot be developed *conceptually* out of the general form of value. As Marx emphasizes, it is only "social custom" (162) that leads to the equivalent form permanently adhering to a specific commodity. That means that nothing more than the *actions of commodity owners* establish the transition from the general form of value to the money form.

ADDENDUM: Marx offers a systematic treatment of commodity owners and their actions only in chapter 2. In that sense, his presentation of the money form here constitutes something of an anticipation. In chapter 1 of the first edition of *Capital*, where Marx separates the different levels of presentation more consistently, the money form does not come after the general form of value. The concluding part of the original value-form analysis is contained in Appendix 3. Marx first uses this sequence incorporating the anticipation of money in the "schoolmasterly" appendix of the first edition.

In the third paragraph, Marx explains what the *price form* is about: the *simple relative expression of value* of a commodity using the commodity that functions as a money commodity. The price of a commodity is nothing other than its value expressed in the money commodity.

In the course of the conceptual development, we now arrive for the first time at the price form of the commodity, which common sense always associates with commodities. Marx began his analysis with a non-empirical object, constructed by the "power of abstraction" (90): the commodity without price form (see 126–127). He has not simply *taken up* the price form as an empirical fact, but has *developed* it categorically: he has explained what the expression of price means and in what sense it is *necessary* for the commodity.

The price form of a commodity is a specific *simple relative form of value*. In the section on the simple form of value, Marx already examined this quantitative determination (144ff.), establishing that the change in a commodity's magnitude of value does not have to be reflected in its relative expression. The same is obviously true of the price form. For example, if productivity increases in specific sectors, the value of the respective commodity declines. If productivity increases just as strongly in the sector producing the money commodity, then we will have a general decline in value, but a constant price level (this corresponds to scenario III, 146). If productivity in producing the money commodity rises to an above-average level, then the money commodity's value declines faster than that of the other commodities. In this case, a general *decline in magnitudes of value* goes along with *rising prices* (corresponding to scenarios ii and iii. 145f.).

ADDENDUM: As will be demonstrated later in *Capital*'s first volume, it is intrinsic to capital to develop the productivity of labor. That means there is an intrinsic tendency for values to decrease in magnitude. As the preceding commentary makes clear, such a decline in values is *not necessarily* reflected in declining prices. When reading the first and second volumes of *Capital*, keep in mind that Marx's arguments usually refer to *value* and not *price*.

Our arriving at the money form raises the question of how up to date Marx's analysis is. In Marx's argument, the money form is linked to a commodity, the money commodity (gold, for Marx). However, the contemporary monetary system no longer bears any relationship to a money commodity, neither *de jure*—for example, with banknotes requiring complete or partial coverage by a commodity, as in the nineteenth century—nor de facto, which might express itself in commodity owners not accepting money that isn't covered by a money commodity, or accepting it only at a markdown. We can thus ask if Marx's analysis is obsolete, or if there is still some kind of indirect linkage to a money commodity today.

ADDENDUM: We have so far followed only the initial steps of Marx's account—dealing with the relation between commodity and money but in abstraction from capitalist production. However, we are not finished with these first steps; two more chapters remain before Marx begins analyzing capital in chapter 4. Even so, further categories are required for the analysis of the modern capitalist monetary system. These include interest, credit, and credit-money, which are first dealt with in the third volume of *Capital*. I provide a brief initial discussion of the problem of the money commodity in my *Introduction* (Heinrich 2012: 69, 161). A more extensive discussion can be found in Heinrich 1999:233ff., 302ff.; and in Stützle (2006).

In the last paragraph of the money form section, Marx takes a brief retrospective look at his reasoning:

> The only difficulty in the concept of the money form is that of grasping the universal equivalent form, and hence the general form of value as such, form C. Form C can be reduced by working backwards to form B, the expanded form of value, and its constitutive element is form A: 20 yards of linen = 1 coat or x commodity A = y commodity B. The simple commodity form is therefore the germ of the money form. (163)

The simple commodity form Marx refers to here is synonymous with the simple form of value. Back on page 154 he stated that "the simple form of value of the commodity is at the same time the simple form of value of the product of labour." He also asserted that the simple form of value is the "embryonic form" of the price form, which has now been explained. Several issues demand our attention. Marx emphasizes here that it is the *inner logic* of the forms of value, the way one form is already contained in another, that underlies their "comprehension." It is not a question of any kind of *historical* interrelation of the forms of value. (He is even more emphatic about this when concluding the presentation on the value form in the first edition's chapter 1; see Appendix 3).

This retrospective look at the conceptual development's inner logic takes us from the end result back to the simple form of value: it is the actual core of what has to be understood. Thus, at the end of his presentation of the forms of value, Marx is able to justify what he merely *claimed* to be true at the beginning of in the analysis of the simple form of value: "The whole mystery of the form of value lies hidden in this simple form" (139).

Now, as was said in the introductory passage to the value-form section, the "origin of the money-form" (139). has been demonstrated. However, Marx makes no mention of the "mystery of money" that he earlier proposed to solve by demonstrating this origin. Still, it's not hard to see that Marx has solved the mystery of money, even if he doesn't explicitly say so. The mystery was how we can buy everything with money. The answer, *because money has value*, is obviously insufficient, since other commodities also have value. Nor can the explication rely on the *material* of money (for example, gold), since that has changed many times in history. The solution to the mystery resides in the money *form*. Nevertheless, since the money form exhibits no *differences in form* from the general form of value, then the mystery of money's solution must already be found there. Marx in fact emphasized that the general equivalent only has "the form of direct exchangeability with all other commodities," that is, it can purchase anything, *because* all other commodities *relate* to it as their expression of value. It's only this act of "relating" within the world of commodities that makes a certain commodity into the general equivalent, thus endowing it with the ability to buy everything. Importantly, this "relating" is not at all accidental or arbitrary; it is *necessary*, for only by relating to a general equivalent can commodities relate to each other as values.

The analysis of the simple form of value has already shown how this becomes a "mystery": the commodity in the equivalent form only has its property of general exchangeability *within* the value relationship. However, since a thing's properties do not usually arise from its relationships, but rather independently of them, the equivalent commodity appears to have the form of direct exchangeability "by nature." That is what accounts for the "riddle of the equivalent form" (150): the *result* of a *relationship* appears to be the *property of a thing*, therefore becoming a mystery.

4. The Fetishism of the Commodity and Its Secret (163–177)

In the title of this subsection, Marx speaks for the first time of the "fetish character of the commodity." He also refers to a "secret." It remains to be seen what this fetishism consists of, and how it conceals a secret.

Using the terms "fetish" and "fetishism" is widespread today. One speaks of "brand fetishism" if somebody only buys a particular brand, or speaking of certain sexual practices as "fetishism." This general usage of *fetish* to mean "something of exaggerated importance" was not usual in Marx's time. Hence, we can't subsume his concept of *fetish* to the current usage. A German lexicon from 1840 states: "Fetishism is the divine worship of (usually lifeless) objects, powers, or natural phenomena. In fetishism, which is the lowest level of religious thought, the cult object is the sensuous object itself (not its hidden source), insofar as it expresses its power to people's best disadvantage or advantage. The characteristic of this form of religion is arbitrary choice and arbitrary rejection or variation." (*Allgemeines deutsches Conversations-Lexicon für die Gebildeten eines jeden Standes in 10 Bänden*, vol. 4:F–G, Leipzig 1840, 79.)

This quotation demonstrates that fetishism was regarded as something primitive and irrational, from which bourgeois society—

which understood itself to be completely rational—sorely wanted to take distance. For that reason, Marx's characterizing capitalist relations as fetishistic, thereby questioning their rationality, was a much greater provocation in the nineteenth century than it is today, when there is widespread talk of fetishism.

Marx's reasoning is very dense, especially in the first few pages of the fetish section (163-69). Every single sentence requires precise reading. That's why the commentary on these pages is very thorough.

a) "Whence, then, arises the enigmatic character of the product of labour, as soon as it assumes the form of a commodity?" (163-65)

> A commodity appears at first sight an extremely obvious, trivial thing. But its analysis brings out that it is a very strange thing, abounding in metaphysical subtleties and theological niceties. (163)

Two important claims are implicit in these initial sentences of the section on fetishism. The first concerns the *level of argumentation*. It is linked to *Capital*'s very first two sentences (125): the "analysis of the commodity" announced there has now been carried out, including an examination of the substance of value, the magnitude of value and the value form. Now, Marx will draw certain conclusions from the *analysis that has taken place*: "its analysis brings out."

The other implicit statement concerns the *content of the arguments*. The section title refers to the "secret" of fetishism, and we must carefully attempt to locate that secret. Marx says that the commodity is not "at first sight" something mysterious (we are all familiar with commodities); rather, it is the *analysis* that brings out the secret—"metaphysical subtleties" and "theological niceties." Analysis hasn't solved a mystery, because there was no mystery calling for a solution. Rather, it has shown us that there is something mysterious. And that mystery is now the issue.

Marx begins to track down the mystery by briefly reviewing the course of the analysis: in the first paragraph he notes two things: (1) there is nothing mysterious about the commodity as a *use-value* (for example, a table), which remains an "ordinary, sensuous thing" (163); (2) things are different when we consider the table as a commodity:

> But as soon as it emerges as a commodity, it changes into a thing which transcends sensuousness [corrected translation: it

Commodities and Money 145

> changes into a sensuous, extrasensory thing, *ein sinnlich übersinnliches Ding*]. (163)

How can Marx refer to the commodity as "a sensuous, extra-sensory thing"? Inasmuch as the commodity is a use-value, it is "sensuous," that is, perceivable with our five senses. Yet as a commodity, it has a dual nature, of being use-value and value, and Marx stated at the beginning of chapter 1 that the objectivity of value was a "phantom-like objectivity" (128). It remained "impossible to grasp" in the case of the individual commodity (138). This is why Marx could speak of value as not a natural but "supra-natural property" of things (149). Marx is obviously referring to these earlier characterizations in speaking now of "extrasensory" things and of the commodity's "metaphysical subtleties" and "theological niceties." This demonstrates that Marx's earlier language—involving terms such as "phantom-like" or "spectral" and "supra-natural"—was not merely a question of stylistic idiosyncrasy. Instead, it expressed a specific state of affairs that he will now address systematically.

However, as the next paragraph shows, value-objectivity's "extra-sensory" dimension is not easily grasped.

> The mystical character of the commodity does not therefore arise from its use-value. Just as little does it proceed from the nature [correct: content, *Inhalt*] of the determinants of value. (164)

The first sentence merely repeats one of the previous paragraph's findings. Marx will argue the second sentence's claim in the following. So far, there has been no mention of the "determinants of value." Yet Marx is obviously referring to the three determinations of value that he has analyzed up to now: the substance of value, the magnitude of value, and the value-form. Now he will discuss their "content."

Marx first speaks of the "physiological fact" (164) that, regardless of how different the useful labor activities are, they are always the expenditure of brain, nerve, and muscles. He thus alludes to the second subsection of chapter 1 where abstract human labor is determined as "an expenditure of human labour-power, in the physiological sense" (137). Next, Marx identifies the second determination's content as the "quantity of labour" (164), which must interest people in all kinds of societies. Third, when people work for each other in some manner, their labor also acquires a "social form" (164). Marx thereby alludes to an idea developed earlier in the value-form section: in commodity production, the product is only "social" if it becomes a commodity; and it becomes a commodity when it acquires a value-form and its value is expressed objectively. (The appendix to the first edition of *Capital* states this more clearly; see the passage from that appendix quoted in the commentary on the third peculiarity of the equivalent form). Under the conditions of commodity production, labor is thus only social if its product acquires a value-form. In that sense, we can say that the "content" of the value-form is the social character of labor.

It's certainly true that there's nothing "mystical" about the three "contents" Marx refers to. But is this really about the "content" of the determinants of value?

The "content" of value, the substance of value, is not simply labor, but *abstract human labor*—a social reduction, through exchange, of the various acts of labor. In the commentary on the second subsection's last paragraph, we pointed out that it's problematic to equate abstract human labor with labor expenditure in the physiological sense.

In a similar way, it's problematic to take simply the duration of labor time as a measure for the magnitude of value. What can be measured is no more than the individual labor-time expended in a concrete type of labor. The "duration" of abstract labor is always bound to *average social conditions*, so it cannot be measured directly.

And finally, the "content" of the value-form is not simply the "social form" of labor, but rather the social form of labor that is expended as (commodity-producing) *private labor*. The latter is socialized as "equal human labor."

What Marx calls the "content" of the "determinants of value" are in fact *transhistorical* determinations applying to *every* society. In all societies, in the first place, there is work and thus expenditure of brain, muscle, and nerves. Second, every society must also concern itself with the duration of labor expenditure. Third, in every society, individuals' labor activities must be related to each other somehow. These three transhistorical determinations, however, do not immediately become the "content" of the determinants of value; rather, they become that content only in *historically determinate* forms: the first as abstract human labor (the result of a social process of abstraction); the second as the duration not of concrete but abstract labor, based upon the formation of specific social averages; and the third as the social form of a specific type of labor, namely (commodity-producing) private labor. This means that the "content" of the determinants of value is itself *socially generated* in a specific manner and is not at all something trans-historical. Marx made that clear in the earlier analysis, but not in the language he uses here.

Commodities and Money 147

So far, Marx has only identified *what does not explain* the mysterious character of the products of labor when they assume the commodity form. Now, in the third paragraph on page 164, comes the answer: "Clearly, it arises from this form itself." Hence the secret of the commodity lies in the commodity *form*. Through the commodity form, the "content" of the determinants of value—that is, the properties of the acts of labor, their equality as human labor, their duration, and the relations of producers—become, in turn, objective properties of the products of labor (value-objectivity, the magnitude of value) and social relations among those products.

The next paragraph explains what this means in detail (164–65). Its first sentence calls for a close reading:

> The mysterious character of the commodity-form consists therefore simply in the fact that the commodity reflects the social characteristics of men's own labour as objective [*gegenständliche*] characteristics of the products of labour themselves, as the socio-natural properties [*gesellschaftliche Natureigenschaften*] of these things. Hence it also reflects the social relation of the producers to the sum total of labour [*Gesamtarbeit*] as a social relation between objects, a relation which exists apart from and outside the producers. (164–65)

If one simplifies this sentence somewhat, then it states that the mysterious character of the commodity-form consists in the fact that the "social character of labor" is "reflected" as "objective characteristics of the products of labor." Let's turn now to the various expressions that show up in this sentence.

The reference to labor's "social characteristics" means that acts of labor are socially interrelated; that their products are useful *for others*; that as human labor, one's own labor counts as *qualitatively* equal to other acts of labor; and that it does so *quantitatively* in a specific measure.

These social characteristics of labor are reflected as "objective characteristics of the products of labor." Whether others recognize a product of labor as useful is demonstrated, under the conditions of commodity production, by it possessing "value" at all. The quantitative relation that the labor expended to produce it bears to other labor activities is demonstrated by its "magnitude of value." Both value and magnitude of value appear to inhere to labor products "objectively" (that is, as an object) in a similar manner to its physical attributes.

Marx specifies here that these "objective characteristics" are "socio-natural properties." What does that mean? "Natural properties" are usually taken to be something independent of human beings and society, something existing in nature without society playing a role. In that sense, "nature" and "society" are often treated as opposites: "society" is created by human beings, but "nature" is independent of them. Marx now joins the terms. Even without analyzing "value" scientifically, it's clearly not a natural property like weight or hardness, meaning that it's something social. Yet it is out of people's control just like a *natural property* such as a diamond's hardness. Value only exists in society, but it operates there like a natural property of labor products.

A caveat: It's not Marx who claims as a result of his analysis that "value *is* a socio-natural property," rather, Marx states that the commodity form "reflects" the social characteristics of labor as a "socio-natural property." The verb "reflects" expresses, on the one hand, something objective—a process independent of human manipulation—and, on the other hand, suggests a degree of distortion (a real mirror always reproduces things as an inverted reflection and, depending on its construction, might enlarge, reduce, or warp them). We will come back to this when dealing with the next sentence.

First, we have to deal with the remainder of this sentence, which states that "the social relation of the producers to the sum total of labour" is reflected as "a social relation between objects, a relation which exists apart from and outside the producers." Marx introduces the expression "the sum total of labour" (*Gesamtarbeit*) here, but does not further explain it. Only a few paragraphs later do we get more details about "the aggregate labour of society" (*gesellschaftliche Gesamtarbeit*)—it is the same German term but differently translated (165). For now, we can only say: individual producers expend their labor privately, independently from one another. Still, in a society characterized by a division of labor, they *objectively* depend on one another (see the commentary on the equivalent form's third peculiarity). Nevertheless, the relation of their private acts of labor to all the other private acts of labor, that is, the sum total of labor, confronts them only as an objective property of their labor products: as "value" and the "magnitude of value." In that sense, "the social relation of the producers to the sum total of labour" becomes "a social relation between objects."

The next sentence states:

> Through this substitution, the products of labour become commodities, sensuous things which are at the same time supra-sensible or social. [Corrected translation: Through this quid pro

quo, the products of labor become commodities, sensuous, extrasensory (sinnlich übersinnlich) or social things.] (165) [14]

The reflection is a *quid pro quo*: *social* relationships turn into *objective* properties. In a quite literal sense, the fact that social relationships appear as objective properties of commodities is precisely what is "extrasensory" about commodities: our senses cannot perceive *this kind of* objective property of commodities.

But *why* does substitution of this kind come with the commodity form? Why does the commodity form reflect the social character of labor as objective characteristics of the products of labor? No answer is provided in this passage (it follows in the next few paragraphs, which point B of this commentary addresses). Instead, Marx merely *says* that it's so but without explaining why.

Marx devotes the rest of the paragraph to the *specific* character of this quid pro quo. He relies on two comparisons. The first relates to how the optical nerve creates the image of an external object. Light stimulating the optic nerve presents itself to us—those who are looking—not as stimulation of the optic nerve, but as an object external to the eye. That means that "seeing" involves a substitution, since by no means do we have the sensation that the optic nerve is being stimulated, but instead perceive something at a certain distance from us. What is special about the commodity form, nevertheless, is not the quid pro quo itself—that one thing stands for another—but rather the kind of quid pro quo taking place. In seeing, light is transmitted from one object to another (the eye); therefore it's "a physical relation between physical things." In the case of the commodity form, however, it is precisely not the case:

> It is nothing but the definite social relation between men themselves which assumes here, for them, the fantastic [correct: phantasmagoric, *phantasmagorisch*] form of a relation between things. (165)

What does Marx mean by the relationship's "phantasmagoric form"? The editors of MEW 23 explain phantasmagoric as meaning "magical,

---

14. Marx uses the term "quid pro quo," originally from the legal context, several times in *Capital*. It means that *one thing stands for another*, which is not the same as *one thing being substituted for another*. Additionally, Fowkes's translation obscures Marx's using exactly the same wording here as on page 163, "sensuous, extrasensory" (*sinnlich übersinnlich*).

illusory" (*zauberhaft, trügerisch*; MEW 23: 921). However, that doesn't entirely capture the word's significance in the nineteenth century. The expression arose around 1800 in Paris where it referred to new, complex techniques used in theater performances. Projections, reflections, enlargements, and so on, were used to generate spectacular visual effects—such as the invocation of ghosts—which appeared quite real to the audience (see Albrecht Schöne's commentary on *Faust* in Goethe 1999: 483ff.). These effects were real to the extent that the audience didn't simply imagine them, though they did depend on technical equipment invisible to the audience.

Because of the "phantasmagoric" relation residing in the commodity, the analogy to light's impression upon the optic nerve is inadequate. According to Marx, an adequate analogy is only to be found in the "misty realm of religion":

> There the products of the human brain appear as autonomous figures endowed with a life of their own, which enter into relations both with each other and with the human race. So it is in the world of commodities with the products of men's hands. (165)

Marx picks up here on a central theme from the critique of religion as carried out by philosopher Ludwig Feuerbach. The definition of fetishism quoted above from the nineteenth-century lexicon stressed that the "sensuous object itself" (a piece of wood, leather, etc.), which is a manmade thing, becomes the cult object. Feuerbach emphasized that the great religions, including Christianity, do basically the same thing. These religions' gods are products of the human mind (the gods are idealizations of real human beings), and human beings in turn submit to their own products. Marx compares the *human mind*'s products (the gods of the religions), which have become independent of their creators, with the *human hand*'s products (commodities), which have taken on a life of their own:

> I call this the fetishism which attaches itself to the products of labour as soon as they are produced as commodities, and is therefore *inseparable from the production of commodities*. (165, emphasis M.H.)

This last sentence clearly shows that Marx does not view commodity fetishism as merely a phenomenon of consciousness that can be dispelled

Commodities and Money 151

by explanations. Instead, fetishism is the *necessary consequence of a specific social practice*, commodity production, which is then reflected in consciousness. Only when that social practice disappears will fetishism disappear.

The first few pages of this subsection (163–65) are just a sketch of what Marx means by "commodity fetishism." They point out how social relationships among commodity producers are reflected back as labor products' objective properties. Many presentations of fetishism go no further than this observation. However, the subsection comprises twelve more pages of the book, which don't just provide additional information but are actually necessary to understanding commodity fetishism.

B) The "Peculiar Social Character of the Labour Which Produces Commodities": Retroactive Socialization (second paragraph 165 to second paragraph 166)

> As the foregoing analysis has already demonstrated, this fetishism of the world of commodities arises from the peculiar social character of the labour which produces them. (165)

"The foregoing analysis" obviously doesn't refer to the immediately preceding pages, devoted to Marx's understanding of "commodity fetishism," but rather to the analysis in the first three subsections of chapter 1. However, those sections do not mention the fetish character of commodities. Therefore, the "foregoing analysis" only implicitly demonstrated what is now made explicit. This means that no new analysis follows, but rather certain conclusions are drawn from the foregoing analysis.

Labor activities occurring in a social context have a "social character." However, this social character is not the same in all societies, but rather depends on the structuring of that social context. The next two paragraphs briefly summarize "the peculiar social character of the labour which produces [commodities]" (165).

The beginning of the next paragraph elucidates the meaning of the "aggregate labour of society":

> Objects of utility become commodities only because they are the products of the labour of private individuals who work independently of each other. The sum total of the labour of all these private individuals forms the aggregate labour of society [*gesellschaftliche Gesamtarbeit*]. Since the producers do not

come into social contact until they exchange the products of their labour, the specific social characteristics of their private labours appear only within this exchange. In other words, the labour of the private individual manifests itself as an element of the total labour of society [*gesellschaftliche Gesamtarbeit*] only through the relations which the act of exchange establishes between the products, and, through their mediation, between the producers. (165)

Marx does not use the term "aggregate labour of society" in a transhistorical sense—to designate, for example, all the productive activity a society carries out. Instead, he is concerned with the aggregate labor *in a commodity-producing society*. There, the particular labor activities are not yet social when they are carried out. There is no prior coordination that would make the particular labor activities into components of the social fabric from the beginning. In fact, because of the social division of labor, the labor activities do stand in a relationship of *objective* interdependence, but they are undertaken *privately, that is, independently of one another*.

In the second sentence, Marx refers to how these private labor activities constitute the aggregate labor of society. As the previous sentence made clear, that does not mean that *all* privately expended labor contributes to the aggregate labor of society, but only those labor activities whose products are actually *exchanged*. Only private labor activities of that kind "manifest themselves as an element of the total labour of society." And they do so "only through the relations which the act of exchange establishes between the products." Labor-creating products not intended for exchange or products that do not find buyers on the market do *not* enter into the aggregate labor of a commodity-producing society.

In effect, Marx has already addressed this special summing up of private labor in the first subsection of chapter 1, when he explained the concept of "socially necessary labor-time." There Marx observed that "the total labour-power of society, *which is manifested in the values of the world of commodities*, counts here as one homogeneous mass of human labour-power" (129, emphasis M.H.). The activity of this "one homogenous mass of human labour-power" is precisely the historically specific aggregate social labor under discussion here.

If Marx includes only those private labor activities whose products are exchanged in the aggregate social labor, he is not arbitrarily excluding other labor activities. Rather, the excluding of other types of labor reflects the specific kind of socialization, that is, the way social cohesion is created, under the conditions of commodity production: the social bond only takes place via exchange.

ADDENDUM: The question of what contributes to aggregate social labor is particularly important for the debate about reproductive labor in the household (which is still primarily done by women). Labor of that kind is crucially necessary for the maintenance and reproduction of human life. However, *under the conditions of commodity production*, labor activities only contribute to the aggregate labor of society when performed outside the household setting, since the products of labor (material goods such as meals, but also care and education) are consumed in the household without ever taking on the form of commodities. To be part of the aggregate social labor requires that the products and services be offered and sold as commodities.

In the quote's third sentence, Marx addresses what is so peculiar about this form of socialization: social contact between producers *first occurs in exchange*, and *that's why* the "social characteristics" of private acts of labor first show themselves here. How do these "social characteristics" of *private* acts of labor reveal themselves? Marx doesn't say so here, but we already know how: they show themselves as *objective* characteristics of the *products* of labor.

On page 164, Marx claimed that *the commodity-form* "reflects" the social characteristics of private labor as objective characteristics of the products of labor. He did not, however, explain how this *reflecting* happens. The third sentence of the quotation above implicitly provides the explanation: under the conditions of commodity production, the social characteristics of labor first show themselves in exchange, because "the producers do not come into social contact until they exchange the products of their labour." But in exchange, producers do not relate directly to one another. Instead, they relate the products of their labor to one another. For that reason, the social characteristics of private acts of labor *can only* show themselves as objective characteristics of the products of labor.

Only *retroactively*, through the *exchange* of labor products, are the individual private acts of labor actually socialized. This has an important consequence that Marx addresses in the paragraph's last sentence:

> To the producers, therefore, the social relations between their private labours appear as what they are, i.e. they do not appear as direct social relations between persons in their work, but

rather as material [*dinglich*][15] relations between persons and social relations between things. (166)

Marx therefore does not consider commodity fetishism a question of false consciousness: the relationships among producers' private labor activities may appear to them as a social relationship between things, but these relationships appear to the producers "as what they are." In a commodity-producing society, there are no *direct* social relationships among producers. People are *private producers*, independent of one another, who do not coordinate their labor. It is only *things* that stand in a social relation, which is mediated by the "extrasensory" quality of value. Commodity fetishism is not an illusion. It is a real phenomenon, if only *within a commodity-producing society*.

The next paragraph elaborates on the last assertion: that the social relationships among producers' private labor activities appear to them as what they are, a social relation among things.

It is only by being exchanged that the products of labour acquire a socially uniform objectivity as values, which is distinct from their sensuously varied objectivity as articles of utility. This division of the product of labour into a useful thing and a thing possessing value appears in practice only when exchange has already acquired a sufficient extension and importance to allow useful things to be produced for the purpose of being exchanged, so that their character as values has already to be taken into consideration during production. (166)

Earlier in this commentary, I mentioned the debate about when products become commodities and acquire value-objectivity: whether it first occurs within exchange or in the production process. Traditional Marxism usually holds that it occurs in the production process. Marx assumes a clear position in this passage, similar to that of the revision manuscript "Ergänzungen und Veränderungen" for *Capital* (commented below in Appendix 4): products acquire value objectivity "only by being exchanged." Marx's claim here is not an arbitrary one. Rather, it expresses the specific social character of commodity-producing labor. Such labor

---

15. Fowkes wrongly inserted the German word *dinglich* here. Marx did not use "*dinglich*" but rather "*sachlich*" in this sentence, which is more general than "*dinglich*."

Commodities and Money 155

is private labor, and its socialization first occurs *retroactively*, through the exchange of products.

Although a society based upon commodity production produces goods with a view to exchanging them, this doesn't imply that those objects possess value-objectivity before exchange. Marx expresses that very precisely when writing that "their character as values has already to be *taken into consideration* during production" (166, emphasis M.H.). The character of these products as values is not already *present*, but rather "taken into consideration."

So far, nothing else has been said about the details of production. From the first sentence of chapter 1, we know that Marx is dealing with *capitalist* production. That the character of commodities as values is "taken into consideration," as Marx says, powerfully shapes the production process and working conditions, which are often destructive for workers. (The first volume of *Capital* offers a thorough treatment of these working conditions.) What Marx means by "taking into consideration" relates to the producers, who under capitalist conditions are not the workers actually producing things, but rather the capitalists commanding production. Based on their knowledge of the market and the production conditions, these producers expect that their products can be exchanged and that when they are exchanged, their value will have a specific magnitude. However, this isn't to say that their expectations are actually met. If, for example, there are surprisingly many products on the market that are produced under better technical conditions, it reduces socially necessary labor-time, meaning that the products possess a much smaller value than projected. Precisely because a product's magnitude of value depends upon multiple *average social conditions*, it cannot be determined by a *single* product's conditions of production prior to exchange. Marx continues:

> From this moment on, the labour of the individual producer acquires a twofold social character. On the one hand, it must, as a definite useful kind of labour, satisfy a definite social need, and thus maintain its position as an element of the total labour, as a branch of the social division of labour, which originally sprang up spontaneously. On the other hand, it can satisfy the manifold needs of the individual producer himself only in so far as every particular kind of useful private labour can be exchanged with, i.e. counts as the equal of [*gleichgilt*], every other kind of useful private labour. (166)

"From this moment on" refers to the point in time when exchange becomes developed enough to have things' value character be "taken into consideration" during production. From that time forward, we can speak not only of commodity *exchange*, but also of commodity *production*. This does *not* mean that the individual product *automatically* becomes a commodity, but rather that production takes place *only* for the purpose of exchange. The product *is intended to be a commodity from the very beginning*, and that aim also shapes the whole of production.

What does the "twofold social character" of private labor refer to? When private labor is being carried out, it is not yet a component of the aggregate labor of society. It first becomes so when it acquires both characteristics mentioned above. The first characteristic, that as useful labor it satisfies some kind of social need, has to be fulfilled in *every* society based on the division of labor in production. The second characteristic is that every particular useful private labor activity is *exchangeable* with every other useful private labor activity and therefore "counts equal of" (*gleichgilt*) it. The latter only exists in a society based upon commodity production. About this equal counting, Marx writes:

> Equality in the full sense between different kinds of labour can be arrived at only if we abstract from their real inequality, if we reduce them to the characteristic they have in common, that of being the expenditure of human labour-power, of human labour in the abstract. (166)

This "equal counting" of the various types of labor is not something preexisting. It must first be created through a "reduction" of the various labor activities to the characteristic of being expenditure of human labor-power—a reduction that "abstracts" from "real inequality." In that sense, equality is only present to the extent that an abstraction from the real differences and the reduction to abstract human labor actually take place.

ADDENDUM: In Marx's revision manuscript "Ergänzungen und Veränderungen" for the second edition there is a sentence following this passage that was later incorporated into the French translation:

> The reduction of various concrete private acts of labor to this abstraction of equal human labor is only carried out through exchange, which in fact equates products of different acts of labor with each other. (MEGA II/6: 41; French edition, MEGA II/7: 55)

Commodities and Money 157

Here again Marx clearly states that it is *only through exchange* that the abstracting from real inequality takes place, creating the equality of labor activities. Therefore, the "abstraction of equal human labor" only exists in exchange. However, if commodities' values are "crystals" (128) of this abstract human labor—which only exist through the reduction occurring in exchange—then neither does value exist prior to exchange. It can at most be estimated, that is, "taken into consideration."

At the paragraph's end, Marx points out that private producers perceive the dual social character of commodity-producing labor (he says that their brains reflect it). They perceive it, however, "only in the forms which appear in practical intercourse, in the exchange of products" (166). And there, the social characteristics of labor appear not as *determinations of labor*, but as *material properties of labor's products*: the social usefulness of private labor appears as the labor products' usefulness to others, while the equality of private labor activities appears as the value-objectivity shared by labor products.

The "peculiar" social character of commodity-producing labor mentioned on page 165 has thus been explained: it is a *retroactive* socialization of labor, in which the *social* determinations of labor become *objective* determinations of labor products (see point F and Appendix 2). In this way, the previous paragraph's concluding statement, that the relationships between private producers appear to them as "what they are" (166)—namely not as direct social relationships between people, but as social relationships between things—is now thoroughly clarified.

c) Knowledge of Value and "Objective Semblance" (third paragraph 166)

Marx now draws some conclusions about everyday knowledge of value:

> Men do not therefore bring the products of their labour into relation with each other as values because they see these objects merely as the material integuments of homogeneous human labour. The reverse is true: by equating their different products to each other in exchange as values, they equate their different kinds of labour as human labour. They do this without being aware of it. (166)

In a commodity-producing society, people regard the products of their labor as "values." They might have quite disparate ideas about what's behind these values, and labor may or may not enter the picture.

However, the equating of different labor activities in consciousness is *not a precondition* for the act of exchange taking place; it is its *objective result*.

In the original German version of the sentence "they do this without being aware of it," "*Sie wissen das nicht, aber sie tun es*," Marx echoes a famous Bible passage. According to Luke, Jesus' last words on the cross were "Father, forgive them, for they know not what they do" (Luke 23:34), which is a much-quoted phrase even today.[16] Hence, Marx characterizes those engaged in exchange as ignorant like those who mocked and tortured Jesus. This phrase depicts, at the most general level, the *unconscious character* of socialization—that is, the forming of the social bond—in an economy based upon commodity production. Socialization takes place through individuals' conscious activity, but the individuals by no means have to be aware of the structures and forms of this socialization. They do it without really knowing what they're doing.

ADDENDUM: Marx's basic insight that people engaged in exchange don't know what they're doing marks a fundamental difference with classical political economy and neoclassical economics. The latter assume that economic actors know what they're doing, and that the economic fabric emerges from their conscious activity. Thus Adam Smith, who attributed commodities' value to the labor time used in making or acquiring them (but without distinguishing between abstract human labor and concrete useful labor), argued that, for example, a beaver exchanges for two deer, *because* people *know* that hunting beaver requires twice as much labor as deer (Smith 1776: 73).

Friedrich Engels based his notion of a pre-capitalist "simple commodity production"—developed in the "Supplement and Addendum" to the third volume of *Capital*—on a similar reflection: people make exchanges based on the labor-times expended in commodity production, because they *know* what these times are (*Capital* III: 1035). With this conception of "simple commodity production," Engels wanted to present pure value relations (not yet capitalistically determined ones) in a clear way. However, the notion of "simple commodity production" is questionable in a *historical* sense, because there were no pre-capitalist societies in which commodity production without capital played a dominant role. Additionally, the idea is questionable in a *theoretical* sense if it's taken as the content of Marx's analysis of commodities: since Engels's "simple commodity production" assumes *knowledge* on the part of the people acting, instead of their *lack of awareness*, it does

---

16. However, these are not the only last words attributed to Jesus. Instead of the serene sentence from Luke, Matthew and Mark have handed down the despairing "My God, my God, why hast thou forsaken me?" Finally, in John there is just the sententious phrase: "It is finished."

not capture Marx's object of investigation at the beginning of *Capital* (for more, see my *Introduction*, Heinrich 2012: 81ff.).

If people were aware of what they were doing in their economic activity, then the economy would be a transparent sphere in which nothing were hidden. Marx's frequent references to "mysteries" and "enigmas" and his emphasizing of concepts such as "fetishism," "inversion," and "mystification" are not simply questions of literary style. He uses this language quite consciously, to demonstrate that the capitalist economy's supposed transparency and rationality is merely a superficial appearance that conceals something in need of deciphering. Marx appends footnote 29 to the sentence just quoted—"they do this without being aware of it"—and indicates briefly there once more why this is so (a detailed explanation appears on 165–66). The note refers to the Italian economist Galiani, who wrote that value is a relation between people. Marx observes that he should have added "a relation concealed beneath a material shell" (167n29). In this way, Marx points out the *specificity* of this kind of human relation: it is *mediated by objects*.

ADDENDUM: Marx repeatedly points out that the mediation of human relations by objects is characteristic of all economic relationships in capitalism. In the *Contribution to the Critique of Political Economy*, for example, he characterizes the difficulties economists have in grasping capital:

> The phenomenon that they have just ponderously described as a thing reappears as a social relation and, a moment later, having been defined as a social relation, teases them once more as a thing. (MECW 29: 276)

For many leftists, too, the core of Marx's analysis is that economic categories such as value, money, and capital are the expressions of certain relations between human beings. They emphasize that these relations, far from being peaceful and harmonic, represent a permanent struggle, ultimately a struggle between social classes. However, that perspective merely highlights what capitalist society has *in common* with all other class societies. Marx, by contrast, is concerned with the *specificity* of capitalist social relations, that is, how those relations *differ* from the relations of other societies: this specificity consists precisely in economic relationships between people being "concealed beneath a material shell," as Marx has just pointed out in reference to Galiani.

ADDENDUM: In the *Communist Manifesto*, which was published in 1848, almost twenty years before the first volume of *Capital*, there is no evidence yet of this insight into capitalism's specificity. Whereas after the well-known prologue, "There is a specter haunting Europe . . .", Marx began his analysis with the famous sentence "The history of all hitherto existing society is the history of class struggles." In *Capital* the chapter on classes was to form the conclusion of the third volume. In the *Manifesto*, Marx assumed that classes and class struggles are the self-evident starting point, from which everything else can be explained. In *Capital*, by contrast, he has come to understand that, precisely because human relations are "concealed beneath a material shell," classes and class struggle cannot be the starting point of his presentation, but are rather the results to be reached. If we take the essential feature of Marx's *Capital* to be the discovery that categories such as value and capital refer to economic structures that express social relations, then we reduce the analysis in *Capital* to the level of that of the *Communist Manifesto*.

Since people equate the products of their labor as values without knowing what they're actually doing, namely, equating their diverse labor activities, Marx claims that value transforms labor products into a "social hieroglyphic" (167) and that people then try to decipher the hieroglyphic. Eventually, the work of deciphering produces results:

> The belated scientific discovery that the products of labour, in so far as they are values, are merely the material expressions of the human labour expended to produce them, marks an epoch in the history of mankind's development. (167)

With the phrase "belated scientific discovery," Marx is by no means referring to his own work, but rather the "labor theory of value" as already formulated by economists such as William Petty, Adam Smith, and David Ricardo with varying degrees of clarity. However, Marx points out that this was not enough, because their discovery

> by no means banishes the semblance of objectivity [corrected translation: objective semblance, *gegenständlichen Schein*] possessed by the social characteristics of labour. (167)

What does it mean to say that the "objective semblance" does not disappear? Value is being traced back to labor, but without asking the question of why the labor expended is reflected as an objective property of a product. The economists deciphered the content of value, but took it to be natural that this content is expressed as "value": an objective property of labor products. Marx continues:

Something which is only valid for this particular form of production, the production of commodities, namely the fact that the specific social character of private labours carried on independently of each other consists in their equality as human labour, and, in the product, assumes the form of the existence of value, appears to those caught up in the relations of commodity production (and this is true both before and after the above-mentioned scientific discovery) to be just as ultimately valid as the fact that the scientific dissection of the air into its component parts left the atmosphere itself unaltered in its physical configuration. (167, emphasis M.H.)

With this, we come to a central point of Marx's argumentation. Marx critiques a mix-up here. "Something which is only valid" under commodity production (the specific social character Marx mentions here is the second social characteristic of private labor he referred to on page 166) appears "to those caught up in the relations of commodity production" as "ultimately valid." That is, for them, the products of labor appear to have the character of value in *every* society, as if value were, as Marx says above, a "socio-natural property." Why do things appear this way? Because people immersed in capitalist relations do not grasp the objectivity of value as resulting from *specific* social relations, as something socially *mediated*. Instead, they take it to be something *immediate*, so that the objectivity exists independently of specific social relations: whenever people work, they seemingly create "value."

When Marx speaks of an "objective semblance" (*gegenständlicher Schein*), he does *not* mean that the objectivity of value does not exist. It exists and exercises a material force that functions as an objective compulsion, *but only in a commodity-producing society*. The "semblance" consists in regarding this specific social relation as a definitive and unchangeable relation, as if people could not relate to the products of their labor as anything other than values, as if the objective compulsions of commodity production were humanity's inevitable fate.

d) The Society's Movement Taking on a Life of its Own, and Its Content (second paragraph 167)

This paragraph is still concerned with how the objective semblance consolidates itself, but it simultaneously addresses how the social fabric *takes on a life of its own*.

Marx says that those engaging in exchange are initially interested in the quantitative proportions of exchange. Then he continues:

> As soon as these proportions have attained a certain customary stability, they appear to result from the nature of the products. . . . The value character of the products of labour becomes firmly established only when they act as magnitudes of value. (167)

Marx contends that it is a consequence of the stability of exchange proportions—that is, the relations among value *quantities*—that the products exchanged acquire, alongside their use-value characteristics, a "value character," meaning that the *quality* of "value" is attributed to them. About the magnitudes of value, the next sentence states:

> These magnitudes vary continually, independently of the will, foreknowledge and actions of the exchangers. (167)

Whereas Marx emphasizes the "stability" of value relations in the first sentence, he stresses their constant change in the second. How can both claims be true? Obviously, Marx is talking about two distinct levels of social development in these last two quotes.

The first level is that of the *emergence of commodity production*. As long as the exchange of products is rather rare and accidental, then coincidence, luck, and differences in knowledge of exchange are all decisive. It is only when exchange attains a certain regularity that coincidence and luck fade into the background in determining exchange proportions. This occurs in markets, where not only individual exchangers of products but numerous exchangers, not just individuals, encounter one another. The exchange proportions now appear "to result from the nature of the products." If this happens, then the production and circulation of commodities have come to dominate at least part of the society's production. Marx has emphasized this in the second paragraph on page 166.

The second quote refers to this new level of development, which is that of *widely established commodity production*. Now if value magnitudes change it is not a return to the coincidental nature of exchange proportions. A change in the magnitude of value no longer means that one seller of wheat receives a lot while another receives little, but rather that wheat's magnitude of value changes for *all* buyers and sellers. Hence, Marx says about those involved in exchange:

Commodities and Money 163

> Their own movement within society has for them the form of a movement made by things, and these things, far from being under their control, in fact control them. (167)

The social bond is formed by the people living in society—"their own movement within society." But under the conditions of commodity production, their interconnectedness is not only, as observed above, created *unconsciously* (those exchanging know not what they do). For those involved in exchange, it also *takes on a life of its own*: it controls the people, instead of them controlling it.

But what is the exact nature of this societal movement that has taken on a life of its own? This is briefly outlined by Marx in the compound sentence that follows. The first part of the sentence lays out the conditions under which the nature of the movement can be recognized, namely that "the production of commodities must be fully developed." Then comes a concise characterization of the nature of the movement:

> all the different kinds of private labour (which are carried on independently of each other, and yet, as spontaneously developed branches of the social division of labour, are in a situation of all-round dependence on each other) are continually being reduced to the quantitative proportions in which society requires them. (168)

In commodity production, labor activities occur independently of one another as private labor. However, these diverse labor activities are objectively interdependent, since they are branches of the social division of labor. This interdependence entails a certain *proportionality* of the diverse labor activities. If, for example, a carpenter is to produce a certain number of tables, somebody must produce the necessary amount of wood and offer it on the market. Again, if the carpenter, after selling his tables, is to buy new clothes with his income, somebody must produce and offer this clothing, and so on. With the division of labor, the diverse labor activities must thus stand in a specific quantitative relation— "quantitative proportions," as Marx describes it. However, under the regime of commodity production, this proportion is not known in the phase of production. To stick to our example: the wood producers don't know how much wood the carpenters will require; carpenters don't know how many tables will be required; and clothing makers don't know how much clothing the carpenters will need. Of course, every producer attempts to estimate (paying) demand, but in the last instance he doesn't know what that will be. His estimates may prove wrong, which has consequences both for those who supply his inputs and for those who produce the commodities he would have otherwise consumed. If the carpenter falsely estimates the need for tables, then he will buy less wood and less clothing in the future, dashing the expectations of other producers.

It is precisely the proportions of individual types of labor, unknown during production, that asserts itself in this "movement of things" that has taken on a life of its own with regard to people. And how do these proportions assert themselves? They do it this way:

> In the midst of the accidental and ever-fluctuating exchange relations between the products, the labour-time socially necessary to produce them *violently* asserts itself as a regulative law of nature. (168, emphasis M.H.; the word "violently" or "forcefully" (German: *gewaltsam*) is omitted from the English translation.—*Trans*.)

The text says that "socially necessary labor-time" asserts itself like a "regulative law of nature." What does that mean? The first subsection of chapter 1 characterized "socially necessary labor-time" as the time needed to produce a use-value "under the conditions of production normal for a given society and with the average degree of skill and intensity of labour prevalent in that society" (129). This means that if more than the socially-necessary labor time is used, it does not add to the amount of value-creating abstract labor. The first subsection also stated that a product is only a commodity if it possesses both use-value and "use-values for others, social use-values" (131). As a result, if the use-values produced exceed (paying) demand, then not all the labor-time expended in producing these use-values counts as value-creating, abstract labor. Marx draws this conclusion explicitly in chapter 3 (201f.). Hence, to see how the "labor-time socially necessary for production" asserts itself, both aspects have to be considered: the necessary labor-time as determined by the conditions of production and the labor-time needed to cover the paying demand. Both magnitudes are unknown to producers in advance. Only on the market is the individual producer informed about whether his conditions of production correspond to the social average and whether his branch as a whole has produced too many products (the magnitude of value of his commodity conveys the information to him). The process by which "socially necessary labor-time" asserts itself in exchange is the same process by which the individually spent private labor is reduced to

Commodities and Money 165

its "quantitative proportion," that is, its share, according to the conditions of production and demand, in the aggregate social labor expended under the division of labor.

Still, in what sense does Marx speak here of a "natural law"?

ADDENDUM: In a letter to Ludwig Kugelmann on July 11, 1868, Marx likewise deals with the way that socially necessary labor time asserts itself. Usually, this passage from the letter is quoted in order to show that Marx was not concerned with a "proof" of value theory. But what interests us here is the way Marx speaks of "natural laws."

> The chatter about the need to prove the concept of value arises only from complete ignorance both of the subject under discussion and of the method of science. Every child knows that any nation that stopped working, not for a year, but let us say, just for a few weeks, would perish. And every child knows, too, that the amounts of products corresponding to the differing amounts of needs demand differing and quantitatively determined amounts of society's aggregate labour. It is SELF-EVIDENT that this *necessity* of the *distribution* of social labour in specific proportions is certainly not abolished by the *specific form* of social production; it can only change its *form of manifestation*. Natural laws cannot be abolished at all. The only thing that can change, under historically differing conditions, is the *form* in which those laws assert themselves. And the form in which this proportional distribution of labour asserts itself in a state of society in which the interconnection of social labour expresses itself as the *private exchange* of the individual products of labour, is precisely the *exchange-value* of these products. (MECW 43: 68)

What Marx describes as a "natural law" here are necessities that are valid for all societies, which cannot simply be abolished by human beings. Nevertheless, the form in which these natural laws assert themselves changes in diverse modes of production. In commodity production, the proportionality between various labor activities does not assert itself by means of a traditional division of labor or a conscious plan by the members of society, but rather through "socially necessary labor-time" determining the commodities' magnitude of value.

Marx uses "natural law" here in a somewhat different sense than in the Preface. There the term referred to the objective character of social development. However, just as in our commentary on the Preface, here too it should be remembered that natural laws had a different meaning in Marx's time than in today's social science.

At the end of the compound sentence on page 168, Marx stresses that the proportions among private labor activities assert themselves "violently" (*gewaltsam*): "In the same way, the law of gravity asserts itself when a person's house collapses on top of him." Marx thus indicates how the process does not occur harmonically and gradually, but rather in a *crisis-ridden* and destructive way. However, until we have analyzed capitalist production relations, nothing more exact can be said about this.

Talking of a "law of nature" asserting itself "violently" carries a critical undertone. Since producers do not arrive at the necessary proportions of their individual labor activities' through a consciously coordinated process, but rather in a way that is mediated through the exchange of products (whereby those exchanging don't know what they're doing), it means that the entire process is just as strange and self-regulating to human beings as a natural process. As a result, the *self-regulating way* that the proportional distribution of labor asserts itself is not at all due to the "natural law," since such a proportional distribution is necessary in every society, but rather due to the *social conditions* under which the law operates. What is key is the "lack of awareness"—"*Bewusstlosigkeit*" or "unconsciousness"—of the social process, which Marx emphasizes in footnote 30, where he cites Engels's first economic work.

The lack of awareness of the social process does *not* refer to people not knowing the *content* or outcome of this process (the proportional distribution of labor). The point is that this distribution *asserts itself* "unconsciously"—not as a result of producers consciously cooperating but rather through the unconscious functioning of the market. Thus Marx writes at the end of this paragraph (echoing the last sentence of the first paragraph on page 167):

> The determination of the magnitude of value by labour-time is therefore a secret hidden under the apparent movements in the relative values of commodities. Its discovery destroys the semblance of the merely accidental determination of the magnitude of the value of the products of labour, but by no means abolishes that determination's material form. (168)

This "material form" (value-objectivity) is not a mere phenomenon of consciousness; it is real and efficacious as long as people relate to the products of their labor as commodities.

e) "Objective Forms of Thought" (*Objektive Gedankenformen*) (second paragraph 168 to second paragraph 169)

In the next two paragraphs, Marx focuses on the *scientific* knowledge of value. He observes that both "reflection on the forms of human life" and "scientific analysis" of these forms first begin *post festum* (retrospectively), which means:

> The forms which stamp products as commodities and which are therefore the preliminary requirements for the circulation of commodities, already possess the fixed quality of natural forms of social life before man seeks to give an account, not of their historical character, for in his eyes they are immutable, but of their content and meaning. (168)

What are the "forms which stamp products as commodities"? A product of labor becomes a commodity if it results from *private labor* and is exchanged on the market for other products. Then it attains the form of an object of value of a specific magnitude. Expending labor as private labor, behaving as if the products of private labor are private property, and exchanging them on the market—all of these forms appear, once established, as "natural forms of social life." This means that the forms seem so self-evident that we no longer perceive them as *specific social* forms, but rather as forms in which life in *every society must* necessarily take place. Thus, according to Marx, when we contemplate social life, we do not discuss them as historical, mutable forms; we only examine what is expressed within these forms.

ADDENDUM: What Marx states here in rather general terms about the conception of historically specific forms as "natural forms of social life" applies very well to Adam Smith. At the beginning of Smith's main work, *The Wealth of Nations*, he maintains that the essential difference between human beings and animals is that humans engage in exchange, but animals don't. Humans have a "propensity to truck, barter, and exchange" which distinguishes them from animals (Smith 1776: 29ff.). But if it's characteristic for human beings to exchange, then this means that it is "natural" for human beings to regard their products as commodities: to the extent that people live in a society, the products of their labor automatically become commodities. Hence Smith regards the market economy based upon exchange as the "natural order." Smith doesn't question the commodity form. What he's interested in is the content expressed in this form, that the labor-time necessary to produce the commodity determines its value.

This tendency to naturalize a historically specific mode of economy persists among today's economists. The group appointed by the German federal government called the German Council of Economic Experts (the press fondly refers to them as the "economic wise men") stated in its annual report for 1999–2000: "Politicians can no more override the objective compulsions and human behavior arising from the laws of the market than they could override the law of gravity" (221). In other words, the laws of the market are just as immutable and natural as the laws of gravity.

Marx next states that the analysis of the content of these forms begins with the "finished form," the money-form. The analysis of commodity prices leads to the determination of the magnitude of value, while "the common expression of all commodities in money" leads to "the establishment of their character as values" (168).

This implies that economic analysis's historical course of development differs considerably from Marx's presentation of the sequence of the categories. Historically, this development proceeds from money and finds the underlying determinations of the commodity. By contrast, Marx proceeds from the commodity's determinations and develops the money-form as a necessary form of value. As the next sentence makes clear, this is not just a difference in the *direction* of the argument, since it is the

> finished form of the world of commodities—the money-form—which conceals the social character of private labour and the social relations between the individual workers, by making those relations appear as relations between material objects, instead of revealing them plainly. (168f.)

What "conceals" refers to is how the social relations between private laborers are represented as relations between things. For this reason, it's no longer visible, hence concealed, that they are relations between private laborers. Because Marx does not begin his presentation from the "finished form," but for him it is a *result*, he undoes this concealment.

The rest of the paragraph deals with the "absurdity" (*Verrücktheit*, or "madness") generated by this concealment. Here Marx essentially picks up on the second peculiarity of the equivalent form, that is, a specific concrete labor activity becomes the form of appearance of abstract labor, and connects it to the general form of value—a specific concrete labor activity becomes the *general* form of appearance of abstract labor. In itself, the linen is by no means the "universal incarnation of abstract labor"; just like a coat, boots, and so on, it is the embodiment of a specific concrete labor. Only in the expression of value, or more precisely as the general equivalent, does the linen "count" as the "universal incarnation of abstract labor." What is "absurd" is that a thing counts as something it is not.

Commodities and Money

Marx now points out that "absurd forms" [*verrückte Formen*] are widespread in bourgeois economics:

> The categories of bourgeois economics consist precisely of forms of this kind. They are forms of thought which are socially valid, and therefore objective [*objektive Gedankenformen*], for the relations of production belonging to this historically determined mode of social production, i.e. commodity production. (169)

For the second time, the term "bourgeois economics" shows up here. It is not as passing a mention as on page 139, but there is still no explanation.

ADDENDUM: In the Postface to the second edition of *Capital*, Marx provides an explanation for the term "bourgeois economics." There he states that political economy qualifies as bourgeois

> in so far as it views the capitalist order as the absolute and ultimate form of social production, instead of as a historically transient stage of development. (96)

Marx doesn't describe the discipline as "bourgeois economics" because it consciously sides with capital, but rather because it doesn't recognize capital's historicity. The term does not refer to the *intentions* of individual economists but to a certain *type* of theory.

When Marx calls the categories of bourgeois economics "absurd forms," he is conceiving bourgeois economics somewhat more broadly than in the Postface just quoted. Economics is "bourgeois" if it cannot break through the appearance (mentioned at the beginning of the second paragraph on page 168) of viewing the social forms that "stamp products as commodities" as "natural forms" pertaining to all social life. Hence, Marx is characterizing any type of political economy that regards *commodity production* as permanent as bourgeois.

Marx hints at the difficulty of breaking through this appearance when he makes reference to "forms of thought which are socially valid, and therefore objective." In effect, commodity production's social forms structure our perception and thoughts. It appears to be a matter of course that people expend their labor as private labor, that they exchange their products, that these products have not only use-value but also have value, that this value is expressed in money, etc. In effect, we can hardly imagine anything different. For people involved in commodity production, the forms themselves are not thematized but, as Marx states above, only the content expressed in those forms.

The forms themselves are socially objective, but only in a society based upon commodity production. What is illusory is how they seem to be something valid in *all* societies (see the conclusion of the first paragraph on page 167). Precisely because this is a semblance that *commodity production* generates, Marx now turns briefly to *other* forms of production.

f) Forms of Production Not Based on Commodity Production (third paragraph 169 to last paragraph 173)

In the following sketches, do not lose sight of their purpose, which is to illustrate the "mysticism of the world of commodities." Marx describes other forms of production here only insofar as they contrast with the world of commodities.

He begins with Robinson Crusoe on his island. Robinson undertakes diverse useful labor activities that are "different modes of human labour" (169). He must decide how much time to spend on each activity, and this will depend upon how much time is needed to achieve a specific outcome. Marx summarizes:

> All the relations between Robinson and these objects that form his self-created wealth are here so simple and transparent. . . . And yet those relations contain all the essential determinants of value. (170)

This requires close reading: Marx does not claim that value relations exist on Robinson's island. Because of the absence of exchange, this would be pure nonsense. Instead, he says that the "essential determinants of value" are present. These "essential determinants" obviously refer to the circumstances just listed in the text. This is the transhistorical "content" of value determination that is referred to at the very beginning of the section (163ff.). The Robinson Crusoe example shows that this content is by no means indissolubly bound to the form of value. In particular, the example demonstrates that the proportional distribution of society's total labor among the particular branches of production can assume different forms. If that distribution asserts itself under commodity production as a "movement made by things" (167) independently of the knowledge and will of those engaging in exchange, in Robinson's case it is a result of conscious decisions.[17]

Next, Marx considers social relations of the Middle Ages, characterized by a generalized personal dependence. In relations of "personal" dependence, we find obligations that are not based on contracts cancelable by either side, as in the wage labor relation. Instead, such dependence is part of the person in question's status and is usually immutable: a serf is obligated to his lord for his whole life, and the lord in turn must also protect and legally represent his serf during a lifetime.

In the Middle Ages, besides such relations of personal dependence, there was also some commodity production. At first it was limited but then gradually expanded. Also, serfs' payments in kind were slowly converted to money payments in the late Middle Ages, forcing dependent peasants to engage in commodity production. However, Marx leaves all this aside. He is only interested in the Middle Ages insofar as they contrast with commodity production. Hence his simplified picture of serfs producing only use-values for their own subsistence, together with their duties to lords and church, but without commodity production. In that spirit, Marx says that "there is no need for labour and its products to assume a fantastic form," that is, as abstract human labor and as value respectively, "different from their reality," that is, their sensually perceivable natural existence as concrete useful labor or a specific product. Why don't they have to take on this fantastic form? Marx's answer:

> The natural form of labour, its particularity—and not, as in a society based on commodity production, its universality—is here its immediate social form. (170)

In commodity production, too, labor is always carried out as a particular useful labor activity, but it is done so privately. Private labor of this kind first becomes a component of the aggregate social labor *retroactively* through the exchange of products: by recognizing the product in exchange as an object of value, the labor that created this product is also recognized as abstract human labor. It is not in its initial "particularity" as a specific concrete useful labor but only in its

---

17. The Herr M. Wirth mentioned in the text is German economist and journalist Max Wirth (1822–1900), whose works were rather well known in Germany during the second half of the nineteenth century. As can be gleaned from the second edition's Postface (95), Marx insisted that the German economists of his time were completely unoriginal.

"universality" as abstract human labor that the labor of commodity producers become social. Because a serf delivers part of his product as a tribute or performs specific concrete labor activities as payment in kind without further mediation, his particular labor is already a component of the aggregate labor of (Medieval) society. For this reason, Marx observe that in these (simplified) Medieval relations:

> The social relations between individuals in the performance of their labour appear at all events as their own personal relations, and are not disguised as social relations between things, between the products of labour. (170)[18]

In these (convention-based) medieval relations the "natural form of labor" is simultaneously its "immediately social form." (This contrasts with commodity-producing labor, where the only labor that has an immediate social form is that which produces the body of the general equivalent, e.g. gold.) However, that a serf's labor possesses an immediate social form by no means implies that it is "labour in *common*, i.e. directly associated labour" (171). Marx refers here to labor that is also carried out in common. His example of the latter is a peasant family that produces food, clothing, and so on for its own need. Here again, Marx simplifies by disregarding the petty trade that is typically present in these circumstances to offer the clearest possible contrast with commodity production. The peasant family's diverse products "confront the family as so many products of its collective labour, but they do not confront each other as commodities" (171). The various kinds of labor "are already in their natural form social functions; for they are functions of the family, which, just as much as a society based on commodity production, possesses its own spontaneously developed division of labour" (171).

Finally, Marx considers an "association of free people"[19] working with the means of production held in common, and expending their many different forms of labour-power in full self-awareness as one single "social labour force" (171). Evidently, this "association of free people"

---

18. The original German of this sentence begins with Marx speaking for the first time of "character masks"—poorly translated in the Penguin edition as "roles"—without further comment. Marx will return to this term at the beginning of chapter 2.
19. Here the Penguin edition's translation uses a somewhat sexist phrase: "an association of free men." By contrast, the original German phrase, "einen Verein freier Menschen," is gender-neutral.—Trans.

refers to a *communist* society.[20] Still, Marx does not further describe the society, limiting himself to remarking on its differences from commodity production. In this society, there is clearly neither private property of the means of production nor private labor. Individual acts of labor are coordinated from the get-go, and thereby also form part of the aggregate labor of society from the outset. Thus the total product of the society is a "social product" (171); individual products of labor do not have to first be recognized as values. A part of the total product is used as means of production while another part is consumed by the society's members and has to be distributed among them. Marx doesn't say anything about how the society makes decisions about which part of the product is to be used as means of production and which new products to produce. Nevertheless, regarding distribution for consumption, he assumes "only for the sake of a parallel with the production of commodities that the share of each individual producer in the means of subsistence is determined by his labour-time" (172). Marx does not claim that things must actually be done this way in a communist society. On the contrary, the immediately preceding sentence points out that the manner of distribution will change as the society develops. Here, Marx is concerned merely with maintaining the greatest possible parallel with commodity production. The parallel resides in the dual function of individual labor-times: on the one hand, they must be allotted among the various branches of production; on the other hand, they measure the individual producer's share in the product that is to be consumed.

Under commodity production, the distribution of labor among branches of production is a process playing out "independently of the will, foreknowledge and actions" of the producers (167). Labor's non-proportional distribution among the different branches of production can lead to the affected producers not having their products recognized in exchange as values—or recognized as values of lesser magnitude. This affects their share in the total product, allowing them to purchase fewer means of production and subsistence than needed.

It is otherwise in the "association of free people," where the distri-

---

20. Marx did not develop a detailed conception of communist society. On the contrary, his isolated statements about it were usually offered in the course of criticizing capitalist relations. In the last chapter of my *Introduction* (2012), I summarize what one can glean from Marx's dispersed comments regarding his conception of communism. For another discussion of Marx's various suggestions in this regard, especially those found in *Capital*'s section on fetishism, see Iber 2005: 74ff.

bution of individual labor activities among the diverse branches of production occurs "in accordance with a definite social plan." Additionally, the share of the product destined for consumption is distributed according to a specific social rule, such as distributing it proportionally to working hours. In commodity production, value mediates both processes. The social relationships among the private labor activities therefore present themselves as social relationships among things. By contrast, in the association of free people, the "social relations of the individual producers, both towards their labour and the products of their labour, are here transparent in their simplicity" (172).

In summary, we may say that in all the forms of production under consideration, various types of labor are performed, in proportions determined by the social division of labor. Labor-time plays an essential role in all, but in none must the *different* types of labor be reduced to *equal* human labor. That only happens in commodity production. Only there do individual acts of labor need to have the *twofold* social character mentioned on page 166, both satisfying a social need *and* being equal to other acts of labor. In all other forms of production, individually expended labor-time in its *particularity* is already part of the aggregate labor of society; it merely has to satisfy a social need. In commodity production, however, labor is expended as *private labor*. Only *retroactively*, insofar as it is reduced to equal human labor in exchange—and this means in its *universality*—does it become a component of society's aggregate labor (which will be discussed in Appendix 2).

G) Religion and Mode of Production
(second paragraph 172 to first paragraph 173)

After this quick review of forms of production not based on commodity production, Marx addresses the connection between religion and relations of production. According to Marx, "Christianity with its religious cult of man in the abstract" is "the most fitting form of religion" for a "society of commodity producers" who relate their private labor to each other as "homogeneous human labor" (172).

Marx does not claim that commodity production brought about Christianity. He merely points to a *correspondence*. In commodity production, diverse types of labor are equated to one another. However, these are only equal in abstraction from their differences, as abstract human labor. The same is the case for commodity owners: if we consider people as commodity owners, we abstract from every concrete determination, and their differences become mere coincidence. The situation is similar with Christianity: differences between people are merely coincidental, all being equal before God as his creations. In that sense, Marx perceives a correspondence: fundamental religious ideas match fundamental social structures. He sees the greatest correspondence between Protestantism and Deism, which conceives a divine creator who does not intervene in the world, since there the Christian God is stripped of Medieval imagery and becomes a largely abstract principle.

The "ancient social organisms of production"—those that are not based upon commodity production—are "much more simple and transparent than those of bourgeois society" based upon commodity production. But Marx continues:

> They are conditioned by a low stage of development of the productive powers of labour and correspondingly limited relations between men within the process of creating and reproducing their material life, hence also limited relations between man and nature. These real limitations are reflected in the ancient worship of nature, and in other elements of tribal religions. (173)

ADDENDUM: In this paragraph, Marx posits an unspecified connection between the level of the forces of production, the relations of production among people, and their conceptual world. In doing so, Marx picks up on claims from the Preface to his *Contribution to the Critique of Political Economy*. There Marx presented the following as a "general conclusion" of his research:

> In the social production of their existence, men inevitably enter into definite relations, which are independent of their will, namely relations of production appropriate to a given stage in the development of their material forces of production. The totality of these relations of production constitutes the economic structure of society, the real foundation, on which arises a legal and political superstructure and to which correspond definite forms of social consciousness. The mode of production of material life conditions the general process of social, political and intellectual life. It is not the consciousness of men that determines their existence, but their social existence that determines their consciousness. (MECW 29: 263)

Traditional Marxism used the brief sketch in this preface and a few other texts as the basis of "historical materialism" (a term not found in Marx's work), which was frequently understood as a comprehensive explanation of history. Typically, the way the "base" was supposed to "condition" the "superstructure" was understood as determination. Nevertheless, Marx primarily emphasizes the idea of "correspondence": not every "superstructure" is compatible with a given "base"; the superstructure must *correspond* to the base in a certain sense, but is not completely *determined* by it. Incidentally, Marx rarely used the terms "base" and "superstructure"—in contrast to the spokespeople of traditional Marxism.

It is precisely this idea of "correspondence" that Marx attempts to make clear in the passage of *Capital* just discussed: depending on the economic relations and material conditions of life, certain ideas become more *plausible*. For example, some religious notions (but also legal, ethical, and political ones) appear to people to be particularly insightful. The point, then, is not to explain the *emergence* or even conscious conceptualization of such ideas, but rather the social conditions for their *assertion*.

In the last part of the paragraph, Marx says that "religious reflections of the real world" can only vanish when relations between people and toward nature become transparent and rational. He does not claim that religion would automatically vanish in a communist society. Marx merely notes that there would no longer be any *social* grounds for its plausibility. We cannot assume that religion would actually vanish, since human beings may also use such beliefs to process personal suffering that cannot be excluded from any form of society.

At the end of the paragraph, Marx emphasizes that these transparent and rational relations will only emerge when the process of production "becomes production by freely associated men, and stands under their conscious and planned control" (173): that is, in the "association of free people" mentioned above, or communist society. Such a societal condition, however, requires "a series of material conditions of existence" which are themselves "the natural and spontaneous product of a long and tormented historical development" (173).

ADDENDUM: Marx picks up here on an idea from the Preface to the *Contribution to the Critique of Political Economy*. There he wrote:

> At a certain stage of development, the material productive forces of society come into conflict with the existing relations of production or—this merely expresses the same thing in legal terms—with the property relations within the framework of which they have operated hitherto.... No social formation is ever destroyed before all the productive forces for which it is sufficient have been developed, and new superior relations of production never replace older ones before the material conditions for their existence have matured within the framework of the old society. (MECW 29: 263)

The first half of the second sentence is problematic. It's not clear what determines the extent of the forces of production for which a given social formation is "sufficient." On the one hand, capitalism has proven extraordinarily flexible in this sense. On the other hand, people have frequently revolted against capitalism's impositions despite its being far from exhausting all possible development of its productive forces.

Nevertheless, what is decisive is the second half of the sentence: the "material conditions of existence" (also mentioned in the passage from *Capital*) of a new mode of production must emerge "within the framework of the old society." A new mode of production cannot simply be dreamed up and then implemented; it must always base itself on something already existing. The question that must be discussed again and again, however, is what exactly this "something" is.

h) Commodity and Value in Political Economy: The Analysis of Fetishism as a Precondition for a Critique of Political Economy (second paragraph 173 to 177)

This part's first paragraph is of central importance to understanding why Marx subtitled his work, "Critique of Political Economy." For the first time, he explicitly criticizes political economy as a whole, not just individual authors. This paragraph stretches from page 173 to page 175 and has three long footnotes (33–35) that elaborate some of the claims. For reasons of clarity, my commentary focuses first on the paragraph, then on the three footnotes.

In the first sentence, Marx credits political economy with having both "analysed value and its magnitude" and "uncovered the content concealed within these forms." The next sentence makes clear that the "content" mentioned is labor. The analysis is "incomplete," however, and footnote 33 explains how Marx understands its incompleteness.

In the next sentence, Marx makes a fundamental critique of political economy:

> But it has never once asked the question why this content has assumed that particular form, that is to say, why labour is expressed in value, and why the measurement of labour by its duration is expressed in the magnitude of the value of the product. (174)

Marx does not accuse political economy's analysis of yielding an *incorrect result*—on the contrary, he concedes that its result is largely correct—but rather of *missing a question*. This amounts to a much deeper critique. Having to rectify incorrect results through scholarly debate is a matter of course in the scientific process. However, if we observe the absence of certain questions, not as the isolated error of a few scholars, but as a systematic problem within an entire science, this is very different. It puts on trial the foundations of the science, that is, the hitherto unquestioned system of conceptual coordinates of that science. On pages 165 and 166, Marx already answered, in a brief way, the question of *why* labor assumes the form of value. There he pointed out that only the products of individual private labor become commodities, and because producers only enter into contact through exchange, the specific social character of their labor first appears there as an *objective* property of their labor products (see my commentary under point B). Therefore it is a specific sort of social interconnectedness that causes labor to be represented as value, causing this content to take on that form. In footnote 34, Marx goes on to identify the reason that political economy was unable to pose the question of "why."

That political economy did not pose this question means that these forms appeared to it as completely self-evident:

> Formulas, which bear the unmistakable stamp of belonging to a social formation in which the process of production has mastery over man, instead of the opposite, appear to the political economists' bourgeois consciousness to be as much a self-evident and nature-imposed necessity as productive labour itself. (174f.)

ADDENDUM: The word "formulas" (*Formeln*) here is probably a printing error in the second and subsequent German editions. In the preceding sentence, only "forms" (*Formen*) are mentioned. In the first edition and in the French translation (corrected by Marx), "forms" is used instead of "formulas" (see MEGA II/5: 49; MEGA II/7: 61).

The phrase used to characterize these forms, "The process of production has mastery over man, instead of the opposite" (175), alludes to the state of affairs described on page 167. That is, under the conditions of commodity production, our "own movement within society" has "the form of a movement made by things." It controls people, rather than people controlling it (see the commentary under point D). These historically specific (and therefore mutable) forms, which "bourgeois consciousness" sees as a "self-evident and nature-imposed necessity,"

Commodities and Money 179

are the fetishistic forms of the world of commodities. In other words, Marx criticizes political economy for remaining caught up in the fetishism of the world of commodities, that it is unable to penetrate. This also illustrates Marx's claim in the letter to Lassalle that was quoted in commenting on *Capital*'s subtitle: *A Critique of Political Economy*. In that letter, Marx emphasized the need to formulate a critique by means of an exposé (MECW 40: 270). The exposition of the commodity fetish serves at the same time as a critique of the category of "value" within bourgeois economics.

Now, the question emerges as to whether bourgeois economics recognized any "pre-bourgeois" forms of production, that is, not based upon commodity production, whose existence would call into question the "self-evident and nature-imposed necessity" of bourgeois forms. Political economy knew of such forms, but according to Marx it treated them "in much the same way as the Fathers of the Church treated pre-Christian religions" (175). The Fathers of the Church (the Church doctors from the first decades after Christ) felt competition from the pre-Christian religions. They treated each as a cluster of absurdities, to be contrasted with the one true religion: Christianity. This is further explained in footnote 35.

FOOTNOTE 33

This footnote deals with political economy's "incomplete" analysis of value. Marx states that "classical political economy" (footnote 34 has information on this term) failed to recognize the dual character of the labor that produces commodities: nowhere did it "explicitly" distinguish between concrete useful labor, which generates use-values, and abstract human labor as the substance of value. This was a distinction that Marx described as "crucial to an understanding of political economy" in the second subsection (132). However, Marx does concede that classical political economy made the distinction "in practice" insofar as it spoke, on the one hand, of labor in a qualitative sense and, on the other hand, in a purely quantitative sense, since merely quantitative differences presuppose a qualitative equality.

Failure to make explicit the difference between the two characteristics of commodity-producing labor leads to a number of misunderstandings and problems. The rest of the footnote is dedicated to an example of this: Ricardo's debate with Destutt de Tracy, a French economist. Actually, the example contains another misunderstanding: Tracy regarded the "value of labor" as responsible for the value of the commodities it creates.

According to Marx, Ricardo understands Tracy to mean that *labor* is represented in value—and not "the value of labor." Marx describes Tracy's conception as "the commonplace error of the vulgar economists, who assume the value of one commodity (here labour) in order to use it in turn to determine the values of other commodities." The notion of the "value of labor" has been discussed above (see my commentary on page 137, footnote 16) and it plays a central role in *Capital*'s chapter 19. Smith sometimes confused the determination of value by labor with the "value of labor." Ricardo doesn't recognize that Tracy fell into the same mix-up.

FOOTNOTE 34

This note explains the reasons economic science failed to pose the question of "why this content has assumed that particular form." Marx contends:

> One of the chief failings of classical political economy is that it has never succeeded, by means of its analysis of commodities, and in particular of their value, in discovering the form of value which in fact turns value into exchange-value. (174)

Classical political economy's main deficiency is that it failed to do what Marx proposed with his analysis of the value-form: to demonstrate that value requires an independent value-form. Still, the question arises as to *why* classical political economy failed here. Additionally, there is the question of why it *did not even attempt* to do so, as Marx indicated in the introduction to the value-form section (139). It is not only because of political economy's interest in the *magnitude* of value (a reason Marx has given before, see footnote 17 on Bailey, 141). Rather it is primarily due to the following:

> The value-form of the product of labour is the most abstract, but also the most universal form of the bourgeois mode of production; by that fact it stamps the bourgeois mode of production as a particular kind of social production of a historical and transitory character. If then we make the mistake of treating it as the eternal natural form of social production, we necessarily overlook the specificity of the value-form, and consequently of the commodity-form together with its further developments, the money form, the capital form, etc. (174)

Marx speaks here of the "value-form of the product of labor," although to be precise Marx should say the "value-form of the commodity," since it is only when the product of labor exists as a commodity that it make sense to talk about the value-form. He calls it "the most abstract" and "most universal" form of the bourgeois mode of production. It is the most abstract form, since the value-form does not presuppose any further relations, as, for example, capital does. It is the most universal form of the bourgeois mode of production, since "production for exchange"—which means that labor products become commodities and the commodities' value obtains an independent form—is the most typical feature of this mode of production. Now if production for exchange is not seen as a specific mode of production but rather as "the most eternal natural form of social production," then the specificity of the value-form and all the form determinations of key economic categories that build upon it are overlooked.

Marx used the expression "bourgeois economics" on page 169. In commenting on that passage, I pointed out that Marx considered political economy to be "bourgeois" because it conceives of the specific social forms that make labor products into commodities as "natural forms of social life." What Marx is pointing to in this footnote is precisely this "bourgeois" character of economics, which prevents it from adequately grasping the value-form.

ADDENDUM: In the late 1840s, Marx was already criticizing political economy for regarding capitalism as eternally valid, rather than a historically transitory mode of production. At that time, he was unable to explain how bourgeois economists arrived at this ahistorical conception. Additionally, he was still convinced that Ricardo, among the political economists, had on the whole correctly explained the capitalist mode of production's way of functioning. In the late 1840s, Marx therefore relied on Ricardo's theory in both his critique of capitalism (for example in his lecture series "Wage Labor and Capital") and in his debate with Proudhon. At this time, Marx was critically *applying* bourgeois economics, but he did not yet have a *critique of its categories*. The critique of its categories first began in the early 1850s. Hence, Marx criticized Ricardo's theory of money for the first time in 1851 (see Marx's letter to Engels, February 3, 1851, MECW 38, p. 273–278). Marx developed this critique of categories comprehensively in subsequent years. However, he first recognized the importance of fetishism in the late 1850s.

Understanding fetishism allows Marx to explain how political economy is prone to an ahistorical approach: it is the bourgeois mode of production itself that makes social relationships into objective properties of things, and that, in turn, generates the illusion that what is valid for this mode of production applies to every type of social production. The unhistorical conception of the bourgeois mode of production also affects how economic relations are analyzed: if we conceive the bourgeois mode of production as "the eternal natural form of social production," then we may examine its "content" (such as the determination of value by labor), but we can no longer see the historically specific features of its forms, that is, why labor is expressed as value, why the value of the commodity requires an independent manifestation in the value-form, etc. We miss the specificity of both the value-form and the categories that build upon it: the money-form, the capital-form.

ADDENDUM: For a long time, the value-form failed to enter into the Marxist discourse. That discourse emphasized the historical character of the capitalist mode of production, concentrating on the content but neglecting the forms and their characteristics. This is exactly what Marx criticized in bourgeois economics. That Marxists had a restricted conception of Marx's analysis was partly fostered by the "paradigm shift" (a change in fundamental conceptions) that occurred in bourgeois economics. In the last third of the nineteenth century, classical political economy, which still held value to be determined by labor, gave way to "marginalism," which in the end based value on "marginal utility" (see my commentary on *Capital*'s title). Marx could concede to classical political economy that it more or less correctly grasped the "content" that determined value, but this was no longer true for marginalism. In debating with marginalism, Marxists therefore insisted upon this content, meaning that the debate between Marxists and bourgeois economists fundamentally turned on the question of whether value was determined only by labor or by (marginal) utility. The value-form disappeared from the debates.

Earlier, in footnote 33, Marx uses the expressions "vulgar economists" and "classical political economy." Now, at the end of footnote 34, he clarifies his use of these expressions. According to Marx, classical political economy "investigated the real internal framework [*Zusammenhang*] of bourgeois relations of production" (174f.). By contrast, the vulgar economists "only flounder around within the apparent framework [*scheinbaren Zusammenhang*] of those relations, ceaselessly ruminate on the materials long since provided by scientific political economy, and seek there plausible explanations of the crudest phenomena for the domestic purposes of the bourgeoisie" (175).

There are two important points here. First, Marx does not dispute the scientific character of classical political economy (in contrast to vulgar economics). Second, Marx distinguishes between the "internal framework" and the mere "apparent framework" in capitalist reality. He distinguishes between classical political economy and vulgar economics not on the basis of the economists' *intentions*, but rather their focus, that is, their object of study.

ADDENDUM: With regard to the second point, there's a slightly different emphasis than in the second edition's Postface. There, Marx relates the development of political economy to the level of class struggle, contending that political economy "can only remain a science while the class struggle remains latent or manifests itself only in isolated and sporadic phenomena" (96). He says that in England and France class struggle assumed "threatening forms" from 1830 onward, with a consequence:

> It sounded the knell of scientific bourgeois economics. It was thenceforth no longer a question whether this or that theorem was true, but whether it was useful to capital or harmful, expedient or inexpedient, in accordance with police regulations or contrary to them. In place of disinterested inquirers there stepped hired prize-fighters; in place of genuine scientific research, the bad conscience and evil intent of apologetics. (97)

This is a highly simplified perspective. In the first place, Marx observed in "Theories of Surplus Value" that there were also forms of vulgar economics in the period before 1830 and scientific approaches afterward. Moreover, here he reduces the difference between science and apologetics, that is, the justification of existing conditions, to an author's *intentions*: "disinterested" inquiry, on the one hand, and "hired prize-fighters," on the other. The pointed language of the Postface aims to present the critique of political economy as the sole legitimate heir to classical political economy (98). This grossly simplifies Marx's reasoning in the fetishism section, which differentiates projects within bourgeois economics on the basis of their *object* and not the economists' *intentions*. This simplified view has influenced many Marxists, who frequently regard all bourgeois economists after Marx as embodying the vulgar economics of "hired prize-fighters." Contemporary talk shows and newspapers' business sections may be full of such figures, but the whole of bourgeois economics cannot be reduced to apologetics.

FOOTNOTE 35

This footnote appears in a paragraph on pages 173–75 dealing with bourgeois economics' treatment of pre-bourgeois modes of production. (This question arises because Marx said that bourgeois economics conceives of the capitalist mode of production as eternally valid.)

Marx describes their approach to pre-bourgeois modes of production by quoting from his earlier text, *The Poverty of Philosophy* (1847): for bourgeois economics, pre-bourgeois institutions are "artificial," in the sense of not being appropriate to human beings, but bourgeois institutions are "natural," corresponding to human beings' "nature." Even today, there are similar justifications of the market economy. And what Marx intended here as parody—"Thus there has been history, but there is no longer any"—would take on a new life at the beginning of the 1990s. At that time, when capitalism seemed to have finally asserted itself worldwide, Francis Fukuyama would advance the idea explicitly and uncritically in his much-quoted essay on the "End of History."

At the end of the footnote Marx addresses a critique of his general statements about society and history in the preface to *Contribution to a Critique of Political Economy* (discussed above briefly in the commentary on pages 172–73). As a kind of introduction to the subsequent discussion, Marx refers first to the French economist Frédéric Bastiat (1801–1850), about whom he wrote in the second edition's Postface that he was "the most superficial and therefore the most successful representative of apologetic vulgar economics" (98). Bastiat stressed the capitalist market's beneficial effects and the fundamental harmony among the interests of social classes, which is why he is still esteemed today. Marx liked to poke fun at the superficiality of Bastiat's arguments, as he does here: even if one accepts Bastiat's claim that the Greeks and Romans lived primarily from plunder, something still had to be produced that could be plundered. Production is an indispensable precondition for all human life and therefore also of social life.

Marx next mentions an anonymous critic's objection, launched against the Preface to the *Contribution*, which he does not dispute: that in the Middle Ages and Antiquity, Catholicism and politics respectively "dominated" each society. However, he confronts that objection with the thesis that it's the relations of production among people—"the manner in which they gained their livelihood"—that explains the dominant roles of politics and Catholicism in each of those societies. The reference to Don Quixote shows that Marx's claim in the Preface to the *Contribution* that there is a certain correspondence between base and superstructure is not an especially profound truth. This is because it is obvious to all readers that the non-correspondence of Don Quixote's imagined superstructure with Spain's economic base at the time is what makes the novel comic.

Returning to the main text, the rest of the chapter deals with fetishism's consequences for bourgeois economics (176–77). Marx sees the debate about nature's role in the "formation of exchange-value"[21] as due to the illusion generated by fetishism: value's "objective semblance" (*gegenständlicher Schein*, which Fowkes translates as "objective appearance") deceives some economists into seeking even a physical cause of value.

The next paragraph makes it clear that fetishism is not limited to the commodity: there are also fetishes of money and capital.

ADDENDUM: Some Marxist literature trades rather liberally on the term "fetishism"; we read of the "wage fetish" and sometimes even of the "state fetish." In fact, Marx speaks of "mystifications" and "inversions" in a variety of contexts, but he uses the term fetish only in reference to the commodity, money, and capital. At the end of the commentary on chapter 2, I briefly address what these three fetishisms have in common.

This paragraph also indicates that there are different degrees of difficulty in seeing through the various forms of fetishism. About commodity fetishism, Marx says that it's "still relatively easy to penetrate" (176). The case of money fetishism is not so simple, but Marx concedes that "modern political economy" seems free from the "illusions of the Monetary System" (the idea that gold and silver naturally possess value). By contrast, the fetishism of modern economics becomes "quite palpable when it deals with capital."

Since we have not yet dealt with money and capital, the reflections above are no more than an anticipation and thus not further elaborated here. However, it should be recognized that Marx concedes that at least part of bourgeois economics partially sees through fetishism. Based on Marx's earlier statements (167, 169, and 174), one might get the impression that he sees bourgeois economics as completely caught up in fetishism. However, that's not the case. Fetishism is not a universal web of delusion that nobody can escape, but more like universal background lighting. Still, even though bourgeois economics managed to partially escape the effects of fetishism, it never perceived fetishism for what it is. That's why it was unable to ask what characterizes fetishism. The question with which Marx introduced the fetish section—What is the secret of the commodity form?—is not posed by bourgeois economics, since for it the commodity form never assumes the status of a problem.

---

21. Marx should say "formation of value": he copied the paragraph where this phrase occurs directly from *Capital*'s first edition. There, Marx did not always maintain the terminological distinction between exchange-value and value, even if he grasped the distinction conceptually.

That the commodity fetish is easier to penetrate than the other fetish forms does not mean that the entirety of bourgeois economics has actually seen through it. In the remainder of chapter 1, Marx provides two striking examples of how one can be misled by fetishism (176–177). He quotes an anonymous author and Samuel Bailey, already known to us from the subsection on the value-form. Both see use-value as a relation between humans and things, but see value as a property inhering in things themselves which becomes apparent when commodities relate to each other in exchange. Marx counters this notion of value's materiality with a simple observation: "So far no chemist has ever discovered exchange-value either in a pearl or a diamond" (177). (Again, Marx should have used "value" instead of "exchange-value.") His parting shot picks up the words of a figure from Shakespeare's comedy, *Much Ado About Nothing*. This is Dogberry, a somewhat dim, overeager constable whose statements are unintentionally comic. By comparing Bailey and the anonymous author to a figure like Dogberry, Marx makes a subtle but scathing criticism. In a similar way, he earlier used a literary allusion to mock Proudhon (see the commentary on footnote 26).

In footnote 38, appended here, Marx observes that the Ricardians were unable to provide a compelling answer to Bailey's critique of Ricardo, "because they are unable to find in Ricardo's own works any elucidation of the *inner connection between value and the form of value, or exchange-value*" (177, emphasis M.H.). Here Marx emphasizes that the noncomprehension of the "inner connection between value and the form of value" is Ricardo's key deficiency. In *Capital*, this connection is the theme of the third subsection on the value-form. In the first edition of *Capital*, Marx also stressed at the end of the value-form analysis that "what was decisively important" was "to discover the inner, necessary connection between value-form, value-substance, and value-amount" (Dragstedt 1976: 34). In effect, Marx claims to have accomplished exactly what he accuses Ricardo of essentially failing to do.

Footnote 38 seems to suggest (as footnote 34 did) that the decisive difference between classical political economy's labor theory of value and Marx's value theory is to be found in the analysis of the value-form. However, this difference is a qualitative one: the analysis of the value-form is a precondition for decoding the fetishism of the world of commodities. This, in turn, allows the categories of bourgeois economics to be grasped as expressions of the *objective forms of thought* (*objektive Gedankenformen*, 169) caught up in this fetishism. That is, analysis of the value-form is what makes possible Marx's "critique of political economy."

Chapter 2: The Process of Exchange (178–187)

A) The New Level of Abstraction in Chapter 2

In every new chapter of *Capital*, one should try to comprehend the argument's level of abstraction, and its relation to the level of abstraction in previous chapters. This chapter's title identifies *the process of exchange* as the object of investigation. *Capital*'s first chapter made frequent mention of the exchange-*relation* of commodities, but never the exchange *process*. A clue to the difference between the *exchange-relation* and the *process of exchange* appears in the introductory sentences:

> Commodities cannot themselves go to market and perform exchanges in their own right. We must, therefore, have recourse to their guardians, who are the possessors of commodities. (178)

Marx now wants to examine the "possessors of commodities," making it even clearer that commodity *owners* so far have not been the object of investigation. As the title of chapter 1 indicates, this object was the *commodity*. The exchange *process* consists in the following: Commodity owner U exchanges his commodity xA with the commodity yB of commodity owner V. By contrast, we obtain the exchange-*relation* of the commodities by abstracting from commodity owners U and V, leaving only: x commodity A = y commodity B, or x commodity A is worth y commodity B.

Chapter 1 focused on the commodity within the framework of the exchange-relation (and, building upon that, within the framework of the value-relation). Although the exchange-relation does not exist in reality without the exchange process, Marx's *analysis* of the commodity initially *abstracted* from commodity owners and therefore from the process of exchange (on abstracting from commodity owners, see page 62 of this commentary). The section on fetishism was the first to mention people engaged in exchange. However, it was not concerned with their actions, but rather with the way commodity exchange affects the representation of their social relationships. It is chapter 2, then, that addresses the actions of commodity owners in the exchange process for the first time.

b) The Process of Exchange and Commodity Owners (Private Owners) (178 to first paragraph 179)

After two introductory sentences, Marx begins his investigation. The next two sentences indicate that the commodity owner's relation to the commodity includes a relation of *force*. The second sentence echoes a line from Goethe's famous poem "Der Erlkönig": "*Ich liebe dich, mich reizt deine schöne Gestalt / Und bist du nicht willig, so brauch ich Gewalt*" ("I love you, your beautiful form tempts me; and if you are not willing, I'll need force"). Marx's mentioning force here might seem banal, but it becomes less so if we recognize that not only things and services become commodities, but even labor-power itself. That is, the capitalist purchases labor-power, a worker's capacity to labor, and this purchase implies the power of command over the sellers of labor-power. Marx initially claims that the commodity as a thing is subordinated to the will of the commodity owner, but that's not all there is to the relation between the commodity and its owner.

> In order that these objects may enter into relation with each other as commodities, their guardians must place themselves in relation to one another as persons whose will resides in those objects, and must behave in such a way that each does not appropriate the commodity of the other, and alienate his own, except through an act to which both parties consent. The guardians must therefore recognize each other as owners of private property. (178)

Marx's use of the term "property" here does not refer simply to retaining a thing to use it, but rather to an exclusive right of retaining it that excludes all others from doing so. In the former case, I might lie on a sunny beach, excluding others to the extent that I partly make their use of it impossible: they can't lie down on the same stretch of beach that I'm occupying. In the latter case, I'm the owner of the beach and can exclude all others from using it, regardless of whether I'm using the beach or not. Moreover, the exclusion extends as far as my property, not being limited to the small surface I need to lie down. One can indeed speak of private property, state property, and so forth, depending upon who the owner is. However, the essential feature of property is not the kind of owner, but rather the exclusion of non-owners.

It's not a new insight that people engaging in exchange are *private property owners*. It formed the foundation of bourgeois social philosophy from John Locke to Hegel. What is new, however, is Marx's way of connecting exchange and private property. "*In order that these objects may enter into relation with each other as commodities ... the guardians must therefore recognize each other as owners of private property*"—that is the core of the statement quoted above. It means that human beings are by no means naturally owners of private property who then start to exchange. On the contrary, only in a society based on exchange must they mutually recognize one another as private property owners, that is, accept their mutual exclusion from the disposition of a thing.

There is a striking parallel here with the first paragraph of chapter 1. The object of that chapter was the commodity and the first paragraph made clear that the commodity form assumed by the product of labor is not transhistorical, but rather a specific social form of wealth. In a similar manner, the first paragraph of chapter 2 points out that ownership of private property—exclusively retaining a thing so as to exclude others—is not a transhistorical or quasi-natural property of human beings, but rather a historical construction that is bound to specific social conditions.

ADDENDUM: Marx's historicization of private property implies a radical critique of bourgeois social philosophy. Locke, Smith, and Ricardo took for granted an *isolated* human being who relates to things in his environment as an "owner." If people come into contact with one another, they already do so as private property owners, and their "natural" form of intercourse is exchange. In the "Introduction" from 1857, Marx argues:

> The individual and isolated hunter and fisherman, with whom Smith and Ricardo begin, belongs among the unimaginative conceits of the eighteenth-century Robinsonades, which in no way express merely a reaction against over-sophistication and a return to a misunderstood natural life, as cultural historians imagine.... It is, rather, the anticipation of "civil society," in preparation since the sixteenth century and making giant strides towards maturity in the eighteenth. In this society of free competition, the individual appears detached from the natural bonds etc. which in earlier historical periods make

him the accessory of a definite and limited human conglomerate.... Only in the eighteenth century, in "civil society" do the various forms of social connectedness confront the individual as a mere means towards his private purposes, as external necessity. But the epoch which produces this standpoint, that of the isolated individual, is also precisely that of the hitherto most developed social (from this standpoint, general) relations. (Marx 1973, 83f.)

Bourgeois social philosophy's seemingly natural starting point, the isolated individual—also understood as a private property owner—is nothing other than an idea arising in bourgeois society that is based on the commodity owner.

Marx doesn't take the existence of private property as something self-evident, and then identify what owners can do with their property, such as make exchanges. Rather, he begins with exchange and determines what exchange requires: the guardians of commodities must both acknowledge each other as owners of private property and accept exchange as a *common act of will*:

This juridical relation, whose form is the contract, whether as part of a developed legal system or not, is a relation between two wills which mirrors the economic relation. The content of this juridical relation (or relation of two wills) is itself determined by the economic relation. (179)

Exchange is based on the exchangers' willed action—the commodities are subjugated to them—yet *what* the exchangers want, the "content" of this relation of two wills, is not coincidental or arbitrary, but rather based on the "economic relation": the commodity's determinations condition the actions of those possessing commodities.

In footnote 2, Marx uses this insight to continue the critique of Proudhon that he began in footnote 26 of chapter 1. Marx makes a double accusation against Proudhon: first, that Proudhon takes his "ideal of justice" from "the juridical relations that correspond to the production of commodities," thereby transforming something historical into something ideal and eternal; second, that he wishes to reform "the actual production of commodities and the corresponding legal system" according to that ideal.

Marx criticizes a certain *mode* of critique here: it consists in measuring actually existing relations against an ideal, against ideas of how these relations should be. Marx is frequently accused of this mode of critique as well. However, the footnote clearly shows that Marx is criticizing not only Proudhon's specific ideal, but rejecting an entire mode of critique. If Marx had wanted only to criticize Proudhon's ideal, he would have offered his own ideal. Instead, using chemistry as an example, he asks the rhetorical question of what one would think of a chemist if, rather than examining the "laws governing molecular interactions" in order to solve certain problems, he proposed to remake molecular interaction according to "eternal ideas." Marx obviously thinks that the critique of political economy does not require ideals of that kind any more than chemistry does.

ADDENDUM: Marx has specific *aims*, such as abolishing capitalism and replacing the society based on the competition of atomized individuals by a "free association" of human beings who cooperate according to a plan. He provided certain arguments for pursuing these aims, such as his proofs that capitalism's regular mode of functioning entails enormous social and ecological "costs." (Marx frequently makes such arguments in analyzing the capitalist process of production.) But in offering such proofs, he is not complaining about capitalism violating any kind of norm or ideal. He does not appeal to moral sentiment, conscience, or anything of the sort, but rather to the existential interests of *those who must bear these costs* in the hope of motivating people to struggle against the social conditions that generate them.

Returning to the main text, we find Marx drawing general conclusions from his argument so far:

> Here the persons exist for one another merely as representatives and hence owners of commodities. As we proceed to develop our investigation, we shall find, in general, that the characters who appear on the economic stage [corrected translation: that the economic character masks of the persons] are merely personifications of economic relations; it is as the bearers of these economic relations that they come into contact with each other. (178f.)

After casually referring to "character masks" (*Charaktermasken*) on page 170, where it was translated as "roles," Marx uses the term again here, translated above as "characters," in a more general sense. With the term "character masks," and later "economic characters" (*ökonomische Charaktere*) on for example page 206, translated as "economic characteristics," he refers to specific economic roles assumed by individuals, the logic of which arises from certain economic relations. The *commodity owner* is one such role. Commodity owners' actions are decided by their wills, but when acting as commodity owners, the content of their chosen actions is derived from the economic relation: people act according to "character masks," and the person is thus the "personification" of the "economic relations," as Marx pointed out in the Preface (92).

ADDENDUM: With these observations, Marx implicitly formulates a profound critique of Hegel's philosophy of right (Hegel 1821), which generalizes bourgeois economics' conception of human beings as owners. Hegel sees the *person* as an individual who bears an abstract relation to himself—abstracted from his particularities, his concrete characteristics. The person's central feature is the *will* (§ 35). His will can be directed at anything, making that thing into the person's property (§ 44), if it is not yet the property of someone else. The person thus gives himself an "external sphere of freedom" (§ 41). From the relation of human beings to things—basically their relation to nature—Hegel derives a specific sociality, namely that of the property owner. Against this, Marx implicitly maintains that the (Hegelian) person is a *personification* of an economic relation. His status as property owner is not simply a product of his will regarding the things of nature, but instead involves a specific social relation, the exchange relationship. The economic relation is not based on the will, but rather the reverse: the content of the will is based on the economic relation.

This isn't the only place in *Capital* where Marx criticizes bourgeois social philosophy's fundamental assumptions. The criticism continues, for instance, at the end of chapter 6; in Part 6 on wages; in the part of chapter 24 dealing with "the inversion of property laws"; and in chapter 48 on the "trinity formula" at the end of the third volume.

c) The Contradictory Requirements of the Exchange Process and Its Solution: Money
(179 to first paragraph 181)

A preliminary remark on the course of Marx's argumentation: In chapter 1, Marx implicitly distinguishes between the money-*form* as a specific form of value and *money* as the material bearer of that form of value. The *general equivalent form* (and the *money-form* is nothing more than the general equivalent form tied to a specific commodity) was recognized as something produced by the world of commodities. In the general form of value, the whole world of commodities relates to a single commodity as an equivalent; this commodity, then, is the bearer of the general equivalent form (158–59). Chapter 2 is no longer dealing with the money-form's determinations. Instead, it deals with *money* as the result

Commodities and Money 193

of the exchange process, and it does so on two levels. On the one hand, it considers money as the result of the *contemporary* exchange process in capitalist societies (179–81; commented upon below under point C). On the other hand, it looks at the *historical* process leading up to the contemporary state of affairs (181–84; commented upon below under point D).

> What chiefly distinguishes a commodity from its owner is the fact that every other commodity [corrected translation: commodity body] counts for it only as the form of appearance of its own value. . . . The owner makes up for this lack in the commodity of a sense of the concrete, physical body of the other commodity by his own five and more senses. (179)

Here Marx reprises the distinction posited in chapter 2's first two sentences between the commodity (chapter 1) and commodity owners (chapter 2). When we consider the exchange-relation between two commodities, their respective use-values are irrelevant (see chapter 1.1, point D in this commentary). This ceases to be true when we consider commodity owners: a commodity that is to be exchanged does not have any use-value for its owner (otherwise, he wouldn't exchange it); his commodity only has use-value for others. This basic situation in exchange leads to two contradictory requirements for it to take place.

Since the commodity is not a use-value for its owner, it must be exchanged before it can be "realized" as a use-value, that is, before it can be consumed. In exchange, however, commodities are related to each other as values. For that reason, Marx says that the commodities "must be realized as values before they can be realized as use-values." At the same time, "they must stand the test as use-values before they can be realized as values" (179). According to Marx, this is because

> the labour expended on them only counts in so far as it is expended in a form which is useful for others. However, only the act of exchange can prove whether that labour is useful for others, and its product consequently capable of satisfying the needs of others. (179f.)

The reference to labor "counting" is obviously about its counting as value-creating labor. At the end of the first subsection of chapter 1, Marx emphasized that one only produces a commodity if one produces "use-values for others, social use-values" (131). We're thus caught in a circle:

to be realized as use-value, the commodity must be realized as value, but for it to be realized as value, the commodity must stand the test as use-value.

The contradictory requirements, however, are not yet over. In the second paragraph on page 180, Marx points out that for every individual commodity owner exchange is both an *individual* and *social* process. Every commodity owner wishes, on the one hand, to exchange his commodity for a certain other commodity that satisfies *his individual* need. On the other hand, every commodity owner also wants his commodity to be exchangeable with every other random commodity, that is, he wants it to be generally *socially* recognized. In other words, every commodity owner demands something from all other commodity owners—they should accept his commodity in exchange—something that he himself is *not* prepared to do since he only accepts those commodities that satisfy his needs. It's evident that these requirements cannot be simultaneously fulfilled for all commodity owners.

In the next paragraph, Marx characterizes this state of affairs using the concepts developed in the analysis of the value-form. Tellingly, in this brief excursus at the level of value-form analysis, Marx no longer speaks of "desire" on the part of commodity owners, as in the previous paragraph, but rather of "counting." For *every* commodity owner, his own commodity "counts" as a general equivalent. The result is a paradoxical form of value, in which *every* commodity would be the general equivalent. However, that is by no means possible. (In the first edition of *Capital*, Marx ended the analysis of the value-form with precisely this paradoxical form of value; see Appendix 3.)

> But since this applies to every owner, there is in fact no commodity acting as universal equivalent, and the commodities possess no general relative form of value under which they can be equated as values and have the magnitude of their values compared. (180)

The second part of the sentence, that the general form of value is necessary for commodities to be generally compared as values, was one of the key results of Marx's examination of the value-form (see the commentary on page 158). The lack of a general equivalent here has drastic consequences for the commodities that are supposed to be exchanged:

> Therefore they definitely do not confront each other as commodities, but as products or use-values only. (180)

Commodities and Money 195

The contradictory requirements of the exchange process—which are not arbitrary requirements but rather arise from the basic situation of exchange—appear to make the exchange process impossible. Nevertheless, the exchange process occurs, and Marx presents the solution with a well-known turn of phrase:

In their difficulties our commodity-owners think like Faust: "In the beginning was the deed" [*Am Anfang war die Tat*]. They have therefore already acted before thinking. (180)

Since Marx makes this emphatic reference to Faust, we should consider the context of the *Faust* quote. In Goethe's tragedy, Faust wants to translate the New Testament, and reads the first sentence of the Gospel of John: "In the beginning was the Word. . . ." Faust does not agree with this statement and plays with various possibilities, finally concluding that the only suitable sentence is "In the beginning was the deed."[22] For both Faust and Marx, the point isn't a *temporal* beginning but rather an *objective priority*. What has primacy? Knowledge based upon thought or action not yet based on understanding?

ADDENDUM: Although they are not mentioned in this passage, Marx's quotation from *Faust* is directed against contractual theories of money, which have been part of the bourgeois theoretical canon since John Locke. Locke maintained that people, when still in a pre-governmental "state of nature," agreed to attribute "value" to a specific object and use it as money (Locke 2003: 120–21). Locke and other contractual theorists do not assume the existence of a real historical event, such as a meeting where people voted to introduce money. Rather, the contract in the "state of nature"

---

22. 'Tis written: "In the beginning was the Word!"
Here now I'm balked! Who'll put me in accord?
It is impossible, the Word so high to prize,
I must translate it otherwise
If I am rightly by the Spirit taught.
'Tis written: In the beginning was the Thought!
Consider well that line, the first you see,
That your pen may not write too hastily!
Is it then Thought that works, creative, hour by hour?
Thus should it stand: In the beginning was the Power!
Yet even while I write this word, I falter,
For something warns me, this too I shall alter.
The Spirit's helping me! I see now what I need
And write assured: In the beginning was the Deed!

is a methodological construct that aims to reveal money's essential properties: such theorists see money as essentially the result of a common insight on the part of those engaged in exchange. To them, at the beginning is not the "deed" but rather the insight from which the deeds follow.

But how is it possible that there is this "deed" occurring before thought, as Marx contends? His succinct answer is:

> The natural laws of the commodity have manifested themselves in the natural instinct of the owners of commodities. (180)

The phrase "natural instinct" is obviously used ironically, since being a commodity owner is precisely not a "natural" characteristic of human beings. At the same time, this expression points to something important. Instinct means a behavior that is not consciously controlled, and this is precisely the idea here: a behavior derived from the "natural laws of commodities" (analyzed in chapter 1), which commodity owners must follow if they wish to exchange:

> They can only bring their commodities into relation as values, and therefore as commodities, by bringing them into an opposing relation with some one other commodity, which serves as the universal equivalent. We have already reached that result by our analysis of the commodity. But only the action of society [corrected translation: the social deed, *die gesellschaftliche Tat*] can turn a particular commodity into the universal equivalent. (180)

However, this explanation is unsatisfactory. Commodities cannot universally relate to one another as values without a general equivalent, which in turn can only result from a "social deed," but that does not prove that this social deed *actually* occurs. The argument becomes even more difficult if one assumes, as Marx does, that the "social deed" occurs without previous knowledge of the interrelations of commodities and money. So why is it that the "social deed" is in fact the solution to the problem of exchange?

First of all, recall that Marx is not concerned with a *temporal* beginning. It's not about societal activity that transforms commodity production *without money* into commodity production *with money*. Marx is always analyzing both the commodity and the exchange process *in capitalism*. If he begins by presenting a commodity not determined by price and exchange not mediated by money, he is not assuming that either actually existed at some time. Rather, both the commodity not determined by price and exchange not mediated by money result from the process of abstraction that Marx mentioned in the Preface of *Capital*.

Marx is not addressing a problem of temporal origins but rather a problem structurally present for those engaged in exchange: for every person engaged in exchange, exchange must simultaneously be an individual *and* social process. The exchangers solve this problem in the deed, without thinking, through their "natural instinct" as commodity owners; they stick to what they know, the *fetishism* of the world of commodities (which they do not see through as fetishism). Marx does not explicitly mention commodity fetishism here, but it is clearly the source of that "natural instinct."[23] The producers' social relations are reflected back to them as an *objective* characteristic of their products of labor, as their value. Commodity owners wish to objectively retain these values in exchange, since for the owners, it's not the use-value of their commodity that is decisive—it doesn't have any use-value for the owner, otherwise he wouldn't exchange it—but rather its value. For that reason, commodity owners are prepared—without thinking—to relate their commodities to an independent manifestation of value, and exchange them for it. But it is only through all commodity owners relating their commodities to another commodity as an independent manifestation of value that the commodity becomes the general equivalent.

Money, the permanent general equivalent, is the result of a *contemporary* social process, in which we all participate when buying or selling, that is repeated again and again. It is not a consciously coordinated process but one enforced by the "natural laws of the commodity."

> Through the agency of the social process it becomes the specific social function of the commodity which has been set apart to be the universal equivalent. It thus becomes—money. (180f.)

Immediately after this statement, Marx puts in two sentences without any transition from the Apocalypse, or Book of Revelation (the two sentences are found in distinct chapters, and Marx switched their order).[24]

---

23. Dieter Wolf has emphasized the importance of the subsection on commodity fetishism for understanding chapter 2 of *Capital* (Wolf 1985: 206ff.).
24. In the MEW and the Penguin edition, the quote from the Apocalypse is placed in its own paragraph. In Marx's original, and the editions of *Capital* that Engels

The Book of Revelation is the final and most controversial book of the New Testament. Its vivid prophecies—the arrival of the Four Horsemen, the plagues, the appearance of the Anti-Christ, and the imminent end of the world—greatly stimulated people's imaginations and art during the Middle Ages and Early Modern Period. The Apocalypse also played an important role for both sides in the disputes between the Catholic Church and the popular movements it denounced as heretical. Today, the "number of the beast" mentioned in the quote (666) is usually encountered in horror movies about Satanic cults.

If one takes the "beast" in the Apocalypse as a metaphor for money, then the quote expresses an important insight obtained from Marx's analysis of the exchange process. Human beings transfer their power to the "beast" (money) but then must submit to its power, since one can only buy and sell that which bears the "number" of the beast. People indeed carry out the exchange process. However, they do not relate directly to one another but to money. Through this mediating function, money acquires a power to which people must then submit.

d) The Historical Development of Commodity Exchange and Money (third paragraph 181 to third paragraph 184)

> Money necessarily crystallizes out of [corrected translation: The money-crystal (*Geldkristall*) is the necessary product of] the process of exchange, in which different products of labour are in fact equated with each other, and thus converted into commodities. (181)

By emphasizing the money-*crystal* (*Geldkristall*), Marx indirectly draws attention to the difference between the money-*form* and the material bearer of that form. In chapter 1, in the section on the value-form, Marx showed that commodities can only universally relate to one another as values if their values can be expressed by a general form. If the general equivalent form is connected over the long term to a specific commodity, the general value-form becomes the *money-form*. Thus far chapter 2 has shown that commodity owners must act in accordance with these attributes of the value-form in the real exchange process because only if the exchangers relate to a general equivalent can the contradictions of the exchange process be resolved, and the

---

edited, the quote appears at the end of the previous paragraph, making clearer its connection to thoughts expressed there.

commodity that permanently takes the role of a general equivalent becomes *money*.[25]

Here again Marx stresses that it is only in the process of exchange "in which different products of labour are in fact equated with each other, and thus converted into commodities." That is, before exchange they are simply *products*, but not *commodities*.

Both the form analysis of the commodity in chapter 1 and the analysis of commodity owners' actions at the beginning of chapter 2 presuppose the commodity as the general form of wealth, as Marx says in reference to "societies in which the capitalist mode of production prevails" (125). The *historical* development of money in pre-capitalist conditions, which has not yet been dealt with, now becomes the object of analysis. What we discovered in relation to the historical appearance of the forms of value (158) also applies here. The results of the analysis are not derived from the historical development. On the contrary, it is the analysis of the fully developed relations that provides the key to understanding the historical emergence of the corresponding forms.

Right at the beginning, Marx takes a sweeping look at the whole historical development:

> The historical broadening and deepening of the phenomenon of exchange develops the opposition between use-value and value which is latent in the nature of the commodity.... At the same rate, then, as the transformation of the products of labour into commodities is accomplished, one particular commodity is transformed into money. (181)

Marx appends footnote 4 here criticizing "petty-bourgeois socialism." This is an allusion to Proudhon's "philistine utopia" which was criticized in footnote 26 of chapter 1 (161). In terms of substance, this note adds nothing new to the previous one—there is even the same comparison between money and the Pope.

---

25. In traditional Marxism, the analysis of the commodity was frequently reduced to the connection between value and labor. For a long time, almost no one paid attention to the analysis of the value-form and money. In the 1970s, Hans-Georg Backhaus stressed the central importance of the interrelation between value-theory and the theory of money in his "Materialien zur Rekonstruktion der Marxschen Werttheorie" (Backhaus 1997). In this work, Backhaus presents Marx's value theory as a critique of "pre-monetary" theories of value. In Heinrich 1999, I examined the character of Marx's theory of value as a "monetary theory of value."

The next two paragraphs outline the two transformation processes mentioned in the last sentence quoted.

Marx describes the difference between the simple expression of value (x commodity A = y commodity B) and the direct exchange of products (x use-value A = y use-value B) by pointing out that in the case of direct exchange:

> The articles A and B in this case are not as yet commodities, but become so only through the act of exchange. (181)

In the previous paragraph, Marx made virtually the same statement with regard to commodity exchange; it takes exchange, he said, to transform the products of labor into commodities (181). The difference, however, becomes clear in the next sentence: the only prerequisite for exchange is that individuals mutually recognize each other as the owners of private property, but "this relationship of reciprocal isolation and foreignness does not exist for the members of a primitive community of natural origin" (182). In a society based on exchange, useful things are produced with a view to exchange, their value character being "taken into consideration" during production (166). However, in the "primitive community of natural origin" that Marx has in mind here, this is not the case. In the first scenario, exchange "in fact" makes commodities out of things that were produced with the intention of their being commodities (181). However, in the second scenario—the "community of natural origin"—exchange makes something new out of these objects of utility. For this reason, as Marx emphasizes, the exchange proportions when such products are exchanged are entirely coincidental. Exchanges of this type (the first paragraph on page 182 refers to "the exchange of commodities" but it would be more precise to say "the exchange of products that develops into the exchange of commodities") do not begin within the community. Instead, they begin with foreign communities or their members, since only with them does that "relationship of reciprocal isolation and foreignness exist" through which private property owners acknowledge one another.

However, the regular repetition of exchange between communities starts to affect them internally; they begin to make a distinction between immediate utility and utility for exchange. The quantitative exchange-relation, no longer coincidentally determined, leads to the establishment of fixed magnitudes of value (see also the passage 167–68, which is quite similar in terms of content despite the different context).

After tracing the historical transformation of labor products into commodities, Marx outlines the parallel transformation of the commodity into money:

> In the direct exchange of products, each commodity is a direct means of exchange to its owner, and an equivalent to those who do not possess it, although only in so far as it has use-value for them. At this stage, therefore, the articles exchanged do not acquire a value-form independent of their own use-value, or of the individual needs of the exchangers. (182)

In this situation, exchange remains limited. For exchange to expand a general equivalent is needed. However, as Marx explains, "The problem and the means for its solution arise simultaneously" (182). Exchange of one's own products with those of others only occurs if all the products are commensurable with a third commodity, which temporarily assumes the form of the general equivalent. Over the course of history, diverse commodities have taken on that form, until it is finally attached to certain kinds of commodities. In this way, the general equivalent form "crystallizes out into the money-form" (183).

My commentary on the value-form section of chapter 1 mentioned historicist interpretations that take Marx's presentation of the "origin of the money-form" as a somewhat abstract depiction of the historical emergence of money (139). Yet this kind of historical account appears on pages 182–84 only after Marx has presented both the value-form's development in chapter 1 and the problem of exchangers' actions at the beginning of chapter 2. Historicist interpretations mix up these *three* levels, which Marx clearly distinguishes from one another and which have a hierarchical relationship in the argument. In these interpretations, the argument's different levels in chapters 1 and 2 can no longer be kept apart. For many authors holding these views, chapter 2 serves merely to make the concepts in chapter 1 more concrete, although it is unclear why that is necessary.

With regard to the historical dimension of Marx's sketch, twentieth-century research indicates that money's emergence was actually a more complex process than Marx assumed based on the state of knowledge in the nineteenth century. For example, Karl Polanyi (1957) points out that in early advanced civilizations, the various functions of money, such as its role as a medium of exchange or store of value, were initially distributed among quite different material supports. Also, the claim that slaves served as money (183) is historically dubious.

The second and third paragraphs on page 183 deal with the precious metals, gold and silver, to which the money form finally adhered. The reason, according to Marx, is the "appropriateness of their natural properties" (184) to money's functions as a form of appearance of value. That is, in order to serve as an expression of value, the different exemplars of the body of the money-commodity must be of uniform quality, easily divisible, and capable of being reassembled from their parts. All of that is true of the precious metals.

In both paragraphs, Marx points out properties that money acquires when monetary relations are fully developed. The use-value of the money commodity doubles. Alongside its properties as a physical commodity (the use-value referred to at the beginning of chapter 1) there is the "formal" use-value "arising out of its specific social function." For example, gold has natural properties making it useful for tooth fillings. As money, however, gold has the additional use-value that it can "buy" things.

ADDENDUM: This observation might smack of hairsplitting. Nevertheless, as Marx further explores the functions of money, he will more fully characterize this formal use-value of money. The section on interest-bearing capital in *Capital*'s third volume examines money as a "sui generis" commodity that not only serves as a medium of exchange but which is itself traded.

Additionally, Marx states that individual commodities are only "particular" equivalents of money and that money is their "general" equivalent. This leads to the conclusion that individual commodities relate to money as "particular commodities" relate to the "general commodity."

What does that mean? Individual commodities and the money commodity are all objects of value. Individual commodities are merely *particular* expressions of value, that is, value expressed in iron or wheat or boot polish. By contrast, the money commodity is not a particular expression of value (expressed in gold) but rather—as long as gold is money and continues to be so—the *general* expression of value, hence the immediate expression of value. This argument basically expresses the first peculiarity of the equivalent form, but now, in relation to the general equivalent form, use-value becomes the *general* expression of value.

e) Money-Form and Money Fetish
(Last paragraph 184 to 187)

In the three paragraphs remaining in chapter 2, there are a few long

Commodities and Money 203

footnotes consisting almost entirely of quotations. Marx uses these to substantiate his brief references to various economists' conceptions of money. Only if one were dealing with these authors in detail would it make sense to discuss these quotations. Instead, Marx's arguments in the main text are what demand our attention.

In the first of the three paragraphs, Marx notes a fundamental mix-up occurring in many theories of money:

> The process of exchange gives to the commodity which it has converted into money not its value but its specific value-form. Confusion between these two attributes has misled some writers into maintaining that the value of gold and silver is imaginary. (184f.)

Marx already pointed out that economists usually mix up value and value-form in footnote 17 on page 141. To understand what Marx is saying in the above quote, we must carefully specify the difference between value and value-form. On the one hand, commodities are *values* to the extent that, in exchange, an abstraction is made from their properties as use-values, so that they only represent an amount of abstract human labor. Every commodity, whether gold or iron, is an object of value. On the other hand, a commodity has a specific *value-form*, because other commodities relate to it in a specific way. Gold has the money-form because all other commodities use the material of gold to express their own value. In exchange, iron is just as much an object of value as gold, but the other commodities do not relate to iron as the expression of their value. For that reason, gold has a different value-form than iron.

Since the specific *value-form* of money results merely from the relationship of commodities to the money-commodity and this relationship can in principle change at any time (if another commodity becomes the money commodity), one can fall prey to the notion—if one does not distinguish between value and value-form—that money's value is merely "imaginary."

Marx mentions a further mix-up. Since money can, in certain uses, be replaced by "symbols of itself," it has been conceived of as a "mere symbol." What does that mean? If gold is the money-commodity, but exchange is done not directly for gold, but for a paper bill representing it, then exchange occurs not for money, that is to say, gold, but rather for a "symbol of itself"—a symbol of gold, which serves as money. Thus, a symbol serves as money. Some have concluded from this that money itself is merely a symbol. However, if one explains money as a mere symbol, Marx continues, then one declares it to be "the arbitrary product of human reflection" (186), that is, something derived from conscious human thought.

After pointing out in the next paragraph that gold's value as money is not determined any differently from other commodities' values, Marx summarizes:

> The difficulty lies not in comprehending that money is a commodity, but in discovering how, why and by what means a commodity becomes money. (186)

Marx's reflections on 184–86, which we have just discussed, assume the existence of a money *commodity*, in this case gold. If a *commodity* functions as money, then the value of the money commodity is no more imaginary than the value of other commodities. In such cases, we must indeed endeavor to understand how and by what means that commodity becomes money. The matter is more complicated in the contemporary monetary system, where different countries' currencies are no longer tied to a money commodity (see the commentary on the money-form in chapter 1). However, even in the case of a non-commodity money, that which functions as money can only do so because all other commodities relate to this non-commodity money as the expression of their value. The core of Marx's analysis does not depend on whether we're dealing with a commodity money or a non-commodity money.

The final paragraph of chapter 2 (187) deals with the *money fetish*. In contrast to his treatment of the commodity fetish, Marx addresses the money fetish briefly, and the term only appears in the chapter's final sentence. In the section on the commodity fetish, Marx began by asking what is mysterious about the commodity; he took the reader by the hand, so to speak, and gradually explored this mysteriousness and its consequences. With the money fetish, however, he proceeds very rapidly. Marx is obviously relying on being able to seamlessly build on his earlier presentation of the commodity fetish. We should therefore make an effort to recall what commodity fetishism is all about.

In this last paragraph Marx traces how the money fetish arises from the exchange process. In doing so, he goes all the way back to the value-form analysis in chapter 1: the reflections there on the value-relation of two commodities, abstracted from the exchange process. In the simple form of value, the commodity that functions as the equivalent appears to possess the equivalent form as "a social property inherent in its nature" [corrected translation: a socio-natural property, *gesellschaftliche*

Natureigenschaft] (187). I commented on Marx's first use of this latter expression on page 165, where the better translation "socio-natural property" was used.

When analyzing the simple form of value, Marx spoke of "the mysteriousness of the equivalent form, which only impinges on the crude bourgeois vision of the political economist when it confronts him in its fully developed shape, that of money" (149). Since the properties of things usually do not arise from their relations to other things, the commodity functioning as the equivalent appears to have the equivalent form "by nature" (149).

> We followed the process by which this false semblance became firmly established, a process which was completed when the universal equivalent form became identified with the natural form of a particular commodity, and thus crystallized into the money-form. (187)

The semblance is "false," because it inverts the real relation: a feature resulting from a relationship seems to be an objective property of a thing, *independent* of this relationship. With the simple form of value, this semblance was not yet "firmly established": if we consider just two commodities, then it's clear that one is the equivalent only because the other commodity relates to it. Things are different with money, the commodity to which all other commodities relate:

> What appears [corrected translation: seems] to happen is not that a particular commodity becomes money because all other commodities express their values in it, but, on the contrary, that all other commodities universally express their values in a particular commodity because it is money. The movement through which this process has been mediated vanishes in its own result, leaving no trace behind. (187)

The last sentence aptly expresses the basis not only of the money fetish but also the commodity fetish (and, as we will see later, the capital fetish). Thus the *result* of a social mediation presents itself in such a way that the mediation is no longer visible; it seems to be unmediated. The properties that the thing possesses only due to this mediation seem to belong to the thing itself. If one inquires into the causes of these properties, the mediating "movement" does not even come into view.

From this, it also becomes clear that the use of money in no way presupposes that people *know* what money is. By repeatedly relating their commodities to another commodity as their universal equivalent, people make that commodity money. "They do this without being aware of it" (166) was said in the section on the commodity fetish, but it applies just as well here.

In the section on commodity fetishism, Marx also pointed out that political economy begins its analysis with the "results of the process" (168). In effect, it is a problem to begin with "this finished form of the world of commodities—the money-form—which conceals the social character of private labour and the social relations between the individual workers, by making those relations appear as relations between material objects, instead of revealing them plainly" (168f.). Political economy starts with the results of a process that is socially mediated, without however understanding them as mediated results. Consequently, its answers to questions about the content of these "finished forms" tend to remain within the limits of fetishism. (This is generally, but not always, the case; see the end of the section on the commodity fetish.)

Not recognizing that money is the result of a mediating process leads to the following distorted perception:

> This physical object, gold or silver in its crude state, becomes, immediately on its emergence from the bowels of the earth, the direct incarnation of all human labour. Hence the magic of money. (187)

The expression "all human labour" refers to all commodity-producing labor, since only its products are exchanged for money. That gold and silver are money *by nature* is just one of the common explanations of money (though it's not so important these days). However, Marx addressed another explanation in the paragraph on 184–86: the idea that money is simply a symbol, its use deriving from an agreement or arbitrary ruling. These two basic perspectives are also called, in turn, "metallism" and (monetary) "nominalism." It's important to recognize that Marx opposes both viewpoints, although chapter 2's final paragraph only deals with metallism. What the perspectives have in common is that both are unable to perceive the mediating "movement" that turns something into money. In its place something else is substituted: in one case *nature*, which supposedly makes gold and silver into immediate incarnations of value, and in another case *society* (or the state's institutions) which can consciously rule that anything is money. At the end of this paragraph,

Commodities and Money

Marx looks at the social basis of that process of mediation, which is not recognized by either economic perspective.

> Men are henceforth related to each other in their social process of production in a purely atomistic way. Their own relations of production therefore assume a material shape which is independent of their control and their conscious individual action. This situation is manifested first by the fact that the products of men's labour universally take on the form of commodities. The riddle of the money fetish is therefore the riddle of the commodity fetish, now become visible and dazzling to our eyes. (187)

The claim here that people relate to one another "in a purely atomistic way" in the production process means that people expend their labor as private labor, separate from one another, and allow only exchange to mediate economic intercourse, thus making their labor products into commodities. As values, however, the commodities can only be widely related to one another if they all relate to a general equivalent. And when the general equivalent attaches to a specific commodity, it becomes money. In that sense, Marx writes that the "riddle of the money fetish" is merely the "riddle of the commodity fetish" become visible. This last statement holds regardless of whether we are dealing with a commodity money or a non-commodity money—such as state-issued paper money that is not backed by a commodity, which is therefore not merely the representation of a money commodity. Hence, it is by no means true that the disappearance of the money commodity entails the disappearance of the money fetish.

Chapter 3: Money, or the Circulation of Commodities (188-244)

With every new chapter of *Capital*, we should clarify what the subject matter and level of abstraction are, based on Marx's chapter title and any introductory remarks. The title of chapter 3, "Money, or the Circulation of Commodities," is a mixture of old and new elements. In chapter 1, Marx spoke of the "money-form," and in chapter 2, he spoke of "money." By contrast, the expression in the title phrase "circulation of commodities" has not appeared until now. For this reason, it is not immediately clear why the chapter title should connect "money" and "circulation of commodities" with an "or." Moreover, there is no further information here about this chapter's subject matter, since after the initial subheading the text immediately turns to addressing the money commodity's "first function."

ADDENDUM: By contrast, the *Contribution to the Critique of Political Economy* does deal with the connection between this chapter of *Capital* and the preceding material. There, at the end of his examination of the exchange process, Marx states:

> As they develop, the interrelations of commodities [corrected translation: the processing relations (*Die prozessierenden Beziehungen*) of the commodities to each other] crystallise into distinct aspects of the universal equivalent, and thus the exchange process becomes at the same time the process of formation of money. This process as a whole, which comprises several processes, constitutes [corrected translation: is] *circulation*. (MECW 29: 292)

In this quote, it's clear what the "circulation of commodities" means. It refers to the *totality of all exchange processes of commodity owners*. Chapter 2, which yielded the category of money as a result of the commodity owner's activity, dealt with the *process of exchange*, which is a part of the totality of the exchange processes that was

Commodities and Money 209

obtained by means of abstraction. For its part, chapter 1 addressed the *exchange-relation* of the commodity, which is a part of the exchange process that was obtained by abstracting from the commodity owners. This shows that Marx's chosen starting point for the presentation in *Capital*, the commodity, is not something immediately given, but rather results from a previous abstraction. Marx discovered that this starting point made sense through his research process. For us, by contrast, it is only in the course of the presentation that we can judge whether this starting point makes sense or not.[26]

But why should one examine the processes of exchange *as a whole* after examining the individual act of exchange? The first sentence of the quote above provides an answer: "The processing relations of the commodities" condense into "distinct aspects of the universal equivalent." Marx deals with the general equivalent's three fundamental "aspects" (*Bestimmungen* or "determinations") in the three subsections of chapter 3; they then take on concrete form in the individual "functions of money," although a single money *determination* can include more than one money *function*. The connection of the relationship between commodities in circulation and the fundamental determinations of money—a connection that is merely claimed at this point, not yet demonstrated—explains the "or" in the title: the examination of money's determinations coincides with the analysis of the circulation of commodities, since these determinations come out of the latter analysis.

Something else becomes clear here as well. When beginning his examination of the value-form, Marx pointed out that the commodity in the relative form of value plays an active role, whereas the commodity in the equivalent form plays a passive one. One commodity expresses its value, while the other serves as material for the expression of value. This distribution of active and passive roles does not stop here: a commodity can only be in the *general* equivalent form and ultimately the *money-form* because all other commodities actively relate to it. This is the only way a specific commodity can become *money*: a commodity becomes money because all commodity owners relate their commodities to this particular one. Here, the same is being claimed about the *functions of money*: these functions result from the "processing relations" of commodities. Neither money nor its functions are simply given. However, this "movement" of the processing relations, as Marx writes at the end of chapter 2, "vanishes in its own result, leaving no trace behind" (187). As a consequence, it seems that money is simply there, or that states and governments could simply create it by fiat. And the same goes for the functions of money, which are seemingly there, as givens. Most bourgeois economists thus simply accept money's functions as given facts, merely enumerating them and failing to grasp that they

---

26. See Marx's distinction between the *method of presentation* and the *method of inquiry* in the Postface to the second edition of *Capital, Volume 1,* page 102. I also refer to it in my commentary on the first paragraph of chapter 1.

are a *result*. For a long time, Marxists fell prey to this inverse error. The world of commodities led them not to take money seriously, with labor's role in determining value appearing to be the only important thing. What many Marxists overlooked then was that money is a *necessary* result of circulation, which cannot be circumvented (more on this under 1a).

The *Contribution to the Critique*'s second chapter (which corresponds to the content of *Capital*'s third chapter) has a brief introduction that defines its object of analysis:

> The principal difficulty in the analysis of money is surmounted as soon as it is understood that the commodity is the origin of money. After that it is only a question of clearly comprehending the specific form [corrected translation: form-determinations] peculiar to it. . . . During the following analysis it is important to keep in mind that we are only concerned with those forms of money which arise directly from the exchange of commodities, but not with forms of money, such as credit money, which belong to a higher stage of production. (MECW 29: 303f.)

Capital's third volume deals with these additional forms of money. Chapter 3 in the first volume thus does not conclude the examination of money. Here again, it becomes clear that the three volumes of *Capital* constitute a whole, and one must therefore read them all.

1. The Measure of Values

Marx's first sentence in chapter 3 not only makes clear that he presupposes *gold* to be the money commodity, but also that he is considering a monetary system based on a money *commodity*.

ADDENDUM: When dealing with the money-form, I pointed out that the contemporary monetary system is neither de jure nor de facto based on a money commodity. I referred to Heinrich 2012 (69, 161), Heinrich 1999 (233ff., 302ff.), and Stützle 2006 for a deeper treatment of this question. These works attempt to show how the central features of Marx's conception of money remain valid even after the money commodity disappears. For a critique of this conception, see Knolle-Gruthusen/Krüger/Wolf (2009); these authors make a twofold claim. On the one hand, they reject the idea that Marx's analysis of the commodity and money can do without reference to a money commodity. On the other hand, they contend that the contemporary monetary system remains based on a money commodity—even if invisibly so and in a way that nobody notices, gold is still supposed to be the money commodity. However, since a commodity can only become a money commodity when all commodity owners express the value of their commodities in this special commodity, it seems absurd to speak of a money commodity not being noticed as a money commodity.

Under the heading "The Measure of Values," Marx begins to investigate the "functions" of money. It's easy, on the basis of our everyday experience, to enumerate money's key functions, such as being a measure of value and a means of both circulation and hoarding. These functions of money also form the basis of the dominant economic theories. But whereas these usually *begin* with a brief list of money functions and then quickly proceed to considering more complicated relations (banks, financial markets, currencies), Marx looks at these functions of money only *after* examining the relation of commodities and money, at a fundamental level, in the first two chapters of *Capital*. We can see, based on the scope of chapter 3, that Marx's concern here goes beyond listing money's various functions.

Marx says that money's "first function" is as the measure of values, but he doesn't explain why this function should be considered the first among money's various roles.

ADDENDUM: The *Contribution to the Critique of Political Economy* has a more detailed account:

> The first phase of circulation is, as it were, a theoretical phase preparatory to real circulation. Commodities, which exist as use values, must first of all assume [corrected translation: create, *schaffen*] a form in which they *appear* to one another nominally as exchange values [here it should say: values],[27] as definite quantities of objectified *universal* labour time [that is, *abstract* labor time]. (MECW 29: 303-4)

"Real circulation" here refers to commodities actually changing hands. If this changing of hands is to be an exchange of *commodities*, and not mere *products*, then the products must have a form allowing them to confront each other as values, and their value must be *expressed*. The original German has commodities "creating" this form, but this is strictly speaking wrong, since commodities don't *do* anything!

---

27. In the *Contribution*, Marx did not yet distinguish terminologically between *value* and *exchange value* (the form of appearance of value). In the quoted passage, the point is that commodities appear to each other as values, in that their values take the form of prices. Here and in some of the quotations that follow from the *Contribution*, the reference should be to *value* instead of *exchange value*.

There is an explanation for this unclear language: Marx's presentation in the *Contribution to the Critique of Political Economy* had not yet clearly differentiated form determinations (the necessity of which is deduced) from actions (in which these form determinations are realized). Even in this earlier text, however, the distinction itself was in substance quite clear to him.

a) Immanent Measure of Value and Money as Its Necessary Form of Appearance (188)

> The first main function of gold is to supply commodities with the material for the expression of their values, or to represent their values as magnitudes of the same denomination, *qualitatively* equal and *quantitatively* comparable. It thus acts as a universal measure of value, and only through performing this function does gold, the specific equivalent commodity, become money. (188, emphasis M.H.)

Marx identifies two facets of money's function as a measure of values: a qualitative one and a quantitative one. First, the values of commodities are presented as *qualitatively equal*, because they are measured in the same material: gold. Second, the values are *quantitatively commensurable*, because they are all expressed in quantities of gold. However, it's not something that gold *does* that allows it to function in this way. Marx states:

> It is not money that renders the commodities commensurable. (188)

ADDENDUM: Marx does not make clear in this passage of *Capital* whose theory he is arguing against. In the corresponding section of *A Contribution to the Critique of Political Economy* (MECW 29n306), however, he mentions Aristotle. Aristotle had explained that money makes things commensurable in exchange, but that this is only a practical and expedient measure, since things "in truth" are incommensurable. Marx follows up on the last remark in his excursus on Aristotle in the value-form analysis (see 151f.).

> Because all commodities, as values, are objectified human labour, and therefore in themselves commensurable, their values can be communally measured in one and the same specific commodity, and this commodity can be converted into the common measure of their values, that is, into money. (188)

Commodities and Money 213

Marx makes two claims here about the cause-and-effect relation: 1) that gold, as the measure of values, can *measure* at all is due to commodities having already been reduced to a common dimension in which they can be compared and measured; 2) that gold is the *common* measure is not due to gold itself, but because all commodities jointly relate to gold. Marx's earlier analysis of the value-form yielded both results (on commensurability, see chapter 1, the last paragraph of page 140 and the first two paragraphs of page 141; on the general equivalent form as "the joint contribution of the whole world of commodities," see chapter 1, the first paragraph of page 159).

> **Money as a measure of value is the necessary form of appearance of the measure of value which is immanent in commodities, namely labour-time. (188)**

The distinction between an "immanent" measure and the external "form of appearance" of this measure is not an intuitive, everyday one.[28] The question arises: If labor-time is already the measure of value, then why do we still need money as an independent measure? Or does money measure value, because it simply represents hours of labor-time? Marx does not mean the latter. In footnote 1, he raises the question

> why money does not itself directly represent labour-time, so that a piece of paper may represent, for instance, x hours' labour. (188n1)

This addresses a question that did not come up explicitly in the earlier value-form analysis. (Marx came closest to dealing with this problem in his critique of Proudhon in chapter 1, 161n26.) The question emerges, however, because Marx has just emphasized that commodity values are commensurable as "objectified human labour." So, why not just measure value directly with labor-time? The answer that Marx provides in footnote 1 initially appears rather unsatisfactory. The question raised

> comes down simply to the question why, on the basis of commodity production, the products of labour must take the form of commodities. This is obvious, because their taking the form

---

28. See Schlaudt (2011) for a detailed discussion of Marx as a "theorist of measure."

> of commodities implies their differentiation [corrected translation: doubling, *Verdopplung*] into commodities [on the one hand] and the money commodity [on the other]. (188n1)

This last claim, that products as commodities must double themselves into commodities and the money-commodity, was precisely what the question puts into doubt. Merely asserting that it happens is not an especially convincing answer. Nor does the next sentence offer much more than a hint:

> It is also asked why private labour cannot be treated as its opposite, directly social labour. (188n1)

So far Marx has only mentioned "labor in directly social form" (151) in his discussion in chapter 1 of the equivalent form's third peculiarity: the labor that produces the equivalent form's material body is "labor in directly social form" because its product does not require any mediation and is instead immediately social. Marx's cursory remark leads us to the following question: why can't the products resulting from the many different acts of private labor, that is, individual commodities, be at the same time products of directly social labor, that is, commodities taking the equivalent form? Obviously, Marx doesn't intend to provide an exhaustive answer here: rather, he refers to the *Contribution to the Critique of Political Economy*, meaning that we have to consult that work. In the passage that Marx quotes here from the *Contribution*, he is criticizing the ideas of John Gray, who wanted to abolish money and make labor-time the immediate measure of value. Marx's main counter-argument is that commodities

> are only comparable as the things they are. Commodities are the direct products of isolated independent individual kinds of labour [corrected translation: isolated, independent kinds of private labour], and through their alienation [*Entäußerung*][29] in the course of individual exchange they must prove that they are general social labour, in other words, on the basis of commodity production, labour becomes social labour only as a result

---

29. In the *Economic-Philosophical Manuscripts* of 1844, the notion of "*Entfremdung*" (to get estranged from an essence or an inner substance) is crucial. In the quote here, Marx uses the term "*Entäußerung*" (to get rid of something). Unfortunately, both German terms are usually translated with the same English word: *alienation*.

of the universal alienation [*Entäußerung*] of individual kinds of labour. (MECW 29: 321f.)

This quotation deals with precisely the condition that, in my commentary on commodity fetishism in chapter 1, I called "retroactive socialization." Commodities are products of *private labor*. These acts of private labor are not yet components of society's total labor—they are still to become "*social labor.*" This *only* happens in exchange "as a result of the universal alienation [*Entäußerung*]."

How do private acts of labor become components of society's total labor? This occurs *insofar as individually expended, private labor is reduced to abstract human labor in exchange*. Before exchange, private producers, independently of each other, *individually* expend certain amounts of *concrete* labor. For example, carpenter X dedicates five hours of carpentry labor to manufacturing a table; carpenter Y, in order to produce a similar table, requires six hours of labor; tailor U requires four hours of tailoring labor for a pair of pants, and so on. These amounts of concrete labor that producers individually expend during the production process are all that can be measured with a clock. What constitutes value, however, is not *individually* expended *concrete* labor, but rather *abstract human* labor. It's therefore not simple labor-time that is the "immanent measure of value," but abstract human labor-time. However, it is only in exchange that concrete labor is reduced to abstract labor. Only in exchange do we find out whether the "socially necessary labour-time" (129) is closer to the five hours required by carpenter X or the six hours required by carpenter Y. And furthermore only there do we find out in what relation—in respect to the distinction between complicated and simple labor—the labor of the tailor stands to that of the carpenter, the different extent to which both of these kinds of labor count as "multiplied" (135) simple labor.

The labor-time that can actually be measured *prior* to exchange— which is individually expended, concrete labor—does not help us determine value. Value only exists in the universal, reciprocal relationship that commodities have to each other in exchange. As the analysis of the value-form in *Capital*'s chapter 1 and of the exchange process in chapter 2 demonstrated, this universal, reciprocal relationship is only possible if commodities can relate to a *general equivalent*. So the "immanent" measure of value, which is (abstract human) labor-time, and its "form of appearance," which is money, do not exist in a *temporal* sequence, in which one can simply choose which measure to use. Instead, money as the measure of values is the "necessary form of appearance" of the immanent measure of labor-time, and the immanent measure (abstract human labor) *cannot appear otherwise* than as money. That's why in the *Contribution*, Marx refers to money as the "immediate form of existence [*unmittelbare Existenzform*]"[30] of the labor alienated [*entäußert*] in exchange (MEW 13: 42), that is, of abstract labor.[31]

ADDENDUM: In the *Contribution*, Marx criticizes Proudhon's conception of socialism (abolishing money but retaining commodity production) on the basis of these conclusions:

> But it was left to M. Proudhon and his school to declare seriously that the degradation of money and the exaltation of commodities was the essence of socialism and thereby to reduce socialism to an elementary misunderstanding of the inevitable correlation existing between commodities and money. (MECW 29: 323)

In substance, the same basic misunderstanding is found among all those who believe that the value of a commodity is determined solely by its process of production. If this were the case, then it would be difficult to see why money is value's necessary form of appearance. Basically, the claim that value is determined purely in production advances a Proudhonian position (with the inconsistency of not drawing Proudhon's conclusions!).

As a twofold result, we can affirm: (1) it is not money that makes commodities commensurable (commodities are commensurable as values); (2) but this does not mean one can dispense with money as a measure of value. Rather, money is the *necessary*, inevitable form in which the value of commodities appears.

Incidentally, it may be observed here (188), as in chapter 1 (128, 148),

---

30. Both MECW 29: 297 and the Charles H. Kerr edition of the *Contribution to the Critique of Political Economy* (1904, 64) translate "*unmittelbare Existenzform*" as "direct embodiment," which is a less-than-satisfactory translation. However, the MECW volume also commits the more egregious error of translating the passage from MEW 13; 42 in a manner that suggests that Marx criticizes Benjamin Franklin for *falsely* regarding money as the immediate form of existence of abstract labor: "[Franklin] is bound to mistake money for the direct embodiment of this alienated labour" (MECW 29; 297). In fact, Marx accuses Franklin of *not recognizing* that money is the immediate form of existence of this alienated [*entäußerte*] labor.—Trans.

31. It comes to light here once again (see the commentary on 181f.) that Marx's theory of value is a "monetary" theory of value: the substance of value, abstract labor, cannot appear at all without relating to money.

Commodities and Money 217

that Marx speaks of a "form of appearance," without referring to that which appears as an "essence." Evidently, he continues to be cautious about using the term "essence."

b) Price and Ideal Money[32] (189–190)

Marx begins by repeating his characterization of the price-form on page 163 of chapter 1. In the price-form, value is expressed in the money commodity. In contrast to the general relative form of value in which a series of commodities express their value in the general equivalent, now the simple, isolated relative form of value suffices. Only the money commodity itself has no price-form.

In the next paragraph, Marx formulates a new thought: price is something distinct from the commodity body and is just a "purely ideal or notional form [corrected translation: purely ideal or imaginary form, *rein ideelle oder vorgestellte Form*]" (189). Despite being "invisible," value exists "in these very articles"—to the extent that they are exchanged as commodities, it should be added—and is "signified [corrected translation: imagined, *vorgestellt*] through their equality with gold." It is, however, an equality, that "exists only in their heads." For that reason, the custodian of a commodity must make its value visible by sticking a price tag on it. Footnote 2, attached to this paragraph, testifies to Marx's power of association but contributes little to the argument. From a contemporary perspective, it stands out how uncritically Marx adopts the then-common manner of speaking about "savages and semi-savages."

The ideal quality of the price-form has consequences:

> Since the expression of the value of commodities in gold is a purely ideal act, we may use purely imaginary or ideal gold to perform this operation. . . . In its function as measure of value, money therefore serves only in an imaginary or ideal capacity [corrected translation: money therefore serves only as imaginary or ideal money, *dient das Geld daher nur als vorgestelltes oder ideelles Geld*]. (189f.)

To express a commodity's value, money does not have to be physically

---

32. Two different German adjectives, "ideal" and "ideell," usually have the same English translation: "ideal." Whereas the German "ideal" means absolutely perfect, "ideell" means that something is imagined, at the level of ideas. Several times in chapter 3, Marx uses the term "ideelles Geld" which is translated as "ideal money."

present. In this sense, money as the measure of value is only "ideational money." However, it does matter *what* is functioning as money: the same value expressed in gold yields a different measure than when expressed in silver. As Marx emphasizes on page 190, having a double standard of value (such as gold and silver) is rather impractical, since gold and silver prices evolve differently, if the ratio between the two metals' values changes.

When commenting on the beginning of chapter 3, I discussed the claim from the *Contribution to the Critique of Political Economy* that the determinations of the general equivalent derive from the relationships that commodities have to each other. This state of affairs becomes evident here, with regard to the way money as the measure of value has an ideal existence. Its ideal existence *results* from the fact that the commodities in the price-form only relate to money ideally.

ADDENDUM: Generalizing, Marx notes in the corresponding passage of the *Contribution to the Critique of Political Economy*:

> The distinct form in which gold crystallises into money depends in each case on the way in which the exchange values [it should say: *values*, see footnote 27 of this book] of commodities are represented with regard to one another. (MECW 29: 307)

But here Marx takes the analysis a bit further:

> Commodities now confront one another in a dual form, really as use values and ideally as exchange values [again it should say: *values*]. They represent now for one another the dual form of labour contained in them, since the particular concrete labour actually exists as their use value, while universal abstract labour time assumes an imaginary existence in their price. (MECW 29: 307)

In this passage, Marx is not simply repeating what is already clear, namely that both commodities and the labor represented in them have a dual character. Rather, the point here is *how* this dual character shows up *within the price-form*. As a use-value, the commodity is "really" present in the sense of sensuously, objectively present, and the concrete labor that creates use-value also "actually exists." By contrast, the value of the commodity and thus the abstract labor represented in it are only "imaginary" in the price.

In the *Contribution*, Marx also addresses Adam Smith's unsatisfactory approach to the commodity's dual existence. Smith understood labor to be the measure of

Commodities and Money 219

value, but he did not distinguish between concrete and abstract labor. He referred to labor as the "real price" and money as the "nominal price" of commodities (Smith 1776: 34ff.), thus trivializing money's significance. Just as neoclassical economics does today, Smith treated money as only a technical aid to exchange. For this reason, he considered money important in everyday practice, but without a crucial role in theoretical analysis. Marx criticizes Smith's conception by noting:

> The difference [between labor as real price and money as nominal price] is on the other hand so far from being simply a nominal difference that all the storms which threaten the commodity in the actual process of circulation centre upon it. (MECW 29: 307f.)

Marx then points out how the contradiction contained in the commodity form becomes clear here, because

> the particular labour of an isolated individual [which s/he has expended in production] can become socially effective only if it is expressed as its direct opposite, i.e. abstract universal labour. (MECW 29: 308).

Moreover, this social character can only be expressed when there is exchange-for-money and not before. Marx emphasized this a few sentences earlier, when he wrote:

> The particular individual labour contained in the commodity can only *through alienation* [corrected translation: through the process of externalization, *durch den Prozess der Entäußerung*] be represented as its opposite, impersonal, abstract, general—and only in this form social—labour, i.e. money (MECW 29: 308, emphasis M.H.).

c) Measure of Values and Standard of Prices
(191 to second paragraph 195)

Commodities represent their values in specific quantities of gold (if gold is the money commodity); in that way, gold serves as the *measure of values*. For their part, the amounts of gold also must be measured. The measuring is done with multiples of a specific weight of gold. This gold weight becomes the *measure of prices*. The measuring of values and the measuring of prices are two completely different functions of money:

> It is the measure of value as the social incarnation of human labour [more precisely, of abstract human labor]; it is the standard of price as a quantity of metal with a fixed weight. (192)

The difference between these two functions becomes clearer as they become more fully specified: as the measure of prices, the unit of measurement has to be *fixed*, so that the proportions don't change. That is to say, "a handful of gold" is not an appropriate unit of measurement. Instead, it should be one gram or one ounce, which constantly expresses the same amount of gold.

As the measure of values, however, gold's value is indeed mutable. That is, over the course of time, a gram of gold can be the "social incarnation" of *different* amounts of abstract human labor. In the paragraphs that follow, Marx discusses the effects of the measure of values' mutability.

A change in the money commodity's value does not affect the unit of measurement of prices: twelve ounces of gold still possess twelve times as much value as one ounce, despite changes in the gold's value. (Marx's reference to a decline in the value of gold by "1,000 per cent" on page 192 is an error. If gold's value declined by more than 100 percent, it would be negative. What he probably means is a decline to 1/1000 of the previous value.)

Nor does a change in the money commodity's value inhibit its function as the measure of values, since changes in its value simultaneously affect all commodities. When Marx mentions "the laws of the simple relative expression of value which we developed in an earlier chapter" (193) he is referring to what was presented in chapter 1 under the heading "The Quantitative Determinacy of the Relative Form of Value" (144–46). There we saw the effects of changes in values of both the commodity in the relative form of value and the commodity in the equivalent form. Marx repeats some of the results of that investigation in chapter 3 on page 193.

However, the claim that changes in the money commodity's value do not interfere with money's measuring function is only valid when comparing the *simultaneous* values of different commodities. If we consider measurements that have occurred at *different points in time*, then a change in the money commodity's value during the interim would mean that the measurements of value can no longer be *directly* compared. In these cases, commensurability depends on correctly calculating the changes in the money commodity's value.

ADDENDUM: Some readers might be surprised by Marx's drawn-out discussion of how the mutability of the money commodity's value affects its function as a measure of prices and values. The reasons for Marx's thoroughness probably derive from the history of economic theory. Ricardo had searched for an unchangeable measure of value. In *Theories of Surplus Value*, Marx dealt with Ricardo's reflections

Commodities and Money

on this matter (see MECW 32: 320ff.). Marx's discussion in *Capital* also responds to Ricardo's concerns, showing that the mutability of the measure of values does not pose any fundamental problems.

From the last paragraph on page 193 to the bottom of page 195, Marx discusses how money-names take on a life of their own. The words for metal weights, for example "pound," originally served as money-names, designating a specific quantity of money. The names endured, but with time they separated from the original weights. The result is that "pound" both designates a weight and serves as a money-name. Ultimately, money units are established purely by law, and the aliquot parts acquire legal names such as taler, pound, or penny. These "legally valid names . . . made for the purpose of reckoning" (194f.) are used to express commodity prices,

> and money serves as money of account whenever it is a question of fixing a thing as a value and therefore in its money-form. (195)

In footnote 12, Marx points out how these names of account have caused confusion in history. Legally established names for money can be used to express the metal weight of gold, which is the basis for measuring prices. The account name of gold was called its "mint-price," and it appeared that the state was fixing the price of gold. However, the state had merely established another name for the unit of measurement. Marx then concludes, without further comment:

> On the other hand, it is in fact necessary that value, as opposed to the multifarious objects of the world of commodities, should develop into this form, a material and non-mental one [corrected translation: non-conceptually objective form, *begriffslos sachlichen Form*], but also a simple social form. (195)

Expressing value through a money-name is "non-conceptually objective" because value is expressed as an object, without relying on the concept of value: if one says "a certain commodity is worth one taler," then the value is expressed as an object, but without saying anything about what "value" is. The form is a "simple social" one, because it is simple and socially *valid*. To talk of a "necessary" development of value, as Marx does here, is problematic, since it seems like historical determinism. Yet Marx's point is that generalized commodity production *requires* a "simple social" expression of value. It would have been more exact to say:

if commodity production is generalized, *then* developing this social form becomes necessary.

d) Price and Value
(last sentence of 195 to 198)

> Price is the money-name of the labour objectified in a commodity. (195)

With this, Marx summarizes what he has established so far, based on value, about price. But there is more:

> Although price, being the exponent of the magnitude of a commodity's value, is the exponent of its exchange-ratio with money, it does not follow that the exponent of this exchange-ratio is necessarily the exponent of the magnitude of the commodity's value. (196)

Marx uses "exponent" here, not in the mathematical sense, but to mean a "representative" or "indicator." A price indicates the magnitude of a commodity's value, but this indication is not always correct. This passage does not tell us anything about the circumstances in which the price might correctly or incorrectly indicate the magnitude of value. The topic here is a different one: the *conditions of possibility* for their being a difference between the price, on the one hand, and the magnitude of value, on the other:

> The magnitude of the value of a commodity therefore expresses a necessary relation to social labour-time [corrected translation: aggregate social labour-time, *gesellschaftliche Gesamtarbeitszeit*] which is inherent in the process by which its value is created. With the transformation of the magnitude of value into the price this necessary relation appears as the exchange-ratio between a single commodity and the money commodity which exists outside it. (196)

This makes clear once again that *magnitude of value* and *price* are categories located at *conceptually distinct* levels:

- The *magnitude of value* of a commodity expresses the extent to which the individual concrete labor expended in creating it counts as social

labor-time. This is the commodity's aforementioned relationship to society's aggregate labor.
- *Price* expresses a commodity's exchange relation with the money-commodity. In this role, it is a form of appearance, a mode of expression of the magnitude of value; we can also say, based on the arguments at the beginning of chapter 3, that it is a *necessary* form of appearance of value's magnitude (see page 188).

This means that, in a *qualitative sense*, price and magnitude of value are by no means identical and are thus not *directly* commensurable.

Marx writes that "this relation," the exchange-relation of the commodity with the money-commodity, the price,

> may express both the magnitude of value of the commodity and the greater or lesser quantity of money for which it can be sold under the given circumstances. The possibility, therefore, of a quantitative incongruity between price and magnitude of value, i.e. the possibility that the price may diverge from the magnitude of value, is inherent in the price-form itself. (196)

Previously in footnote 21 on page 146, Marx spoke of a "lack of congruence between the magnitude of value and its relative expression." What he meant was that a commodity's magnitude of value can develop *in a different direction* from its relative expression—but this does not necessarily mean that the expression is incorrect. For example, if the value of the money-commodity declines, then the commodity's price increases, even if the commodity's magnitude of value remains unchanged. However, here the incongruity dealt with is a different one: the price can *incorrectly* reflect the magnitude of value in a *quantitative sense*. That's why now, in contrast to footnote 21, Marx speaks of a "quantitative incongruity."

If Marx speaks of a "quantitative incongruity" here it might appear, contrary to our conclusion from Marx's distinction of value and price on page 196, that magnitude of value and price are not directly commensurable, that it is precisely their commensurability he has in mind. However, pay close attention to what Marx is actually comparing in this quote. It's not the *magnitude of value* and *price*, but rather *two different prices*: on the one hand, a price that adequately expresses value and, on the other, a price expressing what the commodity can be purchased for at the moment. Keep in mind this meaning of the "quantitative incongruity between price and magnitude of value" in what follows. Marx continues:

> This is not a defect, but, on the contrary, it makes this form the adequate one for a mode of production whose laws can only assert themselves as blindly operating averages between constant irregularities. (196)

Marx's section on fetishism in chapter 1 mentioned that in commodity production economic "laws can only assert themselves as blindly operating averages." There Marx stated:

> In the midst of the accidental and ever-fluctuating exchange relations between the products, the labour-time socially necessary to produce them asserts itself as a regulative law of nature. (168)

Marx's reference to "accidental and ever-fluctuating exchange relations" means the commodity prices are constantly fluctuating but only coincidentally express the magnitudes of value correctly. Only in the course of these fluctuations do the magnitudes of value impose themselves as "blindly operating averages."

ADDENDUM: These reflections could lead one to believe that a commodity's *empirically* visible prices fluctuate around an average price that correctly expresses its magnitude of value. In chapter 5, however, Marx explicitly states that this is not the case (269n24; similarly 329n9). To put things differently, the prices being discussed here—at a level of presentation that still abstracts from capital—are not identical with empirical prices in everyday life. Only in Volume 3 of *Capital* does Marx deal with the prices that are formed through competition among capitals.

In the next paragraph, Marx explains that the price-form not only makes possible a "quantitative incongruity" between the magnitude of value and price, but

> it may also harbour a qualitative contradiction, with the result that price ceases altogether to express value, despite the fact that money is nothing but the value-form of commodities. (197)

A commodity only has value to the extent that it is the product of abstract, value-constituting labor. If something that is not a product of labor is exchanged, then it has a price *but no value*.

The "qualitative contradiction" that Marx speaks of here thus consists

Commodities and Money

in the fact that money, the value-form of commodities, can become the expression of a non-value. This means that

> the expression of price is in this case imaginary, like certain quantities in mathematics. (197)

ADDENDUM: In mathematics, "imaginary" numbers are multiples of the number i, which is the square root of minus one. In early nineteenth-century mathematics, it was not clear if these were actual existing numbers or dubious inventions. Hence the designation "imaginary" numbers in contrast to "real" numbers, that is, all numbers that can be represented as finite or infinite decimal fractions. Contemporary mathematics retains this designation, despite no longer making such distinctions with regard to the "reality" of individual numbers. Unlike the magnitudes of mathematics, however, there is a fundamental difference between prices that (correctly or incorrectly) express magnitudes of values and prices that are applied to things that are not objects of value.

With regard to "imaginary" expressions of price, Marx makes a fundamental distinction. On the one hand, there are imaginary prices of things "which in and for themselves are not commodities, things such as conscience, honour, etc." (197). Here Marx is alluding to the different forms of corruption. On the other hand, "The imaginary price-form may also conceal a real value-relation or one derived from it" (197).

ADDENDUM: As an example of the second case, Marx mentions uncultivated land, which is not a product of labor and therefore has no value. In Volume 3 of *Capital*, Marx shows that land prices are generally derived from the ground rent that can be obtained for the land and the market interest rate. Other examples of imaginary prices that conceal real value-relations—or are derived from them—are the prices of shares and bonds in the stock market, also dealt with in the third volume of *Capital*.

In section b above, Marx emphasized that the price-form is an "ideal form." Now he builds on this claim: alongside the commodity's "real shape," that is, its useful shape, it has "an ideal value-shape ... in the form of its price" (197). For the owner of the commodity, however, this ideal value-shape is not sufficient. If the commodity is to really function as value for the owner—to serve him as a "general equivalent—the commodity must really be transformed into money. Marx speaks of its transformation into gold, since he assumes gold to be the money commodity. For this transformation, Marx casually uses the term "transubstantiation," a concept I will address when commenting on page 203. He alludes in this passage to the various difficulties of this transformation, using language that is both philosophical (Hegel's concept) and theological (Saint Jerome). The next subsection will look at these difficulties. Now Marx summarizes:

> The price-form therefore implies both the exchangeability of commodities for money and the necessity of exchanges. (198)

Then he formulates a new thought:

> On the other hand, gold serves as an ideal measure of value only because it has already established itself [corrected translation: it has already operated—*sich umtreibt*] as the money commodity in the process of exchange. Hard cash lurks within the ideal measure of value. (198)

At the beginning of chapter 3, Marx emphasized that the "first function" of the money commodity is to be the measure of values. Only by performing this function does the specific equivalent commodity (gold, here) become money. Now, however, Marx is claiming that gold's function as an ideal measure of value presupposes that it "operates" in the exchange process. So what is really primary: the "measuring" or the "operating"?

In terms of the objective dependence of one category on another, it's the measuring function that comes first. Only *because* commodities express their values in a common material, for example, gold, does this material acquire the money-form. Due to this objective dependence, the measuring function has to be examined first (in the first subsection of chapter 3) before looking at gold's operation in circulation; that is, the function of money as a means of circulation (second subsection of chapter 3). In social interaction, however, both of these functions presuppose each other: on the one hand, gold can only function as a means of circulation because it is a measure of values. On the other hand, gold is the measure of values—and can only be so—because it functions as a means of circulation.

2. Means of Circulation

ADDENDUM: In the *Contribution to the Critique of Political Economy*, an introductory paragraph makes clear the relationship between the first and second subsections of this chapter:

> When, as a result of the establishing of prices, commodities have acquired the form in which they are able to enter circulation and gold has assumed its function as money, the contradictions latent in the exchange of commodities are both exposed and resolved by circulation. (MECW 29: 323)

Circulation presupposes the existence of both *price-determined commodities* and *money*. The first subsection dealt with these presuppositions: a commodity acquires a price by expressing its actual or imagined value in the money-commodity; and the money-commodity becomes money, because it functions as the measure of values.

a) The Metamorphosis of Commodities

"Metamorphosis" comes from the Greek word for a change of form. Marx probably had in mind the *Metamorphoses* of the Roman poet Ovid (43 BC – ca. 17 AD), which formed part of the canon of humanist education in the nineteenth century. Since his school days, Marx had been familiar with this text, which he appreciated. He alludes to it on page 194, observing that, in the course of history, "the more precious metal extrudes the less precious from its function as measure of value. Silver drives out copper, gold drives out silver, however much this sequence may contradict the chronology of the poets." The "chronology of the poets" refers to the sequence of the five Ages of Man from Ovid's *Metamorphoses*, beginning with the idyllic Golden Age and ending with the present-day Iron Age, full of hardship and discord.

The Social Metabolism and Its Form Aspect
(198 to third paragraph 199)

The first four paragraphs of part a) are an overall introduction to the subsection on money as a means of circulation:

> We saw in a former chapter that the exchange of commodities implies contradictory and mutually exclusive conditions. The further development of the commodity does not abolish these contradictions, but rather provides the form within which they have room to move. This is, in general, the way in which real contradictions are resolved. (198)

It's common to refer to this passage when dealing with the concept of contradiction in Marx's work or the relationship between Marx's and

Hegel's dialectics. However, what interests us here is not these sentences' possibly far-reaching philosophical implications, but rather their concrete meaning in the present argument.

In the first sentence, Marx refers to "the exchange of commodities." Let's recall that in chapter 1 Marx dealt with the "exchange-relation of commodities"; he analyzed commodities' form determinations but not the behavior of commodity owners. Marx first does so in chapter 2, "The Process of Exchange," where he shows that people's actions have to follow the commodity's previously analyzed form determinations if they want to act and exchange as commodity owners. In the rest of chapter 3, the analysis of the commodity and money's form determinations and the analysis of the commodity owners' actions are still separated in terms of *content*, with the analysis of the form determinations remaining primary. However, in the *presentation* both levels are now frequently intertwined.

The first sentence refers to the contradictory requirements commodity owners bring to the exchange process, which Marx examined in chapter 2 (see 180ff.). That chapter presented the owners all relating their commodities to money as a solution to these contradictions. Here the problem will be investigated further. The second sentence above mentions the "further development of the commodity." This does not refer to a *historical* development, but rather to the *conceptual* development of the commodity's further determinations, as can easily be seen in what follows. Those further determinations do not eliminate the contradictory relationships, but rather provide "the form within which they have room to move." That, at least, is Marx's claim, but he still has to demonstrate that it is actually the case.

The quote's third sentence merely emphasizes that Marx does not consider his point—that contradictions are not abolished, but rather find a form in which to move—to be anything unusual. The example that follows in the text refers to the movement of two bodies under the influence of gravitational force. The bodies' movement depends upon their mass, speed, and direction of movement. There are basically three possibilities: (1) the bodies fall toward each other and collide; (2) the bodies approach each other, but do not collide, and are deflected in their orbits, moving away from each other; (3) the lighter body approaches the heavier body and is deflected, but does not possess enough energy to permanently move away from the heavier body. The smaller body thus moves in an elliptical course around the larger one. This is the case, for example, in the orbits of the planets around the sun. Marx has this last possibility in mind when mentioning the ellipse as the form of motion in which the "contradiction is both realized and resolved" (198).

Commodities and Money

> In so far as the process of exchange transfers commodities from hands in which they are non-use-values to hands in which they are use-values, it is a process of social metabolism. The product of one kind of useful labour replaces that of another. (198)

Here, pay close attention to the language. Marx does not write: "the process of exchange *is* social metabolism," but rather "in so far as the process of exchange." This implies that the process of exchange has many aspects, but "in so far" as it transfers products from one person to another, it is a process of "social metabolism."

Marx thus far has only mentioned metabolism in *Capital* in one other passage. On page 133[33] he referred to "useful labor" as a condition of human existence, independent of all social forms, that mediates "the metabolism between man and nature." Here he is not speaking of metabolism alone, but rather "social metabolism," the changing of hands of products that occurs wherever there is a social division of labor.

All societies with a division of labor require a "social metabolism." However, there are different social forms in which this metabolism can occur; the exchange of commodities is just one of these (distribution by a guiding authority or the associated producers themselves would be another form of social metabolism). Once more, Marx is emphasizing the difference between *material content* and *social form*. (He addressed this difference for the first time on page 126, presenting use-values as the material content of wealth, which in capitalist societies takes on the social form of a "collection of commodities.") The social metabolism, that is, products changing hands, is the material content of the process, whereas its specific social form is the exchange of commodities.

> Once a commodity has arrived at a situation in which it can serve as a use-value, it falls out of the sphere of exchange into that of consumption. But the former sphere alone interests us here. We therefore have to consider the whole process in its formal aspect, that is to say, the change in form or the metamorphosis of commodities through which the social metabolism is mediated. (198f.)

Our focus now is the *form aspect* of the social metabolism, that is, the

---

33. Therefore, the translator's comment on page 198 of *Capital* that this is the first use of "metabolism" is wrong.

process of commodity exchange. However, Marx uses the term *form* in a dual sense here. On the one hand, he contrasts the process's *social form* to its material content. On the other, the social form examined here (commodity exchange) involves a *change of form*—the exchanged commodity's form changes. For that reason, the subsection bears the title "The Metamorphosis of Commodities."

In the next paragraph, Marx accuses economists of "very imperfectly" grasping "this change of form," thus indirectly emphasizing his own investigation's originality. In explaining the economists' imperfect understanding, he mentions their lack of clarity concerning the concept of value. On the other hand, he criticizes how they only pay attention to the material aspect in the exchange of the "ordinary commodity" with "the money commodity." This amounts to overlooking "what has happened to the form of the commodity" (199). In other words, in dealing with money, they overlook the money-*form*. We should recall that, when introducing the section on the value-form in chapter 1, Marx indicated that he wished to demonstrate the "origin of this money-form" (139), which is something that bourgeois economists never even attempted. If Marx's claim about bourgeois economics is correct, that on the level of the exchange-relation (presented in chapter 1) the money-*form* was overlooked, then it's hardly surprising that when the economists consider the process of exchange, they also neglect the money-*form*.

In the next paragraph, Marx sketches the starting point for the commodity's change of form. In doing so, Marx is picking up on what he said earlier with regard to the exchange process (182f.): it produces a doubling of the commodity into, on the one hand, commodity and, on the other, money,

> an external opposition which expresses the opposition between use-value and value which is inherent in it. In this opposition, commodities as use-values confront money as exchange-value. (199)

Note that here (and further below), it would be more correct to say "value" than "exchange-value."[34] Yet how is this confrontation possible between commodity as use-value vs. money as value, if on both sides

---

34. As in the *Contribution to the Critique of Political Economy*, Marx in the first edition of *Capital* did not yet strictly distinguish between value and exchange-value. He first did so in the second edition, but there he only somewhat revised the text of chapter 3, in contrast to chapter 1, with the result that this terminological inexactness persists in many passages of the former.

Commodities and Money 231

there is only a commodity, hence the *unity* of use-value and value? Marx's answer:

> But this unity of differences is expressed at two opposite poles, and at each pole in an opposite way. This is the alternating relation between the two poles. (199)

On the side of the commodity, we can see that:

> the commodity is in reality a use-value; its existence as a value appears only ideally, in its price, through which it is related to the real embodiment of its value, the gold which confronts it as its opposite. (199)

The claim that the commodity is "in reality" a use-value means that our senses can grasp its physical, useful properties. This also holds, by the way, if the commodity is a service. I can observe and feel how a barber cuts my hair. By contrast, our senses cannot grasp the commodity's value-objectivity. The price "ideally" expresses this value-objectivity, in an "imaginary form" (see 189 corrected translation). The commodity's "real" (sensually tangible) value shape is the gold that confronts it as money, and the commodity relates to it through its price. Marx claimed that the "first peculiarity" of the "equivalent form" is that "use-value becomes the form of appearance of its opposite, value" (148).

On the side of the gold confronting the commodity as money, we encounter:

> Inversely, the material of gold ranks only as the materialization of value, as money. It is therefore in reality exchange-value [more exactly: *value*]. Its use-value appears only ideally in the series of expressions of relative value within which it confronts all the other commodities as the totality of real embodiments of its utility. (199)

Marx chooses his words carefully here. He does not write that the material of gold "is" the materialization of value, but rather that it "ranks as" (*gilt als*) the materialization of value. Assuming the relationship of validation, money is then "in reality" value: as gold, value can be grasped by the senses, and in this sensuous shape gold "counts" (*gilt*) as the materialization of value.

The use-value of money that Marx mentions now is *not* the use-value of the money *material*. The money material that Marx is considering, which is gold, has the use-value of serving as jewelry and tooth fillings. Gold has this use-value independently of its being the money-commodity. When gold is *money*, however, it has the *additional* use-value. In chapter 2, Marx refers to a "formal use-value" (184) of being directly exchangeable for all other commodities. Marx refers here to the expanded relative form of value, because it makes visible this formal use-value of money.

In the paragraph's final sentence, Marx anticipates something that must be confirmed in the upcoming analysis:

> These antagonistic forms of the commodities are the real forms of motion of the process of exchange. (199)

Let's summarize these "antagonistic forms":

- Commodity: real use-value (based on the commodity-body) vs. ideal value (based on the expression of value in price)
- Money: real value (based on a relationship of validation) vs. ideal use-value (the formal use-value of being exchangeable for all other commodities only exists ideally, in money's relative form of value).

ADDENDUM: In the *Contribution to the Critique of Political Economy*, Marx characterizes this kind of confrontation between the commodity and money in the exchange process as a

> dual and opposite relation in which each extreme is nominal where its opposite is real, and real where its opposite is nominal. (MECW 29: 326)

He aptly describes the relation as "presenting commodities as bilateral polar opposites" (MECW 29: 326). It was during his investigation of the simple form of value that Marx first spoke of poles in chapter 1 of *Capital* (139). My commentary on this explained what Marx means by poles: two aspects that mutually condition, but also mutually exclude, each other. Here, we are dealing with *two* connected polar antagonisms: real use-value vs. ideal/nominal use-value and ideal/nominal value vs. real value. For that reason, he calls the relation "dual."[35]

---

35. Dieter Wolf (1985, 271ff.) thoroughly deals with this dual-polar antagonism.

Commodities and Money 233

Introduction to the Investigation of the Metamorphosis of the Commodity (last paragraph 199 to fourth paragraph 200)

After the general introduction to section 2, on which I have just commented, the final paragraph on page 199 and the first four paragraphs on page 200 introduce the treatment of the metamorphosis of the commodity. By emphasizing the role of the commodity owner—"Let us now accompany the owner of some commodity, say our old friend the linen weaver"—Marx makes clear that he will present people's actions and the underlying form-determinations together. He uses the example of the linen weaver, who first exchanges linen for money and then this money for a Bible. Here Marx explains that the commodity's exchange process is "accomplished through two metamorphoses of opposite yet mutually complementary character—the conversion of the commodity into money, and the re-conversion of the money into a commodity" (200).

In a footnote to this passage, Marx quotes Ferdinand Lassalle (1825–1864), commenting that he "erroneously makes money a mere symbol of value" (200n16). This statement anticipates what is to come. So far Marx hasn't used the expression "symbol of value," which is a theme that the next section, "Coin: The Symbol of Value," will treat for the first time. It's likely that Marx's main motive in mentioning Lassalle's text is that he wanted to distance himself from the latter's views, which were popular in the German labor movement.

For the linen weaver, the commodity metamorphosis means that "instead of his original commodity, he now possesses another of the same value but of different utility" (200). The exchange of commodities C – M – C is for him merely a way to mediate the exchange of products, C – C.

Let's recall how chapter 1 of *Capital* begins. Marx's subject matter was the commodity in capitalism (opening sentence, 125). Nonetheless, he began his investigation of exchange-value by considering the exchange relation C – C, which is not typical of capitalism. Marx abstracted from the *price determined* commodity familiar to us in everyday life, since the categories of money and price did not yet exist at this early stage of the presentation. However, the *exchange-relation* C – C examined then was not a random abstraction, but rather the content of the *exchange process* C – M – C. Since then, the categories *money* and *price* have been developed, and now we are dealing with the exchange process involving *price-determined* commodities. (The presentation in this chapter's first subsection, "The Measure of Value," yielded the price-determined commodity as one of its results.) Hence, it is *only now* that we come to treat the apparently simple relation that is familiar to us in everyday life.³⁶

C – M. The First Metamorphosis: Sale (Supply and Demand on the Market for Commodities, Realization of the Price of the Commodity, Realization of the Ideal Use-Value of Money) (last paragraph 200 to first paragraph 205)

In a single long paragraph that begins on page 200 and ends on page 202, Marx deals with the many difficulties that sale involves. Here, for the first time, he deals more lengthily with *market relations* and the role of *demand*. It is by no means true, as is sometimes claimed, that Marx disregards these questions. However, for Marx the market is not an entity that can be taken for granted. The dominant economic theories, both in Marx's time and today, regard markets as simple, almost natural institutions where the sellers and buyers of products meet and prices are formed. Next, they usually examine the different forms of markets (competitive, monopolistic, oligopolistic, etc.) and their influence on price formation. Or they look at and evaluate the consequences of market participants having disparate information. The market itself, however, is taken to be something completely natural and self-evident. Marx characterizes the market as the "scene of action" (199), but for him commodity owners' actions are anything but natural. Their actions result from the commodity's form-determinations. Markets thus have a number of preconditions—preconditions that prevailing economic theories generally ignore.

ADDENDUM: The sketch of market relations in chapter 3 is far from complete. So far, only the form-determinations of the commodity and money have been developed. After having presented capital's basic form-determinations, Marx will return to market relations in chapter 10 of the third volume of *Capital*.

First, Marx recaps the commodity owner's basic problem. As part of the social division of labor, he usually only produces one type of product. However, the owner's needs are manifold, leading him to depend on other producers' products, which he can only obtain through exchange.

---

36. Footnote 3 on page 54 of this book pointed out that some authors fundamentally misunderstand Marx's presentation when they claim that, at the very beginning of *Capital*, Marx is dealing with a relation that is familiar to us from everyday life.

This *forces* the commodity owner to engage in exchange. Therefore, "the product of his labour serves him solely as exchange-value" (201). Here, the term exchange-value is correct: the commodity owner's product should be an exchange-value for all the products required to satisfy his needs, so that their owners are willing to exchange their products for our commodity owner's product. However, his product is merely a *single* equivalent: "It cannot acquire universal social validity as an equivalent-form except by being converted into money" (201).

In chapter 2, Marx's argument already reached this point. Every commodity owner would like his commodity to be the general equivalent. But since not all commodities can simultaneously serve as the general equivalent, one commodity must be singled out to play this role on its own: it becomes money (see page 180f.). All of this is now assumed. Now we are dealing with the difficulties that every commodity owner encounters when he wishes to transform his particular commodity into money. These difficulties are of both a qualitative and quantitative nature.

Qualitative: Does it stand the test as a use-value? The commodity "must above all be a use-value for the owner of the money. The labor expended on it must therefore be of a socially useful kind" (201). Under the conditions of commodity production, the division of labor "is an organization of production which has grown up naturally, a web which has been, and continues to be, woven behind the backs of the producers of commodities" (201). Hence, it is only in retrospect that one learns whether the commodity satisfies a money owner's need or not. Marx distinguishes between two cases here. First, the product doesn't satisfy any need of a money owner, and therefore cannot be exchanged. Second, the type of product, linen in this case, satisfies a need, but that doesn't mean that the 20 yards of linen of *our* linen weaver satisfies a social need, since the social need may have already been met. In both cases, the linen weaver's product is "superfluous, redundant and consequently useless" (201). But what does that mean? If the product is useless, it does not possess any use-value, at least not "use-value for others." However, as Marx observed in chapter 1, having use-value is a precondition of the product being a commodity (131). Hence we can conclude that a useless product is not a commodity, and therefore does not possess value, regardless of how much labor was expended in its production.

ADDENDUM: In chapter 7, Marx discusses how this unused product is useless and therefore only a "possible," but not "real" use-value (289).

Quantitative: If the product is actually exchanged as a commodity for money, there is still the question: For how much money? The price of the commodity expresses this "how much." However, it's not certain that *the price anticipated by the commodity owner* actually expresses the commodity's *value*. What constitutes value is not individually expended labor-time, but rather "socially necessary" labor-time (129), which depends upon the normal conditions of production. However, what counts as *normal* changes over time. It's possible that, in the market, our linen weaver discovers that what had previously been normal conditions of production are no longer so. If he expended more than the socially necessary labor-time, then his commodity has a lower magnitude of value than he anticipated with his price.

Nevertheless, even if all the linen offered on the market was manufactured under the same normal conditions of production, the total sum of this linen can still contain too much labor-time:

> If the market cannot stomach the whole quantity at the normal price of 2 shillings a yard, this proves that too great a portion of the total social labour-time has been expended in the form of weaving. The effect is the same as if each individual weaver had expended more labour-time on his particular product than was socially necessary. (202)

If the total amount of linen produced exceeds what is socially necessary (or more precisely, if it goes beyond the paying demand), then not all the labor expended in this sector actually created value. However, the value of an individual yard of linen "is also nothing but the materialization of a part of the quantity of social labour expended in the whole amount of the linen" (202n (asterisk footnote)). This means that an individual yard's value is also lower. (The commentary for the first subsection of chapter 1 already dealt with the influence of paying demand on the amount of value-creating labor [see pages 75–76 of this book].)

The sentence from the page 202 asterisk footnote just quoted, corrected by Marx, is more precise than the original sentence in the text of page 202, asserting that the value of an individual yard of linen is "the materialization of the same socially determined quantity of homogeneous human labour." In fact, it's only "the same socially determined quantity," because what counts is not the labor-time *individually* expended upon *this* yard of linen, but rather the proportionate part it represents of the aggregate socially necessary labor-time that produces linen.

Both the commodity's above-mentioned qualitative determination and the quantitative determination of its transformation into money show that the 20 yards of linen's value is not determined on the basis of its individual production process. Instead its value is only determined *with* the production process and the relations to all other commodities that occur in exchange. Only in exchange is it revealed whether a product is useful at all and therefore a commodity. Moreover, only there do we discover what counts as "normal" production conditions and whether the quantity that was produced actually represents a "use-value for others."

In the next paragraph, Marx uses a Shakespeare quote to summarize the difficulties of transforming a commodity into money. The quote comes from the comedy *A Midsummer Night's Dream*, at a moment when the lovers first come together after a series of complications. Marx points here to parallels in the "love affair" between the commodity and money, indicating the general cause of these problems:

> The quantitative articulation [*Gliederung*] of society's productive organism, by which its scattered elements are integrated into the system of the division of labour, is as haphazard and spontaneous as its qualitative articulation. The owners of commodities therefore find out that the same division of labour which turns them into independent private producers also makes the social process of production and the relations of the individual producers to each other within that process independent of the producers themselves; they also find out that the independence of the individuals from each other has as its counterpart and supplement a system of all-round material dependence. (202f.)

It is somewhat misleadingly stated here that the "division of labor" makes commodity owners independent private producers. The next paragraph's beginning is also not quite correct: "The division of labour converts the product of labour into a commodity" (203). In the second subsection of chapter 1, Marx pointed out that the social division of labor can accompany quite different modes of production (132). It's not the social division of labor that transforms products into commodities or creates private production. Rather, it is that the products of *private labor* can only confront one another as commodities. And on the basis of private commodity production, the quantitative and qualitative configuration of the production process is "haphazard and spontaneous."[37] As private commodity producers, individual producers are independent of each other; they decide what and how much to produce at their own discretion. Even so, the social division of labor creates a social connection between them: an "all-round material dependence." The connection among producers is, however, not consciously produced and planned. Therefore it is a matter of chance whether an individual's product fits into this configuration, and will be transformed into money, and if so, how much. That's what Marx means when he writes that "the social process of production and the relations of the individual producers to each other within that process" is independent of the producers. He thus takes up a basic idea already expressed in chapter 1's fetishism section (167f.): under the conditions of commodity production, the social process of production takes on a life of its own, independent of the producers.

ADDENDUM: In the *Grundrisse* (158), Marx characterizes the way the social process of production takes on a life of its own in a dramatic way: "Individuals are subsumed under social production; social production exists outside them as their fate."

In the next paragraph, Marx states that, in what follows despite these difficulties, he assumes that the commodity successfully transforms into money, since here "we have to look at the phenomenon in its pure shape" (203). Without any further explanation, Marx describes the transformation of the commodity into money as "transubstantiation" (203). This is an important concept in Roman Catholic theology—which Marx already used on page 197—referring to how bread and wine transforms into Christ's body and blood. In the Catholic view, an actual metamorphosis occurs in the Mass: bread and wine essentially cease being bread and wine (they only look like it) and actually become Christ's body and blood. By using the term transubstantiation, Marx connects with the commodity's "theological niceties" (163) mentioned in the fetishism section. If all this sounds rather abstruse to a non-Catholic, it is nevertheless a hard reality in capitalist economies, where commodities *are transformed* into money.

In the two paragraphs that follow on page 203, Marx considers the commodity's transformation into money, paying attention only to its change of form. The commodity and money's changing hands in

---

37. The original German is *naturwüchsig zufällig*, which is more accurately translated as "uncontrolled randomly, like nature."

exchange is "striking,"[38] in the sense that anyone can perceive it. Now Marx poses a question that may initially appear superfluous:

> But what is the commodity exchanged for? (203)

If Marx had answered "for money," then the question would indeed have been superfluous, since that simply describes what everyone sees anyway. However, Marx's answer is:

> For the *universal* shape assumed by *its own* value. (203, emphasis M.H.)

What is claimed here is not directly visible, but rather represents the results of an investigation. Marx's analysis of the value-form in chapter 1 demonstrated that commodities must express *their own* value in another commodity, and that this expression of value is only adequate if it is *universal*. Money is the shape of the commodities' *own* value and as the first part of this chapter shows, money is also the *necessary* manifestation of value. With the mere exchange of products, one product exchanges for some other product. However, in the case of *commodity* exchange, a commodity exchanges for *its own* value-shape.

Likewise, Marx asks what gold is exchanged for and answers:

> For a particular form of its own use-value. (203)

As the money-commodity, gold has the universal (formal) use-value of being exchangeable for *all* other use-values. If it now exchanges for a special commodity, then it exchanges for a "particular form" of its universal use-value. Marx now relates both processes to each other.

> The commodity is divested of its original form through its sale. . . . The realization of a commodity's price, or of its merely ideal value-form, is therefore at the same time, and inversely, the realization of the merely ideal use-value of money. . . . This single process is two-sided: from one pole, that of the commodity-owner, it is a sale, from the other pole, that of the money-owner, it is a purchase. In other words, a sale is a purchase, C – M is also M – C. (203)

---

38. The original German is "*sinnfällig*," meaning "obvious to the senses."—*Trans.*

What Marx states in the last two sentences (which might be all that strikes one in a quick read) is not a new or particularly original insight. In a footnote, Marx quotes the French economist Quesnay, who formulated this insight a hundred years before him. What is new and original here is, however, Marx's analysis of the *change of form*. We see the movement of the "bilateral polar opposites" (MECW 29: 326) or "antagonistic forms" (199): the realization of the commodity's merely ideal form of value, its transformation into real value, is at the same time the realization of money's merely ideal use-value. What Marx announced somewhat cryptically on page 199, that the antagonistic forms of the commodity are "the real forms of motion of the process of exchange," is now clearer.

Marx refers for the first time here to the "realization of price," and in the remainder of the chapter he uses this expression several times though he is *not* talking about a realization of value, which is nevertheless an expression often used in the literature about Marx. In Volume 1's later chapters, Marx indeed speaks of the "realization of value" in a few places. However, he does so only in contexts where the categorical difference between value and price (on this difference see the commentary on page 196) does not play a role (see for example p. 681).

In the next paragraph, Marx looks at the source of the money into which the commodity is transformed. In doing so, he cannot consider all the relations that come into play, but only those reached by the *level of presentation so far*:

> Up to this point we have considered only one economic relation between men, a relation between owners of commodities in which they appropriate the produce of the labour of others by alienating [*entfremden*] the produce of their own labour. (203)

Here Marx characterizes buying and selling with very general language, saying that a buyer can only "appropriate" something else by "alienating" something of his own. By contrast, in relationships not based upon exchange—such as a peasant's tribute to a lord, a present made to another person, or transferences from an already existing fund—it is possible to appropriate something without alienating something of one's own.

ADDENDUM: Appendix 1 points out the central role of the concept of "alienation" in the *Economic and Philosophical Manuscripts* of 1844. There, Marx assumes that the "essence of human beings" consists in objectifying themselves in labor to develop their

Commodities and Money 241

abilities as a species. Under capitalist conditions, however, workers do not control the labor process, nor do they dispose of the products of their own labor. The upshot is that they are "alienated" from their human species-being. However, Marx criticizes the notions of a "human essence" and the idea of "alienation" from this essence in the *Theses on Feuerbach* (1845) and in *The German Ideology* (1845–46). Moreover, in texts written after 1845, he no longer employs the notion of "human essence." Still, some literature on Marx claims that the young Marx's discourse on alienation continues more or less without interruption in *Capital*. However, in *Capital* Marx uses the expressions "alienated" or "alienate" only in a few passages, and employs the terms in a very general sense, no longer having anything to do with alienation from a human essence. That's the case here: alienation of one's own product literally means making it somebody else's product, through sale. There is no mention of a "human essence" here.

Assuming that the only economic relations are those between commodity owners, there are only two possible ways to own money (if gold is the money-commodity):

> Leaving aside its exchange for other commodities at the source of production, gold is, in the hands of every commodity-owner, his own commodity divested [*entäußert*] of its original shape by being alienated [*veräußert*]; it is the product of a sale or of the first metamorphosis C – M. (204)

The latter, the selling of commodities, is the more common way of obtaining money: money is the "divested shape" of the "alienated commodity," that is, the shape left over after the commodity's divestment from its original shape. This means that the act of selling is not only simultaneously the act of buying, as Marx's last paragraph claimed. This act of buying is only possible because *another* act of selling preceded it.

As a sort of interim balance, Marx now notes how each of the form-determinations of money developed so far results from a relationship that commodities have to money:

> Gold, as we saw, became *ideal money, or a measure of value*, because all commodities measured their values in it, and thus made it the imaginary opposite of their natural shape as objects of utility, hence the shape of their value. It became *real money* because the commodities, through their complete alienation [corrected translation: sale, *Veräußerung*], suffered a divestiture or transformation of their real shapes as objects of util-

ity, thus making it the real embodiment of their values. (204, emphasis M.H.)

Since all commodities make money the manifestation of their value, money doesn't reveal which particular commodity it is the manifestation of value at a given moment. However, because the money in C – M is the manifestation of the value of an additional commodity, Marx can say:

> The first metamorphosis of one commodity, its transformation from the commodity-form into money, is therefore also invariably the second, and diametrically opposite, metamorphosis of some other commodity, the retransformation of the latter from money into a commodity. (205)

M – C. Second Metamorphosis: Purchase
(second paragraph 205 to first paragraph 206)

These two paragraphs don't really tell us anything new:

> Money is the absolutely alienable [corrected translation: saleable, *veräußerliche*] commodity, because it is all other commodities divested of their shape, the product of their universal alienation [corrected translation: sale, *Veräußerung*]. (205)

Here Marx picks up on the results from his earlier analysis of the general equivalent form: a commodity only occupies the general equivalent form because all other commodities make up the general relative form of value, expressing their value in it (159). Here, however, we're no longer at the level of form analysis, as in chapter 1, but that of the exchange process: the real relationship of commodities to one another. For that reason, the equivalent commodity is no longer simply the material of the *expression of value* of commodities. Now that the other commodities are actually *exchanged* for the general equivalent, it becomes the "divested shape" of the other commodity and as a result the "absolutely saleable commodity." Why so? Because every sale is simultaneously a purchase. If every commodity is alienable for money, then money is likewise alienable for every commodity, therefore becoming the "absolutely saleable commodity"—the general equivalent "has the form of direct exchangeability with all other commodities" (161). Nevertheless, the prices of commodities show gold "the limit of its convertibility, namely its own quantity" (205).

Commodities and Money 243

As Marx emphasizes here, there are no *qualitative* limits to what money can purchase—it can buy everything—but a *quantitative* limit remains.

At the end of the analysis of C – M, Marx emphasized that one commodity's initial metamorphosis C – M is at the same time another commodity's concluding metamorphosis M – C (the linen's initial metamorphosis was at the same time the wheat's concluding metamorphosis). Now that Marx is explicitly considering the concluding metamorphosis (the money obtained for the linen is transformed into a Bible), he points out that this concluding metamorphosis is *another* commodity's initial metamorphosis (the purchase of brandy follows the sale of the Bible).

The Completed Metamorphosis as a Whole
(second paragraph 206 to second paragraph 207)

"The completed metamorphosis of a commodity as a whole" consists of the "two opposite and complementary movements": C – M and M – C. Marx emphasizes that the commodity's change of form can only be consummated through two opposite actions being carried out by commodity owners. As in the case of the sequence of chapters 1 and 2, here the analysis of *economic form-determinations* precedes the analysis of people's *actions*.

The actions of commodity owners "are reflected in the antithetical economic characteristics" (206), those of the *buyer* and the *seller*. However, these are not "fixed roles, but constantly attach themselves to different persons in the course of the circulation of commodities" (206).

In the next paragraph Marx summarizes what the completed metamorphosis of the commodity as a whole presupposes:

- "four denouements," meaning the endpoints of both C – M and M – C
- "three dramatis personae"; there are only three actors, because the seller in the first action is also the buyer in the second act (206).

ADDENDUM: In the *Contribution to the Critique of Political Economy*, Marx looks more deeply into the economic characteristics of the buyer and seller and how they are misinterpreted:

> The commodity owners entered the sphere of circulation merely as guardians of commodities. Within this sphere they confront one another in the antithetical roles of buyer and seller. . . . These distinctive social characters are,

> therefore, by no means due to individual human nature as such, but to the exchange relations of persons who produce their goods in the specific form of commodities.... It is therefore as absurd to regard buyer and seller, these bourgeois economic types, as eternal social forms of human individuality, as it is preposterous to weep over them as signifying the abolition of individuality. They are an essential expression of individuality arising at a particular stage of the social process of production. (MECW 29: 331)

After looking at the buyers' and sellers' actions, Marx returns to analyzing the form-determinations. The two partial processes of the commodity's metamorphosis form a *circuit*: "commodity-form, stripping off of this form, and return to it" (207). Here the commodity begins as a non-use-value for its owner, but at the endpoint becomes a use-value for its owner. In contrast, money starts as a "solid crystal of value," only to disappear again: "it dissolves into the mere equivalent-form of the commodity."

In the above, it was evident that the two partial metamorphoses of a commodity's circuit represent the inverse partial metamorphoses of the circuit of two other commodities. This allows Marx to conclude:

> **Hence the circuit made by one commodity in the course of its metamorphoses is inextricably entwined with the circuits of other commodities. This whole process constitutes the circulation of commodities. (207)**

The term "circulation of commodities," which forms part of this chapter's title, is introduced here systematically for the first time (see the explanations above regarding the chapter heading).

ADDENDUM: In the *Contribution to the Critique of Political Economy*, Marx emphasizes:

> But each individual sale or purchase stands as an independent isolated transaction, whose complementary transaction, which constitutes its continuation, does not need to follow immediately but may be separated from it temporally and spatially. (MECW 29: 330)

That has an important consequence that *Capital* does not explicitly mention:

> In the real process of circulation C – M – C, therefore, represents an exceedingly haphazard coincidence and succession of motley phases of various complete metamorphoses. The actual process of circulation appears, there-

> fore, not as a complete metamorphosis of the commodity, i.e. not as its movement through opposite phases, but as a mere accumulation of numerous purchases and sales which chance to occur simultaneously or successively. The process accordingly loses its distinct form [corrected translation: "The *form-determination of the process is thus extinguished,*" emphasis M.H.]. (MECW 29: 330)

On pages 198 and 199, Marx emphasized the importance of this change of form, but commented that it had been "imperfectly grasped." This "imperfect grasp" is not due to the incompetence of individuals. Instead, it's the process of circulation itself that invisibilizes the change of form, "extinguishing" it.

The Difference Between the Circulation of Commodities and the Exchange of Products, "Socio-natural Connections," the Possibility of Crisis (third paragraph 207 to 209)

> The circulation of commodities differs from the direct exchange of products not only in form, but in its essence. (207)

Marx's reflections on page 200, where he shows that the material content of C – M – C is C – C, might lead one to believe that this is just a formal difference. However, Marx now shows that this only holds for a commodity owner considered in isolation: the linen weaver has exchanged linen for the Bible, but this does not apply to the Bible salesman; he exchanges his Bible for brandy. Even if the exchange of products is completely consummated between two people, concluding for both of them at the same time, there are nevertheless three participants in each "metamorphosis" of C – M – C. Only for one of them does it represent the complete metamorphosis of his commodity. Every single metamorphosis C – M – C presupposes past metamorphoses and leads to future ones. From this, Marx now draws two very different conclusions:

> We see here, on the one hand, how the exchange of commodities breaks through all the individual and local limitations of the direct exchange of products, and develops the metabolic process of human labour. On the other hand, there develops a whole network of social connections of natural origin [corrected translation: a whole network of socio-natural connections, *gesellschaftlicher Naturzusammenhänge*], entirely beyond the control of the human agents. (207)

The first conclusion has to do with the *material content* of exchange: products changing hands, which occurs in every society characterized by a division of labor, is something constantly expanding. For individual producers, this means that the number of different products they can exchange constantly increases. However, this development takes place within a specific *social form-determination*: the products are produced as commodities. This form-determination entails the second consequence: that the expansion of products changing hands takes the shape of a "network of socio-natural connections" beyond the control of people.

The section on commodity fetishism in chapter 1 pointed out that human beings do not control their own social dynamic under commodity production (168). Moreover, Marx has already discussed how the social process of production becomes an entity independent of human beings (202). Now, he speaks of a "network of socio-natural connections." Despite being a product of human beings, society becomes a (second) "nature" under the conditions of commodity production. That is, it becomes a force standing above human beings governed by its own objective laws (which are not something that a human legislator consciously dictates), and people must submit to these laws just as much as to the objective laws of (first) nature. Here Marx follows up on his earlier use of the term "socio-natural properties" (165), not just in terms of the choice of words, but also thematically. Marx earlier pointed out that a fundamental feature of commodity fetishism is that, for producers, the social character of their labor is reflected "as objective characteristics of the products of labour themselves, as the *socio-natural properties* of these things. Hence it also reflects the social relation of the producers to the sum total of labour as a social relation between objects, a relation which exists apart from and outside the producers" (165, emphasis M.H.). In the discussion of the money fetish, Marx also spoke of how a thing appears to possess the general equivalent form as "a socio-natural property [corrected translation]" (187). Now, with the phrase "network of socio-natural connections," Marx is pointing to a new level in the autonomization of the social relations between producers.

Marx observes another difference between the circulation of commodities and the exchange of products. The difference concerns the behavior of money. At the end of the metamorphosis C – M – C, individual commodities ultimately fall out of circulation, disappearing in consumption. Not so with money, which occupies the "point in the arena of circulation vacated by the commodities." Marx sums this up:

> When one commodity replaces another, the money commod-

ity always sticks to the hands of some third person. Circulation sweats money from every pore. (208)

If the process of circulation continues, then the money that "sweats" out of circulation will eventually flow back into it. However, it can't be assumed that this happens automatically. In the long paragraph that follows (208f.), Marx criticizes the "dogma" that there is an "equilibrium between sales and purchases" which also plays an important role—as Say's Law—in contemporary neoclassical theory. Marx begins by examining what "equilibrium" might mean.

If it means only that there are exactly as many purchases as sales, then it's a "flat tautology." A tautology is a statement that's always correct—for example, "tomorrow it will either rain or not rain"—but for that reason conveys little information (the example doesn't help us decide whether to take an umbrella tomorrow). The statement Marx refers to is tautological, because every act of purchase is simultaneously an act of sale. In that sense, the number of purchases is always equal to the number of sales. However, this "flat tautology" is not what is meant:

Its real intention is to show that every seller brings his own buyer to market with him. (208)

Marx's assertion here is not entirely correct. Literally, it would mean that no seller is ever unsuccessful, since he would always find a buyer for his commodity. Yet neither classical nor neoclassical economics would go so far as to make such a claim.

ADDENDUM: In the *Contribution to the Critique of Political Economy*, Marx describes more fully what he means by "dogma" here. There, Marx recaps James Mill's views:

There can never be a lack of buyers for all commodities. Whoever offers a commodity for sale wants to obtain another in exchange for it, and is therefore a buyer through the mere fact of being a seller. Thus, the buyers and sellers of all commodities taken together must, through a metaphysical necessity, balance each other. Hence if there are more sellers than buyers of one commodity, there must be more buyers than sellers of another commodity. (MECW 29: 333)

This is not a literal quote from Mill (in particular, Mill does not refer to a "metaphysical necessity"), but rather Marx's summary of Mill's ideas (for the original passages of Mill that Marx summarizes see MEGA II/2, 386f.). However, the summary aptly captures the dogma's driving idea: it is not that every single act of sale is successful, but rather that, on the market, total supply equals total demand. If there is a surplus of supply for one type of commodity (for example, linen), then there must at least be a surplus of demand for another commodity (for example, brandy). Marx directs his critique at this claim.

In the next two sentences, Marx lays out the conditions under which purchase and sale are identical, and under which conditions they are not:

> Sale and purchase are one *identical* act, considered as the alternating relation *between two persons who are in polar opposition to each other*, the commodity-owner and the money-owner. (208, emphasis M.H.)

The weaver's selling the linen is identical to its purchase by the former wheat owner (Marx's example is on page 204). Nevertheless, the people participating are "in polar opposition to each other": one person is a commodity owner (seller), the other a money owner (buyer).

> They [sale and purchase] constitute *two acts, of polar and opposite character*, considered as the transactions of one and *the same* person. (128, emphasis M.H.)

The same person, our linen producer, appears as both a seller (he sells the linen) and as a buyer (he purchases a Bible). For the same person, then, purchase and sale are *not identical*, but rather "two acts of polar and opposite character." This non-identity of purchase and sale for the same person is, however, not something that is merely formal and unimportant. In fact, it has far-reaching consequences:

> No one can sell unless someone else purchases. But no one directly needs to purchase because he has just sold. (208f.)

In the previous paragraph (208), Marx already emphasized that circulation constantly "sweats" money, and money "sticks to the hand of some third person." The sale of the linen (as the concluding metamorphosis of the wheat) leaves money "stuck" to the linen weaver's hand; the sale of the Bible (as the concluding metamorphosis of the linen) leaves money "stuck" to the Bible salesman's hand. The money can get stuck for a shorter or longer period of time. If the linen weaver does not want to buy a Bible right away with the money he received, then the Bible salesman is left with

Commodities and Money 249

his book. The brandy seller is now also left with his beverage, since the Bible salesman has no money with which to buy it.

Marx now arrives at the key conclusion:

> To say that these mutually independent and antithetical processes [sale and purchase] form an internal unity is to say also that their internal unity moves forward through external antitheses. [Why? Because they confront each other "independently." M.H.] These two processes lack internal independence because they complement each other. Hence, if the assertion of their external independence [äusserliche *Verselbständigung*] proceeds to a certain critical point, their unity violently makes itself felt by producing—a crisis. (209)

Here we have before us the most general conceptualization of a crisis. In everyday understanding, an economic crisis is a matter of businesses not selling their products, bankruptcies, worker layoffs, and fall in incomes. Here, however, Marx emphasizes that a crisis asserts the "unity" of the autonomous parts of an interrelated whole. The sale and purchase of commodities belong together, forming part of the social metabolism—not of the social metabolism as such, but of social metabolism when it takes place under the commodity regime. Here, however, they have become autonomous from one another. If many people retain money, that interrupts considerably the circulation of commodities. A linen weaver may want to constantly sell his linen without purchasing anything. However, he will soon be stuck with his linen if others likewise cease to purchase things. Consumer reluctance (on a large scale) leads to an overall excess in commodity supply. In a crisis, this excess supply is "forcefully" eliminated when the producers go bankrupt. This is a way of asserting, for the time being, the inner unity of purchase and sale, supply and demand.

In the sentence that follows, Marx enumerates all the contradictions (the terms "antithesis," *Gegensatz*, and "contradiction," *Widerspruch*, are used interchangeably) that become the forms of motion of the metamorphosis of commodities. In this way, Marx follows up on what he said in the introductory paragraph to the "Means of Circulation" subsection. There he spoke of how the commodity's (conceptual) development demonstrates the form in which its contradictory determinations have room to move (see 198). Marx has already dealt with all the contradictions enumerated here. However, two expressions that he uses to characterize the last contradiction are new: "the conversion of things into persons and the conversion of persons into things" (209). Nevertheless, it's clear that this phrase refers to the fetish character of the commodity. In the fetishism section, Marx had emphasized that the fetish is real. For commodity producers, "the social relations between their private labours appear as what they are, i.e. they do not appear as direct social relations between persons in their work, but rather as material relations between persons and social relations between things" (166). These things, which have acquired social properties, are thus "personified," made into quasi-acting persons. By contrast, individuals do not *directly* relate their labor to one another. They do so only through the *mediation of things* and are subordinated to the movement of these things (as Marx makes clear on page 168). In that sense, one can speak of "the conversion of persons into things." Marx concludes with an important restriction:

> These forms [the antitheses involved in the metamorphoses of commodities] therefore imply the possibility of crises, though no more than the possibility. For the development of this possibility into a reality a whole series of conditions is required, which do not yet even exist from the standpoint of the simple circulation of commodities. (209)

Separating purchase and sale—such as when no further purchase follows the sale of the linen—is initially just a *possibility*. It is not yet clear how and why this possibility sometimes becomes a reality. At the level of presenting the commodity and money, we are still abstracting from capital and here for the first time Marx describes this level of presentation as "the simple circulation of commodities." At this level, we can only ascertain the "possibility of crises." That possibility is rooted in the characteristic that distinguishes commodity circulation from the direct product exchange: the mediation of money.

ADDENDUM: The *Contribution to the Critique of Political Economy* is clearer on this matter: "Although circulation of money can occur therefore without crises, crises cannot occur without circulation of money" (MECW 29: 332).

In footnote 24 on page 209, Marx briefly touches on the "method of the bourgeoisie's economic apologists," that is, the defenders of capitalist relations. On the one hand, they tend to identify commodity circulation with the simple exchange of products. This is the case with the "dogma" (Say's Law) that Marx just criticized. According to this doctrine, there is an equilibrium between sale and purchase and thus crises are impossible. The claim is justified by abstracting from money and dissolving commodity circulation into the exchange of mere products. On the other hand, Marx continues, the apologists tend to reduce the capitalist production process to the relationships of simple commodity circulation. This claim anticipates later material in *Capital*, since we have not yet arrived at the analysis of the capitalist process of production.

Footnote 24 contains the following important observation:

> The production and circulation of commodities are however phenomena which are to be found in the most diverse modes of production, even if they vary in extent and importance. If we are only familiar with the abstract categories of circulation, which are common to all of them, we cannot know anything of their differentia specifica, and we cannot therefore pronounce judgment on them. (209n24)

We have already brought up Engels's conception of "simple commodity production," dealing with the idea in my commentary on the sentence "They do this without being aware of it" (166) (see pages 158–59 of this book). In footnote 24, Marx makes clear that he does *not* assume that "simple commodity production" existed in history as an independent mode of production. Commodity production and the circulation of commodities appear in different modes of production, but as subordinate aspects and with different characteristics. A sentence from the section on fetishism points in exactly the same direction:

> As the commodity-form is the most general and the most undeveloped form of bourgeois production, it makes its appearance at an early date, though not in the same predominant and therefore characteristic manner as nowadays. (176)

The expression "means of circulation" appeared above in the heading of this chapter's second part. Now in the concluding sentence of subsection a), "The Metamorphosis of the Commodity," Marx returns to the expression and refines it: "As the mediator of the circulation of commodities, money obtains the function of the means of circulation" (MEW 23: 128).[39]

---

39. This sentence is completely omitted from the English translation in the Penguin edition.—Trans.

Nota bene: these days another expression is often used for this function of money, namely "means of payment." Marx also uses the expression in section 3 of this chapter, but in a different sense.

b) The Circulation of Money

The Circulation of Commodities and the Semblance Generated by It (210 to third paragraph 212)

On pages 207–8, Marx briefly addressed the commodity and money's different forms of motion. The linen that the weaver sells returns to him in the shape of a Bible, but the money he spends to purchase the Bible no longer returns to him. If the weaver receives money again, it is only through the renewed sale of linen—that is, by repeating the process. Within the framework of the transformation C – M – C, the commodity moves in a *circuit*: it leaves its starting point but returns to it in a different shape. By contrast, money merely moves away from its starting point; it is characterized by *circulation*.

As it circulates, money constantly repeats the same process. It functions as "a means of purchase by realizing the price of the commodity" (211). However, this visible process hides something:

> That this one-sided form of motion of the money arises out of the two-sided form of motion of the commodity is a circumstance which is hidden from view. The very nature of the circulation of commodities produces a semblance of the opposite. (211)

The first metamorphosis of the commodity, its sale, is still visible as one of its movements. But then, as a use-value, the commodity drops out of circulation into consumption. What remains in circulation is only the commodity's value shape (Marx refers to this as its "skin" and "monetary larva"). However, it is no longer visible as the *manifestation of a commodity's value*, but only as money, which goes on buying.

> Hence the result of the circulation of commodities, namely the replacement of one commodity by another, appears not to have been mediated by its own change of form, but rather by the function of money as means of circulation. As means of circulation, money circulates commodities, which in and for themselves lack the power of movement. . . . Hence although the movement of money is merely the expression of the circu-

lation of commodities, the situation appears to be the reverse of this, namely the circulation of commodities seems to be the result of the movement of money. (211f.)

ADDENDUM: The *Contribution to the Critique of Political Economy* explains the significance of this reversal more fully:

> Just as commodity owners presented the products of individual labour as products of social labour, by transforming a *thing*, i.e. gold, into the direct embodiment of labour time in general and therefore into money, so now their own universal movement by which they bring about the exchange of the material elements of their labour confronts them as the specific *movement of a thing*, i.e. as the circulation of gold. (MECW 29: 336, emphasis M.H.)

In *Capital*, Marx referred to the first point—a thing becoming the embodiment of labor time in general—as the "money fetish" (187), and here he is dealing with a further development of money fetishism. When addressing commodity fetishism in *Capital*, Marx said that if value is indeed a relation among people, one should not forget to add: "a relation concealed beneath a material shell [corrected translation: beneath the shell of a thing, *unter dinglicher Hülle*]" (167n29). Here, we see an extension of money fetishism: not only is the relationship between people concealed under the shell of a thing, but their *own movement* confronts them *as the movement of a thing*.

In the next paragraph, Marx explains:

> Hence its [money] movement, as the medium of circulation, is in fact merely the movement undergone by commodities while changing their form. (212)

What is most fundamental is the commodities changing their form. The movement of money is dependent upon this transformation and merely expresses it. However, Marx emphasizes:

> It is in any case evident that all this is valid only for the simple circulation of commodities, the form we are considering here. (212)

As on page 209, Marx is emphasizing the presentation's level of abstraction. Consequently, in more developed relations, the relationship between the commodity and the movement of money may have characteristics completely different from those addressed so far.

The Amount of the Means of Circulation, Critique of Quantity Theory
(final paragraph 212 to 220)

Whereas commodities constantly drop out of circulation, money remains in circulation functioning as a means of circulation. The question arises: how much money is required? Before Marx addresses this, he specifies that "in the direct form of circulation being considered here, money and commodities always come into physical confrontation with each other" (213). In effect, he is assuming that payments are made in cash, excluding from consideration deferrals of payment on the part of the buyer, which transforms seller and buyer into creditor and debtor respectively (a possibility considered in this chapter's third section). Given this assumption, the sum of the commodities' prices will determine the amount of means of circulation required: to buy commodities priced at 100 pounds sterling, one needs money in the amount of 100 pounds sterling. Marx next qualifies this general statement in three regards, taking into account the value of money (213–15), the prices and amount of commodities (214), and money's velocity of circulation (215–17)

The value of money. Here Marx picks up on his reflections on pages 144–46, where he looked at how the relative form of value is determined in a quantitative sense. A change in the value relation of commodities A and B in turn alters the quantitative expression of value of commodity A in commodity B. As far as prices are concerned, this means that with "the values of commodities remaining constant, their prices vary with the value of gold (the material of money), rising in proportion as it falls, and falling in proportion as it rises" (213). For example, if the value of gold is halved, but the value of commodities remains the same, one will have to pay two ounces of gold for all commodities that previously cost one ounce. Additionally, twice as much gold will be required for circulation. This is now explained more generally:

> First the price of the commodities varies inversely as the value of the money, and then the quantity of the medium of circulation varies directly as the price of the commodities. (213)

A change in commodity prices leads to a change in the amount of money. But the former is due to a change in the value of money. Hence Marx concludes:

> This change in the quantity of the circulating medium is cer-

tainly caused by the money itself, yet not in virtue of its function as a medium of circulation, but rather in virtue of its function as a measure of value. (213)

In reference to the discovery of new sources of gold and silver in the seventeenth and eighteenth centuries, Marx mentions the "false conclusion" that commodity prices rose then because more gold and silver entered into circulation (214). In fact, exactly the reverse happened. Gold and silver could now be extracted with less labor from the newly discovered sources, causing the money material's value to decline. For that reason, prices increased, and the rise in prices led to more means of circulation being required, which in turn was actually extracted from the sources. (*Contribution to the Critique of Political Economy* deals more extensively with this, MECW 29: 392–96.). Marx will return to this "false conclusion" again on page 220. In the following, he presupposes that money's value remains constant.

Prices and the Amount of Commodities. If money's value remains constant, then the sum of the commodities' prices determines the amount of means of circulation. The sum of prices, in turn, results from the amount of commodities and their price levels. There are then two possibilities that can cause changes in the sum of commodity prices and thus the amount of means of circulation:

- If the prices of the commodities remain constant, then the sum of prices depends on the amount of commodities circulating.
- If the amount of commodities remains constant, then the sum of prices depends on the commodity prices, although, as Marx emphasizes, it doesn't matter whether the price changes express a real change in commodity values or mere fluctuations of market prices (215).

Velocity of Money's Circulation. Individual sales occur not only simultaneously, but successively. Hence, the same piece of money can realize multiple prices, reducing the required amount of means of circulation. Marx presents a formula expressing this relationship, which in the Penguin edition is transformed into a sentence (216):

$$\frac{\text{the sum of the prices of the commodities}}{\text{the number of times coins of the same denomination turn over}} = \text{the quantity of money functioning as means of circulation}$$

There are three things to note about this formula. *First*, since there are monetary units and coins of different value in circulation, the denominator on the left side should contain the weighted average of their various turnover times. Today this average is referred to as money's "velocity of circulation." Contemporary economic theories use this formula or similar ones, referring to it as "Fisher's equation" (named for the American economist Irving Fisher, 1867–1947). *Second*, on the right side, Marx's language is very precise. He refers to the quantity of *money functioning as the means of circulation*; that is, not the total amount of money, but only that part of money in circulation. *Third*, the equation only speaks for the equality of two magnitudes, but says nothing about causal connections, nothing about *why* the magnitudes are equal. For example, if the number of theater attendees equals the number of seats in the theater, I don't know whether other potential attendees were refused when the theater filled up or if all were allowed in by providing additional seats. The same is true here. The equation does not explain whether the total means of circulation adjusts to the sum of prices and velocity of circulation or, on the contrary, the sum of prices and velocity of circulation adjust to the total means of circulation. Marx, nevertheless, has a clear position on this question. Above, he described the idea that variations in the amount of means of circulation cause changes in price as a "false conclusion."

ADDENDUM: Marx makes his own view on the causal relationship explicit in the *Contribution to the Critique of Political Economy*:

> If the velocity of circulation is given, then the quantity of the means of circulation is simply determined by the prices of commodities. Prices are thus high or low not because more or less money is in circulation, but there is more or less money in circulation because prices are high or low. (MECW 29: 341)

In the following paragraph Marx summarizes his fundamental argument for this causal relation—for a given value of money, the amount of means of circulation depends on the sum of prices and velocity of circulation:

> Just as the circulation of money is in general merely a reflection of the process of circulation of commodities, i.e. their circular path through diametrically opposed metamorphoses, so too the velocity of circulation of money is merely a reflection of the rapidity with which commodities change their forms, the continuous interlocking of the series of metamorphoses. (217)

Based on this last claim, Marx draws another conclusion:

> Inversely, when the circulation of money slows down, the two processes become separated, they assert their independence and mutual antagonism; stagnation occurs in the changes of form, and hence in the metabolic process. The circulation itself, of course, gives no clue to the origin of this stagnation. (217)

If the total means of circulation results from the sum of prices of the commodities (which in turn depend on the amount of commodities and their prices) and the velocity of money's circulation, then very different outcomes are possible. Marx addresses a few of these on pages 218 and 219. Due to the large number of these possibilities, a change in the price of commodities doesn't necessarily mean that there has been a corresponding change in the amount of means of circulation. Commodity prices can remain the same, and the amount of means of circulation can nonetheless change. However, it can also occur that commodity prices change, but the total means of circulation remains constant. Both cases are possible, because other factors are involved. Only abstracting from these factors does the relationship between the sum of prices and the total means of circulation become clear.

In the last paragraph, Marx summarizes his conclusion:

> The law that the quantity of the circulating medium is determined by the sum of the prices of the commodities in circulation, and the average velocity of the circulation of money, may also be stated as follows: given the sum of the values of commodities [more precisely, *the sum of prices of the commodities*, since as Marx pointed out on page 215, price changes even without changes in value have the same effect] and the average rapidity of their metamorphoses, the quantity of money or of the material of money in circulation depends on its own value. (219)

Marx describes, by way of contrast with his conclusion, the conception underlying the "false conclusion" mentioned above:

> The illusion that it is, on the contrary, prices which are determined by the quantity of the circulating medium, and that the latter for its part depends on the amount of monetary material which happens to be present in a country, had its roots in the absurd hypothesis adopted by the original representatives

> of this view that commodities enter into the process of circulation without a price, and money enters without a value, and that, once they have entered circulation, an aliquot part of the medley of commodities is exchanged for an aliquot part of the heap of precious metals. (220)

In footnote 31, Marx presents Montesquieu as a "representative" of this view. He dealt more extensively with Montesquieu in the part of the *Contribution to the Critique of Political Economy* dealing with the history of theory (MECW 29: 390ff.).

Today's neoclassical economic theory also promotes the idea, under the name of the "quantity theory of money," that the total money in circulation determines the level of prices. In countries like Germany, where there is a great fear of inflation, the belief that an increased amount of money automatically leads to price increases forms part of everyday consciousness, influencing many debates on economic policy.

Marx clearly rejects the "quantity theory" here, but that doesn't mean the topic is settled. We have to recall the level of abstraction at which his arguments take place: that of the "simple circulation of commodities" where the commodity and money are considered in abstraction from capital. Moreover, we continue to assume "the direct form of circulation" (without any form of credit) in which "money and commodities always come into physical confrontation with each other" (213).

ADDENDUM: Ricardo promoted a quantity theory of money that would play a role in English banking legislation in the 1840s. In Volume 3 of *Capital*, Marx deals with this legislation and its consequences for the credit system.

c) Coin. The Symbol of Value

> Money takes the shape of coin because of its function as the circulation medium. (221)

For the real circulation of commodities, their "money-names" (as Marx calls their prices here) are not sufficient; the commodity must find itself face-to-face with actual *coin*. In this chapter's first part, "The Measure of Values," Marx dealt with coin in the course of his discussion of money as the standard of price: he pointed out that the individual weights of gold (as the money commodity) acquire their own money-names, which are ultimately set by the state. The state also undertakes the minting of gold into coins, so that the coins are universally recognized.

Coin in the Process of Circulation
(second paragraph 222 to second paragraph 224)

Marx is concerned here with the effects of *actual* use on coins. The "real content" of the coin (the actual gold it contains) comes to deviate from its "nominal content" (what it should contain according to its face value). Nonetheless, the coins still circulate for a while. Marx describes this as the "natural and spontaneous tendency of the process of circulation to transform the coin from its metallic existence as gold into the semblance of gold, or to transform the coin into a symbol of its official metallic content" (222). This lends itself to the possibility "of replacing metallic money with tokens made of some other material, i.e. symbols which would perform the function of coins" (223): silver and copper tokens substitute for gold for small sums, although the metallic content of these tokens no longer has anything to do with the value stamped on them (in this case, one speaks of "small change"). Marx sums this up:

> In its form of existence as coin, gold becomes completely divorced from the substance of its value. Relatively valueless objects, therefore, such as paper notes, can serve as coins in place of gold. This purely symbolic character of the currency is still somewhat disguised in the case of metal tokens. In paper money it stands out plainly. (223f.)

In the next paragraph, Marx makes an important qualification regarding paper money:

> Here we are concerned only with inconvertible paper money issued by the state and given forced currency. This money emerges directly out of the circulation of metallic money. Credit-money on the other hand implies relations which are as yet totally unknown, from the standpoint of the simple circulation of commodities. (224)

Paper money issued by the state and given forced currency refers to paper money that the state issues and must be accepted in making payments (the state also has to accept it in tax payments). By contrast, *credit-money* consists of promises to pay (promissory notes) that can themselves be used as payment: I can pay person B with a promissory note obtained from person A. Hence credit-money presupposes credit relations, which reach their fullest form in the banking system. Here, however, at the level of presentation of simple commodity-circulation, we are only dealing with the relationship between commodities and money.

Up to this point, Marx's argument follows historical developments. It no more than ascertaining the facts of the historical process: the money-commodity being replaced by less valuable—and, finally, worthless—symbols in the process of circulation. However, Marx has not yet answered the questions of *what makes this process possible at all*, and what it means for the analysis of money. He first deals with these questions at the end of the current subsection "c) Coin. The Symbol of Value."

The "Law Peculiar to the Circulation of Paper Money" (third paragraph 224 to first paragraph 225)

So far, Marx's presentation of commodity circulation has assumed that the money commodity itself circulates. Now we come to paper money, which the state puts into circulation to replace gold. Here the question comes up of whether there are laws specific to paper money's circulation (not juridical laws, but economic ones). Marx's answer:

> In so far as they [paper bills] actually circulate in place of the same amount of gold, their movement is simply a reflection of the laws of monetary circulation itself. A law peculiar to the circulation of paper money can only spring up from the proportion in which that paper money represents gold. In simple terms the law referred to is as follows: the issue of paper money must be restricted to the quantity of gold (or silver) which would actually be in circulation, and which is represented symbolically by the paper money. (224)

Why should the issuing of paper money be restricted to this quantity? Marx responds on the next page:

> If the paper money exceeds its proper limit, i.e. the amount in gold coins of the same denomination which could have been in circulation, then, quite apart from the danger of becoming universally discredited, it will still represent within the world of commodities only that quantity of gold which is fixed by its immanent laws. (225)

If a larger amount of paper money is brought into circulation than could be circulated as gold coins, then the paper money is devalued, Marx believes, and the prices expressed in paper money increase. This means that *for paper money*, Marx accepts precisely the quantity theory that he earlier called an "absurd hypothesis" (220) in relation to metallic money.

However, Marx does not provide a justification for his accepting a quantity-theory style "law peculiar to the circulation of paper money." In the first place, it's obvious he has in mind "inconvertible notes": paper money that the state has no obligation to redeem for gold. If the state guaranteed a corresponding amount of gold for every paper note it received, then there could be no law peculiar to the circulation of paper money, since the paper bills could be immediately cashed in for metal if the price of a commodity were higher in paper money than in gold.

Even with the assumption of inconvertible notes, however, the "law" is by no means self-evident. If, for example, the supply of goods is reduced, then presuming that prices and the velocity of circulation remain the same, more money will be available than necessary for circulation. Some of the money remains with the commodity owners who have sold their commodities, thereby reducing the amount of money in circulation. Initially, it doesn't matter whether gold or paper money serves as the means of circulation. The devaluation of paper money that Marx anticipates only occurs if the commodity sellers are not willing to hang on to the paper money for a while, and instead immediately try to spend it. In this case, demand would not adjust to the reduced supply of goods. Demand for commodities based upon paper money would exceed supply, with the consequence that prices (expressed in paper money) would increase, with paper money being devalued in relation to gold. However, the precondition for this whole process is commodity owners being unwilling to hold on to paper money, in contrast to gold money.

Here Marx was probably thinking of the assignats that were issued during and after the French Revolution and of England's temporary suspension of the obligation to redeem pound notes at the beginning of the nineteenth century. The assignats, issued on a large scale to meet the revolutionary government's financial needs, lost much of their value. The devaluation in the case of pound notes, which hadn't been issued in such a large number, wasn't as strong. However, both types of paper money were seen as anomalies at the time. Only metallic money and paper money with a redemption obligation were considered "normal." Removing this obligation made people suspicious of paper money, which was only accepted as payment with a surcharge. But in order for the "peculiar" law that Marx formulates to hold for *every* non-redeemable state paper money with a legal rate of exchange—including those that aren't just issued in exceptional situations—*commodity owners must use all non-redeemable paper money exclusively as a means of circulation.*

ADDENDUM: In the *Contribution to the Critique of Political Economy*, Marx affirms just this:

> Once the notes are in circulation it is impossible to drive them out, for the frontiers of the country limit their movement, on the one hand, and, on the other hand, they lose all value, both use value and exchange value, *outside* the sphere of circulation. Apart from their function they are useless scraps of paper. (MECW 29: 353f.)

In *Capital*, this kind of claim is no longer found. We will soon see that it does not easily fit with what this chapter's third section argues. *Moreover, if paper money can also continue to exist outside of circulation, then Marx's law "peculiar" to paper money's circulation loses its basis.*

The Symbol of Money (second paragraph 225 to 227)

As a mere symbol, paper money represents gold money. Marx concludes from this:

> Only in so far as paper money represents gold, which like all other commodities has value, is it a symbol of value. (226)

Why does Marx give so much importance to this point? In the history of economic theory, there is a longstanding dispute about how to understand money. Many authors have claimed that money does not itself have value, but is only a symbol of value. For Marx, this view was found in Ferdinand Lassalle (200n16). Marx assumed that he himself had deciphered money's nature: it is a commodity like any other commodity and therefore an object of value like other commodities, not merely a symbol of value. What is special about the money-commodity is its *value-form*: the general equivalent form. The money-commodity has this special value-form not due to its intrinsic properties, but rather because all other commodities relate to it as the expression of value. Unlike the money-commodity, paper money *is actually* a symbol of value, but only to the extent that it is a symbol of the money-commodity, with the money-commodity itself being an object of value.

In footnote 35, Marx criticizes John Fullarton, an author he otherwise appreciated. Marx accuses Fullarton of concluding, based on paper

Commodities and Money 263

money replacing the money-commodity in circulation, that the money-commodity is also superfluous as the measure of values. Marx obviously considers this inference to be absurd, and in fact it would be wrong, since the function of money as a means of circulation is distinct from its function as a measure of value. However, Fullarton by no means makes such an inference. He does not claim that, *because* a symbol can replace money in one of its functions, therefore it is also replaceable in another function. Fullarton merely formulates the *suspicion* that non-redeemable notes could render an independent measure of value unnecessary. He does not offer any logical arguments to justify this suspicion. Instead, he refers to historical examples (though not in the part of the text Marx quotes): non-redeemable paper money in Europe (for example the assignats during the French Revolution) and temporarily non-redeemable paper money in England. Nevertheless, Fullarton does not present a categorical grounding for the *possibility* of these empirical facts. For that reason, one cannot accuse him of a logical error, but rather of lacking a theoretical analysis. As it turns out, Fullarton was correct in his suspicion: the contemporary monetary system no longer has a money-commodity, and no object of value serves as the measure of values.

So far Marx has only considered mere symbols replacing the money-commodity as a simple historical fact. Only now does he pose the question of

> why gold is capable of being replaced by valueless symbols of itself. (225)

To better understand Marx's answer, we should recall how bourgeois economists usually answered this question. According to their view, those engaged in exchange accept symbols as payment, because (and as long as) they are sure that other participants in the market will also accept the symbols as payment. If one inquires into the source of their certainty, bourgeois economists typically point to the state. On the one hand, the state compels acceptance of the symbol through legal forced currency (though the state cannot force anyone to *sell*). On the other hand, it protects the "value" of the symbol by making it as counterfeit-proof as possible and by limiting the extent of the symbol's legal manufacture. This explanation thus operates at the level of an institutional and action theory. We will soon see that Marx locates his explanation at a completely different level.

Marx begins by specifying once again the function in which the money commodity is replaced: as an independent means of circulation, that is, as money that *only* serves as a means of circulation (226). It is not single coins that are independent in this way (since they can always perform multiple functions), but rather the minimum mass of money that is constantly in circulation. But why can this money that is constantly in circulation, which is reduced to a mere means of circulation, be replaced by a symbol? Marx's answer:

> The presentation of the exchange-value [more exactly, of *value*][40] of a commodity as an independent entity [in money] is here only a transient aspect of the process. The commodity is immediately replaced again by another commodity. Hence in this process which continually makes money pass from hand to hand, it only needs to lead a symbolic existence. Its functional existence so to speak absorbs its material existence. Since it is a transiently objectified reflection of the prices of commodities, *it serves only as a symbol of itself*, and can therefore be replaced by another symbol. (226, emphasis M.H.)

Marx's explanation here operates on the level of the analysis of forms, not the actions of individuals. In the process C – M – C, in which the commodity simply changes form, money already functions as a mere *symbol*, as a "symbol of itself." Yet if the money-commodity, in its function as the means of circulation, already functions as a mere symbol, then it can—in this function—also be replaced by actual symbols. The individual actors can only do this because it's *possible* to replace the money-commodity with symbols. The state's forced currency gives "objective social validity" (226) to the various symbols (which, as Marx emphasizes, are limited to the sphere of a given community). In doing so, the state *does not make possible* the replacement of money by mere symbols. Instead, it merely *confirms* and *secures* this replacement, which the process's form makes possible.

ADDENDUM: In the *Contribution to the Critique of Political Economy*, Marx points to the specific kind of explanation he has given:

> Our exposition has shown that gold in the shape of coin, that is, tokens of value divorced from gold substance itself, originates in the process of circulation itself and *does not come about by arrangement or state intervention.* (MECW 29: 351, emphasis M.H.)

---

40. See my explanation about the use of *value* and *exchange value* in footnote 34 on page 230 above.

Commodities and Money 265

When considering both the economic actions of individuals and those of the state, Marx distinguishes between, on the one hand, the rationality of the actions and, on the other, the specific forms of economic relations that make these economic actions "rational" in the first place.

3. Money

At first glance, this heading is confusing, since "Money, or the Circulation of Commodities" is the title of this entire chapter. The form-determinations of money should derive from the "processing relations of the commodities to each other" (MECW 29: 292 corrected translation; see the commentary above on this chapter's title). So far, we have dealt with money's key functions as a measure of values and means of circulation, but what is meant here by simply "money"?

Let's briefly look back. Chapter 1 of *Capital* presented the money-*form*: social custom joins the general equivalent *form* to a certain commodity's specific *natural form* (162). Chapter 2 then addressed *money*: a specific commodity comes to have the exclusive function of the general *equivalent*, because of the commodity owners' common activity (which is spontaneous and unplanned). This commodity becomes money (180–81).

Now, under the subheading "3. Money," Marx states succinctly:

> The commodity which functions as a measure of value and therefore also as the medium of circulation, either in its own body or through a representative, is money. (227)

ADDENDUM: In the *Contribution to the Critique of Political Economy,* Marx's account is not so abbreviated:

> In the first place, a commodity in which *the functions of standard of value and medium of circulation are united* accordingly becomes money, or the unity of standard of value and medium of circulation is money. But as such a unity gold [= money] in its turn possesses an independent existence which is distinct from these two functions. (MECW 29: 358, emphasis M.H.)

The claim here is that money, as the unity of the measure of values and means of circulation, is something new that cannot be reduced to the functions already discussed.

Marx only briefly hints at where we can see the operation of this new form-determination of money *as money*. He points to two kinds of situations where money must operate *as money. First*:

> It [gold or silver] functions as money, on the one hand, when it has to appear in person as gold. It is then the money commodity, neither merely ideal, as when it is the measure of value, nor capable of being represented, as when it is the medium of circulation. (227)

The money-commodity's presence is not required for it to function as either a measure of values or means of circulation. To measure values, it must be clear *what* functions as the money-commodity (whether it's gold or something else), but gold does not have to be physically present for a commodity's value to be expressed as a specific quantity of gold. In exchange, *something* must be physically present as a means of circulation, but it doesn't have to be the actual money-commodity, because a representative suffices. Moreover, even if gold is present, "it only serves as a symbol of itself" (226), as Marx said in the previous section. All this means that *we have not yet encountered a situation in which the money-commodity has to be physically present*.

Second:

> On the other hand, it also functions as money when its function, whether performed in person or by a representative, causes it to be fixed as the sole form of value, or, in other words, as the only adequate form of existence of exchange value [more precisely, of value] in the face of all the other commodities, here playing the role of use-values pure and simple. (227)

Here Marx is addressing what money actually is: the sole, independent manifestation of value as distinct from the world of commodities. Money as the sole manifestation of value does not play a direct role in its function as a measure of values or means of circulation. (It does play an *indirect* role, inasmuch as gold becomes the measure of values, only because it counts as the singular manifestation of value with regard to the world of commodities). Importantly, Marx is establishing here that money is able to perform as the *sole manifestation of value*, not only by means of the money-commodity itself, but also through its *representatives*. We will soon come back to the consequences of this.

ADDENDUM: At this point in the *Contribution to the Critique of Political Economy*, Marx identifies two fundamental properties of money *as money*.

Commodities and Money 267

> All prices of commodities signify definite amounts of gold; they are thus merely notional gold or notional money. . . . Gold [as money] is *the material aspect [corrected translation: material existence] of abstract wealth* in contradistinction to commodities which only represent the independent form of exchange value [more precisely, *value*], of universal social labour and of abstract wealth. (MECW 29: 358)

Abstract wealth, value, is not tangible. In money, however, it acquires a "material existence," a material reality, meaning that one can touch and even pocket this abstract wealth.

By contrast, Marx continues, every commodity as a use-value is merely a single element of material wealth, which can only satisfy a specific need.

> But money satisfies any need since it can be immediately turned into the object of any need. . . . Gold [as money] is, *therefore, the material symbol of physical wealth*. (MECW 29: 358)

Based on these two properties, Marx concludes:

> As regards its form, it [gold as money] is the direct incarnation of universal labour, and as regards its content the quintessence of all concrete labour. It is universal wealth in an individual form. (MECW 29: 358)[41]

This points to a change in money's role. As a means of circulation, money was only a mediator, the "servant" of the world of commodities, so to speak. Now, however, this changes:

> The servant becomes the master. The mere underling becomes the god of commodities. (MECW 29: 359)

The sense in which money becomes the "god of commodities," however, will have to be explained in the following.

a) Hoarding

The Hoard as a New Function of Money (227–28)

The first paragraph offers an introductory look at the process of hoarding:

---

41. On the general equivalent as the "individual incarnation" of the universal, see my commentary on the general value form (pages 135–36 of this book) dealing with a similar statement in *Capital*'s first edition (Dragstedt 1976: 27).

the metamorphosis of the commodity is interrupted and coin as means of circulation is retained. Now the second paragraph states:

> When the circulation of commodities first develops, there also develops the necessity and the passionate desire to hold fast to the product of the first metamorphosis. This product is the transformed shape of the commodity, or its gold chrysalis. (227)

The reference to how "the circulation of commodities first develops" above does not point to a *conceptual* but rather *historical* development: the formation of commodity circulation. The next two paragraphs likewise deal with "the very beginnings of the circulation of commodities" and also "more developed commodity production." Marx does not clarify the causes of the "necessity" and "passionate desire" that are supposed to accompany this historical development or even what "passionate desire" is supposed to mean at all. This will only be explained in the following sections, which mention the "lust for gold" (229) and the "hoarding drive" (230).

> Commodities are thus sold not in order to buy commodities, but in order to replace their commodity-form by their money-form. Instead of being merely a way of mediating the metabolic process [*Stoffwechsel*], this change of form becomes an end in itself. (227f.)

Here, an inversion of means and ends takes place: money no longer functions as a means for commodity exchange, the "underling" of commodities (MECW 29: 359). Instead, commodity exchange becomes a means of obtaining money. *Money, the money-form of the commodity, now becomes the end*, the "god of commodities" (referred to in the preceding quote from the *Contribution to the Critique of Political Economy*, MECW 29: 359). This inversion of means and ends is extremely important: Marx discussed the difference between commodity circulation (mediated by money) and the exchange of products on pages 207–8. He pointed out that when money mediates commodity circulation, this means it can be interrupted, which introduces the "possibility of crises" (209). Yet it was still not clear why this possibility should become a reality. Here we have taken a step further: if money is the *aim* of the process, then the metamorphosis of the commodity *must* be interrupted to retain money (though it's still not clear why this should happen on a large scale and generate a crisis).

If this interruption occurs, then money is "petrified into a hoard, and the seller of commodities becomes a hoarder of money" (228). This new form-determination of money as a hoard is accompanied by a new economic "character mask": the "hoarder."

The next two paragraphs deal with the above-mentioned "necessity" of hoarding. When commodity circulation began in history, people only exchanged surplus use-values, so that the gold and silver thus obtained "become of themselves social expressions for superfluity or wealth" (228). As "excess" or "glut," the money's fate was an open question; for example, it could even be buried. This changes, however, with further developed commodity production, when not just surpluses are exchanged:

> With more developed commodity production, every producer is compelled to secure for himself the *nexus rerum* [corrected translation: *nervus rerum*], the "social pledge." (228)

Marx's use of the expression "nervus rerum" plays on the Latin phrase "pecunia nervus rerum": *money is the nerve of all things*. The term in the original German text, "*Faustpfand,*" that is translated here as "social pledge," comes from the right of lien. It refers to a pledge passing over *physically* to the creditor as security for a claim (the creditor then holds the pledge in his fist). The term is used metaphorically here. Since money not only represents value, but value in a directly exchangeable form, it is my "pledge" vis-à-vis society that can be applied anytime.

I need this "pledge" to buy things that can satisfy my needs, even if I have not myself just sold something. Yet to have the money "pledge" in hand, I must have sold something beforehand without buying.

Now, Marx asks how this can be possible "on a general scale." Where is money supposed to come from if commodities are sold on a large scale without buying (hence, with money being taken out of circulation without going back in)? As an answer, Marx mentions the sources of gold and silver production. Gold and silver producers make purchases with these metals, without having sold something beforehand. We can summarize Marx's argument this way: hoarders can remove gold from circulation, because gold producers constantly bring new gold into circulation.

In this way, Marx addresses a topic that today goes under the title "money supply." It's the question of how money comes into circulation at all. If the money system is based on the money commodity gold, then gold production is the initial source for money supply. In fact, the money supply (even for a gold-based currency) is considerably more complicated. Both the credit money of banks and the paper money issued by states play an important role. But here Marx is only dealing with the "simple circulation of commodities," abstracting from capital and credit and therefore also from banks, credit money, and state debt. If Marx is only considering money supply in terms of gold production, that is due to the presentation's level of abstraction.

"The Lust for Gold," "The Hoarding Drive" (229 to third paragraph 231)

> With the possibility of keeping hold of the commodity as exchange-value, or exchange-value [both times, it should be "value" instead of "exchange-value"] as a commodity, the lust for gold awakens. (229)

Marx indeed speaks here of "the lust for gold" and further below of "the hoarding drive." However, we should first clarify the difference between the use of those terms in Marx's time versus their current use. If we speak today of "drives," then we think perhaps of the concept of drive in the psychoanalysis of Sigmund Freud, or remember the concept of instinct of the comparative (human and animal) behavioral research of Konrad Lorenz. Such notions are connected with debates concerned with whether and how human social behavior is already determined by a basic psychological or biological configuration. For that reason, these days one cannot get around immediately further specifying the talk of drives. This was completely different in Marx's time, given that *Capital*'s first volume appeared almost forty years before Freud's *Three Essays on the Theory of Sexuality*, in which he first formulated his theory of drives.

ADDENDUM: Marx did not coin the phrase "the lust for gold." It is clearly a translation of Virgil's phrase in the *Aeneid* "auri sacra fames" (literally, accursed hunger for gold), which was well known among educated people in Marx's time. The analogous passage in the *Contribution to the Critique of Political Economy* has the Latin expression, without indicating the source. There, Marx states that it is relations mediated by money that first engender "the passion for enrichment," lust for gold, and the like:

> Money is not just *an* object of the passion for enrichment, it is *the* object of it. This urge is essentially auri sacra fames. The passion for enrichment by contrast with the urge to acquire particular material wealth, i.e. use values, such as clothes, jewellery, herds of cattle, etc., becomes possible only when general wealth as such is represented by a specific thing and can thus be retained as a particular commodity. Money therefore appears both as the object and the source of the desire for riches" (MECW 29: 365). In the *Grundrisse*, Marx adds: "But greed itself is the product of a definite social development, not *natural*, as opposed to *historical*. (Marx 1973: 222)

As commodity circulation expands, eventually everything becomes for sale: "Circulation becomes the great social retort into which everything is thrown, to come out again as the money crystal" (229). But the inverse is also true, since with money, that "absolutely social form of wealth which is always ready to be used" (229), one can buy anything. However, that's not all:

> But money is itself a commodity, an external object capable of becoming the private property of any individual. Thus the social power becomes the private power of private persons. (229–30)

Here, the money fetish reaches its completion. In chapter 2, Marx explained that money in the general equivalent form becomes a "socionatural property" of a thing (187, corrected translation). When dealing with the circulation of money, we saw how commodity owners' overall activity, which mediates the interaction of their labors, appears as a thing's movement: the motion of money (see 212 and MECW 29: 336f.). Now it's revealed that social power itself is embodied in a thing that I can pocket and carry around!

ADDENDUM: Marx's treatment of this question is somewhat more extended in the *Urtext* (Original Text) for the *Contribution to the Critique of Political Economy*:

> Money is "impersonal" property. I can carry it around with me in my pocket as the universal social power and the universal social nexus, the social substance. Money puts social power as a thing into the hands of the private person, who as such uses this power. The social nexus, the social exchange of matter, itself appears in money as something entirely external, not having any individual relation at all to its possessor, so that the power he wields appears to be something quite incidental and external to him. (MECW 29: 431f)

Social power is always based upon social relations, upon recognition and dependence, and possibilities of disposal. Money's power is also rooted in specific social relations: producers behaving toward their products as if the latter are commodities and their singling out something that everyone recognizes as a general equivalent. However, these social relations are *impersonal* and *objective* (mediated by things). In pre-bourgeois societies, where commodity exchange played only a subordinate role, social power was based, by contrast, on *personal* relations of dependence. For example, slaves were the personal property of their owners and serfs were personally dependent upon specific feudal lords. The modern wage laborer is not *personally* dependent and can terminate his or her employment contract (while remaining *objectively* dependent in that they have to find some employer). Under conditions of commodity production, a person with money disposes of social power, and in principle anyone could do so. This applies on both a large and small scale. Money alters all social relationships, as is affirmed in the Shakespeare quote in footnote 42 on page 229. Money, it says, makes "the hoar leprosy adored; place[s] thieves . . . makes the wappen'd widow wed again."

As Marx points out, ancient and modern society judged money's enormous social impact in completely different ways: "Ancient society therefore denounced it [money] as tending to destroy the economic and moral order" (230).

In societies with time-honored traditions, the spread of money and commodity relations dissolved their established values and social relationships. Many works from Ancient Greece lament this process, and Marx quotes Sophocles to this effect in footnote 43 on page 230.

Nevertheless, things are completely different in modern society:

> Modern society, which already in its infancy had pulled Pluto by the hair of his head from the bowels of the earth, greets gold as its Holy Grail, as the glittering incarnation of its innermost principle of life. (230)

Here Marx is having fun with a gamut of mythological references, although his allusions also carry powerful messages. Pluto is both the god of wealth and of death and the underworld. That modern society "in its infancy had pulled Pluto by the hair of his head from the bowels of the earth" is a metaphor for the sixteenth- and seventeenth-century exploitation of Latin American gold and silver mines. There, both a large part of the indigenous population and the enslaved Africans who were shipped to the "New World" died under miserable conditions. The "Holy Grail" alludes to the medieval Grail legend. The Grail was supposedly the chalice Jesus drank from during the Last Supper with his disciples, and which Joseph of Arimathea later used to collect his blood during the Crucifixion. Kept in a secret place, the chalice is supposed to be able to perform miracles and grant eternal youth. Many medieval poems and legends told of the quest for the Grail, which people saw as a panacea. Marx speaks here for the first time of modern society's "principle of life." He is tying into everyday consciousness, and its awareness that in modern bourgeois society everything revolves around increasing wealth.

Commodities and Money

Now money is no longer (as in ancient society) a dissolving factor. Rather, it is the "incarnation" or embodiment of social power, becoming a new "Grail" that seems to solve all problems. As he did when discussing commodity fetishism, Marx makes clear by means of a religious allusion that modern bourgeois society (which regards itself as enlightened and rational!) has its own faith in miracles.

> The hoarding drive is boundless in its nature. (230)

We discussed above that this "drive" does not refer to an anthropological feature of human beings, but rather a specific social characteristic based upon the regime of commodity circulation and money. Nor does Marx's phrase "in its nature" refer to anything natural. Instead, his idea is that the hoarding drive is essentially boundless, having no intrinsic limit. Why is this so? Marx recycles an argument from page 205: money may be *qualitatively* limitless, because it can be transformed into every type of commodity, but every amount of it is *quantitatively* limited, and thus hits a barrier. That is why Marx concludes:

> This contradiction between the quantitative limitation and the qualitative lack of limitation of money keeps driving the hoarder back to his Sisyphean task: accumulation. (231)

Finally, Marx emphasizes that the hoarder can only heap up treasure if he withdraws money from circulation, buying little and selling a great deal:

> The hoarder therefore sacrifices the lusts of his flesh to the fetish of gold. He takes the gospel of abstinence very seriously. . . . Work, thrift and greed are therefore his three cardinal virtues, and to sell much and buy little is the sum of his political economy. (231)

This is the only place in *Capital* where Marx mentions a "fetish of gold," and it is a passing reference. Since this chapter's first sentence postulates gold as the money commodity, and Marx occasionally speaks of *gold* in place of *money*, we can assume that he is not trying to introduce a gold fetish in addition to the money fetish. Instead, just as gold stands for money, the "fetish of gold" here means nothing other than the money fetish.

The Function of Hoards for the Economy as a Whole, Consequences for the "Law Peculiar to the Circulation of Paper Money" (last paragraph 231)

On page 228, Marx explained how a hoard functions for an individual commodity owner: the individual needs larger or smaller hoards in order to buy independently of his own sales. In the section's final paragraph, Marx turns to how hoards function in the economy as a whole: the amount of money circulating changes along with fluctuations of the commodities in circulation, but hoards generate the necessary balance: "The reserves created by hoarding serve as channels through which money may flow in and out of circulation, so that the circulation itself never overflows its banks" (232).

In the subsection on the "symbol of value," Marx formulated the "law peculiar to the circulation of paper money." Paper money is devalued when the quantity issued exceeds the amount of metallic money that would be in circulation. Marx now argues that hoarding ensures that the amount of money in circulation does not become too great. This implies the specific law of paper money circulation is only correct if paper money *cannot* be hoarded. As explained above, Marx actually argued along these lines in the *Contribution to the Critique of Political Economy* (MECW 29: 353f.). However, after the foregoing analysis of hoarding, it's not clear why state paper money cannot be hoarded, since Marx has pointed out that money can carry out its function as "the sole form of value" by means of a "representative" (see the brief introduction to section "3. Money," on page 227). Therefore, we can conclude in contrast to Marx that the "law peculiar to the circulation of paper money" does not hold! The quantity theory that Marx rejects for metallic money circulation does not apply either for the circulation of paper money. However, this doesn't mean that the state can issue as much paper money as it wants without any consequences. If the amount issued is so great that the hoarded reserves also overflow, then money will remain in circulation and prices increase. However, the price increases are not simply due to the state issuing money. They depend instead on the relation between the amount of money issued and the (variable) size of the hoarded reserves.

B) MEANS OF PAYMENT

Money's New Function, New Economic Characteristics (232 to second paragraph 234)

So far it has been assumed that the commodity and money confront each other directly, but this does not have to be the case. There are many circumstances "under which the alienation [corrected translation: selling] of the commodity becomes separated by an interval of time from the realization of its price" (232). This has consequences for the form-determination of the entire process of exchange:

> The seller becomes a creditor, the buyer becomes a debtor. Since the metamorphosis of commodities, or the development of their form of value, has undergone a change here, money receives a new function as well. It becomes the means of payment. (233)

Here, one must first untangle the terminology: Marx speaks of "means of payment" when the commodity is paid for retroactively. If the commodity is paid for at the time of purchase, Marx calls the money used a "means of circulation." These days, the expression "means of payment" is used for both cases.

> The role of creditor or of debtor results here from the simple circulation of commodities. (233)

ADDENDUM: In the *Contribution to the Critique of Political Economy*, Marx makes clear what he means by the creditor and debtor's economic roles "resulting" from simple circulation:

> The different forms which money assumes in the process of circulation are in fact only crystallisations of the transformation of commodities, a transformation which is in its turn only the objective expression of the changing social relations in which commodity owners conduct their exchange. New relations of intercourse arise in the process of circulation, and commodity owners, who represent these changed relations, acquire new economic characteristics. (MECW 29: 371f)

Marx indicates that the economic roles of "debtor" and "creditor" can also emerge "independently of the circulation of commodities." This clearly refers only to commodity circulation that is *dominated* by *capitalist* production, and does not imply the complete absence of commodity-money relationships. To this effect, Marx writes about creditor-debtor relations in antiquity and the ancient world at the paragraph's end:

> Here, indeed, the money-form—and the relation between creditor and debtor does have the form of a money-relation—was

only the reflection of an antagonism which lay deeper, at the level of the economic conditions of existence. (233)

Here again we see Marx assuming that commodities and money exist in pre-capitalist relations—but in subordinate roles—with the result that the antagonisms of the corresponding relations of production are expressed in money relations. Marx nowhere mentions "simple commodity production" as a mode of production, as Engels suggests (see page 158–9 of this book and the commentary regarding 209n24 on pages 250–51 above).

Now Marx returns to money when it functions as a means of payment in simple commodity circulation. First, money serves as a measure of values. Second, it works as a merely "nominal means of purchase"— nominal because the purchase is made not with money but only the promise of money. Third, the means of circulation was temporarily transformed into a hoard before the payment, since in order to pay at all, the debtor must have sold without subsequently buying. When he finally pays, the money no longer mediates a purchase:

> The means of payment enters circulation, but only after the commodity has already left it. The money no longer mediates the process. It brings it to an end by emerging independently, as the absolute form of existence of exchange-value [more precisely, value], in other words the universal commodity. (234)

Next Marx distinguishes three different purposes that can be connected with the sale of a commodity. First, a *seller* can want to buy a new commodity with the money he obtains, in order to satisfy his needs. Marx considered this case in his reflections on the metamorphosis of the commodity; money functions here as the *means of circulation*. Second, the commodity can be sold in order to hold on to its money form. The seller then becomes a *hoarder*, and the money acquired functions as a *hoard*. Third, the commodity can be sold in order to make a payment. The seller is then a *debtor*, and the money will function as *means of payment*.

In the last two cases, money is "the self-sufficient purpose of the sale" (234), although in the third case the circulation process itself induces this "self-sufficient purpose," that is, the debtor is forced to sell his belongings if he doesn't pay.

In the final paragraph, Marx states that a buyer can transform money into a commodity *before* transforming a commodity into money. This means that his commodity undergoes the second metamorphosis (M – C) before the first one (C – M).

ADDENDUM: On page 199 of *Capital*, Marx analyzed the antagonistic forms of the commodity and money that confront each other in the exchange process. The commodity, which has a real use-value but ideal value, confronts money, which has a real value but ideal use-value. In the *Contribution to the Critique of Political Economy*, Marx explicitly connects his analysis of the means of payment to this "bilateral polar antithesis" (see commentary above regarding page 199):

> The active process of this bilateral polar antithesis is in its turn separated while it is being carried through. . . . On the one hand, the seller actually hands over the commodity as use value without actually realising its price; on the other hand, the buyer actually realises his money in the use value of the commodity without actually handing over the money as exchange value [more precisely, value]. (MECW 29: 372)

When money is used as a means of payment, the commodity first realizes its price, not in money itself, but in the buyer's *promise* of money, "as a title to money in civil law" (234).

ADDENDUM: In the *Contribution to the Critique of Political Economy*, Marx deals with this in greater detail:

> Just as formerly money was represented by a token of value, so now it is symbolically represented by the buyer himself. Just as formerly the value-token as a universal symbol entailed a State guarantee and a legal rate, so now the buyer as a personal symbol gives rise to private, legally enforcible, contracts among commodity owners. (MECW 29: 373)

Marx speaks of both "a title to money in civil law" and "private, legally enforcible contracts." That raises the question of how a title (a claim to something) is to be put into effect, what power is there to enforce it? Marx clearly has *state power* in mind here. Ultimately, state power must enforce mutual recognition between private property owners and the fulfillment of contracts. Here it becomes clear that social intercourse in simple commodity circulation already requires a corresponding state power. However, one must avoid functionalist errors. If the working of simple commodity circulation presupposes a certain state power, that does not yet say anything about how such a state power emerged historically. Nor does it explain the historical processes that led to the state's having long-term modes of operation that are compatible with commodity circulation. Functional need alone is not yet an explanation for a specific institution's existence or its mode of operation.

Means of Payment and Monetary Crisis
(last paragraph 234 to first paragraph 237)

Here Marx points out an important difference between money as a means of circulation and means of payment:

> The flow of the circulating medium does not merely express the connection between buyers and sellers: the connection itself arises within, and exists through, the circulation of money. The movement of the means of payment, however, expresses a social connection which was already present independently. (235)

Why is this difference important? If money were only used as a means of circulation, then if I didn't have any money *now*, I could not buy anything *now* either. The connection between the seller and myself would never have happened. The seller would not have sold anything, and as a result he might now produce less. Things are different with money as a means of payment. I have purchased, but only *promised* to pay. If I don't succeed in raising money, this doesn't change anything about the connection between myself and the seller, which already exists. The seller assumed that he had sold something, and that I would make the payment at a certain date. He may also have deferred payment on raw materials he used, using money as a means of payment. Based on my promise to pay, the seller has himself promised to pay another seller. If I can't pay, then it's possible that he won't be able to pay either, etc. This simple example demonstrates how credit relations permit the expansion of the radius of incomplete economic transactions. If one transaction fails, that can lead to the failure of many further transactions that have already been initiated.

The use of money as a means of payment also affects the *amount of money* that is required for circulation. When considering money as a means of circulation, we saw that the amount required as a means of circulation was by no means equal to the sum of prices to be realized. This is because the same piece of money can circulate many times, and realize the prices in numerous exchanges (see the formula for the quantity of money functioning as a means of circulation above). When money operates as a means of payment, then debt claims can themselves

Commodities and Money 279

be used as payment, with only the differences being paid in money. That is what Marx means when he writes: "There remains only a single debit balance to be settled" (236). This can be illustrated with an example: A has to pay 100 euros to B, B has to pay 120 euros to C, and C has to pay 90 euros to A. B pays C with the debt claim to A, plus 20 euros in cash, and C pays A with this debt claim of 100 euros and receives 10 euros back. To realize the total of 310 euros in prices required only 30 euros in cash (using money as means of circulation would have meant using at least 120 euros in cash). If there are only three sellers, this way of settling claims is unlikely. However, if thousands of economic actors maintain bank accounts, then their claims can be settled among the banks, with the amount of cash needed being reduced enormously. However, a new problem arises now, which Marx addresses in the next paragraph.

> There is a contradiction immanent in the function of money as the means of payment. When the payments balance each other, money functions only nominally, as money of account, as a measure of value. But when actual payments have to be made, money does not come onto the scene as a circulating medium, in its merely transient form of an intermediary in the social metabolism, but as the individual incarnation of social labour, the independent presence of exchange-value [more precisely, value], the universal commodity. This contradiction bursts forth in that aspect of an industrial and commercial crisis which is known as a monetary crisis. (235)

As footnote 50 on page 236 emphasizes, this type of monetary crisis is distinct from monetary crises based on money-capital traded on stock exchanges. Today the latter are called financial crises. The text addresses a type of monetary crisis that only occurs if there is a system for settling payments, so that cash is not required to settle most claims. Money then serves only "nominally" as "money of account." But disruptions in the settlement system mean that "money suddenly and immediately changes over from its merely nominal shape, money of account, into hard cash" (236).[42]

---

42. The type of monetary crisis addressed in the text, expressed by a short-term lack of money, occurred rather frequently in the nineteenth century. Since the mid-twentieth century, however, such crises no longer play an important role. This is because commercial buyers receive credit from banks, and banks through

Although Marx does not emphasize it, we are dealing here (as on page 209) with just "the possibility of crises."

Marx's description of monetary crises here contains a few allusions that require explanation. When he writes the "bourgeois, drunk with prosperity and arrogantly certain of himself [corrected translation: "conceited with Enlightenment," *Aufklärungsdünkel*], has just declared that money is a purely imaginary creation" (236), he is referring to the eighteenth-century critique of mercantilism. Mercantilism associated wealth with money, but the Enlightenment considered this an economic superstition, since money was merely a means of exchange and real wealth consisted of commodities. Yet when the monetary crisis comes, nothing remains of this illusory rationality—or "conceit with Enlightenment":

> As the hart pants after fresh water, so pants his soul after money, the only wealth. (236)

This formulation is based on an Old Testament verse: "As the hart panteth after the water brooks, so panteth my soul after thee, O God" (Psalm 42). Marx substitutes money for God, pointing once again to money's quasi-religious importance.[43]

In footnote 51 on page 236, Marx uncharacteristically quotes himself: "This sudden transformation of the credit system into a monetary system adds theoretical dismay to the actually existing panic, and the agents of the circulation process are overawed by the impenetrable mystery surrounding their own relations." A sense of mystery and awe at one's own social relations can still be felt today, whenever there is a crisis of the euro or the financial markets. Frightened politicians, journalists, businessmen, and financial traders are haunted by the question "How will the markets react?" Marx now summarizes:

---

the "interbank trade" do not hesitate to provide one another with credit and can borrow additional money from central banks over the short term. Nevertheless, the unexpected bankruptcy of Lehman Brothers in September of 2008 threatened once again to generate a large-scale monetary crisis. Interbank trading almost completely collapsed in the face of possible future bankruptcies. In fact, it was only wide-reaching state guarantees—offered by the key capitalist countries—that averted the danger of a short-term lack of money and a subsequent collapse of banks and businesses.

43. Obviously Marx assumed that the reader was familiar with this Psalm. Felix Mendelssohn Bartholdy (1809–1847) also composed a cantata based on the Psalm. It was considered one of his best church compositions and was frequently performed.

> In a crisis, the antithesis between commodities and their value-form, money, is raised to the level of an absolute contradiction. Hence money's form of appearance is here also a matter of indifference. The monetary famine remains whether payments have to be made in gold or in credit-money, such as bank-notes. (236f.)

In chapter 2 of *Capital*, Marx argued that the commodity's doubling into money, on the one hand, and commodity, on the other, in the exchange process is simply an externalization of the immanent antagonism of use-value and value (see page 181). The crisis induces a further intensification of this antagonism.

Marx's claim here that "money's form of appearance" doesn't matter is an important one. The "monetary famine" relates to *money*, and not just its manifestation as gold. As with money's role in hoarding, the means of payment in a crisis can also be assumed by symbols of value.

The Total Amount of Money in Circulation
(second paragraph 237 to 240)

At the top of page 237, Marx presents a formula for the total amount of money in circulation. However, it is somewhat erroneous. The sum given by Marx consists of three addends, two positive and one negative. About the first addend, Marx writes that "for any given turnover rate of the medium of circulation and the means of payment, it is equal to the sum of prices to be realized." However, he already provided the correct formula for this addend on page 216: the sum of commodity prices (paid in cash) divided by the velocity of circulation of the money used as means of circulation. Similarly, the second addend is not simply equal to "the sum of prices to be realized, plus the sum of the payments falling due" (this difference is the balance of payments). Rather, it is this balance divided by the velocity of circulation of the money used as means of payment. And finally, one cannot simply subtract the "number of circuits"—a dimensionless quantity—from these price sums (expressed in a specific currency unit). Rather, we must subtract that part of money that functions both as means of circulation and means of payment. Hence, the correct formula is:

$$M = \frac{P}{V_1} + \frac{B}{V_2} - M_1$$

Here M is the total amount of money in circulation; M_1 is the amount of money that functions as means of circulation *and* means of payment; P is the sum of prices of commodities paid for in cash; B is the balance of payments; v_1 is the velocity of circulation of the money used as a means of circulation; and v_2 the velocity of money's circulation as a means of payment.

This corrected formula does not affect Marx's conclusion that the amount of money in circulation and the sum of prices of the circulating commodities do not have to coincide in any way or stand in a fixed proportion to each other. Further, it can be observed that the amount of money in circulation changes, with changes in the quantitative ratio of purchases by cash payment (money used as a *means of circulation*) versus purchases made with the promise of money (money used as a *means of payment*). If payments made with the promise of money (for example, payment with a credit card) tend to replace cash payments, then for that reason alone, the amount of money in circulation drops down considerably.

Next, Marx briefly addresses *credit-money* (238), already mentioned on page 224. Credit-money "springs" from money's function as a promise of payment, insofar as promises to pay circulate and themselves perform money's functions. Marx does not emphasize it here, but it's clear that credit-money (the promise to pay) will have to be redeemed for real money at some point or replaced by another promise to pay.

Finally, Marx declares that "when the production of commodities has attained a certain level and extent… [money] becomes the universal material [corrected translation: universal commodity] of contracts." That is, even with services and taxes not directly involving the buying and selling of commodities (for example, rent payments on tracts of land or taxes paid to the state), the payment is not made in kind, but in cash. That money is the "universal commodity of contracts" is completely obvious to us these days, but it wasn't always so.

In the last paragraph, Marx points out another important historical change:

> The development of money as a means of payment makes it necessary to accumulate it in preparation for the days when the sums which are owing fall due. While hoarding, considered as an independent form of self-enrichment, vanishes with the advance of bourgeois society [*bürgerliche Gesellschaft*], it grows at the same time in the form of the accumulation of a reserve fund of the means of payment. (240)

Commodities and Money 283

c) World Money

Marx has not used the expression "world money" so far, but its meaning as money used on the world market or for transactions across national borders is almost self-evident. Marx's key claims about world money—and we should bear in mind that we are only at the level of the "simple circulation of commodities"—appear right in the first paragraph:

> When money leaves the domestic sphere of circulation it loses the local functions it has acquired there, as the standard of prices, coin, and small change, and as a symbol of value, and falls back into its original form as precious metal in the shape of bullion. (240)

This sentence describes the situation in Marx's lifetime, when gold actually moved back and forth among various countries. If it were necessary for physical gold to be moved, this would be the first case encountered thus far in which money "has to appear in person as gold" (227), as stated in the brief introduction to this third subsection, "Money." However, Marx has not substantiated that gold *necessarily* has to appear here; he seemingly assumes so as a matter of course. Marx couldn't imagine that a *national* currency could at the same time function as world money on the world market. Yet this is exactly what happened after the Second World War. Since then, a large part of world trade has been conducted in US dollars. Since being introduced, the euro has begun to compete somewhat with the dollar in this regard. A much smaller but growing part of world trade is carried out in euros.

> In world trade, commodities develop their value universally. Their independent value-form thus confronts them here too as world money. It is in the world market that money first functions to its full extent as the commodity whose natural form is also the directly social form of realization of human labour in the abstract. Its mode of existence becomes adequate to its concept. (240–41)

The last statement might sound somewhat Hegelian. However, the preceding sentences show that this is a straightforward matter: money, according to Marx's analysis, is the universal expression of value, which Marx summarized with the three peculiarities of the equivalent form. These three peculiarities come together in the statement that money is the commodity "whose natural form is also the directly social form of realization of human labour in the abstract." Since it is only in world trade that commodities unfold their value "universally" (that is, without bumping up against any borders), the money that confronts them becomes the first "universal" expression of value. Before, this universality ended at a country's borders. It is only on the world market that money's mode of existence—that is, its actual functioning—becomes as universal as indicated in the analysis.

The statement that follows, that a double measure of value operates on the world market, gold and silver, was no longer true at the end of the nineteenth century. Gold had largely displaced silver.

> World money serves as the universal means of payment, as the universal means of purchase, and as the absolute social materialization of wealth as such (universal wealth). Its predominant function is as means of payment in the settling of international balances. (242)

World money functions as the *universal means of payment* if—as occurs in national circulation—it is used to pay for already purchased commodities and mechanisms for settling claims that are in place so that only balances need to be transferred. World money functions as the *universal means of purchase,* if it is used for cash payments. Finally, world money functions as the *"absolute social materialization of wealth as such,"* if wealth in abstract form is transferred from one country to another. In footnote 61 on page 243, Marx mentions subsidies and money loans as examples of the latter. One could also add war reparations, which he deals with in footnote 62.

I will not address the confrontation between the mercantilists and their critics discussed in footnote 60. To evaluate Marx's arguments, we would need to delve deeply into mercantilism and Ricardo's theories.

Next, Marx comments that a country needs reserve funds not just for domestic circulation (see the conclusion of the subsection "Means of Payment"), but also for circulation on the world market. For the latter, "It is always the genuine money-commodity, gold and silver in their physical shape, which is required" (243). This holds only if gold and silver are in fact necessary for world money's functioning. But if a national currency assumes this role, as is currently the case, countries must maintain reserve funds in that national currency for world market circulation. This, in turn, creates constant demand for the national currency in question, helping to make it a "strong" currency.

Commodities and Money 285

Finally, Marx asserts that gold and silver (as world money) have a double movement. On the one hand, these metals spread from their sources (gold and silver mines) over the entire world market, their movement mediated by "the direct exchange of the labour of individual countries which has been realized in commodities for the labour realized in the precious metals by the gold- and silver-producing countries" (244). That means this kind of movement is a consequence of world trade.

> On the other hand, gold and silver continually flow backwards and forwards between the different national spheres of circulation, and this movement follows the unceasing fluctuations of the rate of exchange. (244)

The flows mentioned here, which played an important role in the nineteenth century, require some explanation. In that century, individual countries' currencies had a fixed exchange rate to gold. At the same time, there were fluctuations in the exchange rates between the currencies (these fluctuations were rather small, compared to today's). For example, if the French franc declined against the British pound, then one could obtain more francs for a pound than before. Since the franc had a fixed exchange rate to gold, one could ultimately obtain more gold. If one exchanged pounds for francs, redeeming the francs for gold, and finally transported the gold to England, exchanging it for pounds, then one would have more pounds than initially, assuming the French currency's devaluation was enough that the resulting gain exceeded the transportation costs.

Marx's distinction between the two kinds of money flow is still relevant today. The movement of the world money, the dollar, results on the one hand from trade transactions, and on the other hand from exchange rate fluctuations. For example, if the dollar is somewhat more expensive in Frankfurt than in London, then one can make a profit by exchanging euros for dollars in London and then transforming these dollars into euros again in Frankfurt. Since no physical transportation is necessary for these transactions, which are usually just movements between accounts, the smallest exchange-rate differences (or price differences of the dollar) are enough to generate important profits. Even with a price difference between London and Frankfurt dollars that is only 0.1 percent, the use of 10 million euros in London can generate 10,000 dollars in profit—through an almost cost-free transaction that can be made in minutes over the telephone or with the click of a mouse.

Apart from world trade and exploiting of exchange rate differences, world money's movements can happen for other reasons, such as the exploitation of interest rate differences. However, the latter involves relations that go beyond the simple commodity circulation. Understanding such relations presupposes the analysis of capital and interest. The next chapter will undertake the analysis of capital; an analysis of interest-bearing capital must wait for Volume 3 of *Capital*.

Part Two: The Transformation of Money into Capital

The title of Part Two shows that we are finally dealing with capital, while pointing to the importance of money for understanding capital. Moreover, the expression connecting money and capital in the title—"the transformation"—also played an important role in chapter 3. There, the topic was the commodity's transformation into money. Now it is money's transformation into capital.

Chapter 4: The General Formula for Capital

We don't yet know what is meant by the "general formula" for capital. Furthermore, Marx springs the word *capital* on us in the first sentence without explaining it. He assumes the reader has prior knowledge of the subject that he will build upon. However, it is only in the course of Marx's argument that his concept of capital will become clear.

a) Historical Preconditions and Conceptual Point of Departure (first three paragraphs 247)

> The circulation of commodities is the starting-point of capital. The production of commodities and their circulation in its developed form, namely trade, form the historic presuppositions under which capital arises. World trade and the world market date from the sixteenth century, and from then on the modern history of capital starts to unfold. (247)

What the first three chapters of *Capital* examined was the *capitalist* circulation of commodities. The commodity analyzed was the capitalist commodity, as the first sentence of chapter 1 made clear (125). However, capitalist commodity circulation has been considered until now in abstraction from capital. The categories of commodity and money developed so far by Marx can be used as a foundation for analyzing capital. In that sense, the circulation of commodities forms the *conceptual* point of departure for the analysis of capital.

The existence of developed commodity circulation is also a *historical* precondition for capital's emergence, albeit not the only one: Marx has pointed out many times that commodity production and commodity circulation exist in various modes of production in different degrees (see 176, 209n24). He locates the beginning of the "modern history of capital" in the sixteenth century. We don't yet know what Marx understands by the term "capital." However, his reference to a "modern" history indicates that he distinguishes between a modern form of capital and older, pre-modern forms. That he situates the modern form in the sixteenth century is a claim about history, which only historical research can confirm.

> If we disregard the material content of the circulation of commodities, i.e. the exchange of the various use-values, and consider only the economic forms brought into being by this process, we find that its ultimate product is money. This ultimate product of commodity circulation is the first form of appearance of capital. (247)

If we interpret the first sentence in a historical sense—money is the *chronologically* "ultimate product" of the circulation of commodities—then it's obviously false. The difference between the mere exchange of products and the circulation of commodities consists precisely in the fact that money mediates exchanges in the latter. Chronologically, then, money emerges *simultaneously* with commodity circulation and is by no means its "ultimate product" in a temporal sense. Marx's chapter 3 analyzed those "economic forms" that arise not temporally, but rather conceptually from the circulation of commodities. After money as the measure of values and then as the means of circulation, came money as money. In this third form, which is the *unity* of the previous two, money possesses an independent existence as the manifestation of value (227–244). Money was thus the ultimate *categorical* result of this analysis. It is the "ultimate product" of the *analysis of the (capitalist) circulation of commodities* in a conceptual sense.

But if money is conceptually the "ultimate product of commodity circulation," then the claim that money is capital's "first" form of appearance must also be meant categorically: capital's initial (categorical) form of appearance is money. This statement must still be substantiated. However, observe that Marx does *not* say money "is" capital here. Instead, he says that money is the "form of appearance" of capital, thus raising the question of that appearance's content.

In the next paragraph, Marx points out that capital also appears first as money in history. However, he immediately adds that this retrospective look isn't necessary to recognize that money is capital's first form of appearance, since that sequence plays out before our eyes every day.

In footnote 1 of chapter 4, Marx mentions in passing the very important difference between "personal relations of domination and servitude" versus "the power of money, which is impersonal." The former type of relation is typical of pre-capitalist modes of production (where slaves are another person's property and serfs are personally dependent upon a particular lord). In the latter, a social power becomes the property of a thing (see page 271 of this book). This contrast between personal and impersonal relations of domination generalizes what previous chapters established. There we saw how, under the conditions of capitalist commodity production, relationships among people are concealed "beneath the shell of a thing [corrected translation]," while producers' social activity becomes a movement of things that control them (167n29; 168; see pages 159–60, 163 of this book). Likewise, with the circulation of commodities, "there develops a whole network of socio-natural connections, entirely beyond the control of the human agents" (207, corrected translation).

B) Differences in Form Between C – M – C and M – C – M (last paragraph 247 to third paragraph 250)

> The first distinction between money as money and money as capital is nothing more than a difference in their *form of circulation*. (247, emphasis M.H.)

Through *form analysis*, Marx seeks to distinguish "money as money"— the conceptually "ultimate product of commodity circulation"—and "money as a form of appearance of capital," while tracking down that appearance's content.

The formula C – M – C is typical of the "simple circulation of commodities" (see my chapter 3 commentary about page 209 discussing this term). By contrast, money that goes through the movement M – C – M turns into capital. Marx writes that "we find" this second form of circulation alongside the first one (248). He does not address the inner connection between C – M – C and M – C – M here (or in the remainder of chapter 3), which could generate the impression that these two forms of circulation exist rather coincidentally alongside one another.

ADDENDUM: In the *Urtext* for the *Contribution to the Critique of Political Economy*, Marx deals with the non-coincidental connection between money and capital under the heading "Transition to Capital." Appendix 5 in this book reproduces and comments on important passages of this text that clarify how Marx conceived the transition from the category of money to that of capital.

In the second and third paragraphs on page 248, Marx confronts an obvious objection to the M – C – M formula. In effect, it would be "absurd and empty" to pursue this roundabout route of exchange only to obtain the same amount of money in the end. Why does Marx consider the formula M – C – M? Independently of whether or not there is a different quantity of money at the end, the money in M – C – M undergoes a specific movement that is distinct from that of C – M – C. Marx will first examine this specific movement, contending:

> **This will simultaneously provide us with the difference in content which lies behind these formal distinctions. (248)**

Both circuits, C – M – C and M – C – M, consist of the two opposing phases: C – M and M – C. However, these two phases occur in reverse sequence. From this, Marx deduces that the commodity and money have different functions in the two circuits, which I will only briefly summarize here.

In the simple circulation of commodities, the money obtained transforms into a commodity that serves as a use-value. The money itself is "spent" and gone, while the commodity that stands at the circuit's endpoint is consumed.

In the circuit M – C – M, money is "advanced." The money is transformed into a commodity only with a view to being transformed into money again. The money isn't gone, but rather returns to its starting point. This holds regardless of whether the amount of money has increased or not.

In simple circulation, money only returns to the commodity owner if he begins a new circuit of C – M – C, at the end of which, in any case, the money is again spent. In the circuit M – C – M, however, money's return is part of the circuit.

Based on these observations, Marx can point to the two circuits' distinct *purposes*:

The Transformation of Money into Capital

> The path C-M-C proceeds from the extreme [Marx uses "extreme" to refer to the starting point and endpoint of the exchanges] constituted by one commodity, and ends with the extreme constituted by another, which falls out of circulation and into consumption. Consumption, the satisfaction of needs, in short use-value, is therefore its final goal. The path M-C-M, however, proceeds from the extreme of money and finally returns to that same extreme. Its driving and motivating force, its determining purpose, is therefore exchange-value [more exactly: *value*]. (250)

Importantly, Marx speaks here of goals that are immanent to the two *circuits,* based on their *form.* He does not consider the subjective goals of those engaging in exchange. In effect, people as agents do not yet figure in the account.

c) The Different Content of Each Form of Circuit: Capital as Valorized Value (last paragraph 250 to 253)

Characterizing the different goals of the two circuits now enables us to determine their distinct content. In the case of the simple circulation of commodities, both extremes have the same economic form; both are commodities. However, they are qualitatively different use-values. This "interchange carried out between the different materials in which social labour is embodied, forms here the content of the movement" (250).

In the case of the circulation M – C – M, both extremes also have the same economic form: money. However, there is no possible *qualitative* difference between two sums of money, but only a *quantitative* one. The content of the circuit M – C – M can therefore only be the "quantitative changes" (251) at its extremes. Marx now indicates that he is presenting the circulation of money as capital and introduces the famous prime symbol:

> The complete form of this process is therefore M – C– M′, where M′ = M + ΔM, i.e. the original sum advanced plus an increment. This increment or excess over the original value I call "surplus-value." (251)

Here is where Marx first speaks of surplus-value. For the moment, it is only the name for an increase in value. He continues:

> The value originally advanced, therefore, not only remains intact while in circulation, but increases its magnitude, adds to itself a surplus-value, or is valorized [*verwertet sich*]. And this movement converts it into capital. (252)

Through a form analysis on a general level, Marx thus arrives at a characterization of the concept of capital: capital is "valorized" value. This is the first time that *valorizing value* is mentioned: it means value-adding value. With this initial characterization of capital, we can already see that capital is not a thing—or sum of money—but rather a specific *movement*: the movement of valorizing value. At this point we don't know anything about how this *valorization of value* is possible: that is, how value can increase by moving through the circuit M – C – M'.

Marx mentions that even in the circuit C – M – C, the value of the initial commodity can differ from the value of the final commodity. But this kind of quantitative difference remains purely coincidental for this form of circulation. What is decisive here is the qualitative difference between the use-values. For the circuit M – C – M', however, the quantitative difference at the beginning and end is decisive: without such a difference, the circuit would be pointless.

A long paragraph on pages 252 and 253 deals with the fundamental properties of capital as revealed by the form analysis so far. Since the purpose of C – M – C is the exchange of qualitatively different use-values, Marx observes that this process "is a means to a final goal which lies outside circulation, namely the appropriation of use-values, the satisfaction of needs" (252). The beginning and end of M – C – M', however, are qualitatively the same, and the process's entire purpose is quantitative increase. Moreover, if the process comes to a halt, then the money ceases to be capital—either it petrifies as a hoard or is spent on commodities, which are then consumed. Money can only remain capital through the process's repetition. For this reason, money's circulating as capital is perpetual, or "endless" (252), and the surplus-value gained is included in this perpetual valorization:

> If, then, we are concerned with the valorization [*Verwertung*] of value, the value of the £110 has the same need for valorization as the value of the £100, for they are both limited expressions of exchange-value [more precisely, value], and therefore both have the same vocation, to approach, by quantitative increase, as near as possible to absolute wealth. (252)

If valorizing value is the process's purpose, which is what the somewhat confusing term "need" points to here, then it makes no difference what the available sum of value is. This is because valorization does not aim for a specific sum, but rather *increasing* the amount of value.

Marx noted above that the purpose of C – M – C is use-value, whereas the purpose of M – C – M' is value (250). Now, we can take this differentiation of purposes one step further:

> The simple circulation of commodities—selling in order to buy—is a means to a *final goal which lies outside circulation*, namely the appropriation of use-values, the satisfaction of needs. As against this, the circulation of money as capital is an *end in itself*, for the valorization of value takes place only within this constantly renewed movement. The movement of capital is therefore *limitless*. (253, emphasis M.H.)

The circulation of M – C – M' is an "end in itself" and as such "limitless" (*masslos*) in a very literal sense: it has no measure, no inner limit. If the movement's only purpose is to increase value, there is no point where the increase will be sufficient. That could only happen if there were another purpose, for which the increase in value were merely a means.[44]

In footnote 6 on pages 253–54, Marx shows how Aristotle already grasped the distinct characters of the different forms of circulation. Aristotle contrasted "chrematistics" and "economics." The former, which is the *making of money* (and not the *theory of money* as sometimes claimed), has an autotelic and unlimited character for Aristotle. The latter, which Aristotle used in the original sense of home economics or domestic economy (see my commentary on *Capital*'s title and subtitle), is aimed at satisfying needs. As in his excursus on Aristotle in the value-form analysis (151f.), Marx refers to Aristotle here, who was an important point of reference in the nineteenth century and whom he personally held in high esteem. In fact, the Greek philosopher made the first forays into the analysis of the commodity, exchange, and money.

---

44. In reading groups, the question frequently comes up of whether the capital-relation can be regulated in such a way that this limitlessness is restricted and valorization limited. However, this question cannot be addressed yet. First, one would have to examine how the competition between capitals imposes this limitlessness, which presupposes knowledge of all three volumes of *Capital*. Here, the decisive point is that capital *itself* knows no limit to valorization.

d) The Capitalist (254 to first paragraph 255)

So far, Marx has proceeded solely based on the form determinations of the M – C – M' circuit, but has not yet considered people's actions. Now the capitalist enters the picture for the first time:

> *As the conscious bearer* [Träger] *of this movement*, the possessor of money becomes a capitalist. His person, or rather his pocket, is the point from which the money starts, and to which it returns. The objective content of the circulation we have been discussing—the valorization of value—is his subjective purpose, and *it is only in so far as the appropriation of ever more wealth in the abstract is the sole driving force behind his operations that he functions as a capitalist*, i.e. as capital personified and endowed with consciousness and a will. Use-values must therefore never be treated as the immediate aim of the capitalist; nor must the profit on any single transaction. His aim is rather the unceasing movement of profit-making. (254, emphases M.H.)

Whoever makes the M – C – M' circuit's objective content his own subjective purpose—whoever *wants* to valorize value—is a capitalist. We should observe two things here:

First: It does not matter whether the person actually *owns* the money that will be valorized; they just have to dispose of it. They must, in Marx's carefully chosen words, *possess* money. Whoever actually disposes of a thing is its *possessor*, even if he is not the owner. For this reason, people may function as capitalists even if they just borrow money to valorize it, or if they take on the task, as managers, of valorizing other people's wealth.

Second: People can have very different motives. That's why Marx points out that "only in so far as the appropriation of ever more wealth in the abstract is the sole driving force" is somebody a capitalist. That is, only those who are *concerned with profit* itself—those for whom profit is *the goal* of their activity—operate as capitalists in the strict sense. For example, if a person simply wishes to live well from profits, then he or she does not make profit itself the goal, but merely a means of earning a living. For such a person, the valorization of value is not an end in itself, and thus not a limitless process. Profit is then limited by what the money owner requires for his or her livelihood.

If profit is itself the purpose, then it cannot be fulfilled by a single round of profits, but only by "the unceasing movement of profit-making."

The fact that capital is not a thing, but rather a specific movement, is translated into the capitalist's activity.

> This boundless drive for enrichment, this passionate chase after value, is common to the capitalist and the miser; but while the miser is merely a capitalist gone mad, the capitalist is a rational miser. The ceaseless augmentation of value, which the miser seeks to attain by saving his money from circulation, is achieved by the more acute capitalist by means of throwing his money again and again into circulation. (254f.)

Here the "*drive* for enrichment" does not refer to an innate characteristic of humankind, but rather to a socially produced one, as I argued above in the commentary about the "lust for gold" (229) and the "hoarding drive" (230).

When analyzing the commodity, Marx initially examined the *form-determinations of the exchange-relation* (chapter 1) and then *commodity owners' actions in the exchange process* (chapter 2). Likewise, Marx carries out a form analysis of capital here *before* addressing the capitalist as a person. But whereas in chapter 2 Marx used the contradictory requirements of exchange to show *why* commodity owners must adhere to "the natural laws of the commodity" (180), here in chapter 4 he does not explain why individual money owners must conform to the "unceasing movement of profit-making."

ADDENDUM: The reason for enrichment by no means has to be an individual's inclination toward "greed." When analyzing the capitalist mode of production, Marx argues that *competition forces* individual capitalists to permanently behave as capitalists or go under economically. In chapter 10, after stating that capital, with its unlimited drive for valorization, is ruthless with regard to the worker's health and longevity, Marx says:

> But looking at these things as a whole, it is evident that this does not depend on the will, either good or bad, of the individual capitalist. Under free competition, the immanent laws of capitalist production confront the individual capitalist as a coercive force external to him. (381)

Furthermore, in the section on accumulation, he reprises the comparison between the capitalist and the hoarder, but adds a decisive element to it: the capitalist, as a "personification of capital," shares with the miser an absolute drive towards self-enrichment. But what appears in the miser as the mania of an individual *is in the capitalist the effect of a social mechanism in which he is merely a cog*. Moreover, the development of capitalist production makes it necessary constantly to increase the amount of capital laid out in a given industrial undertaking, and *competition subordinates every individual capitalist* to the immanent laws of capitalist production, as external and coercive laws. *It compels him* to keep extending his capital, so as to preserve it, and he can only extend it by means of progressive accumulation," that is, investing the surplus-value. (739, emphases M.H.)

E) VALUE AS "AUTOMATIC SUBJECT" AND "SELF-MOVING SUBSTANCE WHICH PASSES THROUGH A PROCESS OF ITS OWN" (SECOND PARAGRAPH 255 TO 257)

Chapter 4's remaining paragraphs are very dense. It's a good idea to read them several times and very carefully.

In commodity circulation, money only mediates the exchange of commodities, and the money-form "vanishes in the final result of the movement" (255). One could add that the commodity-form also vanishes, since the final result of C – M – C is the commodity being consumed.

> On the other hand, in the circulation M – C – M both the money and the commodity function only as different modes of existence of value itself.... It is constantly changing from one form into the other, without becoming lost in this movement; it thus becomes transformed into an *automatic subject*. If we pin down the specific forms of appearance assumed in turn by self-valorizing value in the course of its life, we reach the following elucidation: capital is money, capital is commodities. (255, emphasis M.H.).

Here, Marx contrasts mistaken claims about capital with its characterization as an "automatic subject." In contrast to its transient role in simple commodity circulation, value is the goal of the entire process in the circuit M – C – M'. *Commodity* and *money* here are merely alternating "modes of existence" (255) and "forms of appearance" (255) of value. However, if the observer "pins down" one of these forms of value's appearance, then that leads to incorrect claims, such as capital's being money or a commodity. Marx already stated that capital is based upon a *movement* (and thus cannot be reduced to the commodity or to money) when he first introduced the concept of capital on page 252. But what does it mean to state that value is an "automatic subject"?

When one speaks of a subject, it evokes independence and self-determination. A subject posits his or her own purposes and pursues them. It is the opposite for an automaton, which by definition is not independent and self-determined. Value is the subject because its process of adding surplus-value "is its own movement, its valorization is therefore self-valorization [*Selbstverwertung*]" (255). For that reason, value is the subject of the process of valorization. Moreover, value here has no other possible purpose than valorization. Hence, it is an "automatic" subject. Just as an automaton might carry out a single process (a ticket machine can print tickets and no more), so value is only capable of a single process: valorizing itself.

If Marx speaks of value as a "subject," this should not be confused with value being an *actor*. Value itself cannot act, any more than commodities can carry themselves to market (see page 178 in chapter 2). People are the only real actors. It is people's activity, of course, that makes value into an "automatic subject"; their activity, however, conforms to the logic of the form of circulation M – C – M'. Our purpose is to decode this logic, for *only within this framework* can we speak of value as doing something, namely "valorizing itself."

We don't yet know how this self-valorization process is *possible*. Just looking at the movement of value in M – C – M' does not reveal where surplus-value comes from. So far we have only analyzed the movement of valorization's form aspect. At this point in the analysis, therefore, Marx is completely correct in claiming about value:

> By virtue of being value, it has acquired the *occult ability* to add value to itself. (255, emphasis M.H.)

Marx does not immediately begin explaining this "occult ability." Instead, he continues to trace the specific role of value in the valorization process. Inside the valorization process, value alternately takes on the forms of money and the commodity. Yet these two forms do not have equal significance.

As the "dominant subject [*übergreifendes Subjekt*]" of this process,

> value requires above all an independent form by means of which its identity with itself may be asserted. Only in the shape of money does it possess this form. Money therefore forms the starting-point and the conclusion of every valorization process. (255)

To better understand this statement, we need to look at the various shapes in which value has appeared so far.

- For the *commodity*, value is a "factor." (The first subsection of *Capital*'s chapter 1 calls use-value and value the "two factors of the commodity.") The value of an individual commodity, however, is neither visible nor tangible.
- In *money*, value obtains an independent, tangible form and is no longer just a factor. Money is immediately value: value in an independent shape.
- For *capital*, which operates in the circuit M – C – M', value is the subject of a process. It takes on different shapes, changing its magnitude. To remain tangible as value in this fluctuating process, an independent form of value is necessary, which can only be money. For that reason, value's money-form is critical for capital, as the title of Part Two made clear, "The Transformation of Money into Capital."[45]

If *valorizing value* requires the money-form to relate to itself, it does not mean that the commodity form is unimportant. On the contrary:

> The capitalist knows that all commodities, however tattered they may look, or however badly they may smell, are in faith and in truth money, are by nature circumcised Jews, and, what is more, a wonderful means for making still more money out of money. (256)

That commodities are a "wonderful means" of valorization is only a *claim* here. Chapter 6 will explain how they actually function as means of valorization.

The expression "by nature circumcised Jews"—*innerlich* (inwardly) *beschnittne Juden*—alludes to Paul's *Epistle to the Romans*, which deals in part with what it is to be a Jew. Christianity began as a Jewish reform sect, and Paul was the first to explicitly direct the Christian message to pagans (non-Jews), which was rather controversial among Jewish Christians.

---

45. Both classical political economy and modern neoclassical economics usually identify capital with capital goods. In emphasizing that the money-form of value is necessary in order to preserve the identity of the subject of the process of valorization—or to put it another way, that capital can only relate to itself by means of the money-form—Marx is transforming his monetary theory of value into a monetary theory of capital (Heinrich 1999: 253).

Paul defended himself by arguing that circumcision alone does not make one Jewish, since whoever is circumcised but fails to follow God's law becomes uncircumcised. Paul continues: "For he is not a Jew, which is one outwardly; neither is that circumcision, which is outward in the flesh: But he is a Jew, which is one inwardly; and circumcision is that of the heart, in the spirit, and not in the letter; whose praise is not of men, but of God" (Romans 2:28–29).

By means of this "inward circumcision," an uncircumcised pagan can become a Jew and therefore a Christian. Marx draws a parallel here with the commodity. Regardless of how a commodity looks, it can be transformed into money. It is "inwardly" money, and the capitalist therefore esteems it. The gist of the comparison is that it is the concealed interior that counts, not the exterior. However, the comparison is problematic, since it plays on the widespread anti-Semitic stereotypes that associate Jews with money.[46]

Marx begins the next paragraph indicating that value in the circuit M – C – M' is not only "a self-moving substance which passes through a process of its own," as the phrase "automatic subject" already implied:

> But there is more to come: instead of simply representing the relations of commodities, it now enters into a *private relationship with itself*, as it were. It differentiates itself as original value from itself as surplus-value, just as God the Father differentiates himself from himself as God the Son, although both are of the same age and form, in fact one single person. (256, emphasis M.H.)

To illustrate value's "private relationship with itself," Marx again resorts to a religious analogy: the relationship between God the Father and God the Son. As father and son they are different, but since there's supposedly only one God, they must be identical and therefore "of the same age." For capital, the analogy works well. In Marx's example, a sum of £100 is advanced, but it only becomes capital if it yields a surplus-value, for example, £10, thus "differentiating" from itself—the original amount contrasts with the newly generated surplus-value. When the surplus-value of £10 is present, however, it is not qualitatively different from the original value of £100. Both of them constitute a homogenous

---

46. A few passages in *Capital* and a number of statements in Marx's correspondence show that he had a completely uncritical attitude toward the anti-Jewish references in the everyday language of his time.

unity of £110, ready for the next round of valorization. Marx summarizes this in the next paragraph:

> Value therefore now becomes value in process, money in process, and, as such, capital. It comes out of circulation, enters into it again, preserves and multiplies itself within circulation, emerges from it with an increased size, and starts the same cycle again and again. M – M, "money which begets money." (256)

ADDENDUM: The religious analogy here aims to illustrate a special kind of *self-relationship*: the way value as capital stands in a "private relationship with itself." Nevertheless, Marx does not return to this self-relationship until *Capital*'s third volume when he examines profit, average profit, and interest as the "fruit" of capital. At that point, it will become clear that this self-relationship forms the basis of a third and final kind of fetishism, after commodity and money fetishism, the *capital fetish*. For now, however, Marx cannot deal with the capital fetish, since it's not yet clear where surplus-value actually comes from (this will be clarified in chapter 6). Moreover, capital has only been grasped abstractly so far, as the subject of the movement M – C – M'. At the end of Volume 2, however, capital will be characterized in terms of the unity of the production and circulation processes. That, in turn, will allow the abstract formula M – C – M' to be filled with content both from the production process and the circulation process, thereby permitting a more concrete treatment of capital's self-relationship (the relationship of capital to its "fruits").

In the next paragraph, Marx points out that the formula M – C – M' (buying to sell more expensively) does not apply only to merchant capital but also to "industrial" capital, which interpolates a production process between purchase and sale. In the nineteenth-century lexicon, "industry" referred to productive activity in general, not just large factories. The movement M – C – M' is shortened to M – M' in interest-bearing capital, which leads Marx to conclude:

> M – C – M' is in fact therefore the general formula for capital, in the form in which it appears directly in the sphere of circulation. (257)

With that, it finally becomes clear what is meant by Marx's chapter 4 title, "The General Formula for Capital."

ADDENDUM: Marx's description of valorizing value as an "automatic subject"

The Transformation of Money into Capital

and as a "self-moving substance that passes through a process of its own" recalls Hegel's conception of substance as subject (Hegel, *Phenomenology of Spirit*:10). For this reason, some of the literature on Marx claims that there is a close relationship between Marx's and Hegel's arguments. Sometimes it is even argued that Marx's concept of capital corresponds to Hegel's concept of *Geist* (spirit or mind). To meaningfully address these theses, one would have to seriously engage with Hegel's philosophy, but that's not possible here. In the Postface to *Capital*'s second edition, Marx indeed made brief general remarks about the need to "invert" Hegel's dialectic "in order to discover the rational kernel within the mystical shell" (103). However, these remarks are far too vague to substitute for a real engagement with Hegel's philosophy.

Chapter 5: Contradictions in the General Formula

a) Presentation of the Problem (258 to first paragraph 259)

> The form of circulation within which money is transformed into capital contradicts all the previously developed laws bearing on the nature of commodities, value, money and even circulation itself. (258)

The "form of circulation" mentioned here is precisely the general formula for capital: $M - C - M'$. What are the "contradictions" that Marx refers to? A first contradiction is that a presupposition so far in the exchange $C - M - C$ is that equal magnitudes of value are exchanged, so that the magnitudes of value are not altered in the course of exchange. However, the *general formula* involves precisely such a change, namely an increase of value.

Marx states that $M - C - M'$ differs from $C - M - C$ only in terms of the sequence of exchanges. Yet even this new sequence only exists from the perspective of the money owner. If the money owner buys a commodity from A and then sells it to B, then for both A and B these are still normal acts of exchange: a sale for A, a purchase for B. This leads Marx to conclude:

> Thus the inversion of the order of succession does not take us outside the sphere of the simple circulation of commodities, and we must rather look to see whether this simple circulation, by its nature, might permit the valorization of the values entering into it and consequently the formation of surplus-value. (259)

This establishes the program for the rest of the chapter: Marx will explore various possibilities for how valorization could occur.

b) The Circulation of Commodities "In Its Pure Form": The Exchange of Equivalents
(second paragraph 259 to first paragraph 262)

Marx first examines circulation as "the exchange of commodities pure and simple," as when two commodity owners buy directly from each other. He makes three observations about this process: (1) With regard to *use-values*, both parties stand to gain, since they each exchange a use-value that is useless to them for one that is useful. (2) Both can also gain with regard to the *expended labor-time*. In a society with a division of labor, every producer usually specializes in one product. This means he can usually produce that product in a shorter time period than his exchange partner who does not specialize in it. Through exchange, therefore, each acquires a product whose production time would be higher for him than the product he himself produces and sells. (3) With regard to *value*, however, both cannot gain.

Now, Marx drops the requirement of "the exchange of commodities *pure and simple*." When money mediates exchanges, then purchase and sale are separated. However, this changes nothing:

> The value of a commodity is expressed in its price before it enters into circulation, and it is therefore a pre-condition of circulation, not its result. (260)

We must briefly dwell on this statement. At first glance, it seems to contradict Marx's having claimed, on many occasions, that commodities first acquire objectivity as values in exchange (138, 166). That is, *before* exchange, products of labor are not yet commodities and objects of value (see MEGA II/6: 30ff., reproduced as Appendix 4 of this book). Instead, they are only transformed into commodities in the exchange process (181). Money being the necessary, unavoidable measure of value derives from the fact that value cannot be determined without exchange (see the commentary regarding page 188 in chapter 3). Yet Marx seems to be saying the opposite here, that the value of commodities is determined *before exchange* and therefore *exists independently of exchange*! Marx's remarks in the chapters 1 to 3 dealt with the fundamental relation between two levels: the level of production and that of exchange. The social magnitude of value is not solely determined at the level of private production. In fact, only when private acts of labor and their products obtain social recognition is socially necessary labor-time revealed (based on the meaning of "socially necessary," found on pages 129 and

202). Moreover, only then is complex labor actually reduced to simple labor. These social determinations are not established solely in private production, but rather in the relation between production *and* exchange: though value is not *created* in exchange, it only *exists* in exchange.

At this point in Marx's argument, however, he is not dealing with this fundamental relation between production and exchange, but rather with an *individual* act of exchange, which presupposes the above-mentioned social determinations. For those engaged in exchange, value always appears as something given, beyond their influence. Although their actions indeed influence value—as a social relationship—the effect of an individual action is generally so small that it is invisible. An individual seller *anticipates* a commodity's value when setting the price, but even he can be right or wrong. Marx now disregards all difficulties involved in exchange (discussed on pages 201 and 202) and assumes here that prices adequately express values.

Exchange, Marx continues in the next paragraph, is a mere change of form, a metamorphosis of the commodity. The commodity-form is transformed into the money-form, but the mere change of form "does not imply any change in the magnitude of the value" (260). At the end of this paragraph, Marx affirms the following about commodity exchange:

> In its pure form, the exchange of commodities is an exchange of equivalents, and thus it is not a method of increasing value. (261)

When Marx speaks here of a "pure form" (*reine Gestalt*), he is basically distinguishing between two kinds of commodity exchange: an impure one, involving the exchange of non-equivalents—for example, when temporarily favorable or unfavorable market conditions affect exchange relations—versus the "pure form" involving equivalents. Based on what was established in chapter 1, we are focusing here on the pure form.

Referring to the French philosopher Étienne Bonnot de Condillac (1715–1780) and more recent authors, Marx now shows how the claim that both sides can profit from exchange results from confusing use-value, where this mutual gain is possible, and value, where it is not.

c) The Exchange of Non-Equivalents
(third paragraph 262 to second paragraph 266)

Marx wants to consider not only the "pure form" of the circulation process, the exchange of equivalents, but also the exchange of non-equivalents. In exchange, commodity owners differ only as "sellers, those who own

The Transformation of Money into Capital   305

commodities, and buyers, those who own money" (263). Based on this distinction, which leaves out commodity owners' material differences, such as their having different needs and disposing of different use-values, Marx considers a total of four cases of non-equivalent exchange:

1. For whatever reason, sellers are able to sell their commodities *above their value*, for example, with a markup of 10 percent. However, since sellers also occupy the role of buyers, they have to pay the same markup in the second role. This means that what they gain as sellers, they lose as buyers. For this reason, a general price hike of 10 percent results in commodities exchanging for their value, with the only change being in the monetary expression of value.

Marx has passed over one issue here. If there is a general price increase of 10 percent where a gold currency is in use, one obtains fewer commodities with the same amount of gold. In effect, the gold producers are alone in experiencing a disadvantageous effect. However, if we are dealing with a paper currency not tied to a commodity, it will only be the paper expression of value that has increased.

2. Buyers could buy the commodities at 10 percent *below their value*. However, they would lose this profit when they in turn become sellers. (With a gold currency, the gold producers would be the only winners, obtaining more commodities for gold. Yet a paper currency not tied to a commodity entails that only the paper expression of value decreases.)

In this way, Marx arrives at a preliminary result:

> The formation of surplus-value, and therefore the transformation of money into capital, can consequently be explained neither by assuming that commodities are sold above their value, nor by assuming that they are bought at less than their value. (263)

3. Marx next considers the possibility of a class that *only buys*, without selling. If sellers now sell their commodities to this class above their value, then they can make profits they don't have to relinquish. But where does this class, which constantly buys without selling, get its money from?

> The money with which such a class is constantly making purchases must constantly flow into its coffers without any exchange, *gratis*, whether by might or by right, from the pockets of the commodity-owners themselves. To sell commodities at more than their value to such a class is only to get back again,

by swindling, a part of the money previously handed over for nothing. (264f.)

Hence, selling above value doesn't yield any real profit, but only minimizes the losses on money given away to the buying class without exchange. Marx illustrates this possibility with the relationship between the Romans and the towns of Asia Minor that paid tribute to them.

4. In addressing a fourth possibility of non-equivalent exchange, Marx drops the precondition employed up to now of "conceiving people merely as personified categories, instead of as individuals" (265). He imagines a "clever" commodity owner A, who bamboozles his colleague B, but B is unable to do the same. Now A has indeed made a profit, but there is a loss of exactly the same size on B's side. Circulating value has therefore not increased. Only distribution between A and B has changed. Now Marx draws the following conclusion:

> The sum of the values in circulation can clearly not be augmented by any change in their distribution, any more than a Jew can increase the quantity of the precious metals in a country by selling a farthing from the time of Queen Anne for a guinea.[47] The capitalist class of a given country, taken as a whole, cannot defraud itself. (265f.)

Marx's depiction of the coin dealer who sells cheap coins at high prices as a Jew is of a piece with widespread anti-Semitic stereotypes (see the commentary regarding page 256).

Wrapping up his reflections on value and circulation, Marx writes:

> If equivalents are exchanged, no surplus-value results, and if non-equivalents are exchanged, we still have no surplus-value. Circulation, or the exchange of commodities, creates no value. (266)

d) "Antediluvian Forms" of Capital
(third paragraph 266 to 267)

Immediately after asserting that circulation does not create value Marx goes on:

---

47. There are four farthings to a penny, twelve pence to a shilling, and twenty-one shillings to a guinea. This means that a guinea is equal to 1008 farthings.

The Transformation of Money into Capital

> It can be understood, therefore, why, in our analysis of the primary form of capital, the form in which it determines the economic organization of modern society, we have entirely left out of consideration its well-known and so to speak antediluvian forms, merchants' capital and usurers' capital. (266)

Why were merchants' capital and usurers' capital—forms of capital that appear very early in history and are therefore "antediluvian," that is, before the flood—initially passed over? It is not yet clear here, the explanation being reserved for the upcoming paragraphs. Still, Marx makes some interesting statements in this passage about the structure of his analysis. For one, he wants to analyze the "primary form of capital." So far, however, he hasn't yet analyzed any specific form of capital. He has only presented the "general formula" of capital, M – C – M′, although it's still unclear where surplus-value comes from. The analysis is pursuing a form of capital distinct from merchants' and usurers' capital, but we don't yet know what it is. That this fundamental form of capital also determines "the economic organization of modern society," as Marx contends, also still has to be shown. Importantly, Marx once again explains that the object of his analysis is the economy of "modern" society and not, for example, the history of that economy's emergence. The first edition's Preface explained that he aimed "to reveal the economic law of motion of modern society" (92).

Why doesn't Marx consider merchants' capital here? The profit of merchants' capital seems to depend on buying commodities cheap and selling them dear. Yet that is exactly what the exchange of equivalents precludes. Therefore it appears that mercantile capital must be based on merchants "cheating" the commodity producers. Marx now explains why we must delay the analysis of this "antediluvian" form of capital:

> If the valorization of merchants' capital is not to be explained merely by frauds practised on the producers of commodities, a long series of intermediate steps would be necessary, which are as yet entirely absent, since here our only assumption is the circulation of commodities and its simple elements. (267)

This statement makes two things clear. First, the valorization of merchants' capital in "modern society" can be explained without fraud. Second, we still lack the means to explain the valorization of merchants' capital at the level of presentation attained so far.

In usurers' capital, capital's "general formula" M – C – M′ shrinks to M – M′. It is "a form incompatible with the nature of money and therefore inexplicable from the standpoint of the exchange of commodities" (267). To illustrate the bizarre character of interest, Marx goes back to Aristotle again. He regards the Aristotle quote to be so important that he puts it in the main text rather than in a footnote as on page 253. Moreover, instead of contrasting chrematistics to economics as he did earlier, Aristotle is distinguishing between two types of chrematistics: one related to economics (the satisfaction of needs) and the other to the mere proliferation of money. Trade and usury belong to the latter. Aristotle feels he can explain merchant profit; he understands it as cheating (which he rebukes). In contrast, interest involves money creating new money, which for Aristotle is "most contrary to Nature," since money should be used for commodity exchange, but not for the generation of new money. After this illustration, Marx resumes:

> In the course of our investigation, we shall find that both merchants' capital and interest-bearing capital are *derivative forms*, and at the same time it will become clear why, historically, these two forms appear before the modern primary form of capital. (267, M.H. emphasis).

ADDENDUM: Here, Marx is suggesting how the valorization of merchants' capital and interest-bearing capital works under modern conditions. Both are *derivative* forms of capital, which are valorized through participation in another form of capital's valorization. Volume 3 of *Capital* will explain how exactly this occurs.

E) VALORIZATION IN PRODUCTION? (FIRST TWO PARAGRAPHS 268)

Marx summarizes the results so far:

> We have shown that surplus-value cannot arise from circulation, and therefore that, for it to be formed, something must take place in the background which is not visible in the circulation itself. (268)

After Marx has systematically reviewed all the possibilities of surplus-value arising from circulation, finding them infeasible, he concludes that surplus-value comes from outside of circulation. Outside of circulation the commodity owner simply deals with his own commodities—that is, their production.

Through the labor expended in the production process, the commodity maker produces value insofar as his commodity "contains a quantity of his own labour which is measured according to definite social laws" (268). With this remark, Marx reminds us that it is not the amount of individually expended labor that creates values, but only the quantity of labor that is *socially* recognized in exchange for a commodity's production. However, this newly constituted value does not amount to a *valorization* of value:

> The commodity-owner can create value by his labour, but he cannot create values which can valorize themselves. He can increase the value of his commodity by adding fresh labour, and therefore more value, to the value in hand, by making leather into boots, for instance.... The boots have therefore more value than the leather, but the value of the leather remains what it was. It has not valorized itself, it has not annexed surplus-value during the making of the boots. (268)

The increase of value proceeds from the commodity owner's labor—which was applied to the leather—but it is not a result of a *valorization* of the leather. It appears, then, that our commodity owner cannot valorize value outside of circulation either.

f) The Result: Paradoxical Requirements of the Presentation (second paragraph 268 to 269)

The starting point for this chapter was the observation that capital's general formula "contradicts all the previously developed laws bearing on the nature of commodities, value, money and even circulation itself" (258). Marx then played through various attempts to resolve this contradiction. He now summarizes his results, appealing to a further contradiction—which explains the plural "contradictions" in the chapter title:

> Capital cannot therefore arise from circulation, and it is equally impossible for it to arise apart from circulation. It must have its origin both in circulation and not in circulation. (268)

Importantly, these are very different types of contradictions. At the beginning of this chapter, the point was that the valorization of value, which the previous chapter presented as an empirical fact ("we find," page 248), *contradicts our available knowledge about* the commodity, value, and exchange. By contrast, the contradiction Marx has just formulated is an explanatory paradox: the analysis so far points to the *scientific explanation having to fulfill contradictory requirements* if it is to explain capital's valorization.

Based on the foregoing, Marx outlines the conditions that the explanation of capital formation must satisfy:

> The transformation of money into capital has to be developed on the basis of the immanent laws of the exchange of commodities, in such a way that the starting-point is the exchange of equivalents. (268f.)

Why? If the exchange of equivalents represents the norm in capitalist commodity exchange, then the transformation of money into capital should be explained by when the norm is applied and not when it is infringed. This methodological condition has an important political consequence. It was common, especially among socialists, to explain profit on capital as a *violation* of the exchange of equivalents: the capitalist was said to *rob* the worker. The idea was to juxtapose the "fairness" of the exchange of equivalents to the "unfairness" of profit on capital (in this spirit, the followers of Ferdinand Lassalle demanded the "full product of labor" for the workers). With Marx's precise way of framing the problem, he pulls the rug out from under that approach. At the same time, however, he doesn't assume that the exchange of equivalents always predominates in daily life under capitalism, as footnote 24 on page 269 makes clear.

If actual commodity prices deviate from values, one must first reduce them to values "to observe the phenomenon of the formation of capital on the basis of the exchange of commodities in its purity" (269n24). Marx emphasizes that this reduction is not "limited to the field of science"; it also occurs in reality: the oscillations in market prices "carry out their own reduction to an average price which is their internal regulator." Thus the problem of capital formation poses itself as follows:

> How can we account for the origin of capital on the assumption that prices are regulated by the average price, i.e. ultimately by the value of the commodities? I say "ultimately" because average prices do not directly coincide with the values of commodities. (269n24)

This last observation is of fundamental importance for Marx's value theory, since average prices based on observable market prices do *not directly* coincide with values. The commentary on chapter 1 (see page 78 of this book) brought this to our attention: one cannot deduce the value-relation of commodities (commodity A has thrice commodity B's value) from their exchange-relations (commodity A has thrice commodity B's cost). Value-relations cannot be directly observed, meaning that value theory is not empirically verifiable or provable in a direct sense.

ADDENDUM: Marx drops a similar clue somewhat later:

> The calculations given in the text are intended merely as illustrations. We have in fact assumed that prices = values. We shall, however, see in Volume 3 that even in the case of average prices the assumption cannot be made in this very simple manner. (329n9)

Marx first deals with the connection between values and average prices in the second section of *Capital*'s third volume.

After making clear the methodological preconditions for an explanation of capital formation, Marx illustrates the money owner's transformation into a capitalist with the image of a caterpillar emerging as a butterfly. His use of the German word *entpuppen* (to eclose) in this chapter's first sentence foreshadowed this curious image.[48] Again, Marx highlights the paradoxical restrictions on the explanation:

> The money-owner, who is as yet only a capitalist in larval form, must buy his commodities at their value, sell them at their value, and yet at the end of the process withdraw more value from circulation than he threw into it at the beginning. His emergence as a butterfly must, and yet must not, take place in the sphere of circulation. These are the conditions of the problem. *Hic Rhodus, hic salta!* (269)

The phrase "Hic Rhodus, hic salta!" comes from the Greek poet Aesop (ca. 600 BCE). In one of Aesop's fables, a pentathlete boasts about how far he once leapt in Rhodes. A bystander then challenges him: *Here is Rhodes, leap here!* Hegel used this sentence in the preface to his *Philosophy of Right* (which Marx cites many times in *Capital*) when emphasizing that he does not aim to construct the state as it ought to be,

---

48. Translated merely as "transformed" in the English edition.—Trans.

but to understand it as it is. Marx is also trying to precisely characterize a problem with a view to saying: here is exactly where the problem must be solved. He doesn't just do it to illuminate the reader. He is also posing the problem in a very sharp way as an implicit critique of political economists. Their usual explanations of capital gain don't conform to even minimum standards of a correct framing of the problem. These standards can be summarized:

a) In explaining surplus-value, it must be assumed that all commodities are bought and sold at their value.
b) The solution must be located both inside and outside the sphere of circulation. In other words, *a one-sided explanation of surplus-value creation focused on the sphere of circulation is just as wrong as a one-sided explanation focused on the sphere of production.*

Chapter 6: The Sale and Purchase of Labor-Power

A) On the Way to Solving the Puzzle: The Specific Commodity Labor-Power (Free Will and Objective Compulsion) (270 to third paragraph 272)

After specifying how capital formation *cannot* be explained, Marx now takes the first steps toward solving the problem. He returns to the general formula for capital, M – C – M′, which includes only the commodity and money, but with a greater sum of money at the end than the beginning. Marx writes: "The change in value of the money which has to be transformed into capital cannot take place in the money itself." This is because both the first and second acts of circulation involve the exchange of equivalents. Marx thus concludes:

> The change must therefore take place in the commodity which is bought in the first act of circulation, M – C, but not in its value, for it is equivalents which are being exchanged, and the commodity is paid for at its full value. The change can therefore originate only in the actual use-value of the commodity, i.e. in its consumption. (270)

Hence we are looking for a commodity with a very special *use-value*. But what kind of commodity would that be? It must be one

> whose use-value possesses the peculiar property of being a source of value, whose actual consumption is therefore itself an objectification [*Vergegenständlichung*] of labour, hence a creation of value. (270)

So far Marx has been drawing purely *logical conclusions*: the money and the *value* of the commodity exchanged cannot be the sources of valorization. Thus there remains only the commodity's *use-value*, which must have the property of being a source of value. Now Marx affirms, as an *empirical fact* (not a logical conclusion), that the money owner indeed encounters such a commodity on the market: *labor-power*. Marx had already mentioned labor-power at the beginning of chapter 1 (128), but here, for the first time, he explains the term:

> We mean by labour-power, or labour-capacity, the aggregate of those mental and physical capabilities existing in the physical form, the living personality, of a human being, capabilities which he sets in motion whenever he produces a use-value of any kind. (270)

If Marx is now appealing to labor-power and its capacity for production as the source of surplus-value, aren't we returning to the possibility just rejected—that is, of applying labor to the commodity—as an explanation of capital formation (268f.)?

In fact, that earlier situation dealt with a *commodity owner* who manufactures his own commodities. He wasn't relating to his own labor-power as a commodity: he neither purchases his own labor-power, nor sells it, but rather applies it through working. Things are different here with the *money owner* who transforms his money into capital. The latter purchases *another's* labor-power as a commodity, pays its value, and then appropriates the product it produces.

Labor-power should be distinguished from *labor*: labor-power is the capacity to work. Consequently selling labor-power is not interchangeable with selling labor. Note that here and in what follows, Marx refers only to the *sale of labor-power*, but not the *sale of labor*. Nor does Marx refer here to a *wage*, but rather to the *value (and price) of labor-power*. Volume 1's table of contents shows that in chapter 19 Marx begins an in-depth treatment of wages.

It shouldn't be taken for granted that labor-power exists *as a commodity*. Marx specifies two conditions that must be fulfilled for that to happen:

1. The owner of labor-power "must be the free proprietor of his own labour-capacity, hence of his person" (271); he cannot be a slave or serf. To retain his independence, he must only sell his labor-power for a specific time period. If he sells it forever, he is transformed from a free person into a slave and is no longer proprietor of his labor-power.

2. The owner of labor-power will only sell it if lacking the means to produce commodities himself and sell them on the market. To produce commodities himself, he must dispose of both means of production and means of subsistence (to survive the time between production and sale of the commodity). If he lacks these means, his labor-power becomes his *only* sellable commodity, which he or she therefore *must* sell.

Marx's description of the worker as "free in a double sense" summarizes both of these conditions:

> For the transformation of money into capital, therefore, the owner of money must find the free worker available on the commodity-market; and this worker must be free in the double sense that as a free individual he can dispose of his labour-power as his own commodity, and that, on the other hand, he has no other commodity for sale, i.e. he is rid of them, he is free of all the objects needed for the realization [*Verwirklichung*] of his labour-power. (272f.)

As pointed out earlier (pages 200–203), commodity owners are *forced* to exchange their commodities: despite having manifold needs, they usually only produce one product. If exchange is the prevailing form of social intercourse, they *must* exchange to acquire all the products required from others. In other words, the owner of labor-power must be a "free person," in the sense of being *able* to sell his or her labor-power. Additionally, he or she must be "free from" all opportunities to produce on his or her own, *forcing* him or her to sell his or her only commodity: labor-power. In contrast to the slave or the serf, the worker's free will is respected under capitalist commodity production; there is no *personal* dependence relation between worker and capitalist. Nevertheless, capitalism's formally free labor contract is grounded in the *impersonal compulsion of economic relations*, which leave the owner of labor-power no other choice but to sell it.

ADDENDUM: In Part Eight of Volume 1, on "So-Called Primitive Accumulation," Marx speaks of the "silent compulsion of economic relations" which "sets the seal on the domination of the capitalist over the worker" (899).

b) The "Historical Imprint" of Economic Categories (second paragraph 273 to first paragraph 274)

We shouldn't take for granted the existence of workers who are free in a double sense and sell their labor-power as a commodity. They don't exist in all societies. Rather, they are

> the result of a past historical development, the product of many economic revolutions, of the extinction of a whole series of older formations of social production. (273)

A few sentences earlier, Marx stated that the question of why the free worker exists doesn't interest us "for the present." Although the existence of the doubly free worker is the decisive historical precondition for valorizing capital, Marx does not want to examine it any further at this point. Here, we recognize the same procedure Marx pursued with the value-form analysis in chapter 1 (158; see commentary on page 130 of this book, which quoted the relevant methodological remarks from the *Introduction* of 1857) and with the examination of the exchange process in chapter 2 (181f., see commentary on pages 199 and 201 in this book). With both topics, Marx analyzed the developed relation's central form-determinations before turning to the *history* of their emergence. Here, too, Marx's initial focus is on the analysis of capital. As the Volume 1's table of contents reveals, Marx dedicates most of the chapters to come to the various methods of producing surplus-value. Only at the end of the first volume—in Part Eight on "So-Called Primitive Accumulation"—does Marx focus on the history of modern capital's emergence.

ADDENDUM: This centuries-long, extremely violent process was mostly about producing "doubly free" workers. Marx summarizes his sketch of the process as follows:

> *Tantae molis erati* [so great was the effort required] to unleash the 'eternal natural laws' of the capitalist mode of production, to complete the process of separation between the workers and the conditions of their labour, to transform, at one pole, the social means of production and subsistence into capital, and at the opposite pole, the mass of the population into wage-labourers, into the free 'labouring poor,' that artificial product of modern history. If money, according to Augier, 'comes into the world with a congenital blood-stain on one cheek,' capital comes dripping from head to toe, from every pore, with blood and dirt. (925f.)

After indicating that the "free worker" is a historical product, Marx observes in the next two paragraphs that the categories of money and the commodity, examined earlier, also bear a "historical imprint." That is

The Transformation of Money into Capital 317

to say, they express relations that have not always existed, but rather have specific historical preconditions.

"In order to become a commodity, the product must cease to be produced as the immediate means of subsistence of the producer himself" (273). When do most products become commodities? "This only happens on the basis of one particular mode of production, the capitalist one" (273). Marx nevertheless is eager to point out that the "production and circulation of commodities can still take place even though the great mass of the objects produced are intended for the immediate requirements of their producers, and are not turned into commodities, so that the process of social production is as yet by no means dominated in its length and breadth by exchange-value" (273). Marx had already mentioned this on page 209, footnote 24. Importantly, we are not dealing in either case with the "simple production of commodities" of the kind postulated by Engels.

Money likewise bears a historical imprint; its existence presupposes a certain level of commodity exchange. The various forms of money, Marx continues, can still begin to emerge even with weakly developed commodity circulation. Marx points out that there is a great difference between the category of money and that of capital:

> It is otherwise with capital. The historical conditions of its existence are by no means given with the mere circulation of money and commodities. (274)

This means the "historic presuppositions" for the emergence of capital mentioned at the beginning of chapter 4 (247) were far from complete. Marx continues:

> It arises only when the owner of the means of production and subsistence finds the free worker available, on the market, as the seller of his own labour-power. And this one historical pre-condition comprises a world's history. Capital, therefore, announces from the outset a new epoch in the process of social production. (274)

There are three important points here:

1. Marx speaks about "capital" here without qualifying it. However, he is obviously referring to what he earlier called the "primary form of capital, the form in which it determines the economic organization of modern society" (266). This is the *modern form of capital,* which

creates surplus-value by using the specific commodity labor-power. Marx contrasted it with the "antediluvian" forms, merchants' capital and usurers' capital, which are much older. What he writes in footnote 4 holds only for the modern form of capital that involves production:

> The capitalist epoch is therefore characterized by the fact that labour-power, in the eyes of the worker himself, takes on the form of a commodity which is his property; his labour consequently takes on the form of wage-labour. On the other hand, it is only from this moment that the commodity-form of the products of labour becomes universal. (274n4)

2. The claim that the "doubly free" worker's emergence embodies "a world's history" should be understood in two senses. First, it is not only local but worldwide changes that lead to this emergence. To produce the English capitalism examined in Part Eight, English colonialism played as much a role as developments in England. Second, creating these conditions and forming modern capitalism leads to a new chapter in world history. Under the influence of constantly expanding modern capitalism, world history becomes something different than it was before.

3. (Modern) capital generates "a new epoch in the process of social production" that is marked not only by a deepening social division of labor, but also by production in capitalist workshops and factories, where hundreds or even thousands of workers cooperate. This capitalist form of social production increasingly replaces individual production in small agricultural or artisanal units, which were typical of pre-capitalist times.

c) The Value of the Commodity Labor-Power (Class Struggle) (second paragraph 274 to first paragraph 279)

When Marx attempts to determine the value of the commodity labor-power, he first emphasizes what it has in common with all other commodities. As value, "it represents no more than a definite quantity of the average social labour objectified in it" (274). But how large is this quantity of objectified average labor? How do we determine the magnitude of value of the commodity labor-power? At first, Marx's analysis is very brief: labor-power exists only as an ability of the individual; therefore, its production consists in the individual's reproduction. For that to happen, the individual requires a certain amount of means of subsistence (in the broad sense, not just foodstuffs). This leads Marx to conclude:

Therefore the labour-time necessary for the production of labour-power is the same as that necessary for the production of those means of subsistence; in other words, the value of labour-power is the value of the means of subsistence necessary for the maintenance of its owner. (274)

Marx now indicates four important points for determining the commodity labor-power's magnitude of value:

1. Needs vary according to the natural and climatic conditions of a country. But they are also "products of history." Thus they depend upon the respective "level of civilization" as well as "on the conditions in which, and consequently on the habits and expectations with which, the class of free workers has been formed." Marx sums this up:

In contrast, therefore, with the case of other commodities, the determination of the value of labour-power contains a historical and moral element. (275)

He calls this element *historical* because it's a product of history. By contrast, Marx's speaking of a "moral" element does not imply that he espouses a particular moral standpoint. This element is "moral," because it's a matter of the actual acknowledgment of certain basic needs. For example, does a society consider it normal and acceptable that working-class families scrape by with a bare minimum and live in small, damp apartments?

Here Marx refers only to the conditions for forming the class of free workers. This might promote the illusion that this historical and moral element took shape merely in the past. But in fact the range of workers' basic needs accepted as normal and legitimate in capitalist society is always in dispute. This means that labor-power's value is *contested*—never more than momentarily fixed. The money owner seeks to valorize his capital by purchasing labor-power, seeking to pay no more than necessary to secure its use as a means of valorization. For the workers, by contrast, this struggle affects their lives as a whole, which are much more than mere means for valorizing capital.[49] The money owners' demands

---

49. Christian Iber finds a way make this point sharply. He looks at the value of labor-power from two sides: "The question for the capitalist is whether he can make a profit with low or high costs. The level of wages is therefore fixed by how useful they are to the capitalist." From the perspective of the workers, the value of labor-power is not a fixed magnitude, but is determined by their needs, which change with social

of valorization are thus fundamentally hostile to workers' basic needs, stimulating a lasting struggle. The value of the labor-power results from this *class struggle*—even if Marx does not use the term at this point.

ADDENDUM: In chapter 10, where Marx deals with the working day, he explicitly addresses class struggle over its length. The capitalist wants as long a working day as possible. Having purchased labor-power, he wishes to consume its use-value (the expenditure of labor-power) for as long as possible. By contrast, the owner of labor-power aspires to limit the working day. His or her labor-power, which he or she must sell again tomorrow, should not be destroyed by overuse. Both claims are legitimate within the framework of commodity exchange. Marx concludes:

> There is here therefore an antinomy, of right against right, both equally bearing the seal of the law of exchange. Between equal rights, force decides. Hence, in the history of capitalist production, the establishment of a norm for the working day presents itself as a struggle over the limits of that day, a struggle between collective capital, i.e. the class of capitalists, and collective labour, i.e. the working class. (344)

2. The individual owners of labor-power are mortal. If labor-power is to be constantly available on the market, its owners must reproduce. This affects labor-power's magnitude of value:

> Hence the sum of means of subsistence necessary for the production of labour-power must include the means necessary for the worker's replacements, i.e. his children, in order that this race of peculiar commodity-owners may perpetuate its presence on the market. (275)

As is clear from the context, the word "race" here refers to a social group or class. In the German original, Marx uses unthinkingly the androcentric term *Ersatzmänner*, literally "substitute-men," translated here with the neutral word "replacements," but it's clear that for maintaining this peculiar "race," substitute women or "*Ersatzfrauen*" are just as important.

There is an important point here that Marx doesn't mention. The value of labor-power also depends on how many members of a family normally sell their labor-power. If the male-provider family model is

---

conditions. It follows from this that "the value of labor-power depends upon what the workers of a country will tolerate, that is, what they've managed to impose on capital as the customary conditions for their reproduction" (Iber 2000: 128).

dominant, then the value of (male) labor-power must cover the entire family's costs of reproduction. However, if the dual-income family model is dominant, then the family's reproduction costs are a bit higher since less is produced in the household, and more must be purchased on the market. But now two labor-powers share the reproduction costs, and the value of individual labor-power declines.

ADDENDUM: Chapter 15, "Machinery and Large-Scale Industry," addresses these issues explicitly:

> The value of labour-power was determined, not only by the labour-time necessary to maintain the individual adult worker, but also by that necessary to maintain his family. Machinery, by throwing every member of that family onto the labour-market, spreads the value of the man's labour-power over his whole family. (518)

This refers to how women's and children's labor expanded following the introduction of machinery. In a footnote, Marx adds:

> Since certain family functions, such as nursing and suckling children, cannot be entirely suppressed, the mothers who have been confiscated by capital must try substitutes of some sort. Domestic work, such as sewing and mending, must be replaced by the purchase of ready-made articles. Hence the diminished expenditure of labour in the house is accompanied by an increased expenditure of money outside. The cost of production of the working-class family therefore increases, and balances its greater income. (518n39)

3. "In order to modify the general nature of the human organism in such a way that it acquires skill and dexterity in a given branch of industry, and becomes labour-power of a developed and specific kind, a special education or training is needed" (275f.).

Marx has not previously mentioned the "general nature of the human organism." Nor does he say anything else about what it might be. However, Marx frequently refers to the general "nature" of something in his work: the nature of the commodity (174n34, 218n28); of commodity exchange (279); of commodity circulation (211); and much later of capital (400n19, 433). At the beginning of chapter 5, Marx spoke of the "nature of commodities, value, money, and even circulation itself" (258). In effect, Marx uses the term "nature" to refer to important, fundamental properties of the object under consideration. It's hotly contested whether or not Marx assumes a specific "human nature" or "anthropology" in *Capital*. In this passage at least, Marx's saying "the general nature of the human organism" does not involve sweeping anthropological claims about "humans" (but see my commentary on pages 283-84, where Marx characterizes the specifically human labor process). From the context, it's clear that he is simply referring to the elementary physical and mental capacities—for physical coordination, mental concentration, attentiveness, and so on—that an average person possesses without special training. Specific training is needed to develop these capacities and to specialize in a certain branch of labor. The training costs enter into the value of labor-power. Depending on their training requirements, labor-powers with different qualifications have different values:

> These expenses (exceedingly small in the case of ordinary labour-power) form a part of the total value spent in producing it. (276)

The phrase "ordinary labour-power" does not refer to the least qualified labor-power, but rather to that of "ordinary" (usual) qualification in a given society. The level of ordinary qualification rises with time, however, so that today these expenses are not as small as Marx assumes here.

4. "The value of labour-power can be resolved into the value of a definite quantity of the means of subsistence. It therefore varies with the value of the means of subsistence, i.e. with the quantity of labour-time required to produce them" (276).

It's hardly surprising that the value of labor-power changes with the value of the means of subsistence (in the broad sense, not just foodstuffs). A table's value also changes with variations in the value of the wood used to make it. However, it's a peculiarity of labor-power that its value is solely composed of the value of those products necessary for its reproduction that are *purchased on the market*. By contrast, a table's value does not include only the value of the wood used (and other means of production). The carpenter who produces the table also contributes to its value through his labor to the extent that this labor is "socially necessary." In this sense, the determination of the value of the commodity labor-power exhibits a peculiarity.

It is easy to see how this peculiarity is functional for capitalism. If domestic reproductive labor (which in Marx's time, as it is today, was primarily done by women) counted as value-creating labor, entering into labor-power's value, then workers would systematically be paid more than what they spend on the market for reproduction. After a while, workers would no longer completely lack means of subsistence. They might be able to buy simple means of production and would no longer need to sell their labor-power.

Nevertheless, even if a certain state of affairs is functional to capitalism it is not an explanation for its actual existence. One must therefore inquire into the socioeconomic mechanisms ensuring that labor-power's value is limited to the value of the goods that the working-class family must purchase on the market.

ADDENDUM: Part Two of *Capital* does not address these mechanisms. Instead, Marx first treats them in chapter 25, when dealing with, among other things, how wage increases repeatedly run up against the limits that capital generates. If labor-power's value fails to increase, or even declines, it does not mean that the working-class family's standard of living must decline. A living standard depends upon the *quantity* of use-values that are available to consume. When labor productivity increases (leading to a decline in value of individual commodities), a *decline in labor-power's value* can indeed go hand-in-hand with *more use-values* being available for the working-class family's consumption. (This occurs whenever the value of labor-power decreases by a smaller percentage than the increase of average labor productivity in the sectors that produce goods the working-class families consume.)

After these reflections on labor power's magnitude of value, Marx looks at two further issues: calculating the daily value of labor-power (276f.) and its time of payment (277f.).

In a schematic way, he shows how to calculate the daily value of labor-power (a magnitude he will use frequently in what follows): the daily value should include not only the goods required each day, but also a proportion of those purchased for longer periods of time (for example, heating fuel). Assuming this mass of commodities represents six hours of social labor, then these six hours constitute, in turn, labor-power's daily value (276). Marx describes the value of the means of subsistence that are physically indispensable as the "ultimate or minimum limit of the value of labor-power." However, the phrase is inexact. It only constitutes the minimum limit of survival, but not of the value of labor-power, as he immediately points out:

> If the price of labour-power falls to this minimum, it falls below its value, since under such circumstances it can be maintained and developed only in a crippled state, and the value of every

commodity is determined by the labour-time required to provide it in its normal quality. (277)

At the time of purchase, the buyer of labor power has not yet obtained its use-value.[50] "The alienation [*Veräusserung*; corrected translation: "selling"] of labour-power and its real manifestation [*Äusserung*], i.e. the period of its existence as a use-value, do not coincide in time" (277). In all capitalist countries, the norm is to pay for labor-power only after using it for a certain period of time. The buyer's money thus functions as a means of payment, and the worker becomes the capitalist's creditor.

This credit relationship is not just a formality. The possibility of default is quite real (if the capitalist goes bankrupt, he won't pay). But even if the capitalist ultimately pays, the worker must often, while waiting for payment, indebt himself or herself to merchants. In his analysis, however, Marx wants to begin by disregarding how the worker advances credit to the capitalist, assuming instead that he or she is paid immediately (279).

d) Illustration and (Moral) Critique (footnote 14)

Using dramatic examples, Marx's footnote 14 illustrates the effects of the worker becoming a de facto creditor to the money owner. The worker frequently becomes, in turn, a debtor to merchants and must often rely on means of subsistence that are inferior and insalubrious. This long footnote is unnecessary in terms of the pure analysis Marx is carrying out—those "theoretical developments" (90) he mentions in the Preface. So why is it included?

Marx is not just illustrating his theoretical analysis here, but also *showing*, through a kind of social reporting, the miserable living conditions of workers under capitalism. This footnote is the first of several such passages in Marx's presentation. The literature on Marx frequently interprets these passages as proof, despite Marx's ridiculing moralistic critiques of capitalism such as Proudhon's (178n2), that *Capital* also contains a level of moralist argumentation. In fact, it would have been easy here to make moral judgments, indicting capitalism for

---

50. Marx comments that the value of labor-power "like that of every other commodity, is already determined before it enters into circulation" (277). On this, see my commentary on pages 303-4 of this book on Marx's similar remark on page 260 of *Capital*.

violating human dignity, for example. However, Marx forgoes explicit value judgments. Instead, he lets the facts speak for themselves: the footnote consists solely of quotes from official reports or from summaries of such reports. That doesn't mean that Marx's role is that of a neutral observer. The arrangement of the text in the footnote shows that Marx is outraged by such conditions and wants to elicit the same outrage in the reader. He doesn't seek to do so with *arguments* proving that norms of justice or moral principles have been violated (he does not mention any such principles or norms). Instead, both here and in similar passages of *Capital*, Marx tries to *show* the miserable living conditions and suffering that capital brings into being.[51]

ADDENDUM: If Marx abstains from making explicit ethical-moral arguments, it is because he regards moral norms and notions of justice as products of a given society, which makes them unsuitable as standards with which to critique that society. A remark from Volume 3 of *Capital* makes crystal clear Marx's conception of the social contingency of norms:

> It is nonsense for Gilbart to speak of natural justice in this connection (see note). The justice of transactions between agents of production consists in the fact that these transactions arise from the relations of production as their natural consequence. The legal forms in which these economic transactions appear as voluntary actions of the participants, as the expressions of their common will and as contracts that can be enforced on the parties concerned by the power of the state, are mere forms that cannot themselves determine this content. They simply express it. The content is just so long as it corresponds to the mode of production and is adequate to it. It is unjust as soon as it contradicts it. Slavery, on the basis of the capitalist mode of production, is unjust; so is cheating on the quality of commodities. (460f.)

The miserable living conditions that capitalism creates can take quite different forms over the course of history. This means that some of Marx's examples may appear to be obsolete today. Nevertheless, although many of these forms have disappeared in the developed capitalist countries, they can return, even there, in periods of crisis. In one respect, the

---

51. Some would claim that speaking of "suffering" and "misery" itself implies a moral judgment. However, this confuses ascertaining misery with the question of its justification. In a very sophisticated manner, Lindner (2013) tries to demonstrate that Marx's critique of political economy, despite his critique of moral principles, includes an ethical dimension that in no way coincides with such principles.

forms of indebting presented in footnote 14 have changed. In developed capitalist countries today, workers rarely depend on retailers granting them credit. However, this is because most workers pay with credit cards or overdraw on a checking account, borrowing from a credit card company or bank. Consequently, by relying on overdrafts (which are usually very expensive), they can buy the goods they need *before* the payment on their labor-power comes in. In the end, the owners of labor-power extend credit to capitalists by borrowing from a bank at high cost. In fact, workers don't fully dispose of their entire wage, since a portion goes almost automatically to the bank as interest payments.

e) The Use-Value of the Commodity Labor-Power (second paragraph 279 to first paragraph 280)

Concerning the use-value of labor-power, Marx writes that it "manifests itself only in the actual utilization, in the process of the consumption of the labour-power" and this "process of the consumption of labour-power is at the same time the production process of commodities and of surplus-value" (279).

Marx has not yet shown that using labor-power actually creates *surplus*-value. So far, we only know that using labor-power creates *value*—if the buyer of labor-power sells the product on the market instead of consuming it directly. We don't yet know whether consuming labor-power actually creates new value that exceeds the value paid for the labor-power. However, only in that way will the money advanced be valorized, and actually transform into capital. Hence we must now leave the visible sphere of circulation and enter "the hidden abode of production." This step is necessary not for completeness sake, but rather to determine whether and under what conditions valorization is possible. Marx announces what the sphere of production holds for us in the following way:

> Here we shall see, not only how capital produces, but how capital is itself produced. The secret of profit-making must at last be laid bare. (280)

The initial part of this commentary pointed out that the title of *Capital*'s first volume, "The Production Process of Capital," is ambiguous. Marx addresses that ambiguity in the first sentence quoted above, and promises to reveal something about both meanings. The second sentence indicates that the explanation of surplus-value creation is not over yet. The "secret of profit-making" has still not been completely "laid bare."

f) The Sphere of Circulation and the Sphere of Production, Freedom, and Coercion (280)

There is an unmistakable irony in the next paragraph, in which Marx characterizes "the sphere of circulation or commodity exchange" as "a very Eden of the innate rights of man" where "Freedom, Equality, Property and Bentham" (280) reign. However, the freedom and equality he refers to are not merely illusory. There is indeed freedom of voluntary contract: the buyers and sellers of the labor-power "contract as free persons, who are equal before the law" (280). Moreover, there is *equality* among commodity owners: all are equal before the law. This kind of freedom and equality did not exist in pre-capitalist societies, either in the relations between slaves and slave owners or those between serfs and lords. However, the freedom and equality that exists among commodity owners is still connected to coercion and inequality. The worker is *free* to sell his or her labor-power, but he or she is also *forced* to sell it, for lack of other commodities. In a legal sense, the worker is the money owners equal, and each has dominion only over his own property. Materially, it makes an enormous difference that one of them already possesses money and the material conditions of production, while the other needs money to survive. Impersonal relations of force have replaced relations of personal domination. Marx already pointed out this difference on page 247, in footnote 1.

Marx identifies "Bentham" with the celebration of self-interest as something socially useful. It is an idea he finds frankly ridiculous:

> And Bentham, because each looks only to his own advantage. The only force bringing them together, and putting them into relation with each other, is the selfishness, the gain and the private interest of each. Each pays heed to himself only, and no one worries about the others. And precisely for that reason, either in accordance with the pre-established harmony of things, or under the auspices of an omniscient providence, they all work together to their mutual advantage, for the common weal, and in the common interest. (280)

Jeremy Bentham (1748–1832) was an English philosopher who founded modern "Utilitarianism." According to that school—which is the complement to classical political economy in the terrain of social philosophy—man is driven by utility. Actions are morally justified if they promote "the greatest happiness of the greatest number of people." This is best achieved if everyone is free to pursue his or her own benefit, while respecting the property of others. Bentham adamantly rejects interfering in property relations.

ADDENDUM: In chapter 24, Marx says of Bentham that "in no time and in no country has the most homespun manufacturer of commonplaces ever strutted about in so self-satisfied a way.... With the dryest naïveté he assumes that the modern petty bourgeois, especially the English petty bourgeois, is the normal man. Whatever is useful to this peculiar kind of normal man, and to his world, is useful in and for itself. He applies this yardstick to the past, the present and the future." Marx portrays Bentham as "a genius in the way of bourgeois stupidity" (758n51).

Marx not only summarizes Bentham's views on page 280, but also the credo of economic liberalism. The latter is still alive today, with its perennial battle cry for "more markets!" Its underlying dogma is that if each individual pursues his personal advantage and respects the property of others (thereby assuring that his own property is respected), this will serve everybody best, producing an optimal outcome for all. Even today, liberalism has problems justifying its credo. Obviously, neither Bentham nor liberalism's other representatives speak of the "pre-established harmony of things" or the "auspices of an omniscient providence" as factors conducing to the common interest. Instead, Marx makes these ironic references to highlight the irrationality of the whole liberal construction. The first phrase on the "harmony of things" comes from the philosopher Gottfried Wilhelm Leibniz (1646–1716). It means that God bestowed an internal order to the world's many separate units of force, and this order guarantees the harmoniousness of the entire world. Long before Marx, the idea ceased to be taken seriously. The second phrase has a similar meaning: "the auspices ... of providence" refers to a divine power that guides us and is supposed to direct things toward the common interest. All of this amounts to saying that the liberal credo cannot be *rationally* justified.

The kind of "common interest" that commodity exchange generates is fairly evident. The money owner enters the market to transform his money into capital. After engaging in the circuit $M - C - M'$, he gets back both the money originally advanced and an additional sum, which is surplus-value. By contrast, the workers who sell their labor-power go through the circuit $C - M - C$, in which the first "C" stands for their

The Transformation of Money into Capital

labor-power and the second "C" represents the means of subsistence they consume. They come out of this circuit just as lacking in material property as when they entered it. This means that they must sell their labor-power again and create more surplus-value for the owner of money. Hence the resulting "common weal" is quite unequal: the continual reproduction of wealth on one side and poverty on the other.

ADDENDUM: In chapter 23, Marx summarizes the reproduction of social relations as follows:

> Capitalist production therefore reproduces in the course of its own process the separation between labour-power and the conditions of labour. It thereby reproduces and perpetuates the conditions under which the worker is exploited [see the concluding section of the commentary on chapter 7]. It incessantly forces him to sell his labour-power in order to live, and enables the capitalist to purchase labour-power in order that he may enrich himself. It is no longer a mere accident that capitalist and worker confront each other in the market as buyer and seller. It is the alternating rhythm of the process itself which throws the worker back onto the market again and again as a seller of his labour-power and continually transforms his own product into a means by which another man can purchase him. In reality, the worker belongs to capital before he has sold himself to the capitalist. His economic bondage is at once mediated through, and concealed by, the periodic renewal of the act by which he sells himself, his change of masters, and the oscillations in the market-price of his labour. The capitalist process of production, therefore, seen as a total, connected process, i.e. a process of reproduction, produces not only commodities, not only surplus-value, but it also produces and reproduces the capital-relation itself; on the one hand the capitalist, on the other the wage-labourer. (723f.)

In the chapter's final paragraph, Marx points out what happens when the "free-trader *vulgaris*" (like today's neoliberal economists) uses the sphere of circulation as his yardstick. He ends up both idealizing the dominant relations there and concealing that "the society of capital and wage-labour" (280) consists of much more than the sphere of circulation. The sphere of production is also part of that society, and we encounter other economic characters in it. "A certain change takes place," Marx writes, "in the physiognomy of our *dramatis personae*" (208). In the sphere of production, the free and equal owners of commodities now morph into capitalist and wage laborer, which is far more than just a formal change.

At the beginning of chapter 2, Marx stated that "commodities are things, and therefore lack the power to resist man. If they are unwilling, he can use force" (178). The commodity labor-power is not a thing, and it is inseparable from its owner. Nevertheless, in the sphere of production, the capitalist rules over the worker's labor power. He can decide how to deploy it, what its application will be, and so on. For the duration of labor-power's sale, the formerly free and equal exchange partners are transformed into ruler and ruled. In the last sentence, Marx emphasizes how unpleasant this relation of domination is for the seller of labor-power: the worker, who "has brought his own hide to market" can expect nothing else in the sphere of production but "a tanning" (208).

ADDENDUM: In these passages, Marx is battling with those who praise capitalism as a system of freedom and equality. They tend to idealize the relations that operate in the sphere of circulation while denying the relations of domination that exist in the production sphere. What are the consequences of this? Sometimes Marx's critique is said to be an "immanent" one, meaning that it shows how capitalism contradicts its own norms of freedom, equality, and property. For example, Jürgen Habermas takes this position, basing himself mostly on Marx's early writings (Habermas 1963: 110f.), while Georg Lohman develops the position more fully and involves *Capital* in his argument (Lohman 1991). In this view, the goal would be to actually realize what capitalism promises but cannot make good on. Marx argued against such conceptions before, in the *Grundrisse*. There he criticizes

> the foolishness of those socialists (namely the French, who want to depict socialism as the realization of the ideals of *bourgeois* society articulated by the French revolution) who demonstrate that exchange and exchange value etc. are *originally* (in time) or *essentially* (in their adequate form) a system of universal freedom and equality, but that they have been perverted by money, capital, etc. . . . The proper reply to them is: that exchange value or, more precisely, the money system is in fact the system of equality and freedom, and that the disturbances which they encounter in the further development of the system are disturbances inherent in it, are merely the realization of *equality and freedom*, which prove to be inequality and unfreedom. (Marx 1973: 248f.)

The crucial point is that capitalist relations may involve (material) inequality and (objective) lack of freedom, while commodity owners enjoy (legal) equality and (personal) freedom. But there is no contradiction between the two. Rather the former are *consequences* of the latter! For this reason, Marx accuses these socialists of a

> utopian inability to grasp the necessary difference between the real and the ideal form of bourgeois society, which is the cause of their desire to undertake

> the superfluous business of realizing the ideal expression again, which is in fact only the inverted projection [*Lichtbild*] of this reality. (249)

However, the question of freedom and equality doesn't end here. What circulation generates is only a certain kind of freedom and equality. It is the freedom of *atomistic individuals who are indifferent to each other* and make one another into means to their own ends. In the *Urtext*, Marx calls this, with greater precision, the "realm of bourgeois liberty and bourgeois equality" (MECW 28: 464). In contrast, Marx knows of another "realm of freedom," which

> really begins only where labour determined by necessity and external expediency ends; it lies by its very nature beyond the sphere of material production proper. . . . Freedom, in this sphere [that is, in actual material production], can consist only in this, that socialized man, the associated producers, govern the human metabolism with nature in a rational way, bringing it under their collective control instead of being dominated by it as a blind power; accomplishing it with the least expenditure of energy and in conditions most worthy and appropriate for their human nature. But this always remains a realm of necessity. The true realm of freedom, the development of human powers as an end in itself, begins beyond it, though it can only flourish with this realm of necessity as its basis. The reduction of the working day is the basic prerequisite. (*Capital III*: 958f.)

This realm of freedom consists in developing each person's individuality as an end in itself. In capitalism, it is the privilege of a few. For the majority, their "freedom" consists in the compulsion to sell their labor-power, and submit themselves, as a consequence, to a relationship of domination. Only when an "association of free people" (171, corrected translation) can control the production process, instead of being ruled by it, will this realm of freedom become a reality for all. As Marx points out elsewhere in *Capital*, the "ruling principle" of the "higher form of society" (739) that might succeed capitalism is not just the overcoming of suffering and misery, but rather "the full and free development of every individual."[52]

---

52. *The Communist Manifesto* already expressed the key principle of a communism: "In place of the old bourgeois society, with its classes and class antagonisms, we shall have an association, in which the free development of each is the condition for the free development of all" (MECW 6: 506)

Part Three: The Production of Absolute Surplus-Value

As announced at the end of chapter 6, we are now dealing with the production process. *Capital*'s table of contents makes clear that not just Part Three, but also Parts Four and Five, deal with production. Marx does not explain right away what he means by "absolute" surplus-value. This explanation first appears in the fourth section of chapter 12 (432). However, in the conclusion of the commentary on chapter 7 the term will be explained.

Chapter 7: The Labour Process and the Valorization Process

1. The Labor Process

> The use of labour-power is labour itself. The purchaser of labour-power consumes it by setting the seller of it to work. By working, the latter becomes in actuality what previously he only was potentially, namely labour-power in action, a worker. (283)

Marx wrote earlier that labor-power is "the aggregate of those mental and physical capabilities" that a person sets into motion "whenever he produces a use-value of any kind" (270). He thereby evokes a distinction going back to Aristotle between *potentia* and *actu*. Through laboring, the worker applies those capabilities that constitute his labor-power. In that

The Production of Absolute Surplus-Value

way, labor-power actually becomes operative (*actu*), whereas previously it was present only as a possibility (*potentia*).[53]

> In order to embody his labour in commodities, he must above all embody it in use-values, things which serve to satisfy needs of one kind or another. (283)

Back in chapter 1, Marx stated at the end of the first subsection that the universal precondition for transforming labor products into commodities is their being use-values, on the one hand, and use-values for *others*, on the other (131).

> The fact that the production of use-values, or goods, is carried on under the control of a capitalist and on his behalf does not alter the general character of that production. We shall therefore, in the first place, have to consider the labour process independently of any specific social formation. (283)

The first sentence should be read carefully. Marx is *not* claiming that it's irrelevant that the labor process is organized capitalistically. He is only saying that it doesn't change the "general character" of producing use-values. This "general character" of the production process—which is independent "of any specific social formation"—is what Marx now wants to address. However, the labor process always exists within specific social formations. This means that what Marx is considering here are the *abstract elements* of every labor process (as he explicitly emphasizes on page 290).

a) General Characteristics of the Human Labor Process, the "Nature" of Human Beings (Second Paragraph 283 to First Paragraph 284)

> Labour is, first of all, a process between man and nature, a process by which man, through his own actions, mediates, regulates and controls the metabolism between himself and nature. (283)

In chapter 1, Marx wrote this about concrete-useful labor in the second subsection:

---

53. In the original German text Marx uses the Latin words *actu* and *potentia*, which were often used in philosophical discussions about Aristotle.

> Labour, then, as the creator of use-values, as *useful labour*, is *a condition of human existence which is independent of all forms of society*; it is an eternal natural necessity which mediates the metabolism between man and nature, and therefore human life itself. (133, emphasis M.H.)

Marx is looking for *concrete-useful* labor's general characteristics that, regardless of the type of society, are a condition of human existence. About the human being who works, Marx writes:

> He confronts the materials of nature as a force of nature. He sets in motion the natural forces which belong to his own body, his arms, legs, head and hands, in order to appropriate the materials of nature in a form adapted to his own needs. (283)

In saying that humans confront "the materials of nature" as a "force of nature," Marx is emphasizing that human beings are also "nature." They do not stand outside nature, but form part of it.

> Through this movement he acts upon external nature and changes it, and in this way he simultaneously changes his own nature. He develops the potentialities slumbering within nature, and subjects the play of its forces to his own sovereign power. (283)

Marx refers again to human "nature," as he did on page 275, but this time in a less general sense. His claim that human beings develop their own nature by transforming external nature is not valid for "those first instinctive forms of labour which remain on the animal level." Rather it holds only for "labour in a form in which it is an exclusively human characteristic" (283f.). Here, Marx is drawing a dividing line between animals and humans, with a view to characterizing the *specifically human* labor process. Thus he refers to basic human capacities:

> A spider conducts operations which resemble those of the weaver, and a bee would put many a human architect to shame by the construction of its honeycomb cells. But what distinguishes the worst architect from the best of bees is that the architect builds the cell in his mind before he constructs it in wax. (284)

The first human ability that Marx specifies here is *anticipating* the possible results of actions.

The Production of Absolute Surplus-Value

> At the end of every labour process, a result emerges which had already been conceived by the worker at the beginning, hence already existed ideally. Man not only effects a change of form in the materials of nature; he also realizes [*verwirklicht*] his own purpose in those materials. (284)

The second ability is *intentionality*—the human ability to anticipate different results makes it possible to pursue a specific purpose by deciding among various courses of action. The same passage continues:

> And this is a purpose he is conscious of, it determines the mode of his activity with the rigidity of a law, and he must subordinate his will to it. This subordination is no mere momentary act. Apart from the exertion of the working organs, a purposeful will is required for the entire duration of the work. This means close attention. (284)

The third ability is *reflexivity*: I have to reflect on what I do and for what reasons. Only then can I direct my actions according to my intentions, and subordinate my will to my purpose. Together, *anticipation*, *intentionality*, and *reflexivity* constitute the *purposeful activity* that is specific to human beings. Fourth, Marx assumes that human beings, through this specifically human labor process, "change" their own nature and develop "the potentialities slumbering within nature," rather than just simply improving existing abilities. This means he posits a *universal* ability of human beings to learn. It's not just a question of improving the individual labor process (a capacity shared by other highly developed animals). Rather, we develop abilities in one labor process that we can then carry over to other labor processes and combine with other abilities. In fact, Marx's analysis of the specifically human labor process contains the elements of a minimal anthropology. It does not, however, specify a fixed, ahistorical "human essence." Instead, it identifies the conditions for human beings' abilities and needs to constantly develop and change through interaction with external nature.

b) The Object of Labor, Instruments of Labor, Objectified (Concrete) Labor
(second paragraph 284 to second paragraph 287)

Marx now outlines the labor process's basic elements:

> The simple elements of the labour process are (1) purposeful activity, that is work itself, (2) the object on which that work is performed, and (3) the instruments of that work. (284)

Marx has just discussed the first point: labor as purposeful activity. The next two paragraphs will be devoted to characterizing the object and instruments of labor. The *object of labor* is that which is transformed by the labor process. If the object of labor itself results from a labor process, it is called a *raw material*.

The *instruments of labor* are things that the worker interposes between himself and the object of labor to better transform the latter. With a few exceptions (such as picking ripe fruit), the worker first grasps the instrument of labor and not the object of labor itself.

> Thus nature becomes one of the organs of his activity, which he annexes to his own bodily organs, adding stature to himself in spite of the Bible. (285)

"The Bible" possibly refers to Matthew 6:27 or Luke 12:25 according to the MEGA commentary on this passage; these biblical verses seem to be about incrementing one's height or stature. In any case, the real point of these Bible passages is that human beings cannot extend the *temporal* duration of their lives, whereas Marx is concerned with the instruments of labor as extensions of human beings' natural organs.

However, as soon as the labor process develops somewhat, it requires *previously elaborated* instruments of labor. Many animal species *use* instruments of labor (for example, some apes crack open nuts with stones or use sticks to reach distant fruit). But *creating* instruments of labor, in an ever more widespread way, is specific to human beings. Appealing to Benjamin Franklin's definition of man as a "tool-making animal," Marx points to the importance of labor instruments in characterizing the various socioeconomic formations:

> It is not what is made but how, and by what instruments of labour, that distinguishes different economic epochs. Instruments of labour not only supply a standard of the degree of development which human labour has attained, but they also indicate the social relations within which men work. (286)

Marx is not defending any kind of technological determinism here. It is not that instruments of labor determine social relations. Instead, Marx claims that they are "indicators" of these relations. If labor is done only with simple, easily made instruments, then there will be simple social relations with a less pronounced social division of labor. By contrast, labor may be done with a large number of more complex instruments, which themselves result from complex labor processes. This would accompany a pronounced social division of labor and complex chains of dependence that individual producers barely perceive.

In summary, Marx states about the labor process:

> In the labour process, therefore, man's activity, via the instruments of labour, effects an alteration in the object of labour which was intended from the outset. The process is extinguished in the product. The product of the process is a use-value, a piece of natural material adapted to human needs by means of a change in its form. Labour has become bound up in its object: labour has been objectified, the object has been worked on. (287)

In the foregoing there have been many references to labor being "objectified." However, since this was always in reference to value, the objectified labor in question was *abstract human labor*. At the beginning of chapter 1, for example, Marx said: "A use-value, or useful article, therefore, has value only because abstract human labour is objectified [*vergegenständlicht*] or materialized in it" (129). Here, by contrast, we are dealing with objectified *concrete* labor—that is, labor that creates use-values.

c) Product, Means of Production, Productive Labor, and (Concrete) Living Labor
(third paragraph 287 to fourth paragraph 290)

Here Marx introduces two additional terms, "means of production" and "productive labor":

> If we look at the whole process from the point of view of its result, the product, it is plain that both the instruments and the object of labour are means of production and that the labour itself is productive labour. (287)

Marx points out in footnote 8 that his characterization of productive labor as use-value–creating labor—that is, productive labor "from the standpoint of the simple production process"—is not identical with the characterization of productive labor from the standpoint of the capitalist production process.

ADDENDUM: "Productive labor" under capitalist conditions refers to *surplus-value creating labor*. In the first volume of *Capital* this is discussed only briefly in chapter 16 (643f.). However, *Theories of Surplus Value* contains a more in-depth discussion (MECW 30: 306–10, MECW 34: 121–46).

Marx now turns to the *product* of the labor process. Frequently, it becomes a means of production in another labor process. In fact, only a few industries have objects of labor that come directly from nature. Most often the object of labor is already a raw material (a previously worked-on object). The same product could be a raw material in one labor process and an instrument of labor in another. Marx concludes:

> Therefore, whenever products enter as means of production into new labour processes, they lose their character of being products and function only as objective factors contributing to living labour. (289)

Here Marx mentions "living labor" for the first time. The term refers to concrete labor employed in the labor process and contrasts with the labor already objectified in products. But the labor objectified in things is only useful if living labor actually engages with them:

> A machine which is not active in the labour process is useless.... Yarn with which we neither weave nor knit is cotton wasted. Living labour must seize on these things, awaken them from the dead, change them from merely possible into real and effective use-values. (289)

The upshot is:

> If then, on the one hand, finished products are not only results of the labour process, but also conditions of its existence, their induction into the process, their contact with living labour, is the sole means by which they can be made to retain their character of use-values, and be realized. (290)

Marx next distinguishes between two things. On the one hand, the labor process involves "productive consumption" of use-values, leading to an independent product. On the other hand, there is "individual consumption" which "produces" only the consumer. When people refer to "consumption" these days they usually mean individual consumption.

d) Levels of Abstraction of the Presentation (last paragraph 290 to first paragraph 291)

The labour process, as we have just presented it in its simple and abstract elements, is purposeful activity aimed at the production of use-values. It is an appropriation of what exists in nature for the requirements of man. It is the universal condition for the metabolic interaction [*Stoffwechsel*] between man and nature, the everlasting nature-imposed condition of human existence, and it is therefore independent of every form of that existence, or rather it is common to all forms of society in which human beings live. (290)

Here Marx is specifying once more the topic of this section. The section does not deal with a *simple* labor process as against a *complex* labor process. Instead it presents the *simple elements* that characterize *every* labor process, regardless of the *social form* in which it occurs—that is, regardless of whether it's capitalist commodity production or, for example, production for the use of freely associated producers. What Marx describes here applies not only to producing material goods, but also to what is today called "immaterial production." In developing computer programs, for example, we can distinguish between the *objects of labor* (existing programming routines, a graphics library), *instruments of labor* (the computer and its installed programs, the programming languages, etc.), and the *productive labor* (the concrete activity that creates the new program).

Footnote 10 appears to be just a humorous aside, but it has a bearing on contemporary economic theories. Economists often conflate means of production with their specific social form in modern society: capital (valorizing value). Then, since every labor process requires means of production, it follows that a labor process without capital is completely impossible. In this way, economists can prove the eternal necessity of capital and therefore also the necessity of profit on capital.

e) The Labor Process as the Process by Which the Capitalist Consumes Labor-Power (the "Rebel" Workers) (second paragraph 291 to 292)

On subsection 1's last two pages, Marx abandons the preceding material's level of abstraction and returns to the "would-be capitalist" (291) of chapter 6, who purchased both the labor-power and the means of production needed for the labor process. Marx makes two observations. First, if the labor process is carried out for the capitalist, that doesn't alter its "general character." Second, it doesn't "immediately" change the "particular methods and operations" of production either, since the capitalist has to begin with labor-power as it is. However, this does not remain the case forever, since subordination to capital will "later on" alter the production process (Marx addresses this in depth in chapters 13 through 15). In this passage, he limits himself to identifying "two characteristic phenomena" that appear in the labor process when it becomes a question of the capitalist consuming labor-power he has purchased. The first of these phenomena is:

> The worker works under the control of the capitalist to whom his labour belongs; the capitalist takes good care that the work is done in a proper manner, and the means of production are applied directly to the purpose. (291)

At the beginning of this subsection, Marx claimed it is characteristic of the specifically human labor process that the worker realizes his or her purpose in it and thus must subordinate his will to this purpose. Nevertheless, if the labor process becomes a process in which the capitalist consumes labor-power, then it is no longer the aim of the worker, but that of the capitalist, which is realized. The worker must submit to this *external* purpose, and the capitalist *controls* his activity.

ADDENDUM: In *Results of the Immediate Process of Production*, originally intended as Volume 1's final chapter, Marx therefore speaks of how the capitalist process of production is, for the worker, the process of "the alienation [*Entfremdung*] of man from his own labour." Then he continues:

> To that extent the worker stands on a higher plane than the capitalist from the outset, since the latter has his roots in the process of alienation and finds absolute satisfaction in it whereas right from the start the worker is a victim who confronts it as a rebel and experiences it as a process of enslavement. (990)

The Production of Absolute Surplus-Value 341

In this way, the capitalist process of production induces a "rebellious attitude" (*rebellisches Verhältnis*) in the worker. In chapter 13 of the published version of *Capital*, Marx writes in a similar vein:

> As the number of the co-operating workers increases, so too does their resistance to the domination of capital, and, necessarily, the pressure put on by capital to overcome this resistance. The control exercised by the capitalist is not only a special function arising from the nature of the social labour process, and peculiar to that process, but it is at the same time a function of the exploitation of a social labour process, and is consequently conditioned by the unavoidable antagonism between the exploiter and the raw material of his exploitation. (449)

Here Marx leaves open the question of what forms this "rebellious attitude" will take and how the workers will organize their resistance— for example, through trade unions struggling for reforms or revolutionary movements aiming to abolish capital.

The second of the "characteristic phenomena" that appear in the labor process is shown in this passage:

> The product is the property of the capitalist and not that of the worker, its immediate producer. Suppose that a capitalist pays for a day's worth of labour-power; then the right to use that power for a day belongs to him, just as much as the right to use any other commodity, such as a horse he had hired for the day. . . . From his point of view, the labour process is nothing more than the consumption of the commodity purchased, i.e. of labour-power; but he can consume this labour-power only by adding the means of production to it. The labour process is a process between things the capitalist has purchased, things which belong to him. Thus the product of this process belongs to him just as much as the wine which is the product of the process of fermentation going on in his cellar. (292)

In Marx's time, many socialists regarded capitalist profit as "robbery" of the worker; the capitalist takes away from the worker something that actually belongs to him. In contrast to such positions, Marx concedes here that the product of labor indeed belongs to the capitalist, since the labor process is "a process between things" that belong to him. Indirectly, Marx points to the limits of this justification of capitalist appropriation: it's only valid under commodity production and relations of private property.

ADDENDUM: Some critics, such as German economist Adolph Wagner (1835–1917), have attributed this analysis of surplus value to Marx: namely that it amounts to a "robbery" of the worker. In his "Marginal Notes" on Wagner's book, Marx defended himself against such allegations, emphasizing that "the capitalist—as soon as he pays the worker the real value of his labour-power—*would have every right, i.e. such right as corresponds to this mode of production*, to surplus-value" (MECW 24: 535, emphasis M.H.). Here, Marx explicitly contextualizes the capitalist's right.

2. The Valorization Process

The products of the labor process, which become property of the capitalist, are use-values. However, the capitalist is not interested in use-values, but rather in value and surplus-value. It's not just use-values that he needs, but commodities. Marx draws the conclusion:

> It must be borne in mind that we are now dealing with the production of commodities, and that up to this point we have considered only one aspect of the process. Just as the commodity itself is a unity formed of use-value and value, so the process of production must be a unity, composed of the labour process and the process of creating value [*Wertbildungsprozess*]. (293)

a) The Process of Creating Value
(third paragraph 293 to second paragraph 298)

Marx first reminds us that "the value of each commodity is determined by the quantity of labour materialized in its use-value"—more precise would be "the quantity of *abstract* labor." Since this isn't about individually expended concrete labor, he immediately adds: "the labour time socially necessary to produce it" (293). In the commentary on chapter 1, *we* emphasized that value and abstract labor are always features that exchanged commodities hold jointly or in community (*gemeinschaftlich*), and when we speak of an individual commodity having these features, it is simply that we are focusing on one commodity *in an exchange relation* (see pages 66–67 of this book). Here Marx stresses "socially necessary" labor time, a quantity that is defined not only by production but by both production and circulation. This reminds us that in the cursory sketch that follows, Marx is not considering a commodity independently from circulation. Rather, he is considering the production process of a commodity *that is already in an exchange relation*.

The Production of Absolute Surplus-Value

Marx uses yarn production to illustrate the process of creating value: if 10 pounds of cotton are used to produce a specific amount of yarn, then the value of this cotton purchased on the market—let's say 10 shillings—enters into the value of the yarn. If the production process results in 2 shillings of wear and tear on the spindle (the spindle being an example of an instrument of labor), then a total of 12 shillings enters into the value of the yarn, for both the raw materials and the instruments employed. Assuming that the amount of value created by twenty-four hours of labor is 12 shillings, then two (twelve-hour) working days are already objectified in the yarn (294). It doesn't matter that the cotton and spindle were produced long before the yarn. All that matters is that the quantity and quality of the cotton and spindle employed were actually necessary for producing the yarn (294).

Marx now looks at the value that the spinner's work adds to the cotton:

> We have now to consider this labour from a standpoint quite different from that adopted for the labour process. There we viewed it solely as the activity which has the purpose of changing cotton into yarn...the labour of the spinner was specifically different from other kinds of productive labour.... Here, on the contrary, where we consider the labour of the spinner only in so far as it creates value, i.e. is a source of value, that labour differs in no respect from the labour of the man who bores cannon.... Here we are no longer concerned with the quality, the character and the content of the labour, but merely with its quantity. (295f.)

Using different language, Marx is rehearsing the various characteristics of concrete and abstract labor, which he first explained in the second subsection of chapter 1. In considering the labor process earlier in the present chapter, we looked at the labor that produces concrete use-values. Here, by contrast, in considering the valorization process, we are looking at abstract, value-creating labor.

> Not only the labour, but also the raw material and the product now appear in quite a new light, very different from that in which we viewed them in the labour process pure and simple. Now the raw material merely serves to absorb a definite quantity of [value-creating] labour. (297)

For example, if six hours of value-creating labor-time are needed to transform ten pounds of cotton into ten pounds of yarn, then in the valorization process the ten pounds of yarn only represent these six hours of value-creating labor.

Marx now comes to a surprising conclusion (297). We assume that the capitalist pays the daily value of labor-power, which might be 3 shillings. The total capital he must advance to produce the yarn therefore amounts to 10 shillings for ten pounds of cotton, 2 shillings for wear and tear on the spindle, and 3 shillings for the value of labor-power. That makes for a total of 15 shillings. What, then, is the value of the ten pounds of yarn that are produced? The total value is composed of, on the one hand, the value of the means of production (the cotton plus wear and tear on the spindle) of 12 shillings and, on the other, the new value that the spinner creates during the course of six hours. Since above we assumed that two twelve-hour working days, under normal conditions, generate a value of 12 shillings, then here a value of 3 shillings is created, which must be added to the value of the means of production The total value of the product is then 15 shillings. Having advanced a capital valued at 15 shillings, the capitalist has now obtained a product with the same 15-shilling value! The surplus-value is zero, and the money advanced has not been valorized!

B) The "Secret of Profit-Making" Revealed (third paragraph 298 to second paragraph 302)

At the end of chapter 6, Marx announced that "the secret of profit-making" would be "laid bare" in the sphere of production (280). Before revealing the secret, Marx first shows that many explanations of profit on capital are completely inadequate. Faced with the absence of surplus value in the results of the spinner above, Marx's capitalist, "who is at home in vulgar economics" (298), offers a barrage of arguments that are typical justifications of capitalist profit:

- One only advances capital to make more money from it.
- One refrains from consuming one's capital, and this abstinence should be rewarded.
- One provides a service to society by giving the worker a job, and one should get something in return.
- One works by supervising the spinner, and therefore also creates value.

The Production of Absolute Surplus-Value

However, all these claims apply both to a capitalist who actually makes a profit and our capitalist above who does not. Then, since there is no special circumstance preventing the valorization of his capital in the example just mentioned of the spinner, it's clear that none of these arguments really explains profit. Marx obviously assumes that a normal capitalist also sees things this way:

> He leaves this and all similar subterfuges and conjuring tricks to the professors of political economy, who are paid for it. He himself is a practical man, and although he does not always consider what he says outside his business, within his business he knows what he is doing. (300)

So what is the solution to this puzzle? It lies in the difference between the value of the commodity labor-power and its use value, which consists in being able to create new value. The value of the commodity labor-power is set by the value of the means of subsistence required to sustain it. In Marx's example of the spinner, that value is equivalent to six hours, or half a working day. However, the worker can work for considerably longer than six hours. This means that he can create a greater value than is necessary to maintain himself, which is what the buyer of labor-power had in mind from the very beginning:

> The owner of the money has paid the value of a day's labour-power; he therefore has the use of it for a day, a day's labour belongs to him. On the one hand the daily sustenance of labour-power costs only half a day's labour, while on the other hand the very same labour-power can remain effective, can work, during a whole day, and consequently the value which its use during one day creates is double what the capitalist pays for that use; this circumstance is a piece of good luck for the buyer, but by no means an injustice towards the seller. (301)

Just as he did in concluding the first subsection, "The Labour Process," Marx justifies the capitalist's appropriation of surplus-value here—within the legal framework of commodity production. The capitalist only has to procure sufficient means of production for a twelve-hour working day. In Marx's example, twenty pounds of cotton valued at 20 shillings and a spindle capable of sustaining 4 shillings of wear and tear. Now the calculation takes on a different appearance. First, there is the necessary capital advance: 24 shillings (for means of production) and 3 shillings (for the value of labor-power), so 27 shillings in total. Next, we tally the resulting product's total value: 24 shillings (for the means of production used) and 6 shillings (for the value the spinner creates in a twelve-hour working day). The total value of the product thus amounts to 30 shillings, which is 3 shillings more than the capital advanced. "The trick has at last worked: money has been transformed into capital" (301).

At the end of chapter 5, Marx stated that capital formation must be explained on the basis of the exchange of equivalents; paradoxically, it must occur both in the sphere of circulation and not in the sphere of circulation. "These are the conditions of the problem. *Hic Rhodus, hic salta!*" (269). Now Marx has finally provided the explanation and concludes triumphantly:

> Every condition of the problem is satisfied, while the laws governing the exchange of commodities have not been violated in any way. (301)

Marx has finally explained value's "occult ability to add value to itself" (255) by virtue of being value. This ability depends on workers *being able to work longer than is necessary for their own reproduction*, meaning they can *create value that is greater than the value of their labor-power*.

Marx now summarizes his analysis:

> By turning his money into commodities which serve as the building materials for a new product, and as factors in the labour process, by incorporating living labour into their lifeless objectivity, the capitalist simultaneously transforms value, i.e. past labour in its objectified and lifeless form, into capital, value which can perform its own valorization process, an animated monster which begins to "work," "as if its body were by love possessed." (302)

The money owner who wants to become a capitalist first transforms his money into commodities, the value of which represents labor that is past or "dead" (as Marx writes here for the first time). These commodities can only maintain their value-objectivity by entering into a new production process as use-values. In analyzing the labor process, Marx explained how products of past labor only maintain their use-value if "living labor" seizes upon them (289). If the money owner's value is to be transformed into capital, it is therefore a precondition that living labor be incorporated into "lifeless objectivity."

The Production of Absolute Surplus-Value 347

Marx describes valorizing value as an "animated monster," thereby building on the image of capital as an "automatic subject," which first appeared in chapter 4. Capital is something dead which only comes to life with the incorporation of living labor. Then, it becomes an "animated monster." (The obvious comparison to a vampire emerges in later chapters.) Marx says that this monster "works," using scare quotes. Nevertheless, he does not refer to the human labor process analyzed earlier in this chapter, but rather to the unceasing hunt for ever more profit. To express how this hunt has something manic and crazy about it, Marx writes that it is "as if its body were by love possessed." This phrase can only be understood, however, if one is familiar with Goethe's *Faust*. In a scene taking place in Auerbach's Keller, a group of revelers sings about a poisoned rat that races around and rages "as if its body were by love possessed" (*als hätt es Lieb im Leib*). This phrase alludes to how lovers, when rejected, sometimes behave madly, racing around and raging. Marx sees capital operating in the same way: blindly and frenetically pursuing the only goal it knows (see 253), that of constantly increasing profit.

c) Conceptual Demarcations and Simple vs. Complex Labor (fourth paragraph 302 to 306)

The process of creating value and the valorization process: The process of creating value lasts as long as it takes to reproduce the value of labor-power that capital has paid for; the valorization process is merely an extension of the value-creating process (302).

The process of creating value and the labor process: the latter is a *qualitative* perspective on labor that takes into account its method, purpose, and content. By contrast, the value-creating process looks at the labor process *quantitatively*, focusing on the labor-time required. However, what matters here is not the individually expended labor-time that could be measured by a clock. Labor-time counts "only in so far as it is socially necessary for the production of a use-value" (303). Marx lists everything that this entails:

- Labor-power has to function under "normal conditions," that is, according to what's socially typical—the instruments of labor have to be in standard condition, the raw material must be of normal quality, etc.;
- Labor-power itself must "possess the average skill, dexterity and speed prevalent in that trade" (303);
- Labor-power must "be expended with the average amount of exertion

and the usual degree of intensity." Moreover, "the capitalist is as careful to see that this is done, as he is to ensure that his workmen are not idle for a single moment" (303);

- There must be no waste of raw materials or instruments of labor. (Marx's footnote 18, which is concerned with the difference between wage labor and slave labor, connects with the last point. Based on a few examples, Marx argues there that slave labor fails to maintain the instruments of labor. It's questionable, however, whether these examples really justify Marx's generalization.)

In chapter 1, we saw how "socially necessary labor-time" is a social result, not known by individual producers' when producing (129). For that reason, a producer might face an unpleasant surprise when his commodity gets to the market (201f.). Here in chapter 7 we see how, in capitalist production, it's the capitalist who imposes the socially average conditions on the workers (or what he anticipates those conditions to be). Not only is there struggle over the value of labor power (see commentary on pages 274ff. in chapter 6), but also over the manner of its expenditure.

Marx concludes his comparing the process of creating value with the labor process by referring to the "dual character of the labor represented in commodities," which he analyzed in chapter 1. There he argues that the difference between labor that creates use-value and labor that creates value—"discovered by our analysis of a commodity"—continues in the two aspects of the production process: as "unity of the labour process and the process of creating value" it is the production process of commodities; as "unity of the labour process and the process of valorization" it is the *capitalist* production process (304).

Finally, Marx briefly addresses the difference between *simple average labor* and *complex labor*. In effect, it makes no difference for the valorization process's basic mode of functioning if the living labor that labor-power adds is simple or complex labor. In either case, surplus-value will only be generated if the labor process's duration extends enough for the newly created value to surpass the value of the commodity labor-power.

Marx first mentions how "higher costs of training" (*höhere Bildungskosten*)[54] make qualified *labor-power* more expensive, but also make it possible to expend *complex labor*, which creates more value than

---

54. The Penguin edition translates the phrase "Arbeitskraft, worin hörere Bildungskosten eingehn" as "labour-power of a more costly kind," whereas the German original refers to higher costs of *training* (*Bildung*).—Trans.

simple average labor (305). In footnote 19, however, Marx points out that the difference between "skilled" and "unskilled labour" is often based upon illusions or accidental circumstances. We referred to this footnote in our commentary on the second subsection of chapter 1, where Marx first deals with the difference between simple and complex labor.

d) Looking Ahead

Having arrived at the end of chapter 7, my commentary on *Capital* comes to an end. In conclusion, I will address a few concepts such as the "rate of surplus-value" and "exploitation." These concepts are treated in later chapters of *Capital*, but they still connect directly with the foregoing arguments. Importantly, our brief outline of the concepts cannot substitute for reading the subsequent chapters.

In his analysis of the value-creating process, Marx draws a clear distinction between the *objective factors* (the products of past labor), on the one hand, and labor-power being expended as *living labor,* on the other. The value of the objective factors (raw material and instruments of labor) enters into the newly created product's value: this value is preserved. By contrast, living labor creates new value. Moreover, if the working day is long enough, this new value exceeds the value of the labor-power that the capitalist has purchased. With this in mind, Marx divides the entire capital that is advanced into two parts, which play different roles in value-creation:

Constant capital ("c" for short) is Marx's term for the part of capital that is spent on raw materials and instruments of labor. If we assume that the instruments of labor are completely used up within a single period of production, then the entire value of the constant capital enters into the value of the new product.

Variable capital ("v" for short) is Marx's term for the part of capital spent on labor-power. Through the expenditure of living labor, the workers create new value that not only replaces the value of the variable capital but also provides surplus-value ("s" for short).

The total *value of the product* is therefore

$$c + v + s$$

The *value product* newly created by the workers is

$$v + s \qquad \text{(see page 321)}$$

Based on the value product, the working day can be divided into two parts: necessary labor-time and surplus labor-time. In the course of *necessary labor-time*, the worker produces the daily value of his or her labor-power, that is, the value of the daily expenditures in reproducing labor-power. During the rest of the working day, which is called *surplus labor-time*, the worker produces surplus-value. The latter goes automatically to the capitalist, since he owns the product that is created (325).

The concepts *necessary labor-time*[55] and *surplus labor-time* allow us to understand the term "absolute surplus-value," which appears in the title of Part Three. Marx offers his explanation at the beginning of Part Four, "The Production of Relative Surplus-Value":

> I call that surplus-value which is produced by the lengthening of the working-day, *absolute surplus-value*. In contrast to this, I call that surplus-value which arises from the curtailment of the necessary labor-time, and from the corresponding alteration in the respective lengths of the two components of the working day, *relative surplus-value*. (305)

Variable capital generates surplus-value. Marx calls the ratio of the magnitudes s/v the *rate of surplus-value*. It is a measure of the valorization of variable capital (324).[56]

Constant capital does not figure in the rate of surplus value. Volume 3 of *Capital* introduces the concept of the *rate of profit*, which is the ratio of surplus-value to the total capital advanced: s / (c + v). Here, the only important thing is not to mix up the rate of surplus-value with the rate of profit, which is a measure of the valorization of the *total* capital advanced.

The rate of surplus-value is exactly equal to the ratio of surplus labor-time to necessary labor-time. For this reason, Marx concludes: "The rate of surplus-value is therefore an exact expression for the degree of exploitation of labour-power by capital, or of the worker by the capitalist" (326). This is Marx's first mention of the "exploitation" of the worker (also *Exploitation* in the original German). In a later passage that

---

55. This "necessary labor-time" that forms a part of the working day should not be confused with the "socially necessary labor-time" required to produce a certain product.
56. On page 324 the Penguin edition translates the phrase "*Verwertung des variablen Kapitals*" (valorization of variable capital) as "increase in the value of the variable capital." The latter is incorrect since *variable capital* refers only to the money spent on labor-power.—Trans.

The Production of Absolute Surplus-Value

we already referred to above (see page 341 of this book), Marx employs the German expression "*Ausbeutung*" for exploitation (449).

The fact that Marx speaks of "exploitation" is sometimes taken as evidence that *Capital* contains a moralistic critique of capitalism. However, this term does not appear in chapters 4 through 7, where Marx deals with the basics of the relation between labor-power and surplus-value. Only in later passages does Marx speak of *Exploitation/Ausbeutung*, and he does so there in a relatively casual way and without moral emphasis. Marx's later references to exploitation in *Capital* also suggest that this term is not employed in a moralistic way. For example, he will speak of the exploitation of the means of production's "use-value" (442); the exploitation of the laws of electricity and magnetism for telegraphy (508f.); the exploitation of "natural wealth" (754), and so on. In all these cases, *to exploit* means to benefit from existing forces, potentials, or resources for specific ends. The same holds for exploiting labor-power: the capitalist, as the buyer of labor-power, harnesses its potential for his benefit. This does not amount to a moral critique, but it does demonstrate that, for capital, labor-power is just another resource among others, all of which it subordinates to the endless valorizing of value, which is capital's only goal. The only way to stop the damage that this subordination causes to labor-power is to exert pressure on capital. Either the exploited themselves or the state could do so. However, *Capital*'s chapter 10 will show that the state only sets limits to exploitation in order to ensure the process's continuity over the long term.

So far, Marx has dealt systematically with the *value of labor-power*, but has not yet addressed *wages*. Marx examines wages in chapters 19 through 22. Both for everyday consciousness and for most economists, the term "wages" refers to payment for the *labor* a worker performs. However, this is false in two senses. For one, labor itself cannot be sold as a commodity: "It is not labour which directly confronts the possessor of money on the commodity-market, but rather the worker. What the worker is selling is his labour-power. As soon as his labour actually begins, it has already ceased to belong to him; it can therefore no longer be sold by him" (677). Furthermore, given that equivalents are being exchanged, the wage's value would have to be equal to the value of the labor performed, thereby eliminating profit. Living labor itself, however, does not have a value; only by being objectified does it (under certain conditions) *create* value. When analyzing the value-form, Marx earlier emphasized that "human labour-power in its fluid state, or human labour, creates value, but is not itself value. It becomes value in its coagulated state, in objective form" (142). The wage considered as *payment for the value of labor* is therefore an "imaginary expression" (677) in that it expresses something impossible. Nevertheless, it has considerable consequences, by underpinning the idea that the worker, through his or her labor, contributes to the product's value, but with this contribution being completely compensated by the wage. The worker is now in the same position as the provider of raw material. If the raw material provider is paid in full, then the profit on the final product has nothing to do with him. Similarly, if the wage covers the value of the labor performed, then the profit on capital can't be due to exploiting the worker. So the wage is not just another expression for the value of labor-power. The presumption of wages to pay "the value of labor" in fact conceals the actual relation of exploitation between capital and labor-power. It is a concealment, however, that nobody thought up; rather it emerges from "the relations of production themselves" (677), influencing the perception of both workers and capitalists.[57] Marx emphasizes that notions such as wages being payment for labor "are reproduced directly and spontaneously, as current and usual modes of thought." By contrast, the underlying relation "must first be discovered by science" (682).

---

57. This is what Marx writes about wages being payment for labor: "All the notions of justice held by both the worker and the capitalist, all the mystifications of the capitalist mode of production, all capitalism's illusions about freedom, all the apologetic tricks of vulgar economics, have as their basis the form of appearance discussed above, which makes the actual relation invisible, and indeed presents to the eye the precise opposite of that relation" (680).

Appendices

Glossary

Bibliography

APPENDIX 1

Marx's Critical Economic Writings

Of the three "theoretical" books of *Capital* that Marx planned to write, he was only able to finish the first one, dealing with the production process of capital. The other two books, on the circulation process and the process as a whole, remained unfinished. Frederick Engels published them after Marx's death. There is not even a manuscript for the fourth book that Marx planned to write, which was supposed to deal with the history of political economy. *Theories of Surplus Value*, published in the German MEW volumes 26.1–3 with the subtitle "The 4th Volume of *Capital*," is not a draft for the fourth book. Instead, it is an unfinished history of just one category.

In the twentieth century, a whole series of Marx's manuscripts were published for the first time. In the discussions that ensued, some attempted to use these manuscripts to patch the gaps in *Capital* and resolve its ambiguities. Frequently people overlooked the time separating these texts and *Capital*, and the different contexts in which these manuscripts were written. Marx was engaged in politics and research for more than forty years, during which time he developed intellectually and changed many of his conceptions. This holds independently of the controversy over whether Marx's thought developed continuously, or whether it was characterized by one or more deep ruptures, since even a continuous development presupposes changes. Therefore what follows will address the context of Marx's most important texts dealing with the critique of economics. The years after the titles refer to the years the texts were written or, for texts that Marx actually published, the year of publication.

Marx studied law in Bonn and Berlin but was primarily interested in philosophy and history. The philosophy of Hegel and the Young Hegelians, who attempted to politically radicalize Hegel's philosophy, had an important influence on him. After his studies, Marx became editor-in-chief of the *Rheinische Zeitung*, a liberal newspaper opposed to Prussian absolutism, which was ultimately banned. During this period, he had to deal with economic questions for the first time. After the *Rheinische Zeitung*'s closure, Marx went to Paris, and along with Arnold Ruge and Georg Herwegh published the *Deutsch-Französische Jahrbücher*, though only one issue came out (1844). There, Marx published two texts, "On the Jewish Question" and "Contribution to the Critique of Hegel's Philosophy of Law. Introduction." Additionally, this issue contained a text by Frederick Engels, "Outlines of a Critique of Political Economy." How deeply Engels's text inspired Marx can still be measured in *Capital*, which quotes it multiple times.

In the years 1843–44, Marx definitively turned away from the Young Hegelians, and the philosophy of Ludwig Feuerbach (1804–1872) became a strong influence on him. As against the "idealist" philosophy of Hegel, which focused on the diverse manifestations of "spirit," Feuerbach conceived a "materialist" philosophy of "human essence," which he saw as characterized not so much by reason as by "sensuousness" (*Sinnlichkeit*). On the basis of this materialism, Feuerbach criticized religion and Hegel's philosophy. Proceeding from this critique, Marx dealt for the first time with political economy in a profound way, studying the works of Adam Smith, David Ricardo, and James Mill.

Economic-Philosophical Manuscripts (summer 1844; MEW 40, MEGA I/2, English: MECW 3). Left untitled by Marx, this text is also known as the "Paris Manuscripts." It was published for the first time in 1932. The manuscript is unfinished, and a few parts have been lost. In the manuscript's preface, Marx stresses Feuerbach's importance: "Positive criticism as a whole—and therefore also German positive criticism of political economy—owes its true foundation to the discoveries of Feuerbach" (MECW 3: 232). Marx expands Feuerbach's concept of human essence by focusing on labor as an objectification of the human being's essential faculties, and based on this, he gives it a historical dimension, since these essential human faculties unfold historically. He also carries over Feuerbach's critique from philosophy to economics: in capitalism, human beings are "alienated" from their real human essence, since they do not control their own labor (neither the labor process nor its products). By contrast, communism restores this control—it is the overcoming of this alienation. Marx criticizes political economy, since it does not recognize the actual, alienated state of affairs in capitalism as an alienated one, but rather sees it as natural. It is therefore a science that operates within alienation.

In autumn of 1844, Marx wrote ***The Holy Family, or Critique of Critical Criticism*** (MEW 2, English in MECW 4). The text was published in 1845 with both Marx and Engels's names attached, but in fact Engels wrote only a small portion of it. Here Marx subjected the Young Hegelians to a scathing critique, basing himself on Feuerbach's philosophy. However, this "Feuerbach cult," as Marx later referred to his high regard for Feuerbach at that time (see his letter to Engels on April 24, 1867, MECW 42: 360), came to an end in 1845. Then came a renewed critique of the Young Hegelians, this time including Feuerbach.

Theses on Feuerbach (spring 1845; MEW 3, MEGA IV/3, English: MECW 5), ***The German Ideology*** (1845–46, co-authored with Frederick Engels, MEW 3; English in MECW 5). Marx's "Theses on Feuerbach" were first published in 1888 by Engels (in a slightly modified form), whereas *The German Ideology* was published in 1932. Both texts criticize Feuerbach's philosophy of the human essence. They reject "essence" and "alienation" as philosophical constructs; instead, they propose to analyze real economic relations such as forces of production and relations of production. Additionally, the texts criticize both the Young Hegelian's and Feuerbach's conception of history for being "idealist," meaning not based on "real" conditions. In contraposition, they present a "materialist" conception of history.

Sketching his own development, Marx claims in the Preface to the *Contribution to the Critique of Political Economy* (1859) that he and Engels wrote *The German Ideology* to "settle accounts with our former philosophical conscience" (MECW 29: 264). Since the work "settles accounts" primarily with Feuerbach, one may conclude that when Marx says "former philosophical conscience" it refers to Feuerbach's philosophy, which played such a key role for him in 1844. All Marx's subsequent texts no longer mention "human essence," and refer very rarely to "alienation," using that expression only in a very general sense to mean that something becomes alien, but no longer in the sense of alienation from an "essence."

In the twentieth century, there were debates about whether *The German Ideology* constituted an important rupture in Marx's development, with Louis Althusser, especially, defending the discontinuity thesis (see Althusser 1965, Althusser/Balibar 1965). Against this view, many others defended the overall continuity of Marx's work, with quite different justifications being given for the continuity thesis. On the one hand was the claim that the notion of "human essence" retained its significance for Marx, and that the references to "fetishism" in *Capital* were equivalent to his earlier notion of "alienation from the human essence" (for example, Schmied-Kowarzik 1981). On the other hand was the argument that an implicit critique of Feuerbach and de facto overcoming of the notion of human essence was already at work in the *Economic-Philosophical Manuscripts* (for example, SOST 1980). Both variants argue for a fundamental continuity, although what is supposed to be continuous is characterized quite differently, but they have difficulties identifying the "philosophical conscience" with which Marx and Engels themselves claimed to be settling accounts.[58]

The Poverty of Philosophy (1847; MEW 4, English: MECW 6). In 1846, Pierre-Joseph Proudhon, who was quite influential in the socialist movement in France, published his major theoretical work, *The System of Economic Contradictions. Or, The Philosophy of Poverty*. This work was oozing with superficial economic knowledge and moral-religious pathos, and Marx responded to it with *The Poverty of Philosophy*. Marx criticized Proudhon based on the materialist conception of history developed in *The German Ideology* and the economic theory of David Ricardo. At the time, Marx regarded the latter as an essentially accurate analysis of capitalism's mode of functioning. His

---

58. I provide an extensive account of the young Marx's development in Heinrich 1999 (chapters 3 and 4). There, I also present arguments for why *The German Ideology* in fact constitutes a break with the philosophical conceptions in Marx's early writings. However, Marx's transition to a new theoretical terrain is not yet complete by the time of *The German Ideology*. That only happens with the "Introduction" of 1857. Having attained this new theoretical terrain, Marx stages his "critique of political economy" from 1857 forward.

main critique of Ricardo then was that he had not recognized the historicity of capitalism and instead regarded it as human beings' natural mode of production. In this work, Marx *uses* the available political economy with a critical intention, but he is still far from criticizing the basic categories of political economy, which is what constitutes his *critique* of political economy.

Wage Labor and Capital (1847; 1891 edition edited by Engels in MEW 6, English: MECW 9). These are talks that Marx delivered in 1847 to the German Workingmen's Club of Brussels. In 1849 he published the talks as lead articles in the *Neue Rheinische Zeitung*. Later, in 1891, Engels published them as a pamphlet, while updating the terminology to match that of *Capital*. Marx keeps his arguments simple and understandable in these lectures. Like *The Poverty of Philosophy*, however, they are based on Ricardo's political economy, and not the critique of political economy.

Manifesto of the Communist Party (The Communist Manifesto) (1848; MEW 4, English: MECW 6). The *Communist League*, an international workers association, commissioned Marx and Engels with composing a manifesto. The text was published under both of their names, but Marx was the only author. Its sketch of capitalism's trajectory begins with the famous sentence: "The history of all hitherto existing society is the history of class struggles" (MECW 6: 482). The text presents class struggles as the motor of historical development. Class antagonism between the bourgeoisie (capitalists) and the proletariat (wage workers) is what characterizes capitalism: as the bourgeoisie develops capitalism, it produces its own gravediggers in the proletariat. The latter must overcome capitalism in order to maintain itself, since capitalism is not even able to guarantee the exploited class's existence. In the *Manifesto*, as against *Capital*, Marx assumes a tendency to absolute pauperization (the working class's situation will deteriorate absolutely over the long term, not just relatively). As in the earlier texts, here too there is a critical use of political economy, but it is not yet subject to critique.

In the revolutionary year 1848, Marx returned to Germany and took over the management of the newly founded *Neue Rheinische Zeitung*. After the defeat of the revolution, however, he had to leave Germany. He went first to Paris, but was deported. In 1849, he moved to London, where he remained until the end of his life. There, Marx first attempted to analyze the revolutionary events and the failure of the revolution. In the series of articles *The Class Struggles in France 1848–1850* (1850; MEW 7, MEGA I/10, English: MECW 10) and in *The Eighteenth Brumaire of Louis Bonaparte* (1852; MEW 8, MEGA I/11, English: MECW 11), he examined the events in France between 1848 until the coup of Louis Napoleon in 1851. The former work argued that the Revolution of 1848 was a consequence of the heavy economic crisis of 1847–48, and Marx was quick to generalize this claim: "A new revolution is possible only in consequence of a new crisis. It is, however, just as certain as this crisis" (MECW 10: 135). This supposed connection between crisis and revolution was an important motive for Marx to renew his economic investigations. For these studies, London proved to be an excellent place. At the time, England was the most developed capitalist country, and London was its center. Wide-ranging debates concerning economic questions took place in Parliament and in the newspapers, while the British Museum contained the most comprehensive library of economics at the time. Looking back, Marx wrote in 1859:

> The enormous amount of material relating to the history of political economy assembled in the British Museum, the fact that London is a convenient vantage point for the observation of bourgeois society, and finally the new stage of development which this society seemed to have entered with the discovery of gold in California and Australia, induced me to start again from the very beginning and to work carefully through the new material. (MECW 29: 264f.)

Reprising his studies, Marx now created extensive manuscripts. But he didn't just broaden his horizon, he also gradually developed a critique of classical political economy's categories instead of just using these categories critically as he had done so far (on the difference, see my commentary on chapter 1's footnote 34 on page 181 in this book). In the early 1850s, Marx laid plans to write a comprehensive critique of economics. However, it was only in 1857 that Marx actually began what he called the "critique of political economy." He wrote a number of manuscripts, but completed none of them. In the course of revising the manuscripts for publication, Marx constantly discovered new problems, or approached old problems again. Instead of developing a publishable text, Marx's methods of research drove him to repeatedly rework the material.

Introduction (August–September 1857, MEW 42, MEGA II/1.1, English: MECW 28 and Marx 1973). This is not an introduction to the *Grundrisse*, which was written shortly afterward, but rather an introduction to the large planned work of which the *Grundrisse* constitutes only a part. The *Introduction* is famous primarily for its reflections on the method of "rising from the abstract to the concrete." However, Marx composed these reflections on method *before* working out his critique of economics. Therefore they should not be understood as Marx's *final* word on method, as is usually the case. Instead, the text is a summary of Marx's thoughts in this area, based on his studies up to that time. Marx will subsequently modify his methodological approach considerably.

In the autumn of 1857, it became clear that a severe economic crisis would occur. This prompted Marx to finally begin writing his long-planned critique of economics. Since Marx expected that the crisis would result in a revolution, he was plagued by the fear that his book would arrive too late (see his letter to Lassalle, February 22, 1858, MECW 40: 271). Through a tremendous effort, he produced a long manuscript in just a few months, while continuing his bread-and-butter journalistic work and studies.

Grundrisse (1857-58, first published 1939–41; MEW 42, MEGA II/1.1–1.2, English: MECW 28 and 29 and Marx 1973). Marx gave no title to this manuscript, which is also without a proper beginning. It grew out of his engagement with a book by one of Proudhon's students. The process of research and the process of presentation, which Marx distinguishes in the Postface of *Capital*'s second edition, are constantly intertwined in this manuscript, since it is only by attempting to present things that Marx recognizes that many interconnections remain unclear to him. In the manuscript, one can already recognize the rough outlines of the *thematic* structure of *Capital*'s three later volumes: the process of production, the process of circulation, and the process as a whole (here: "Capital and Profit"). Still, Marx struggles with numerous difficulties. In the manuscript, he does not yet address many topics that are dealt with in *Capital*, although there are also a number of reflections here that will not show up in the later work.

It is only in this manuscript (and only in one passage) that one finds a clear "theory of collapse." Marx's argument is that the development of the forces of production leads to living labor becoming less and less important in the production process. Yet living labor is the basis of capitalist production; therefore, its diminishment entails the collapse of the capitalist mode of production (MECW 29: 91 and Marx 1973: 705f.). By contrast, *Capital* presents the development of the forces of production as an intrinsic tendency of capital, but one that by no means leads to the collapse of the capitalist mode of production.[59]

It was while working on the *Grundrisse* that Marx first developed a precise plan for his presentation, which is not an arbitrary construction. According to *Capital*'s second edition's Postface, the presentation should reflect "the inner life of the subject-matter" (102). The entire "critique of political economy" was to encompass six books; the book on capital was to be followed by books on ground rent, wage labor, the state, foreign trade, and the world market. For the book on capital, there was a centrally important distinction between the part dealing with "capital in general"—addressing all the essential determinations of capital, but abstracted from the movement of the multiplicity of individual capitals—and the part addressing the "competition between many capitals" where the determinations of capital express themselves. Underlying this distinction was Marx's insight that competition cannot explain the appearances of capitalism, but instead the nature of competition itself needs to be explained.

Through the mediation of Ferdinand Lassalle, Marx found a German publisher who was willing to bring out his large-scale work as a series of individual booklets. In the second half of 1858, Marx started preparing the first booklet.

The Original Text of the Second and the Beginning of the Third Chapter of "A Contribution to the Critique of Political Economy" (Urtext von Zur Kritik der politischen Ökonomie) (1858, first published in 1941 as an appendix to the *Grundrisse*; MEGA II/2, English: MECW 29). In terms of its themes, this manuscript covers the same material as *Capital*'s first three chapters, which address the commodity and money. However, the beginning of the manuscript has been lost. The manuscript is important primarily because the remaining

---

59. Authors as different as Robert Kurz and Antonio Negri refer to the theory of collapse in the *Grundrisse*. However, the theory was based on an inadequate analysis, which *Capital* later overcame. See Heinrich 1999, 349ff. and, for more detail, Heinrich 2013.

part contains two sections that Marx left out of all subsequent presentations: a section on a law of appropriation in simple circulation and another on the transition from money to capital (see Appendix 5).

A Contribution to the Critique of Political Economy (1859; MEW 13, MEGA II/2, English: MECW 29). This was the first and only booklet of the planned series that Marx actually wrote. In its preface, there is an oft-quoted sketch of the materialist conception of history that is very brief and should therefore be used with caution. (I discuss this sketch in the course of commenting on the fetish section in chapter 1.) The booklet deals with the commodity and money—the same material as *Capital*'s first three chapters—although it sometimes puts emphasis on different things. (Appendix 2 contains a section from the *Contribution* on the specifically social character of commodity-producing labor.)

In a review of this work, Engels comments on Marx's method of presentation (MECW 16: 473–77). He distinguishes between the "logical" and "historical" development of categories and comes to the conclusion that the "logical" development (that is, the conceptual presentation) is the same as the historical development, "only stripped of the historical form and of interfering contingencies" (MECW 16: 475). In the debates about the character of the categorical presentation in Marx's work, which focus mostly on his analysis of the value-form, there is a historicist approach that invokes Engels's text, treating it as an authentic explanation of Marx's procedure. Traditional Marxism regarded Marx and Engels as essentially twins, each of whose statements was valid for the other. However, a close reading of their works reveals not only differences, but also how they dealt with such differences. Marx never mentioned this review, even when the context seemed to call for it, as in the 1873 Postface, which also deals with *Capital*'s method of presentation. Since Marx eagerly quoted Engels's works, one suspects that this ongoing silence points to his having considerable misgivings.

Economic Manuscript of 1861–63, (Continuation of) a Contribution to the Critique of Political Economy (MEGA II/3.1–3.6, English: MECW 31–33; about half of the manuscript contains ***Theories of Surplus Value***, published by Karl Kautsky in 1904–1910). Marx originally planned the whole text as the continuation of the first booklet of *A Contribution to the Critique of Political Economy* published in 1859. However, as was typical for Marx, it quickly turned into a research manuscript. The text begins with the presentation of capital in general, which deals with topics that would later play a role in all three volumes of *Capital*.

At the end of 1862, Marx decided not to publish a continuation of the first booklet of the *Contribution*, but rather to publish an independent work, *Capital*. It was to include three theoretical books and a fourth on the history of theory. In the summer of 1863, Marx ceased working on the 1861–63 manuscript and turned to working on *Capital*. He would no longer mention the six-book plan developed during the writing of the *Grundrisse*. Nevertheless, he integrated a number of topics into *Capital* that were originally supposed to be dealt with in the books on ground rent and wage labor. The formerly central concept of "capital in general" also disappeared. After the summer of 1863, Marx would never use it again, either in the manuscript or in his correspondence. In terms of both content and structure, a new work emerged.[60]

Economic Manuscript of 1863–1865 (MEGA II/4.1– 4.2, volume 4.2 in English in Marx 2017). This manuscript contains drafts for all three "theoretical" books of *Capital*. From the draft for the first book, only the sixth chapter (intended as the final chapter) remains: **Results of the Immediate Process of Production** (MEGA II/4.1, English: MECW 34 and Marx 1976). However, Marx did not incorporate this chapter into the first volume of *Capital*, published in 1867. He wrote nearly complete drafts for the second and third books; yet there was no draft for the fourth book on the history of theory.

The writing of the manuscript of 1863–65 coincided with the founding of the International Workingmen's Association, an international association of workers, later referred to as the "First International," in September of 1864. Marx played a central role in this organization from the very beginning. Among other things, he wrote the International's "Inaugural Address" and its "Provisional Rules" (MEW 16; MEGA I/20; MECW 20).

Value, Prices, and Profit (MEW 16, MEGA II/4.1, English: MECW 20). This is a lecture that Marx delivered in June of 1865 to the central council of the International. In it, he anticipates some of the material of *Capital*, but was only able to present it in a truncated form. For that reason, Marx did not want to publish the text. It was first published in 1898 by his daughter Eleanor.

Capital, Volume 1 (1867; MEGA II/5, first edition not published in MEW or MECW, English translation of first chapter in Dragstedt 1976). On the basis of the manuscript of 1863–1865, Marx developed the first volume of *Capital* in 1866–67. He divided the text into six chapters with very few subsections. Chapter 1 examined the value-form, treating it more expansively than in the *Contribution to the Critique of Political Economy*. On the advice of Engels and Kugelmann, who both read the galley proofs, Marx composed a simplified version of the value-form analysis, which became an appendix to the volume. This appendix exhibits a number of problematic simplifications compared to the treatment in chapter 1, but there are also improvements. Thus, for the first time, Marx both highlights the "peculiarities of the equivalent form" and introduces the excursus on Aristotle. (Appendix 3 presents the concluding part of the value-form analysis from chapter 1 of this edition.)

Ergänzungen und Veränderungen zum ersten Band des Kapitals (Additions and Changes to the First Volume of* Capital*) (December 1871– January 1872; MEGA II/6). At the end of 1871, Marx received a message from the publisher of *Capital* that the first volume had almost sold out. For the second edition, Marx wanted to get rid of the double presentation of the value-form; with this goal in mind, he developed a comprehensive revision manuscript. It

---

60. In the debates on Marx's *Capital*, some contend that the six-book plan and the concept of "capital in general" still form the basis of Marx's account in the final work, even though he had ceased to mention them. See for example Moseley 2007.

contains revisions and commentaries on the first edition's chapter 1, which he divided into three chapters for the second edition. This manuscript is of great significance for understanding value theory, since it contains fundamental reflections on value theory that are not found in the first or second editions of *Capital*. Appendix 4 contains the most important passages.

Capital, Volume 1 (2nd edition 1872–73; MEGA II/6). The second edition of *Capital*'s first volume was published in 1872–73 in serial form and then in 1873 as a complete book. Marx transformed the first edition's *chapters* into *parts*, which he divided, in turn, into numerous chapters and subchapters. He made considerable changes primarily to chapter 1, dealing with the commodity. Marx got rid of the double presentation of the value-form, his new presentation being based largely on the simplified one in the first edition's appendix, even if it is not identical to the latter. In the second edition, Marx made a strict terminological distinction between exchange-value and value, and for the first time dealt extensively with the fetish character of the commodity in what became a separate section (parts of this section were already contained in the first edition, but the treatment wasn't as clear there).

Traditional Marxism maintained that Marx developed his theory in a continuous process of perfection. Hence a later version of something was always seen as a better one. However, critical readings of Marx in the last few decades have seen a few authors confronting this "perfection thesis" with a "popularization thesis." They maintain that, in value theory, Marx later opted for a simplified presentation at the price of argumentative precision and methodological stringency. They apply this argument to both the changes in the value-form analysis from the first edition to the second one (relying, in part, on Marx's own comments and changes in the Preface; see my commentary in Appendix 3) and to Marx's evolution as a whole from the *Grundrisse* to *Capital*.[61] However, Marx's development is far too complex to be reduced to either "perfection" or "popularization." The three versions of the investigation of the value-form make this especially clear, since none of them can be unambiguously labeled the "best" (see commentary at the end of Appendix 4).

Le Capital, Livre Premier (1872–1875; MEGA II/7). The French translation was also published in serial form starting in 1872, and then in 1875 as a book. Marx thoroughly revised this translation, and added material not found in the (second) German edition, primarily in the section on accumulation. As a consequence, he would say (in the 1975 Postface to this edition) that it had its own scientific value (Marx 1976: 105). Marx planned to incorporate the changes from the French edition into the third German edition and an English translation but did not manage to do so in his lifetime.

After finishing the manuscript for Book I of *Capital* in 1867, Marx immediately began preparing Books II and III, which were supposed to follow

---

61. Hans-Georg Backhaus and Helmut Reichelt were the key figures advancing the "popularization thesis" (see for example Backhaus 1997, Reichelt 2002). A good overview of the debate is found in Hoff 2004: 21ff.

quickly. During the years 1868 to 1871, Marx developed a long manuscript for Book II, and a few shorter manuscripts for Books II and III. However, he interrupted his work on these manuscripts to prepare the second edition and French translation of the first volume. Furthermore, in the early 1870s, Marx was heavily involved in the First International. During this time, he wrote, among other things, *The Civil War in France* (MEW 17, MEGA I/22, MECW 22) and an analysis of the Paris Commune. After defeat in the Franco-Prussian War of 1870-71 the residents of Paris took power, forming new council-like revolutionary institutions, with a view to overcoming the bourgeois state's structures instead of merely implementing different policies inside the bourgeois framework. This text was published as a statement by the General Council of the International. During this time, Marx also maintained contact with the Social Democratic Party of Germany (SPD), founded in 1869. When the SPD united with the Lassalleean *Arbeiterverein* in 1875, Marx subjected the joint program agreed upon at the unification congress in Gotha to a severe critique. His *Critique of the Gotha Program* (MEW 19, MEGA I/25, MECW 24) contains a brief, frequently quoted description of socialism and communism.

In the 1870s, Marx wrote additional manuscripts for Book III and especially for Book II. He also maintained notebooks, containing a huge number of excerpts, in which he engaged with new literature that was appearing at the time and carried out further research. Above all, Marx wished to take into account economic developments in the United States and Russia for Book III of *Capital*. Although Marx's plans constantly expanded—he was no longer just preparing available manuscripts for publication—his health continued to deteriorate, making it impossible for him to complete the work.

Randglossen zu Wagner *(Marginal Notes on Adolph Wagner)* (written between 1879 and 1881; MEW 19, English: MECW 24). This is Marx's last economic text. German economist Adolph Wagner had criticized among other things Marx's *Capital* in his textbook. Marx addressed this criticism and along the way offered some interesting comments especially on value theory.

Beginning in late 1881, Marx's health continued to deteriorate, making scientific work impossible. His wife, Jenny, died in December 1881, and his oldest daughter, also called Jenny, died in January of 1883. Marx died soon after, in March. After Marx's death, Frederick Engels published all three books of *Capital*.

Capital, Volume 1 (3rd edition 1883; MEGA II/8, English translation not completely identical with the third German edition 1887, MECW 35; fourth edition 1890, MEW 23, MEGA II/10, English: Marx 1976). For the third edition of *Capital*, Volume 1, published in 1883, Engels used the second edition as a basis and added some changes from the French edition. Engels added still more changes from the French translation—but not all of them— to the fourth edition of volume one that was published in 1890.

Capital, Volume 2 (1885; MEW 24, MEGA II/12; English: MECW 36 and Marx 1979). Engels put together *Capital*, Volume 2, from various manuscripts that Marx had written in the late 1860s and in the 1870s (they are contained in MEGA II/11 and MEGA II/4.3). He did not make use of the oldest manuscript of this volume, written in 1864 and contained in the ***Economic Manuscript of 1863-65***.

Capital, Volume 3 (1894; MEW 25, MEGA II/15, English: MECW 37 and Marx 1981). The only manuscript covering all of *Capital*, Volume 3, is a text that Marx wrote between 1864 to 1865, contained in the ***Economic Manuscript of 1863–65*** (MEGA II/4.2, English: Marx 2017). Engels used it as the basis for his 1894 edition of the volume, but he made changes and reorganized it significantly (apart from reformulations, almost all of the subdivisions and headings are by Engels). Engels pointed only to a few insertions as his own doing; the majority of the changes, many of which affect the work's content, were not indicated as such (see Heinrich 1996–97).

After the publication of the third volume, Engels wrote a long addendum titled "Law of Value and Rate of Profit" (1895, MEW 25, MEGA II/14, English: MECW 37 and Marx 1981). There he develops, among other things, his concept of "simple commodity production." This idea came to influence the reception of *Capital*: Engels transforms the "simple circulation" of commodities and money—which Marx presents in *Capital*'s first three chapters as a surface phenomenon in the capitalist reproduction process—into a pre-capitalist form of "simple commodity production." However, Marx does not refer in *Capital* or anywhere else to "simple commodity production," nor to any such model.

Two things should be kept in mind about the three volumes of *Capital* as they are presented by Engels:

First: Engels edited and revised all three volumes. The first volume is a mixture of the second German edition and the French translation; in it are the fewest direct interventions in the text. However, Engels heavily revised the second and third volumes; to a large extent, he gave these volumes their structure by subdividing and streamlining them, and he intervened extensively in Marx's text, which in some passages led to shifts in meaning. If one wishes to deal in-depth with specific issues, one should go back to Marx's original manuscripts as contained in the MEGA.

Second: There are complexities to *Capital* that go beyond its merely being an unfinished work. It's unfinished both because the fourth book on the history of theory is missing and the *Theories of Surplus Value* is not a substitute, and because the treatment of important topics, especially those appearing in the third volume, such as crises and the credit system, remained incomplete. An additional complexity is that the individual manuscripts that Engels used for the edition of the three volumes were written at different periods and thus represent different stages of Marx's knowledge. Marx himself redacted the first volume and paid great attention to the details; Engels's edition of the first volume is based upon texts from the years 1872 to 1875. The second volume is based upon texts written between 1868 and 1881. Among these texts, those from the end of the 1870s represent the most advanced level of Marx's knowledge; they constitute a fundamental reworking of the manuscript for the second volume from the *Economic Manuscript of 1863–65*. By contrast, the third volume is based almost exclusively on a manuscript from 1864–65, so it is the furthest back in terms of Marx's state of knowledge. When doing an in-depth reading of the second and third volumes, one should consider the unequal character of individual passages in the text.

APPENDIX 2

The Universality of Labor as a Social Characteristic of "Labor that Posits Exchange Value"

Starting in 1857, Marx wrote extensive manuscripts for his critique of political economy, but the only texts that he himself published are the *Contribution to the Critique of Political Economy* from 1859 and the first volume of *Capital* in its first and second editions. The *Contribution* comprises only two chapters. The first chapter, "The Commodity," covers the material of *Capital*'s first two chapters, while the work's second chapter contains the material of *Capital*'s third chapter. In contrast to *Capital*, the *Contribution* also discusses the history of commodity and money theories. Above all, the *Contribution* does not clearly separate the examination of the value-form from the analysis of the process of exchange. There is also terminological vagueness in the work: though Marx indeed distinguishes between value as the objectification of abstract labor[62] and the form of appearance of value as a specific quantity of another commodity, he frequently uses the term "exchange value" for both. Thus, in the fragment of the *Contribution* that follows, Marx speaks of "labor that posits exchange value" (*Tauschwert setzender Arbeit*), in contrast with the more precise language in *Capital*: "labor that constitutes/creates value" (*wertbildender Arbeit*) or "labor represented in commodities" (*sich in Waren darstellender Arbeit*).

The following piece of text is found at the beginning of the first chapter. It deals synoptically with the specific social character of "labor that posits exchange value." A summary of this kind is no longer found in *Capital*. This text from the *Contribution* presents difficulties to readers since it summarizes results that have not yet been presented. However, if one has read *Capital*'s first two chapters, it should not be hard to understand. Here, Marx deals with the specific kind of socialization described in this commentary—in points B and F on the fetish section—as "retroactive socialization." It's a continuous piece of text; Marx's emphases are in italics; the underlining is mine. The following version of the text is from MECW 29: 273–275.

---

62. In the *Contribution*, Marx speaks of "abstract general" labor; he first speaks of "abstract human" labor in *Capital*.

> From the analysis of exchange value it follows that the conditions of labour which creates [corrected translation: posits, *setzt*] exchange value are *social categories* of labour or categories of *social labour*, social however not in the general sense but in the particular sense, denoting a specific type of society [corrected translation: socialization, *Gesellschaftlichkeit*]. Uniform simple labour implies first of all that the labour of different individuals is equal and that their labour is treated as equal by being in fact reduced to homogeneous labour [*gleichartige Arbeit*]. The labour of every individual in so far as it manifests itself [corrected translation: represents itself, *stellt sich dar*] in exchange values possesses this social character of equality, and it manifests itself [corrected translation: represents itself] in exchange value only in so far as it is equated with the labour of all other individuals.

This text uses the term "homogeneous labor" to describe the result of abstracting from all differences in the various acts of concrete labor. In *Capital*, Marx describes this as "abstract human labor." The extent to which this abstract labor must also be "general" is elaborated in the following:

> Furthermore, in exchange value the labour time of a particular individual is directly represented [corrected translation: appears directly, *erscheint unmittelbar*] as *labour time in general*, and this *general character* of individual labour appears as the *social character* of this labour. The labour time expressed [corrected translation: represented, *dargestellt*] in exchange value is the labour time of an individual, but of an individual in no way differing from the next individual and from all other individuals in so far as they perform equal labour; the labour time, therefore, which one person requires for the production of a given commodity is the *necessary* labour time which any other person would require to produce the same commodity. It is the labour time of an individual, *his* labour time, but only as labour time common to all; consequently it is quite immaterial *whose* individual labour time this is. This universal labour time finds its expression [corrected translation: represents itself, *stellt sich dar*] in a universal product, a *universal equivalent*, a definite amount of objectified labour time, for which the distinct form of the use-value in which it is manifested as the direct product of one person is a matter of complete indifference, and it can be converted at will into any other form of use-value, in which it appears as the product of any other person. <u>Only as such a *universal* magnitude does it represent a *social* magnitude. The labour of an individual can produce [corrected translation: result in, *resultieren*] exchange value only if it produces *universal equivalents* [corrected translation: results in a universal equivalent; it is singular in German], that is to say, if the individual's labour time represents universal labour time or if universal labour time represents individual labour time. The effect is the same as if the different individuals had amalgamated their labour time and allocated different portions of the labour time at their joint disposal to the various use-values.</u>

Here Marx specifies an additional characteristic of "labor that posits exchange value": an individual's labor time has to represent itself as "universal" labor-time, expressed in a general equivalent. *Capital* addresses this issue at the end of the section on the value-form, during the analysis of the "general form of value." Here, however, Marx cannot yet draw on the analysis of the value-form—it is yet to come—so he offers a somewhat different argument: it's not the particularity of the individuals that counts, but only what they have in common, and that is their universality.

> The labour time of the individual is thus, in fact, the labour time required by society to produce a particular use value, that is to satisfy a particular want. But what matters here is only the specific manner in which the social character of labour is established. A certain amount of a spinner's labour time is objectified, say, in 100 lbs. of linen yarn. The same amount of labour time is assumed to be represented in 100 yards of linen, the product of a weaver. Since these two products represent equal amounts of universal labour time, and are therefore equivalents of *any* use-value which contains the same amount of labour time, they are equal to [corrected translation: they are equivalents for] each other. <u>Only because the labour time of the spinner and the labour time of the weaver represent universal labour time, and their products are thus [corrected translation: present themselves as] universal equivalents, is the social aspect [corrected translation: social being, *gesellschaftliches Dasein*] of the labour of the two individuals represented for each of them by the labour of the other, that is to say, the labour of the weaver represents it for the spinner, and the labour of the spinner represents it for the weaver.</u>

An individual's labor time only becomes social as universal labor time, but that only happens if the product is transformed into a general equivalent. This shows the importance of money. Money is not merely a technical aid or something convenient in everyday life. It is the medium through which the specific sociality of a commodity-producing economy is mediated. Marx accuses Ricardo (whose work is the culmination of classical political economy) of not having recognized precisely this characteristic of value-creating labor:

> He does *not* grasp the connection of *this labour* with *money* or that it must assume the form of *money*. (MECW 31: 389f.)

The passage above summarizes, in the briefest way, what fundamentally distinguishes Marx's theory of value from that of classical political economy.

Marx now contrasts the specific social character of the "labor that posits exchange value" with relations of production that are not based upon commodity production. In *Capital* such a comparison first occurs in the section on commodity fetishism:

> On the other hand, under the rural patriarchal system of production, when spinner and weaver lived under the same roof—the women of the family spinning and the men weaving, say, for the requirements of the family—yarn and

linen were *social* products, and spinning and weaving *social* labour within the framework of the family. But their social character did not appear in the form of yarn becoming a universal equivalent exchanged for linen as a universal equivalent, i.e. of the two products exchanging for each other as equal and equally valid expressions of the same universal labour time. On the contrary, the product of labour bore the specific social imprint of the family relationship with its naturally evolved division of labour. Or let us take the service and dues in kind of the Middle Ages. It was the distinct labour of the individual in its original form, the particular features of his labour and not its universal aspect that formed the social ties at that time. Or finally let us take communal labour in its naturally evolved form as we find it among all civilised nations at the dawn of their history. In this case the social character of labour is evidently not mediated by the labour of the individual assuming the abstract form of universal labour or his product assuming the form of a universal equivalent. The communal system on which [this mode of] production is based prevents the labour of an individual from becoming private labour and his product the private product of a separate individual; it causes individual labour to appear rather as the direct function of a member of the social organisation. Labour which manifests itself in exchange value appears to be the labour of an isolated individual. It becomes social labour by assuming the form of its direct opposite, of abstract universal labour [corrected translation: the form of an abstract universality, *die Form abstrakter Allgemeinheit*].

An economy based on exchange is made up of precisely these "isolated individuals" (regarded as models by bourgeois social philosophy; see the quote from the *Introduction* of 1857 found in point B of my commentary on chapter 2). That kind of economy also depends on their "private labor," which does not count in its particularity, since it does not belong to a social context that takes this particularity into consideration. The isolated individuals are only connected through the market, which considers the individual to be a component of an abstract universality, so that only this abstract universality counts as social. Hence, the individual's labor does not count as concrete labor, but only as abstract labor. The fact that only the abstract universal counts as social is a characteristic of "society" under capitalist conditions, far beyond the economic sphere.

APPENDIX 3

A Paradoxical Form of Value

Contribution to the Critique of Political Economy (1859) has a very brief presentation of the value-form, and it is not yet separate from the examination of the exchange process. The first detailed treatment of the value-form is found in chapter 1 of the first edition of *Capital* published in 1867. In that edition it exists in two versions: in chapter 1, and, following the advice of Engels and Kugelmann, in a simplified version in the Appendix. In the Preface to the first edition, Marx said about the presentation of the value-form in chapter 1: "It's difficult to understand, because the dialectic is much sharper than in the first presentation"—meaning that of the *Contribution* of 1859. He recommended that the "reader not used to dialectical thinking" skip the corresponding passages in chapter 1 and instead read the Appendix (MEGA II/5:12). Marx did not explain in the Preface what he meant by "dialectic," but we may assume that in such a general context the term refers to *conceptual, scientific reasoning*. That the "dialectic is much sharper" means therefore that the scientific reasoning is much more exact and precise than in the *Contribution*.

The second edition, published in 1872–73, contains only one version of the value-form analysis and it is strongly oriented toward the simplified account in the first edition's appendix. Marx included the first edition's Preface in the second edition, but he deleted both the reference to the now-absent Appendix and the sentence quoted above about the "dialectic" being "much sharper." He evidently assumed that he had achieved greater intelligibility despite the loss of the sharpness in the argument. As I argued above in Appendix 1, none of the three available versions of the value-form analysis can be unambiguously characterized as the best. Both in Marx's Appendix of *Capital*'s first edition and in the second edition, there are improvements compared to the earlier version, but both later versions also lose some things along the way.

One of the differences between the first version of the value-form analysis and all later ones is the structure of the concluding part. Later versions end with the "money-form," but the first version of the value-form analysis has the "general form of value" followed by a paradoxical form of value called "Form IV"; the money-form does not yet show up at all. Here we reproduce, interspersed with comments, the presentation of the Form IV, as well as Marx's concluding remarks, which are also absent from the later versions. It is a continuous piece of text, and all emphases are by Marx. The text is found in *Das Kapital*, First

Edition [1867], MEGA II/5: 42–43. The English translation's source is Dragstedt (1976, 32–34).

> The illusion [corrected translation: semblance, *Schein*] as if the equivalent-form of a commodity resulted from its own corporeal nature instead of being a mere reflex of the relationships of other commodities: this illusion [corrected translation: semblance] strengthens itself with the continuing development of the *singular* Equivalent to the *universal,* because the contradictory vectors of the value-form no longer develop *equally* for the commodities which are related to one another, because the universal Equivalent-form separates a commodity off as something totally secluded from all other commodities, and finally because this (the commodity's form) is actually no longer the product of the relationship of any *singular* commodity.

This synopsis clarifies what causes the "semblance of the equivalent-form." In the second edition of *Capital*, Marx makes reference to the "mysteriousness of the equivalent form" in his analysis of the simple form of value, page 149. It also explains why the semblance "strengthens itself" when we consider the general equivalent and not just a single equivalent. *Capital*'s second and later editions, like the widespread fourth edition (MEW 23) and its translations, no longer explicitly mention the "strengthening of the semblance." The later editions do, nevertheless, discuss how the general equivalent form no longer reveals that it's an "antagonistic form," having the form of general exchangeability because all other commodities do not have this form (161 and footnote 26). In the later versions, there is no more than a brief mention of this "false semblance" becoming "firmly established" (187), and that reference appears in the presentation of the exchange process.

> From our present standpoint the universal Equivalent has not yet by any means ossified, however. What was the way in which linen was metamorphosed into the universal Equivalent, actually? By the fact that it displayed its value, first in one single commodity (form I), then in all other commodities in order in a *relative* way (form II), and thereby all other commodities *reflexively* displayed their values in it in a relative way (form III). The simple relative value-expression was the seed out of which the universal Equivalent-form of linen developed. It changes its role within this development. It begins by displaying its amount of value in *one* other commodity and ends by serving as material for the value-expression of *all* other commodities. What holds for linen holds for every commodity. In its developed relative value-expression (form II)—which only consists of its *many, simple* value-expressions—the linen does not yet figure as universal Equivalent. Rather, every other commodity-body forms in this case *linen's Equivalent,* is thereby immediately exchangeable with it and is therefore able to change places with it.

When we reversed the expanded form of value of the linen, this led to the general form of value, with the linen now as general equivalent. However, it was by no means necessary to consider the expanded form of value of *linen*; it could have been any other commodity's expanded form of value. Marx finds a way to show how, in the linen's expanded form of value, every other commodity-body could switch places with the linen. He begins to run through the possibilities, resulting in "Form IV."

> So we obtain finally:
> Form IV:
> 20 yards of linen = one coat *or* = u coffee *or* = v tea *or* = x iron *or*
>   = y wheat *or* = etc.
> One coat = 20 yards of linen *or* = u coffee *or* = v tea *or* = x iron *or*
>   = y wheat *or* = etc.
> u coffee = 20 yards of linen *or* = one coat *or* = v tea *or* = x iron *or*
>   = y wheat *or* = etc.
> v tea = etc.
>
> But each of these equations reflexively yields coat, coffee, tea, etc. as universal Equivalent and consequently yields value-expression in coat, coffee, tea, etc. as universal relative value-form of all other commodities. It is only in its opposition to other commodities that a commodity turns into the universal Equivalent-form; but every commodity turns into the universal Equivalent-form in its opposition to all other commodities. If every commodity confronts all other commodities with its own natural form as universal Equivalent-form, the result is that all commodities exclude themselves from the socially valid displaying of their amounts of value.

Form IV offers us numerous expanded forms of value, one for each commodity. Each of these expanded forms of value can be reversed, so that one also obtains many general equivalents. However, that is by no means possible, since there can be only *one* general equivalent. What this form of value depicts (on the level of form-determinations) is nothing other than what Marx shows in chapter 2 (on the level of action) to be the fundamental problem for commodity owners in the exchange process. For every commodity owner, the value of his commodity is expressed in the multitude of commodities that confront him. He therefore wishes to reverse his commodity's expanded form of value and use that commodity as the general equivalent. Yet if every commodity owner does this, then no commodity is the general equivalent (180). This original version of the value-form analysis thus includes a derivation of the specific form aspects of commodity owners' contradictory starting points; in that sense, the presentation is more comprehensive than the later one. By contrast, the money-form is missing. In fact, the money-form is somewhat misplaced in chapter 1, given that this chapter's level of abstraction is the analysis of form-determinations: the transition from the general form of value to the money-form is not a development based on the value-form's properties (as in previous transitions). It is the result of "social custom" (162), that is, a result of the activity of commodity owners. However, Marx only begins to treat the activity of commodity owners after the value-form analysis. When, on June 27, 1867, Marx sent Engels an overview of the simplified Appendix's structure, he made an apologetic comment about including the money form as point IV: "The following on the money-form is simply for the sake of continuity—perhaps barely half a page" (MECW 42: 393).

> Obviously, the analysis of the commodity yields all *essential* determinations of the *value-form* and the value-form itself in its contradictory vectors, yields the *universal relative value-form,* the *universal Equivalent-form*, and finally the never-ending *sequence of simple relative value-expressions*—which sequence forms at first a transitional phase in the development of the value-form, in order finally to suddenly shift into the *specifically relative value-form* of the *universal Equivalent.* But the analysis of the commodity yielded these forms as *commodity-forms* in general (which thus also apply to each and every commodity) in a *contradictory* manner, so that if commodity A finds itself to be in one of the contradictory form-determinations, then commodities B, C, etc. adopt the other in opposition to it. What was decisively important, however, was to discover the inner, necessary connection between value-form, value-substance, and value-amount; i.e., expressed *conceptually* [*ideell ausgedrückt*], to prove that the value-form arises out of the value-concept [*Wertbegriff*].

The last sentence makes especially clear what Marx is dealing with in the analysis of the value-form: the interrelation of form, substance, and magnitude of value. He is not presenting an abstract reconstruction of the *historical* development of the forms of value. Marx expresses *conceptually* the contemporary and simultaneous interrelation between value-objectivity, as captured in the *concept* of value, and the value-form. This "conceptual" form of expression is an example of how Marx "coquetted" with Hegel's terminology, as he mentions in the second edition's Postface (103). The notion that a form "arises" from its concept stems from a way of thinking that held that "spirit," which is reflected in concepts, is the actual reality, while the "activity of the concept" is the active, dynamic element. However, in the first edition of *Capital*, Marx not only "coquetted" with Hegel's mode of expression, he also *criticized* Hegel's autonomization of the concept. In this sense, it is telling what Marx says in relation to linen's value being expressed in a coat, with the result that the tailoring that produces the coat only counts as human labor as such. In effect, human labor as such can only exist as a specific type of labor that confronts "external material." Marx throws in a criticism of Hegel here: "It is only the 'concept' in Hegel's sense that manages to objectify itself without external material," and quotes as proof the following sentence from Hegel's *Encyclopaedia*: "The concept, which is only subjective at first, marches ahead in accordance with its own proper activity to objectify itself, without needing any external material or stuff for the purpose" (Dragstedt 1976: 20). Whoever has attentively read the value-form analysis in the first edition's chapter 1 will not believe that what is "conceptually" expressed there amounts to a relapse into Hegelian conceptual speculation.

In the second edition of *Capital*, Marx put the rational kernel of this conceptual form of expression into words: "Our analysis has shown that the form of value, that is, the expression of the value of a commodity, arises from the nature of commodity-value" (152). That is, the value-form does not arise from the *concept* of value, but rather from that which the concept of value expresses scientifically, namely the "nature of commodity-value."

APPENDIX 4

Value-Objectivity as Objectivity Held in Common

On November 28, 1871, the publisher of *Capital*, Otto Meißner, wrote to Marx that the first volume was almost sold out, and suggested that he quickly prepare the second edition. For this purpose, Marx planned various revisions; above all, he wanted to get rid of the double presentation of the value-form analysis. Further, he wanted to subdivide the text of *Capital* into parts. Between December of 1871 and January of 1872, Marx drafted a manuscript that is not a single uninterrupted text, but rather multiple attempts at revision. It is focused especially on developing a new version of the value-form analysis. This untitled manuscript was first published in 1987 in the MEGA with the title *Ergänzungen und Veränderungen zum ersten Band des Kapitals* (Additions and Changes to the First Volume of Capital).

The fragment reproduced here belongs to a revision of the section on the general form of value. It served primarily to aid Marx in understanding the shortcomings of his original presentation, and he therefore did not directly include it in the second edition's text. Nowhere else did Marx reflect in such detail on how value-objectivity is something that is always held in common or communally (*gemeinschaftlich*) by commodities, making it clear that one cannot speak of the individual, isolated labor product as an object of value or as a commodity. We can also observe in this text how Marx changes from "*gemeinsam*" (common) to "*gemeinschaftlich*" (communal), which he used in *Capital*'s second edition. This is a continuous section of text. In it, the italics represent Marx's emphases, whereas the underlining is mine. The text is drawn from *Ergänzungen und Veränderungen zum ersten Band des Kapitals* [1871–72], MEGA II/6: 29–32. Until now this important text has not been translated into English. The language of the German original is bumpy, with some parts looking more like a sequence of notes than full sentences. The translation preserves this character, and sometimes may sound a bit awkward.

> Commodities obtain *value-expression* (value-form) only in *relation* to each other. The *expression of value* of a commodity is therefore constantly only given in its *value-relation* to another commodity. Where does this come from? How does this property common to all forms of value of the commodity arise from the concept of value?

Here Marx raises the exact same question he claimed to have answered at the end of the first edition's analysis of the value-form. He does so with language that flirts with Hegel's philosophy by saying that the value-form *arises from the concept* of value. (For more on Marx's "coquetting" with Hegel, see my commentary at the end of Appendix 3.)

> We originally found the concept of the value of commodities as follows:
> We took an exchange-relation such as *1 coat = 20 yards of linen*. We said: the coat and linen express here something *in common* [*etwas Gemeinsames*], they are equal as representations of it. The equality does not consist in their use-values or as objects of use. As such, they are things different from each other and indifferent to each other. This *common* element that makes them *equal* must therefore have a *social character*. It is not their practical social character as use-values that comes into consideration here. Their equation abstracts from that. It is therefore their character as *products of labor*. As products of labor, they are only *equal*, not to the extent that they represent the actual labor that produces their use-values, since they are different precisely *as use-values*. They are equal as products of labor to the extent that they are products of the same labor, the coat as well as linen thus counting as mere *objectifications of human labor as such*. This is their *being as value* [*Werthsein*].

The phrase "we originally found" refers to Marx's characterization of value in the pages prior to the value-form analysis in chapter 1. In the first edition of *Capital* (MEGA II/5: 19f.), this part was much briefer than in the second edition used in the MEW and most translations. What Marx is offering here is a short version of that argument (127–28).

> Thus the coat and the linen as values, each for itself, were reduced to *objectifications of human labor as such*. But this reduction forgot <u>that neither is in and of itself *value-objectivity* [*Werthgegenständlichkeit*]; they are this only in so far as this *objectivity is held in common* [*gemeinsam*] by them. Outside of their relationship with each other—the relationship in which they count as equal—neither coat nor linen possess *value-objectivity* or *objectivity* as congelations of human labor per se. They only possess this social objectivity as a social relationship (in a social relationship).</u>

When Marx stresses that something was "forgotten" in the "reduction" of coat and linen to objectifications of human labor as such, he is criticizing his own presentation in *Capital*'s first edition. What was it that was forgotten? The fact that value-objectivity does not belong to each exchanged thing "in itself." The exchanged things only held this objectivity "in common." Although the presentation in *Capital*'s second edition is a little bit more extensive, and Marx changed from "*gemeinsam*" (common) to "*gemeinschaftlich*" (in community, communal) as mentioned in this commentary on page 66, many readers still "forget" this specific character of value-objectivity. This is especially true of all those interpretations that claim that individual products of labor acquire value-objectivity just by being produced for exchange, that is, before they enter into an exchange relationship

> If we say: *as values*, the commodities are only objective expressions of *the same unity, different-looking congelations of the same labor substance*, reduced however to their true expression, in that one disregards everything that they otherwise express. A commodity-body does not express anything further, as long as it counts for all other commodity-bodies as an expression of their being communal [*gemeinschaftlich*]), then as such they are related to the same *unity* as such an *objectivity*; they are reduced to abstract human labor to the extent that this counts as their *communal* [*gemeinschaftliche*] unity, as the *social* substance that merely presents itself differently in the various different commodity-bodies. They are thus all already expressed *relatively*, namely *relative to human labor*, the social labor that creates them.

Here too Marx emphasizes that the commodities have value when they are reduced to abstract human labor, as "their communal unity": this means that value is not something that each commodity possesses in itself, but rather something they only possess *in common* or *communally*. Marx pursues this idea in the next paragraph:

> If we look at the determination of the *magnitude of value*, it emerges even more clearly that the value-relation of commodities is already anticipated in the concept of value, or that in their value-objectivity, they are not only reduced to abstract human labor *from the get-go*, but rather abstract human labor as their *unity*, abstract human labor as a *specific* social *form* of labor; <u>not only as their substance, but rather as their substance held in common by one commodity with another commodity.</u> The magnitude of value represents a specific quantity of labor, but this quantity is not the coincidental quantity of labor that A or B expend in the production of a commodity. It is socially determined, the *labor socially necessary* for the production of a thing, that is, the labor that a thing costs at the social average. It is labor, first of all, possessing the average social level of intensity and skill, and secondly labor expended under the socially normal conditions of production. (Competition regulates this level, the social pressure that each and all exert on each other.) Abstract human labor is the expenditure of *human labor-power*, but the human labor-power of the individual counts here only as a part of social labor-power, and the measure of its expenditure is therefore not found in individual labor-power, but rather in relations where it operates as a component of the social labor-power.

Marx deals with the magnitude of value here, claiming that it makes even clearer that "the value-relation of commodities is already anticipated in the concept of value." The "concept of value" is the conceptual understanding of value-objectivity. The nature of value-objectivity is "anticipated" by the "concept of value." And what is the nature of value-objectivity? Value-objectivity has abstract labor as its substance. However, it is not a simple substance (inhering in every commodity individually) but rather a "substance held in common by one commodity with another commodity." And why is this social character more clearly expressed in the magnitude of value? Because the magnitude of value represents a specific quantity of labor, but not "the coincidental quantity that A or B expend in the production of a commodity." What constitutes value is not individually expended labor-time, but rather socially necessary labor-time. This socially necessary labor doesn't pertain to an individual product of labor and its production process, however. For that reason, it becomes clear when dealing with the magnitude of value that value-objectivity involves a relation with other commodities.

> Let's summarize the points:
> *The value-form of the commodity* is given in *the value-relation between different commodities.*
> 1) The production of the commodity-bodies as values reduces them to expressions *of the same unity* (what is common to them, that which is equal in them), to *human labor as such* as their *communal [gemeinschaftliche] substance*. This includes: *the relation* to human labor as *unity, the relation of the commodities to each other,* as expressions of the *same* unity. Or, the relation of the products of labor to each other as expressions of the same unit is their being as value. And only through this relation do mere *products of labor*, useful objects, become *commodities. A product of labor, considered in isolation, is not value, any more than it is a commodity.* It only becomes *value* in its *unity* with another product of labor, or in the *relation* wherein the various products of labor, as crystallizations *of the same unity*, human labor, are equated to each other.

Marx states again rather clearly that the product of labor, taken on its own, is neither value nor a commodity; its value-objectivity only exists through its relation to other products of labor. The relation in which products "are equated to each other" is exchange. Only in exchange are the products of labor commodities and value.

> It thus follows: since the *value* of commodities is nothing other than their *relation to labor* as their communal *[gemeinschaftliche]* substance or their *relation to each other* as the expression of this communal *[gemeinschaftliche]* substance, this value of a commodity can only appear in *a relation* in which it relates to another commodity as value, or only in the *value-relation* between various commodities. Hence the expression of value can only be found, or the commodities can only obtain the form of value, in the *relation between different commodities.* This shows us how the value-form arises from the nature of value.

If value-objectivity is a relation of the product of labor to another such product from the very beginning, then, according to Marx's reasoning, value can only "appear" or tangibly exist in a relation. The value-form as a relation is not something *additional* to value. Rather, it "arises" from the specific nature of value, which itself is a relation.

> If I say, this product of labor is value, because human labor is expended in it, then that merely subsumes the product of labor under the concept of value. It is an abstract expression that includes more than it says. Because this product of labor is merely reduced to this concept of value, in order to reduce it to a *thing of the same* substance as all other products of labor. The relation to other products of labor is thus assumed.
>
> If I say for example, the rock is heavy, *I express* weight as a property that the rock has considered in isolation. But in fact, its weight is a physical property that it only possesses in relation to other bodies. The expression, although it says nothing about this relation, includes it.

These two paragraphs explain what is meant by a phrase like "the value of an individual commodity," which Marx also uses: it's an abbreviated expression that "includes more than it says," since the relation to the other commodity, exchange, is included in it from the beginning.

> 2) *Objectivity included in the concept of value*.
> The reduction of the product of labor to its *being as value*, to its value, is consummated by the abstraction from its use-value. Or it is fixed as *value-objectivity*, in that one disregards the physical properties that make it a specific thing and therefore also a specific useful thing (*use-value*). What remains is a purely chimerical objectivity [*rein phantastische Gegenständlichkeit*]—objectivity of abstract human labor, the *objective form* of abstract human labor, that is, human labor, instead of in a fluid state, in a congealed state, instead of in the form of movement, in the form of rest.
>
> There are two things to note here:
> *First*: the form of *objectivity* is included in the concept of value. These things, iron, wheat, gold are things of value, iron-value, wheat-value, gold-value, etc. These products of labor can therefore not be expressed as *values*, their being as value can only come to light, can only appear—or their value can only obtain *value-form*, a form that distinguishes the being as value of commodities from their being as use—to the extent that it is expressed objectively, that is, only in the body of a commodity itself, since the only objectivity of a commodity is its objectivity as a product of labor—as a commodity-body.
>
> *Second*:

(No further text follows. On the next page of the manuscript, Marx begins a new attempt at presenting the general form of value.)

Marx refers here to the value objectivity that results from abstracting from a labor product's use-value as a "purely chimerical objectivity." In the next paragraph, he claims that this value-objectivity can only "come to light" if it is "expressed objectively." However, it can only be expressed objectively in the body of a commodity.

In the analysis of the value-form in chapter 1 of the first edition, Marx wrote about the "chimerical" character of value-objectivity:

> In order to retain linen as a merely corporeal expression of human labour one has to abstract from all that which makes it to be really a thing. Any objectivity of human labour which is itself abstract (i.e. without any additional quality and content) is necessarily an abstract objectivity—a *thing of thought*. In that fashion, a web of flax turns into a chimera [*Hirngespinst*]. (Dragstedt 1976: 19f.)

In this earlier presentation, Marx turns next to the tangible objectification of this abstract objectivity in another commodity. He then voices his critique of the Hegelian *concept*, which can "objectify itself without external material" (Dragstedt 1976: 20).

Both in chapter 1 of the first edition and in the passage reproduced above from the revision manuscript, Marx seems unsure about how exactly to present the relation between the "purely chimerical" objectivity of value and its tangible form of existence in the shape of another commodity. It's clear that this relation is not to be grasped in the manner of Hegel's philosophy. In fact, Marx first found an adequate solution in *Capital*'s second edition. There, he distinguishes between two levels of investigation:

(1) The examination of the *exchange relation* between two commodities; here, we obtain "an abstraction, value" (141, corrected translation), the value-objectivity, which cannot be grasped in the case of the individual commodity;

(2) The examination of the *value-relation* between two commodities, which already assumes the result of the analysis of the exchange relation in level (1); here the expression of value (for example, "20 yards linen is worth one coat") provides the tangible form of existence of the value of that commodity whose value is to be expressed (on this difference, see the commentary on chapter 1, pages 141–42).

Because Marx now clearly sees the difference between these two levels, his examination of the exchange relation also receives more space in the second edition's chapter 1, and Marx also introduces into that chapter his references to the "spectral objectivity" or "phantom-like objectivity" (128) that remains when one abstracts from all use-value characteristics of the commodity. The problem of how to get from a "purely chimerical" objectivity to the tangible manifestation of this objectivity (without falling into the trap of Hegelian conceptual speculation) has been resolved by distinguishing between the two levels of analysis.

This last point is also evidence for my claim in Appendix 1 about the "perfection thesis" in comparison to the "popularization thesis." There I said that none of the three versions of the value-form analysis is clearly the best. If the second edition's version no longer contains the Form IV that appeared in the first version (reproduced in Appendix 3), this is definitely a flaw. However, the later version's clear distinction between the two levels of analysis is a considerable improvement compared to the previous version.

APPENDIX 5

The "Transition to Capital"

After examining the simple circulation of commodities in Part One of *Capital*, Marx turns in Part Two to the form of circulation M – C – M. He approaches it as an empirical fact: alongside the form C – M – C, according to Marx, "we find another form, which is quite distinct from the first; M – C – M" (248). Marx does not make explicit here whether he considers the relationship between the simple circulation of commodities and the form M – C – M to be a necessary or accidental one. However, in a footnote he indicates that he by no means assumes the connection to be coincidental:

> The capitalist epoch is therefore characterized by the fact that labour-power, in the eyes of the worker himself, takes on the form of a commodity which is his property; his labour consequently takes on the form of wage-labour. On the other hand, it is only from this moment that the commodity-form of the products of labour becomes universal. (274n4)

Hence, the simple circulation of commodities is not only a *precondition* of money's transformation into capital, but commodity circulation only becomes generalized as a *result* of capital. However, this is merely a historical claim and does not show why it is so. Only in the *Grundrisse* (1857–58) and in the so-called *Urtext* or "Original Text of *A Contribution to the Critique of Political Economy*" (1858) does Marx show the *necessary* interrelation of simple commodity circulation and the transformation of money into capital. There, he not only tries to demonstrate that simple commodity circulation leads to the category of money (in the sense of money's third form: money as money), but also that money *must* transform into capital to really exist as an independent manifestation of value. If this connection really holds, then generalized commodity production can only exist as capitalist commodity production. Just as commodity production cannot exist without money (as Marx showed in the value-form analysis of chapters 1 and 2, using the connection to critique Proudhon's conception of socialism), so simple commodity circulation cannot exist without capital. On a categorical level, this implies a fundamental critique of the possibility of "market socialism." (Market socialism proposes eliminating the capital-relation from all enterprises, in favor of cooperatives that would continue to produce commodities and compete on the market.)

In what follows, I comment on several passages from the sixth section of the *Urtext*'s second chapter. A commentary on the entire section, which bears the title "The Transition to Capital," is beyond the scope of this book, because Marx's text is both lengthy and inchoate. Confident presentation and the search for such a presentation alternate, making for many repetitions and new beginnings. Therefore, I have selected those passages where the central arguments for the "transition" to capital are clearest. Moreover, my commentary only addresses what is important for understanding the transition.

In the passages reproduced below, Marx does not yet distinguish terminologically between value and exchange-value (the form of appearance of value). For that reason, "exchange-value" should be replaced by "value" in most of the passages. To improve readability, however, I have refrained from indicating this inside the quotes. In what follows, the page numbers refer to MECW 29. Marx's emphases are in italics, whereas mine are underlined.

> Considered in itself, circulation is the *mediation of preposited extremes*. But it does not posit these extremes. It itself must be mediated as the totality of mediation, as total process. *That is why its immediate being is pure appearance*. It is *the phenomenon of a process running behind its back*. . . .
>
> The repetition of the process from both points, money and commodity, does not spring from the conditions of circulation itself. The act cannot again be rekindled of itself. Circulation does not, therefore, carry within itself the principle of self-renewal. It proceeds from preposited moments, and not from those created by itself. Commodities must be thrown into it again and again, and that from outside, as fuel into the fire. Otherwise, it flickers out in indifference. It would flicker out in money as an indifferent result, in so far as money would no longer have any connection with commodities, prices, circulation, cease to be money and express a production relationship; leaving no more than its metallic being, with its economic being annihilated. (479)

Circulation mediates between the "extremes" of the commodity and money. These are "preposited" in that they exist without circulation's influence. Circulation on its own cannot generate these extremes, which is why Marx says that circulation "does not . . . carry within itself the principle of self-renewal." Hence circulation depends on another process. Because this process is not visible from the perspective of circulation, it is thus "running behind its back."

When Marx says that circulation's "immediate being is pure appearance," he is denying that circulation exists "immediately," that is, without mediation or independent of anything else. Circulation does not exist immediately, but rather is *mediated* by another process. If this other process ceases to take place, then circulation stops, and the money that remains would no longer be money, since there would be no commodities that it could buy.

In a text placed inside brackets,[63] Marx looks briefly at the historical development of circulation:

> The simple circulation, merely the exchange of commodity and money (the exchange of commodities in mediated form), precisely because it is only mediating movement between presupposed points of departure, can (up to the formation of hoards) historically exist without exchange value taking hold of the production of a people, whether on the whole surface or in its depths. At the same time, however, historical development shows how circulation itself leads to bourgeois, i.e. exchange-value-positing, production and creates for itself a basis other than that from which it directly sprang. The exchange of surpluses is commerce creating exchange and exchange value. However, it extends only to the act of exchange itself and runs alongside production itself. But then if the appearance of exchange-seeking intermediaries (Lombards, Normans, etc.) is repeated and regular trade develops under which the producing peoples are engaged only in what could be called passive trade, in so far as the impetus to exchange-creating activity comes from outside and not from the inner structure of production, the surplus of production must no longer be an accidental, occasional one, but a constantly recurring surplus, so that the product itself acquires a tendency towards circulation and creation of new exchange values. (480)

Here, Marx explains how, in the course of history, production that occasionally generates surpluses (which are not for exchange) ultimately leads to production for exchange; he also briefly describes this process in chapter 2 of *Capital* (181f.). Marx could turn next to describing the historical steps leading up to capitalist production. However, as he points out, this is not the issue here:

> At this point, however, we have nothing to do with the historical transition of circulation into capital. The simple circulation is, rather, an abstract sphere of the bourgeois process of production as a whole, which through its own determinations shows itself to be a moment, a mere form of appearance of some deeper process lying behind it, even resulting from it and producing it—industrial capital. (482)

This statement clarifies two things. One is that the phrase "simple circulation"—or the "simple circulation of commodities," as Marx writes in *Capital*—does *not* refer to pre-capitalist relations. Second, we see how Marx's aim is to show how simple circulation, "through its own determinations," reveals itself to be a form of appearance of industrial capital. This means that simple circulation (if it is comprehensive and universal) *cannot be anything other* than

---

63. In his drafts, Marx sometimes put longer notes inside brackets. He would write down a note to preserve a thought, but the brackets indicate that this was not the final place for the note.

Appendices 385

the surface of the capitalist process of reproduction. Marx now explores this second point:

> *What becomes, emerges, is produced in circulation, when its form itself is considered, is money itself and nothing else.* Commodities are exchanged in circulation, but they do not originate in it. Money, as price and coin [meaning the first two forms of money: a measure of value and means of circulation], is already an own product of circulation, but only formally. The exchange value of the commodity is the premiss of price, just as the coin itself is nothing but the self-established form of the commodity as similarly premissed means of exchange. (485)

As Marx pointed out earlier, we are not dealing with a historical transition. The term "originating" does not refer to emerging in history, but rather a process that happens in circulation every day and can be revealed by "considering" the process of circulation. Circulation generates money in an ongoing way. However, the first two functions of money—measure of value, means of circulation—are merely "formal" products of circulation, since they express something that already exists in the commodity.

> But things stand differently with money [meaning the third function of money: money as money]. It is a product of circulation which has grown out of it, as it were, contrary to initial agreement. Money is not merely a mediating form of commodity exchange. It is a form of exchange value growing out of the circulation process, a social product which, in virtue of the relations into which individuals enter in circulation, creates itself. <u>As soon as gold and silver (or any other commodity) have developed themselves as measure of value and means of circulation (as the latter, whether in bodily form or as symbol), they become money without the society's aid or desire.</u> (487)

The third function of money—money as an independent manifestation of value—is the true product of circulation. It is something new, not yet present in the commodity. Value is just one of the two "factors" of a commodity. It is only with money as money that value comes to exist in an independent shape, that is, in a form in which it is not simply present in the commodity. However, we soon see that this is not really independent value at all, since money's

> independent attitude with respect to circulation, its withdrawal from the latter, robs it of both its values: of its use value, since it does not have to serve as metal; of its exchange value, since it possesses this exchange value only as a moment of circulation, as an abstract symbol of the commodities' own value reciprocally opposed to each other; as a moment of the movement of the form of the commodity itself. So long as money remains withdrawn from circulation, it is as worthless as if it lay buried in the deepest pit. But if it re-enters circulation, its intransience is at an end, the value it contains disappears in the use values of the commodities for which it is exchanged, and it once again becomes a mere means of circulation. (488)

Hence money cannot retain its independent value: outside of circulation, as a hoard, it loses both its use-value and exchange-value, while within circulation, it loses its imperishability and therefore its independence. In an earlier passage, Marx made this even clearer:

> Money, as "universal form of wealth", as exchange value become independent, confronts the whole world of real wealth. It is the pure abstraction of the latter, hence, fixed in this way, an imaginary magnitude. Wherever universal wealth appears to exist in an entirely material, tangible form, <u>it has its existence only in my head, and is a pure chimera.</u> As the material representative of universal wealth, money is realised only when it is thrown back into circulation, when it disappears in exchange for the particular species of wealth. In circulation, it is always real only when it is given out. Should I want to hold on to it, it evaporates in my hands as a <u>mere spectre of wealth</u>. Making it disappear is the only possible way of securing it as wealth. The dissolution of the stores in ephemeral gratifications is its realisation. It can now again be stored by other individuals, but then the process starts once again. <u>The independence of money with respect to circulation is mere appearance</u> [corrected translation: semblance, *Schein*]. <u>So in its determination of consummate exchange value, money sublates itself.</u> (479)

Money as an independent manifestation of value results from simple circulation, but at the same time its independence is "mere semblance." *This independence cannot exist within simple circulation.* This means that within the framework of simple circulation, we cannot get all the determinations of money: therefore we need a further determination, another categorical development.

How can money, as an independent manifestation of value, maintain itself as the general form of wealth? Based on the analysis so far, Marx begins to lay out the *requirements* that must be fulfilled:

> If money is to be preserved as money, it must, just as it appears in the form of residue and a result of the process of circulation, be capable of re-entering this process, i.e. of not being converted in circulation into a mere means of circulation disappearing in the form of commodity in exchange for a mere use value. Money, while it is in one determination, should not be lost in the other, i.e. it should remain money also in its being as commodity, and, in its being as money, exist only as a transient form of commodity; in its being as commodity it should not lose its exchange value, and, in its being as money, its relation to use value. <u>Its entry into circulation must itself be a moment of its stay-by-itself, and its stay-by-itself, entry into circulation. Thus, the exchange value is now determined as a process</u> and not merely as a disappearing form of use value indifferent to this use value itself as physical content, and not merely as a thing in the form of money; it is determined as relation to its own self through the process of circulation. (490f.)

If money is to maintain itself as an independent manifestation of value, it cannot just enter circulation and buy any commodity. Instead, money must enter circulation in a specific way. It must do so in a way that allows it to remain an independent manifestation of value. We still don't know what this special way of entering circulation is in a concrete sense. However, Marx concludes that, if this way of entering circulation exists, value must be part of a "process": a *process involving constant changing of form between the commodity and the means of circulation.*

If money as an independent manifestation of value results from circulation and can only exist as a process, then what is this process's *content*? Prior to the passage just quoted, Marx wrote:

> As the aim of exchange, i.e. as movement which has for its content exchange value itself, money itself, the only content [of the process] is an increase of exchange value, *accumulation of money*. (488)

Hoarding itself involves accumulation, but of a merely formal kind. Value that was previously launched into circulation as a commodity is simply withdrawn as money. Here we are looking for something different from merely formal accumulation. This means that a further requirement is that money must enter circulation as an independent manifestation of value

> to reappear in its adequate form as *adequate exchange value*, but simultaneously as *multiplied, increased exchange value, valorised exchange value*. Value valorising, i.e. multiplying, itself in circulation, is in general exchange-value-for-itself which passes through circulation as an end-in-itself. This *valorisation, this quantitative increase of value*—the only process which value can perform as such—appears in the accumulation of money [that is, as hoarding] only as the opposite of circulation, i.e. through its own sublation. Moreover, circulation must itself be posited as a process in which value is retained and valorised. (491)

Yet how can circulation be a process where value preserves itself and grows? Marx continues:

> In circulation, however, money becomes coin and, as such, is exchanged for commodity. If this exchange is to be more than formal, if the exchange value is not to be lost in the consumption of the commodity, so that there is not merely a change in the form of the exchange value (once as its universal abstract being in money, and again, its being in a particular use value of the commodity), the exchange value must in fact be exchanged for a use value, and the commodity must be consumed as a use value, but in this consumption it must be retained as an exchange value, in other words, its disappearance must disappear, and must itself be merely a means for the emergence of a greater exchange value, for the reproduction and production of exchange value—*productive consumption*, i.e. consumption through labour in order to objectify labour, to create exchange value. (492)

Increasing value in circulation can only happen if *consuming* the purchased commodity itself becomes a way of *generating increased value*. This is productive consumption, consumption through (value-creating) labor. However, it is still not clear exactly what commodity must be purchased to carry out this kind of productive consumption. So far Marx has simply formulated the requirement.

Independent value entering into circulation for the sake of valorization is not a one-time process. Marx explains how the process of multiplying value is endless, by appealing to the contradiction between independent value being qualitatively unlimited, but quantitatively limited inasmuch as any particular value has only a limited magnitude:

> As a form of universal wealth, as exchange value become independent, money is incapable of any other movement but the quantitative one: to expand itself. By concept it is the essence of all the use values; but its quantitative limits, as the limits of what <u>is always merely a definite magnitude of value, a definite sum of gold and silver, is in contradiction with its quality</u>. That is why rooted in its nature is a constant drive to go beyond its own limits.... <u>So enrichment is an end-in-itself</u>. The end-determining activity of exchange value become independent can only be enrichment, i.e. its own self-expansion.... <u>So, fixed as wealth, as the universal form of wealth, as value that counts as value, money is a constant drive to go beyond its quantitative limits; an endless process.</u> Its own viability consists exclusively in this; it preserves itself as self-important value distinct from use value only when *it continually multiplies itself* by means of the process of exchange itself. The active value is only a surplus-value-positing value. (495f.)

Marx has now characterized money as *truly* independent value as value *in process*, value that multiplies itself through an *endless* process, which is an *end in itself*. In this way, he has identified capital's key determinations. Marx now concludes:

> Resulting from circulation as adequate exchange value and independent but again entering circulation, in it and through it perpetuating and valorising (multiplying) itself, money is *capital*. <u>In capital money has lost its rigidity and from a tangible thing has become a process</u>. Money and commodity as such, just as the simple circulation itself, exist for capital merely as particular abstract moments of its being in which it just as continually appears, passing from the one into the other, and just as continually disappears. The process of becoming independent appears not only in the form that capital confronts circulation as an independent abstract exchange value—money—but also in that circulation is simultaneously the process of its becoming independent, that it stems from circulation as something become independent. (496)

Marx's work in revealing capital's properties roughly corresponds to what he demonstrates in the form analysis in *Capital*'s chapter 4. However, Marx's starting point in *Capital* is the form of circulation M – C – M (or M – C – M'), the existence of which he simply presupposes. By contrast, the *Urtext* actually demonstrates how these properties of capital follow from the categorical determinations of money's third function. With that, Marx makes good on his claim at the beginning of this subsection of the *Urtext*: he has shown that the very characteristics of simple circulation show it to be a result of a deeper, underlying process (482). Money with its third function—money as money— can only acquire a real existence when it repeatedly enters circulation as part of a valorization process. Otherwise its independent existence will remain illusory, as with hoarding. In this way, Marx demonstrates that the characteristics of generalized simple commodity circulation depend on its being the expression of an underlying capitalist valorization process. If this capitalist valorization process is not present, then simple circulation will not be completely developed; its characteristics will not really exist.

Both in chapter 4 of *Capital* and here, at the end of the *Urtext* section, "The Transition to Capital," value emerges as value-in-process that yields surplus-value. But these determinations of value are still no more than requirements. In the *Urtext*, they emerge as requirements to be fulfilled for money as truly independent value. In *Capital*, the requirements arise from the existence of the circulation formula M – C – M′. However, we still don't know how it is *possible* to fulfill these requirements. The *Urtext* points to "productive consumption," but we still don't know how productive consumption makes value-that-generates-surplus-value possible. In *Capital*, Marx explicitly asks how it is possible to create surplus value, if we assume the exchange of equivalents. In chapter 5, he criticizes a series of inadequate solutions to this problem. In chapter 6, however, Marx finally presents the first part of the answer: it involves the purchase and sale of a special commodity, labor-power. The second part of the answer comes in chapter 7.

In the *Urtext*, Marx still did not clearly distinguish between labor and labor-power—the *Urtext* uses the German phrase *Arbeitsvermögen*, or "labor capacity," whereas in *Capital*, it's *Arbeitskraft* or "labor power." Marx even equates living labor and labor-power in a few passages, and does not make a precise analysis of the commodity labor-power. Instead, in the section that follows, "The Transformation of Money into Capital," he attempts to characterize what constitutes the "opposite" of money-as-capital. It can't be commodities, since money as capital "passes into any form of commodity whatsoever" (502). Because money, as the form of all commodities, represents "objectified labor" its opposite could only be "unreified labor" or "living labor," which only exists as a capacity of the "living subject" (502). However, the *capacity for living labor*—existing in the living subject, independently of whether that subject works or not—must be distinguished from *living labor* itself, which only exists when the living subject actually works.

But Marx does not tell us why the transformation of money into capital can only be explained by an exchange with the "opposite" of capital. Nor is it very plausible to say that commodities can't be this opposite because they exchange for capital, but then explain the transformation of money into capital precisely because it exchanges with its opposite, "labor." Here, Marx is not able to explain fully why capital's exchange with labor is so fundamentally different from capital's exchange with other commodities.

The vagueness of Marx's reasoning becomes especially clear in this passage which summarizes the argument:

> Money exists as capital only in connection with non-capital, the negation of capital, in relation to which alone it is capital. *Labour itself is the real non-capital*. The first step made by money to become capital is its exchange with the labour capacity so as by means of the latter to transform the consumption of the commodities, i.e. their real positing and negation as use values, simultaneously into their actualisation of exchange value.
>
> <u>The exchange through which money becomes capital cannot be its exchange with commodities [in general] but can only be one with its conceptually determined opposite, the commodity which is itself a conceptually determined opposite of it—labour.</u> (504)

In the first paragraph, Marx says that money becomes capital by exchanging for *labor capacity*, but in the second he says that money becomes capital by exchanging for *labor*. Marx is not yet really clear about the difference between exchanging for the commodity labor-power and exchanging for labor, which is not a buyable commodity and also has no value, but rather creates value (see chapter 19 of *Capital* and the concluding part of my commentary on chapter 7). In the *Urtext*, Marx is beginning to chart out an explanation of surplus-value creation, but he hasn't arrived at it yet.

The *Urtext* constitutes an important supplement to the analysis in *Capital*, because in the section "Transition to Capital" it demonstrates the categorical relationship between money and capital. However, the material under the heading "The Transformation of Money into Capital" suffers from an inadequate conception of the commodity labor-power. For this reason, the last considerations fall short of being a truly helpful supplement to Marx's account in *Capital*.[64]

---

64. Both the conception of labor as "non-capital" and the claim that the transformation of money into capital turns on the relationship of capital to its opposite were important for Italian *operaismo* and the texts of Antonio Negri in particular.

APPENDIX 6

Levels of Abstraction and the Course of Argument in the First Seven Chapters of *Capital*

1. What Is Being Abstracted From

What follows is not a summary of *Capital*'s first seven chapters. Instead, it aims only to clarify the *structure* of the argument, and it presupposes familiarity with the chapters.

Capital's object of investigation is the capitalist mode of production, but it begins its account with the commodity. Even so, the very first sentence of chapter 1 indicates that it's the commodity *in capitalism* that's being analyzed (125). *Capital*'s first three chapters deal with both the capitalistically produced commodity and money-as-used-in-capitalism, though still in abstraction from capital itself. In those chapters, Marx examines the simple circulation of commodities, treating it not as an independent mode of production, but as an *abstract sphere of the capitalist process of reproduction* (see MEGA II/2: 68). Chapter 4 is the first to address capital, and does so with the *general formula* of capital M – C – M′, in which the valorization of value is depicted at the level of the simple circulation of commodities. The analysis of the capitalist process of production then begins in chapter 7.

There are no general methodological considerations that could determine in advance whether this sequence of presentation makes sense. That can only be decided by examining the entire course of reasoning in *Capital*'s three volumes. To understand the structure of Marx's argument, it's useful to explore, focusing on certain nodal points, the levels of abstraction and the course of Marx's presentation so far. In the Preface, Marx pointed out that the analysis of "economic forms" does not have microscopes or chemical reagents at its disposal, but only the "power of abstraction" (90). Let us turn, then, to the levels of abstraction in the first five chapters.

Capitalist production is based on purchasing a particular commodity, labor-power. It was an important insight on Marx's part that what is sold is not *labor*, but rather *labor-power*. Both classical political economy and common sense assume that it is labor that is sold. However, buying and selling the commodity labor-power is only a special case of the buying and selling of commodities. If one wishes to examine the peculiarities of the buying and selling of this particular commodity, one must first examine the circulation of commodities in general, abstracting from the peculiarities of both commodity owners. On the one hand, there is the owner of money, who purchases labor-power, and, on the other, the owner of labor-power, who sells it. By considering them only as owners of commodities or money, one gets a view of the simple circulation of commodities—the permanent buying and selling that a capitalist economy appears to be at first glance.

The simple circulation of commodities comprises numerous, interconnected individual *processes of exchange*: commodity owners exchange their commodities for money, while owners of money exchange their money for commodities, with individuals alternately taking on the roles of commodity and money owners. Therefore, examining commodity circulation first requires considering the exchange process in abstraction from this mutual entanglement.

In examining the exchange process, however, one notes that the owners of commodities and money confronting each other in exchange must act in accordance with the already existing properties of commodities and money. Examining the exchange process therefore requires an analysis of these presupposed properties. This in turn leads to an *analysis of the commodity in abstraction from the exchange process of commodity owners*. What is left is the pure *exchange-relation of two commodities*.

Marx begins his presentation in chapter 1 with the *commodity*, treating it as a simple economic form. In the "Marginal Notes on Wagner," Marx characterizes the commodity as "the simplest social form in which the product of labour presents itself in contemporary society" (MECW 24: 544). However, Marx does not begin his presentation with the *price-determined* commodity, which is how *one can see* the commodity in simple circulation. Instead, the commodity Marx considers in chapter 1 is a *result of the process of abstraction* described in the preceding paragraphs. In that sense, what Marx examines in chapter 1 is the *exchange-relation of commodities* underlying the *exchange process between commodity owners*, which is what he will examine in chapter 2.

2. Value, Money, and Fetish at Different Levels of the Presentation

Based on the analysis of commodities' exchange-relations, Marx characterizes the substance of value, magnitude of value, and value-form. The substance of value, *abstract human labor*, is not simply present in the labor process (nor does Marx develop the category by analyzing the labor process). Rather, abstract labor results from the reduction of the *different types of concrete labor*. Just like the value it creates, abstract labor does not come to exist in the labor process. Instead, it exists only in the social relationship where this reduction actually takes place: that is, in exchange, which is what Marx stresses in the manuscript *Ergänzungen und Veränderungen* of 1871–72 and later in the French edition of *Capital*:

> The reduction of various concrete private acts of labour to this abstraction of equal human labor is only carried out through exchange, which in fact

equates products of different acts of labor with each other. (MEGA II/6: 41, and MEGA II/7: 55)

Nor is the *magnitude of value* set in the labor process. What constitutes value is the "socially necessary labour-time" (129) that is required to produce a use-value. However, that is a social result that only emerges in exchange, because it is only in exchange that the standard productivity of labor, addressed in chapter 1, and the size of social need is determined (201f.). It is also there that the reduction of complex to simple labor occurs (135; 304ff.). Note, however, that commodities' empirically average prices *do not* coincide with the magnitudes of their values (269n24).

Since the substance of value only exists as a social relationship, it is not tangible but rather "spectral" or "phantom-like," as Marx observes at the beginning of chapter 1 (128). This raises the issue of the *value-form*, that is, the form in which a commodity's value is expressed. Another commodity, in its concrete useful shape, functions as the expression of value. Marx then works out the three "peculiarities of the equivalent-form": *use-value* becomes a form of appearance of *value*; *concrete labor* a form of appearance of *abstract labor*; and *private labor* a form of appearance of *labor in directly social form*. The general character of value, however, cannot be expressed by a single, random commodity. It takes the *general form of value*—where an individual commodity is singled out as the expression of value of all other commodities—to have an adequate expression of value. Then, if this general equivalent becomes fused with a particular commodity, the general form of value becomes the money-form. Importantly, the value-form analysis of chapter 1 results not in money, but rather in the *money-form*.

Only in chapter 2 does *money* become the object of investigation, with Marx presenting it as the—unconscious and unintentional—result of the *actions* of commodity owners. Here, Marx no longer examines the exchange-relation of commodities, but rather the *exchange process* among commodity owners. If producers are going to behave as commodity owners and exchange commodities, they must mutually recognize each other as the private owners of their respective products. They must also behave according to the commodities' form-determinations: their commodities can only be realized as values if they relate to money as the universal expression of value. If the commodity owners follow the logic of the commodity's form-determinations, then they behave as economic *character masks*. If they fail to do so, they face economic ruin.

Individual processes of exchange are intertwined in simple commodity circulation, C – M – C. The various relationships of commodities to each other result in a crystallization of the fundamental form determinations of money (the measure of values, means of circulation, money as money). Value was initially only one of the two *factors of the commodity*, but in money as money it takes on an *independent shape*.

Part Two remains at the level of simple commodity circulation, but it examines a new figure of circulation, M – C – M. Since its only possible purpose is multiplying value—the creation of *surplus-value*—the formula must be written M – C – M', with M' > M. This represents an endless and limitless multiplication of value (valorization) as an end in itself, and Marx refers to it as *capital*. With this basic determination, capital is characterized not as a simple sum of value, but as *value in process*; it is value that alternately takes on the forms of commodity and money and multiplies in doing so. But money is not just a temporary form that value assumes in the circulation process M – C – M'; money is rather the independent form in which value expresses its identity with itself and its own multiplication. A *capitalist* possesses (but does not necessarily own) a sum of money, and he makes its endless multiplication into his subjective purpose. This multiplication of value is made possible—despite the exchange of equivalents—because of a specific commodity, the commodity *labor-power*. The latter's use-value, living labor, creates new value, when deployed to produce commodities which are then actually exchanged.

Whereas chapters 4 through 6 remain at the level of simple commodity circulation, chapter 7 deals with the *use* of labor-power. Marx first discusses the abstract elements of all *labor processes*, also characterizing the *specifically human labor-process*. He then turns to how the capitalist *process of production* uses labor-power. There, the commodity labor-power is purchased and deployed in commodity production, but it will only generate surplus value, if the productive expenditure of labor lasts longer than required for the reproduction of labor-power. Hence workers work more than is necessary for their own reproduction, which Marx later calls *exploitation*. The *surplus labor-time* expended creates *surplus-value*, which is the purpose of capitalist production.

Marx's presentation of value and money includes, in an integral way, the inversions and forms of fetishism that apply to each of these categories. Chapter 1 deals with the exchange-relations of commodities, and at this level of abstraction Marx develops the *commodity fetish*. The latter is "the fact that the commodity reflects the social characteristics of men's own labour as objective characteristics of the products of labour themselves, as the socio-natural properties of these things" (164f.). These are not forms of false consciousness, but rather "objective forms of thought" (*objektive Gedankenformen*) (169) that are given with commodity production. Fetishism, Marx emphasizes, "attaches" to the products of labor whenever they are produced as commodities (165f.). In the capitalist economy, the fetish is not an illusion. Since relationships between producers really are mediated by things in capitalism, social relationships really are reflected as properties of things (166). What is false, however, is the idea that this must hold for every kind of economy (167).

Marx develops the *money fetish* in chapter 2, where the level of abstraction is the exchange process among commodity owners. What Marx calls the money fetish is that the unconscious result of the commodity owner's activity (the general equivalent) appears as an objective property of a special object:

> What appears to happen is not that a particular commodity becomes money because all other commodities express their values in it, but, on the contrary, that all other commodities universally express their values in a particular

commodity because it is money. The movement through which this process has been mediated vanishes in its own result, leaving no trace behind. (187)

Following his treatment of the commodity fetish and money fetish, Marx's presentation continues at the level of commodity circulation and turns to the increasing autonomization of social relations vis-à-vis the individual (202). This leads him to speak of a "whole network of socio-natural connections" (207, corrected translation). With the third form-determination of money, "as money," the money fetish attains completion: social power becomes "an external object capable of becoming the private property of any individual. Thus the social power becomes the private power of private persons" (230).

Part Two does not mention the capital fetish explicitly—this occurs for the first time in *Capital's* third volume when dealing with interest-bearing capital. Nevertheless, Marx anticipates the capital fetish, when he states that value "has acquired the occult ability to add value to itself" (255). However, this isolated hint is not yet connected with Marx's explanation of how workers produce surplus value through their surplus labor. Later on in his argument, Marx will more fully analyze both the capital relation—in the production process, the circulation process, and in the capitalist process taken as a whole—along with the inversions and mystifications it generates. At the end of *Capital's* third volume, then, Marx will not only have deciphered the connection between surplus labor, on the one hand, and profit, average profit, commercial profit, interest, and ground rent on the other. He will also have shown the reasons why everyday consciousness and mainstream bourgeois economics do not perceive this connection, or do so only in a very distorted way. To grasp this, one must be familiar with all three volumes. Here, after going over the first seven chapters of Volume 1, we are still only at the beginning of the whole investigation.

3. "Theoretical Developments" and Historical Process

The capitalist mode of production does not constitute an eternal condition for human economic activity. Rather, capitalism is a *historical* mode of production, and it is so in two senses. *First*: capitalism developed out of a non-capitalist environment, expanding geographically and subordinating more and more areas to its control until it finally became the dominant mode of production. This means that there is a history of how the capitalist mode of production emerged and imposed itself. *Second*: after becoming the dominant mode of production, capitalism continues to have a history. This is a specifically capitalist history marked by class struggle, accumulation, the development of productive forces, reproduction, and crises. It takes a different course in each specific country, while being simultaneously influenced by developments in other countries.

When Marx examines the capitalist mode of production, he is dealing with a *historical* object. This has led to the misunderstanding that his *presentation* must also be a historical one, an abbreviated and pointed retelling of capitalism's historical development, as Engels suggested in his review of the *Contribution to*

Levels of Presentation of the First Seven Chapters

	LEVEL OF ABSTRACTION	OBJECT OF ANALYSIS	IMPORTANT CONCLUSIONS CONCERNING VALUE MONEY, AND VALORIZATION	FETISH, INVERSION, IMPERSONAL DOMINATION
Chap. 1	Exchange relation between commodities	Form-determinations of the commodity: substance of value, magnitude of value, value-form	-Value as a factor of the commodity -Abstract labor as the substance of value -The money-form of value	Commodity fetish
Chap. 2	Exchange process bet. commodity owners	Form-determined actions (character masks)	-Money as the (unconscious) result of commodity owner's action	Money fetish
Chap. 3	Simple circulation of commodities	Relationships of commodities to each other, form-determinations of money, other economic character masks	-Functions of money -The possibility of crisis -The independent existence of value in "money as money"	-Autonomization of social relations into "socio-natural connections" -Social power becomes a thing as money, which can become the private property of anyone
Chaps. 4, 5, 6	Simple circulation of commodities	Form-determinations of the valorization process, the capitalist as a new economic character mask, valorization and the exchange of equivalents	-Capital: valorizing value (value in process) -Money as the independent form of valorizing value -Valorization is made possible by the purchase and use of a special commodity: labor-power	-The occult quality of capital (inklings of the capital fetish) -(Bourgeois) freedom and equality in the sphere of circulation
Chap. 7	Capitalist production	Abstract aspects of the labor process, value-creation, and valorization process	-The specific human labor process -Valorization occurs by extending the value-creation process	Domination and exploitation in the sphere of production

the *Critique of Political Economy*. People have often seen the first three chapters of the first volume—following Engels's claim in his "Supplement" to Volume 3—as depicting a pre-capitalist "simple production of commodities" (an erroneous construct, as I have pointed out several times in this commentary). In this view, later chapters in Volume 1 present modern capitalism's historical development up to the factory system and the concentration and centralization of capital.

This conception holds that Marx's *Capital*—as Kautsky claimed in his influential introduction to the work—is an "essentially historical work" (Kautsky 1887: xi).

However, such a conception baldly contradicts Marx's claims in the Preface to the first volume. There, he emphasizes that the work deals with "theoretical developments" (90), and that the text makes reference to conditions in England only as an "illustration" of such developments. Marx makes it clear that he is by no means offering a historical depiction: "Intrinsically, it is not a question of the higher or lower degree of development of the social antagonisms that spring from the natural laws of capitalist production. It is a question of these laws themselves" (90). In keeping with this perspective, Marx emphasizes at the end of Volume 3 that he wants to present "the internal organization of the capitalist mode of production, its ideal average, as it were" (970).

This way of defining the object of *Capital* is not arbitrary, nor does it exclude historical developments from the account. On the contrary, the presentation of this "ideal average" is what makes possible an approach to history that is not based on mere anecdotes but rather on scientific analysis.

In the *Grundrisse*, Marx emphasizes that capital's emergence constitutes a completely different object of investigation than developed capital's mode of functioning: "The conditions and presuppositions of the *becoming*, of the *arising*, of capital presuppose precisely that it is not yet in being but merely in *becoming*; they therefore disappear as real capital arises, capital which itself, on the basis of its own reality, posits the conditions for its realization" (459). Marx is not only talking about two different objects. In fact, knowledge of *developed capital* amounts to a precondition for investigating *capital's emergence*, for only if we know *what is coming into being* can we recognize the elements of this formation taking shape in the mass of historical data. In the Introduction of 1857, Marx embodied this idea in the (biologically questionable) claim: "Human anatomy contains a key to the anatomy of the ape" (105).

For this reason, *Capital* presents the historical emergence of capitalist structures only after sufficiently explaining the categories that define these structures. Hence Part Eight of Volume 1, on the "So-Called Primitive Accumulation," deals with capitalist production's emergence in England, but it comes only *after* the analysis of the capitalist process of production. The same holds for the historical chapters dealing with merchants' capital and interest-bearing capital in Volume 3: each of them follows the presentation of the categories corresponding to these forms of capital.

However, theorizing capitalism in its "ideal average" is not only the precondition for recounting the historical emergence of the capitalist mode of production. It also constitutes a precondition for analyzing the history of developed, fully-formed capital. Capital's dynamic is based on the unlimited and endless valorization of value, and the tendency to expand both absolute and relative surplus-value production. This constitutes a specific field where—under certain historical conditions, traditions, and relations of force—class struggle and the struggle of competition between individual capitals plays out. The "theoretical development" of the categories, however, does not just constitute a general background for analyzing concrete struggles. *The categorical presentation itself leads to points where nothing further can be developed conceptually, and we must turn to the contested historical process instead.* Chapter 10 of the first volume, which deals with the working day, demonstrates this in an exemplary way. We cannot determine the limits of the working day based on the "laws of commodity production." Instead, it is the "violence" (*Gewalt*) of class struggle and the state that decides these limits, which are repeatedly brought into question. Hence, there are historical depictions in *Capital* that are not just "illustrations" and go beyond telling how capitalist relations emerged. Nevertheless, the location and meaning of these passages are by no means arbitrary but rather are based strictly on the theoretical development of the categories.

Glossary

In the first two chapters of *Capital*, we encounter a number of terms that might be new for the reader. Marx created some of these terms, and others he discovered, sometimes giving them new definitions. This glossary cannot explain all these terms; I will only address those that have a close connection to commodities and value, as well as labor. The keywords used to group the terms are not arranged alphabetically. Instead, concepts that belong together come one after another. Explanations are kept rather short, and they presuppose familiarity with the preceding commentary. Italicized terms within an explanation indicate that a term has its own explanation. The page numbers point to especially relevant passages of *Capital* dealing with the concept in question.

COMMODITY AND VALUE

Commodity: A thing (or service) that appears in a dual form: in its natural form, as a physical thing, an object of use, and as an object of value (138). Things and services only become commodities because they are produced by *private labor* acts—carried out independently from one another—and are exchanged (166). The commodity form of the product of labor is a specific social form existing only in societies based on exchange.

Use-Value: The usefulness of a thing (or a service) makes it a use-value. It is conditioned by the physical properties of a thing, but presupposes that people know how to use these physical properties (125f.).

Exchange Value: The amount of another thing B that one obtains in exchange for A (126). Exchange value is a form of appearance of *value* (126–28).

Value: The common element of commodities that are exchanged (127); only as values are commodities quantitatively commensurable (141).

Substance of Value: The basis of value. It is a "social substance" that is "common" (or, better translated, "communal") to all commodities (128). This substance is not merely labor, but rather equal human labor, *abstract human labor* (129).

Magnitude of Value: The magnitude of value depends upon the quantity of "value-creating labor" contained in a commodity. This quantity is not identical to the *individual labor-time* that a producer expends; only *socially necessary labor-time* for producing a commodity counts (129).

Value-Objectivity (Wertgegenständlichkeit): With this term, Marx emphasizes that commodities, besides being physical objects, are also objects of value. However, things only obtain value-objectivity, separate from their objectivity as use-values, through exchange (166). *Value* appears as an objective property of commodities, although as a purely social property it cannot be grasped by the senses or in a physical way. Marx therefore speaks of a "spectral" or "phantom-like" objectivity (128) and of value as a "supra-natural" (149) property of the thing. He also refers to commodities as "sensuous, extra-sensory" (*sinnlich* übersinnlich) things (163 and 165); in the first case wrongly translated as "a thing which transcends sensuousness" and in the second case as "sensuous things which are at the same time supra-sensible."

An abstraction, value (Wertabstraktion, wrongly translated as "abstract value"): An abstraction we perform as observers, in which we discover that commodities are objects of value. We have therefore reduced the commodities to their property of being values (141).

Value-Form (Expression of Value, Exchange Value): In the value-form, the *value* of commodity A acquires an objective expression as a specific quantity of another commodity B. Now the value of commodity A is no longer intangible: it comes forth in the relationship to another commodity, becoming tangible as a specific amount of the other commodity (138f., 141f.).

Value-relation: The relationship of commodities to each other as objects of value.

The Fetish Character of the Commodity (Commodity Fetish): Under the conditions of commodity production, the social characteristics of labor appear as objective characteristics of the products of labor. Marx describes this quid pro quo as commodity fetishism. This fetish character is not a conceit of the imagination or an illusion; it is real, originating from "the peculiar social character of the labour which produces [commodities]" (165). However, it is not easy to see that commodities' fetish character originates in the peculiar social relations of commodity production: what is valid only under commodity production appears to people caught up in those social relations to be eternally valid. Here, we are dealing with a false semblance: that labor products are necessarily objects of value in every form of society (167).

Exchange-relation: The relation between two commodities that are exchanged, considered in abstraction from commodity owners. The exchange-relation is examined in chapter 1 of *Capital*.

Exchange Process: The process of exchange carried out by commodity owners. In contrast to the focus of the *exchange-relation*, the concern here is the commodity owners' activity. The exchange process is examined in chapter 2 of *Capital*.

Labor

Labor-power: The ability of people to perform labor.

Labor: The process of applying this ability.

Concrete, Useful Labor: The visible, actual labor process, which takes place in a specific, concrete manner and creates something useful. Concrete, useful labor produces use-values (128, 131ff.).

Abstract Human Labor (Equal Human Labor): In exchange, there is an abstraction from the particularity of various types of labor; these various types of labor are reduced to equal human labor or abstract human labor (128). Whereas *concrete useful labor* that creates *use-values* exists in all forms of society (133), abstract human labor is a specific social determination of labor that only exists in a specific social context: a society based on exchange (166f.; MECW 29: 277f.).

The Dual Character of the Labor Embodied/Represented in Commodities: The fact that commodity-producing labor is both *concrete useful labor* and *abstract human labor* (131ff.).

Individual Labor-Time: The labor-time an individual producer—either an individual person or enterprise—requires to produce a certain product (129).

Socially Necessary Labor-Time: The labor-time necessary to produce a specific use-value under socially normal conditions of production and with the usual level of skill (129). As a supplement to this technical characterization of necessary labor-time, chapter 3 brings demand into the picture: labor-time only counts as socially necessary if it creates a product for which there is social demand (201f.). The individual process of production determines neither what counts as normal conditions of production nor the demand. Both are determined socially in the process of exchange.

Private Labor: Labor carried out independently of other producers, that is, without consultation or coordination. Commodities are products of private labor (132f.). Every producer attempts to estimate market conditions, but it is only in the market that he finds out whether his product is socially accepted and whether his private labor forms part of the *total labor of society* (165). Under the conditions of commodity production, privately expended *concrete useful labor* only becomes a component of the total labor of society when it is reduced to equal human labor, or *abstract human labor*, in exchange.

Total Labor of Society: In generalized commodity production, the total labor of society is made up of the many acts of *private labor*. However, acts of private labor only become components of the total labor of society if their products are actually exchanged (165).

Labor in Directly/Immediate Social Form: Labor in a direct or immediate social form, with its product requiring no further mediation to become a social product. Under the conditions of commodity production, the only *private labor* that is directly social is the labor that produces the general equivalent (151). In social relations not based upon commodity production, but rather on relations of personal domination and servitude, labor in its natural form enters directly into the workings of society as a specific *concrete, useful labor*. Under such relations, labor in its natural form is therefore immediately social labor from the get-go (170).

Immediately Socialized Labor: Here, too, labor in its natural form is already *labor in immediately social form*. It becomes immediately socialized labor because it is expended in common and uses communal means of production. Marx's examples are, on the one hand, the "patriarchal rural industry of a peasant family" and, on the other hand, the "association of free people" (171, corrected translation).

Bibliography

The scope of this work has not permitted me to address, even superficially, the various debates concerning Marx's theory of value and capital. However, Ingo Elbe (2008) and Jan Hoff (2017) present the debates in a very comprehensive and rigorous fashion. Some more recent contributions to the discussion are found in the three works listed below: Hoff et al. (2006), *Beiträge zur Marx-Engels-Forschung* 2007 and 2010; Elbe/Reichardt/Wolf (2008); and Bonefeld/Heinrich (2011). I offer a detailed account of my positions on these debates in Heinrich (1999) and Heinrich (2016).

WORKS BY MARX AND ENGELS

MECW: *Marx-Engels Collected Works,* Lawrence and Wishart, London.
MEGA: *Marx Engels Gesamtausgabe,* Walter de Gruyter Verlag, Berlin.
MEW: *Marx Engels Werke,* Karl Dietz Verlag, Berlin.
Marx, Karl (1867): "The Value-Form," *Capital and Class,* no.4, Spring 1978: 130–150.
Marx, Karl (1973): *Grundrisse: Foundations of the Critique of Political Economy,* New York: Vintage.
Marx, Karl (1976): *Capital, Volume I,* translated by Ben Fowkes, London: Penguin.
Marx, Karl, (1976b): *Value: Studies by Karl Marx,* edited and translated by Albert Dragstedt, London: New Park Publications.
Marx, Karl (1979): *Capital, Volume II,* translated by David Fernbach, London: Pelican.
Marx, Karl (1981): *Capital, Volume III,* translated by David Fernbach, London: Pelican.
Marx, Karl (2017): *Marx's Economic Manuscript of 1864–65,* edited and introduced by Fred Moseley, translated by Ben Fowkes, Chicago: Haymarket.

Althusser, Louis (1965): *For Marx,* London: Verso, 1969.
Althusser, Louis; Etienne Balibar (1965): *Reading Capital,* London: Verso, 1997.
Backhaus, Hans Georg (1997): *Die Dialektik der Wertform,* Freiburg: Ça ira.

Beiträge zur Marx-Engels-Forschung Neue Folge: Geld – Kapital – Wert. Zum 150 Jahrestag der Niederschrift von Marx' ökonomischen Manuskripten 1857–58 Grundrisse der Kritik der politischen Ökonomie (2007), Hamburg: Argument.

Beiträge zur Marx-Engels-Forschung Neue Folge: Das Kapital und Vorarbeiten. Entwürfe und Exzerpte (2010), Hamburg: Argument.

Böhm-Bawerk, Eugen von (1949): *Karl Marx and the Close of His System*, edited and with an introduction by Paul Sweezy, New York: Augustus M. Kelley.

Bonefeld, Werner; Michael Heinrich (2011): *Kapital und Kritik. Nach der "neuen" Marx-Lektüre*, Hamburg: VSA.

Dragstedt, Albert, ed. and trans. (1976): *Value: Studies by Karl Marx*, London: New Park Publications.

Elbe, Ingo (2006): "Between Marx, Marxism, and Marxisms: Ways of Reading Marx's Theory," *Viewpoint Magazine*, https://www.viewpointmag.com/2013/10/21/between-marx-marxism-and-marxisms-ways-of-reading-marxs-theory/.

Elbe, Ingo; Tobias Reichardt; Dieter Wolf (2008): *Gesellschaftliche Praxis und ihre wissenschaftliche Darstellung. Beiträge zur Kapital-Diskussion*, Hamburg: Argument Verlag.

Elbe, Ingo (2008): *Marx im Westen. Die neue Marx-Lektüre in der Bundesrepublik seit 1965*, Berlin: Akademie-Verlag.

Fromm, Erich (1961): *Marx's Concept of Man*, London/New York: Continuum, 2004.

Goethe, J. W. von (1999): *Faust. Kommentare*. Edited by Albrecht Schöne, Frankfurt/M: Deutscher Klassiker Verlag.

Habermas, Jürgen (1981): *Theory of Communicative Action*, 2 volumes, Boston: Beacon Press, 1984.

Habermas, Jürgen (1963): "Natural Law and Revolution," in: Habermas, *Theory and Practice*, Boston: Beacon Press, 1974.

Haug, Wolfgang Fritz (2005): *Vorlesungen zur Einführung ins "Kapital,"* 6, rev. ed., Hamburg: Argument.

Hegel, G.W.F. (1807): *Phenomenology of Spirit*, Oxford: Oxford University Press, 1977.

Hegel, G.W.F. (1821): *Elements of the Philosophy of Right*, translated by H. B. Nisbet, edited by Allen W. Wood, Cambridge: Cambridge University Press, 1991.

Heinrich, Michael (1996/97): "Engels' Edition of the Third Volume of *Capital* and Marx's Original Manuscript," in: *Science & Society*, vol. 60, no. 4, Winter 1996–97: 452–466.

Heinrich, Michael (1999/2020): *Die Wissenschaft vom Wert: Die Marxsche Kritik der politischen Ökonomie zwischen wissenschaftlicher Revolution und klassischer Tradition*, 8, Münster: Westfälisches Dampfboot. (An English translation will be published by Brill 2021.)

Heinrich, Michael (1999a): "Untergang des Kapitalismus? 'Die Krisis' und die Krise," in: *Streifzüge* 1: 1–5.

Heinrich, Michael (2012): *An Introduction to the Three Volumes of Karl Marx's Capital*, New York: Monthly Review Press.
Heinrich, Michael (2013): "The `Fragment on Machines´: A Marxian Misconception in the *Grundrisse* and Its Overcoming in *Capital*," in: Riccardo Bellofiore, Guido Starosta, Peter D. Thomas, eds.: *Marx's Laboratory Critical Interpretations of the Grundrisse*, Leiden: Brill, 197–212.
Heinrich, Michael (2016): "'Capital' after MEGA: Discontinuities, Interruptions and New Beginnings," in: *Crisis and Critique* 3:3: 92–138, https://crisiscritique.org/political11/Michael%20Heinrich.pdf.
Hilferding, Rudolf (1904): *Böhm-Bawerk's Criticism of Marx*, in: Böhm-Bawerk, Eugen von (1896): *Karl Marx and the Close of His System*, edited and with an introduction by Paul Sweezy, New York: Augustus M. Kelley, 1949.
Hoff, Jan (2004): *Kritik der klassischen politischen Ökonomie: Zur Rezeption der werttheoretischen Ansätze ökonomischer Klassiker durch Karl Marx*, Köln: PapyRossa.
Hoff, Jan (2017): *Marx Worldwide: On the Development of the International Discourse on Marx since 1965*, Chicago: Haymarket Books.
Hoff, Jan; Alexis Petrioli, Ingo Stützle, Frieder Otto Wolf, eds. (2006): *Das Kapital neu lesen— Beiträge zur radikalen Philosophie*, Münster: Westfälisches Dampfboot.
Iber, Christian (2005): *Gründzüge der Marxschen Kapitalismustheorie*, Berlin: Parerga.
Kautsky, Karl (1887): *Karl Marx Oekonomische Lehren: Gemeinverständlich dargestellt und erläutert*, Stuttgart.
Knolle-Grothusen, Ansgar; Stephan Krüger, Dieter Wolf (2009): *Geldware, Geld und Währung: Grundlagen zur Lösung des Problems der Geldware*, Hamburg: Argument-Verlag.
Lenin, V. I. (1915): "On the Question of Dialectics," in: *Collected Works*, Volume 38, Moscow: Progress Publishers, 1976.
Lindner, Urs (2013): *Marx und die Philosophie: Wissenschaftlicher Realismus, ethischer Perfektionismus und kritische Sozialtheorie*, Stuttgart: Schmetterling Verlag.
Locke, John (1690): *Two Treatises of Government & A Letter Concerning Toleration*, New Haven: Yale University Press, 2003.
Lohmann, Georg (1991): *Indifferenz und Gesellschaft. Eine kritische Auseinandersetzung mit Marx*, Frankfurt: Suhrkamp Verlag.
Mandel, Ernest (1968): *Marxist Economic Theory*, 2 volumes, New York: Monthly Review Press, 1969.
Moseley, Fred (2007): *Kapital im Allgemeinen und Konkurrenz der vielen Kapitalien in der Theorie von Marx: Die quantitative Dimension*, in: *Marx-Engels Jahrbuch* 2006, Berlin: Akademie Verlag, 81–117.
Polanyi, Karl (1979): *Die Semantik der Verwendung von Geld*, in: *Ökonomie und Gesellschaft*, Frankfurt/Main: Suhrkamp, 317–345.
Reichelt, Helmut (2002): *Die Marxsche Kritik ökonomischer Kategorien:*

Überlegungen zum Problem der Geltung in der dialektischen Darstellungsmethode im "Kapital," in: Fetscher, Iring; Alfred Schmidt (eds.), Emanzipation als Versöhnung: Zu Adornos Kritik der "Warentausch-Gesellschaft" und Perspektiven der Transformation, Frankfurt/M.: Neue Kritik, 142–189.

Rubin, Isaak Illich (1972): Essays on Marx's Theory of Value, Detroit: Black & Red.

Sachverständigenrat zur Begutachtung der gesamtwirtschaftlichen Entwicklung (1999): Jahresgutachten 1999/2000: "Wirtschaftspolitik unter Reformdruck," Wiesbaden: Statistisches Bundesamt.

Schlaudt, Oliver (2011): "Marx als Meßtheoretiker," in: Bonefeld/Heinrich (2011), 258–280.

Schmied-Kowarzik, Wolfdietrich (1981): Die Dialektik der gesellschaftlichen Praxis: Zur Genese und Kernstruktur der Marxschen Theorie, Freiburg: Alber.

Smith, Adam (1776): An Inquiry Into the Nature and Causes of the Wealth of Nations, Chicago: University of Chicago Press, 1977.

Sohn-Rethel, Alfred (1973): Geistige und körperliche Arbeit, 2, rev. ed., Frankfurt/M.: Suhrkamp.

SOST (Sozialistische Studiengruppen) (1980): Entfremdung und Arbeit Ökonomisch-philosophische Manuskripte aus dem Jahre 1844, Kommentar, Hamburg: VSA.

Stützle, Ingo (2006): "Die Frage nach der konstitutiven Relevanz der Geldware in Marx' Kritik der politischen Ökonomie," in: Hoff et al., eds. (2006), 254–286.

Trenkle, Norbert (1998): "Was ist der Wert? Was soll die Krise?," in: Streifzüge 3: 7–10.

Wolf, Dieter (1985): Ware und Geld, Hamburg: VSA. (Reprinted 2002 with the title Der dialektische Widerspruch im "Kapital.")